P9-CCZ-381

National Service: What Would It Mean?

National Service: What Would It Mean?

Richard Danzig
Peter Szanton

Lexington Books
D.C. Heath and Company/Lexington, Massachusetts/Toronto

Library of Congress Cataloging in Publication Data

Danzig, Richard.
National service.

Bibliography: p.
Includes index.
1. National service—United States. 2. Military service, Compulsory—United States. I. Szanton, Peter L. II. Title.
UB353.D36 1986 355.2'236'0973 85-45897
ISBN 0-669-12372-2 (alk. paper)
ISBN 0-669-12374-9 (pbk. : alk. paper)

Published simultaneously in Canada
Printed in the United States of America
Casebound International Standard Book Number: 0-669-12372-2
Paperbound International Standard Book Number: 0-669-12374-9
Library of Congress Catalog Card Number: 85-45897

The paper used in this publication meets the minimum requirements of American National Standard for Information Sciences—Permanance of Paper for Printed Library Materials, ANSI Z39.48-1984. ∞™

86 87 88 89 90 8 7 6 5 4 3 2 1

Contents

To Our Families

Preface

In 1910, William James opened a debate that still captures the popular imagination and is still unresolved. In an essay titled "The Moral Equivalent of War," he proposed that American youth be conscripted into "an army enlisted against nature":

> [t]o coal and iron mines, to freight trains, to fishing fleets in December, to dishwashing, clothes-washing, and window-washing, to road-building and tunnel-making, to foundries and stoke-holes, and to the frames of skyscrapers would our gilded youths be drafted off, according to their choice, to get the childishness knocked out of them, and to come back into society with healthier sympathies and soberer ideas.[1]

Variations of this idea, which has come to be known as national service, have commanded popular and political support ever since. Presidents Wilson, Roosevelt, Truman, Eisenhower, Kennedy, Johnson, and Carter supported some form of youth service. Bills calling for service programs or for commissions to study and propose such programs have been introduced in virtually all recent sessions of Congress. Thirteen states (and several cities and counties) now operate youth service programs, most of which are small and oriented toward environmental conservation. In 1984 the Gallup organization reported that 65 percent of the American people favored a program in which all young men and women would serve for 1 year either in the armed forces or in civilian social work in return for unspecified educational benefits.[2] This was no passing enthusiasm; polls have consistently shown similar support for such proposals ever since the days of the Civilian Conservation Corps of the 1930s.

It is not surprising that the concept of national service should exercise such appeal; it is one of the few innovations on the political horizon that, if adopted in comprehensive form, might transform the conditions of life in the United States. As envisioned by its proponents, a large-scale national service system could simultaneously multiply the labor power available for attacking the nation's social and environmental problems, make the military services both more effective and more representative, and deeply enrich the lives of those who serve. It is also possible, however, that a mandatory system of service would preempt time and energy now devoted to more valid ends, breach the constitutional prohibition against involuntary servitude, produce intrusive new bureaucracies, cost (perhaps waste) large sums of money, and reverse the precept that a democratic state exists to serve its citizens rather than the other way around.

It is striking, therefore, that despite decades of discussion, it is still unclear what is meant by national service. The phrase does not describe a particular program or even a well-defined idea. It merely evokes an ideal, an ideal whose particulars, attractive or repugnant, have not been supplied. Would national service be mandatory, wholly voluntary, or governmentally encouraged? Would it be universal, or would it apply only to youth, males, the fit, or those without dependents? What is its purpose: that youth pay their dues to society through sacrifice and labor, or the reverse, that society meet its obligations to youth through useful, paid employment?

The confusion surrounding the nature and purpose of national service has permitted broad support for the ideal, but has also inhibited examination of the problems and benefits that different systems of service might entail. Consider, for example, the issues raised by a mandatory and universal program imposed on, say, eighteen-year-olds. Annually, almost 4 million Americans become eighteen years of age. Would eighteen-year-old mothers or children who support parents or siblings be required to serve? What would be done with the tens (perhaps hundreds) of thousands of young people who simply refused to serve?

Such unanswered questions have provoked this study. Our purpose is neither to advocate national service nor to attack it. It is to try to understand what national service might mean and how it might work and thereby to help illuminate and focus the continuing debate. We attempt to do this mainly by being specific. We have developed four alternative models of national service. The models embody quite different treatments of several key variables: whether national service would be voluntary or mandatory; whether it would involve only draftable males or all persons of every age and condition; whether only several months or 1 or 2 years of service would be required; whether the program would operate under federal, state, or local authority; whether its intention would be mainly to expand the scope of social and environmental services, to improve the character or employability of the participants, or to strengthen the military. Under each model of national service, we explore a variety of questions. What tasks would the participants undertake? What is the social value of performing those tasks? What needs of the participants might be met in the various forms of service and in the many kinds of assignments? What would be the costs of these programs in dollars and in terms of the alternative activities that participants would not be free to pursue? What kinds of administrative arrangements would be necessary to recruit, train, assign duties for, and supervise the participants? How might service affect labor markets?

Four models cannot capture the almost infinite number of possible variations on the theme of national service. Furthermore, our answers to the questions we pose, like any assertions about the future, amount to no more than informed speculation. And in the end, conclusions about whether national service is a good idea or a bad one, and what forms of it are preferable, depend on choices among competing values. We leave those decisions to our readers. Nonetheless, we hope this book advances the national service debate. Our discussion of the probable costs and benefits of the models, while hardly definitive, should at least suggest the potential and the problems that distinguish them. In addition, since each model represents a broad type of national service, the discussion should shed some light on other forms of service we do not specify but that interested readers may readily construct.

Acknowledgments

If this book approaches our goals, it is largely because we have had much help. We are indebted, first, to our distinguished consultants. Six consultants canvassed the tasks that, in the fields they knew best, might be assigned to the kinds of national service participants generated by each model. They noted the training and supervision requirements those tasks implied, estimated the number of participants likely to prove useful, and commented on the benefits that might flow from such assignments.

Child care questions were examined by Suzanne Woolsey and Susan Gutchess; education, by Theodore Sizer; environmental protection, by Perry Hagenstein; health care, by Dr. Phillip Lee, Lew Butler, Jim Rice, and Margot Smith; military issues, by Gary Nelson, Robert Hale, and Joel Slackman; and a variety of additional social services, by Francine Rabinovitz.

In addition, Michael Maccoby and Cynthia Margolies assessed some of the variables in each model that would determine the psychological impact of service on the participants; Orley Ashenfelter and Ronald Oaxaca analyzed the effects of each model on the labor market; and Edward K. Hamilton, with Arthur Hauptman, commented on possible administrative structures and the probable costs of each model. James Lacy enriched that mix of speculation with a careful review of both the historical debate over national service and the partial precedents for it in U.S. history.

We are also indebted to the members of our advisory board who, in two meetings of the board as a body and through many communications from individual members, kept us sensitive to the profoundly different perspectives they brought to the question of national service. Members of the board were Lori Bailey, Elise Boulding, Alan Bowser, Senator Bill Bradley, Edward Clark, David Cohen, B.T. Collins, Jamileh-Sofia di Guida, William Donaldson, Senator David Durenberger, Representative Jack Edwards, Jane Fleming, Arthur Flemming, Henry Foster, Harry Hufford, William Josephson, Paul Joskow, Roger Landrum, Representative James Leach, Steven Minter, Charles Moskos, Senator Sam Nunn, Representative Leon Panetta, Dr. Chase Peterson, Major General Colin Powell, Charles Prejean, Lisbeth Schorr, John Shattuck, Michael Smith, Max Stier, Lieutenant General Maxwell Thurman, and Scott Thomson. Members of the advisory board are not responsible for the views we present, nor do they represent any agreed view of national service. To the contrary, they were helpful critics exactly because of the diversity of their views.

Others who read some or all of the manuscript in draft and offered helpful comments were Michael Bailin, Martin Binkin, Steven Cimbala, Alex Cook, Alec Dickson, Donald Eberly, Rashi Fein, Andrew Hahn, Clifford Johnson, Sar Levitan, Mark Newell, Neil Singer, Andrew Sum, Robert Taggart, Carl Weisbrod, Wendy Wolf, and Adam Yarmolinski. We are grateful to them all.

Finally, Gordon Berlin, Shepard Forman, and Enid Schoettle at the Ford Foundation (which funded this work) maintained a nice balance between encouragement and exasperation over the 4 years the project took to complete, and Patricia Hanen, Lori Martin, Bernard Wolfson, Sarah Szanton, and Kitty Barrett provided, in turn, project administration, research assistance, word processing, and the determination to move on to other pursuits that brought us finally to the end.

Notes

1. James, "The Moral Equivalent of War," 13–14.
2. Gallup, "National Service in Exchange for Educational Benefits."

1
Plan of the Book

How to Read this Book

This book has four parts. Chapter 1 comprises the first; it offers a brief historical and political background to the debate about national service and explains why and how this study was done.

The second part, composed of chapters 2, 3, and 4, analyzes the theoretical attractions of the concept of national service. Chapter 2 examines the argument that national service participants might be used to augment or improve social services and the environment, and it offers the best estimates we can make of the number of national service participants (often hereafter referred to as NSPs) who could usefully be assigned to those tasks. Chapter 3 discusses another of the traditional arguments for some form of national service, that the experience would confer important benefits on the NSPs themselves. It attempts to identify and assess those benefits for young NSPs and for older persons. Chapter 4 examines how national service might benefit the armed services, either in the current context of an all-volunteer force or under a draft.

Part three is the most distinctive section of the book. There, in chapters 5 through 8, we examine four quite different but plausible forms of national service. We assess the extent to which the potential of the ideal might be captured in practice, and the human and financial costs of each form of service. In chapter 5, we discuss a model that makes the equivalent of 6 weeks of service a prerequisite to graduation from high school. Chapter 6 assumes the reinstitution of a military draft and discusses a system that provides a 2-year civilian service alternative that might be chosen by persons drafted. Chapter 7 evaluates a wholly voluntary system of national service that might be developed by expanding and integrating existing federal and state conservation and public service corps. Finally, in chapter 8, we describe an unusual universal and mandatory program that would require all persons to perform a year of civilian (or a longer period of military) service or to pay an annual tax penalty for failure to serve. In each of these chapters, after describing the model and outlining how it might work, we evaluate the model in terms of its probable impact on unmet social needs, on the NSPs, and on the military. We also assess its constitutional implications and likely costs.

Finally, part four (chapter 9) extracts from the preceding discussion the conclusions we believe most important for future policymaking.

There is at least one defect of this structure: Read straight through, the book may seem highly repetitive. Chapters 5 through 8, for example, contain sections reviewing the impact of each chapter's model of service on social needs and on NSPs. The models differ, as do the affects; still, similarities in impact from model to model produce somewhat similar discussions, and, to make comparative judgments easier, we have made those discussions parallel in form.

One advantage of this structure is that even the most interested reader need not read straight through. Although everyone should skim this first chapter to understand the ground rules on which the book proceeds, the reader may then choose sections or chapters of the book selectively. Thus, a reader mystified by the persistent appeal of national service might have a special interest in chapters 2, 3, and 4. Someone already susceptible to that appeal who wishes to see how various forms of service might work and how the value of service compares to its costs and difficulties might move more directly to any or all of chapters 5 through 8. Some readers may regard only a universal and mandatory system as true national service, so they might proceed directly to chapter 8. Those interested only in a voluntary system might look only at chapter 7. And those interested only in the larger conclusions of this study will find them laid out in chapter 9.

The Persistent Attraction

There are three enduring questions of life in the United States that, when considered together, exercise—as another writer said in another context—an almost electric force among one another.

One of these questions is how the nation can better meet its social and environmental needs: maintaining parks and forests; caring for the very young, the elderly, and the ill; tutoring those who need special attention. Another is whether society should provide its youth not merely an academic education but a broader experience of life, a greater sense of worth, and better preparation for employment and citizenship. A third question is how the military might be made more effective and more representative of the civilian society it serves.

Often when these questions are considered alone, and almost invariably when they are considered together, a vision is generated of some system whereby young Americans (or perhaps all Americans) would be asked (or required) to serve the nation for some period in either a military or civilian capacity. That vision is usually termed national service.

For persons whose concern is military manpower, youth unemployment, or better social services, some form of national service represents a possible solution to a particular problem. But to the general public, national service seems attractive for its potential to accomplish so many ends at once. Indeed, national service has been seen as a way not only to answer the three enduring questions, but also to have youth pay their dues to society; provide young people with jobs; give them settings other than school and home in which to test their capacities and discover their interests; bring them in contact with persons older, younger, and of different backgrounds than themselves; and teach them to work jointly toward a common public goal. Some have seen national service as a kind of shaking of the bottle, a disruption of normal life patterns that would help young people break free of deadening environments. Others believe it might open up to broader public scrutiny the institutions in which the young people would serve.

As one would expect of an idea with so many possible virtues, the notion of national service has long attracted strong interest. William James's 1910 essay, "The Moral Equivalent of War," stimulated considerable discussion of this idea, and support for it has persisted. That interest has been reflected in programs as varied as the church-based work camps of the 1920s; the New Deal's Civilian Conservation Corps and National Youth Administration; the conservation work assigned to conscientious objectors during World War II and the broader social service tasks permitted objectors during the Korean and Vietnam wars; the Peace Corps; several service-oriented job programs sponsored by ACTION in the 1970s; and a growing number of small-scale conservation corps now operated by federal, state, and local authorities. The appeal of the concept is also evident in many proposals that never reached fruition. These include Universal Military Training (UMT), sought by President Truman in the late 1940s, and the National Service Corps, a domestic version of the Peace Corps that was proposed by the Kennedy administration in 1962 and 1963, the latter eventually leading to the establishment of VISTA (Volunteers in Service to America). That appeal has also accounted for the endorsement of the idea by many task forces and commissions.[1]

Similarly, polls consistently have shown that a majority of Americans favor some form of universal service for young men. A 1982 Gallup poll of 1,500 so-called opinion leaders found that 80 percent favored "requiring all young men to give one year of service to the nation, either in the military forces or in nonmilitary work here or abroad, such as work in hospitals or with elderly people."[2] The reasons given for that support varied widely, but among them were the following:

> A forty-six-year-old newspaper publisher from Illinois expressed this view: "I support such a plan, and one advantage would be that it would improve the quality of the military."
>
> Here are the views of a forty-five-year-old business executive: "If one makes a personal investment in this country, he will take a greater interest in being a citizen.
>
> A retired professor of philosophy from South Carolina feels that discussion of this plan would be particularly timely "in view of the fact that the federal government is cutting back on its social services."[3]

More broadly, the Gallup organization calculated from a February 1984 sample that 65 percent of American adults favored a 1-year compulsory national service plan offering educational benefits and that 58 percent of young persons (ages eighteen to twenty-four) also supported it. By quite similar margins the proposal was favored by persons in all age categories, of both sexes, and by both whites and nonwhites.[4]

Reflecting that level of interest, bills have been introduced in almost every session of Congress over the last decade to establish additional youth service programs, civilian service alternatives to a future military draft, programs into which young people could volunteer for military or civilian service, or national commissions to study the idea of national service.[5] Significantly, no such bills have become law, but a number of programs with some attributes of national service have been established.

Precedents

The United States came closest to mounting a comprehensive civilian service program in the 1930s through two initiatives of the New Deal: the Civilian Conservation Corps (CCC) and the National Youth Administration. The CCC, "Roosevelt's Tree Army," was proposed by FDR as he accepted the 1932 Democratic nomination and was established during the first 100 days of his administration:

> I propose to create a Civilian Conservation Corps to be used in simple work, not interfering with normal work, and confining itself to forestry, the prevention of soil erosion, flood control, and similar projects. . . . [M]ore important . . . than material gains will be the moral and spiritual value of such work. . . . [W]e can take a vast army of these unemployed out into healthful surroundings. . . . [W]e can eliminate, at least to some extent, the threat that enforced idleness brings to moral and spiritual stability.[6]

Unemployed men between the ages of eighteen and twenty-five were eligible to participate in the CCC. Initial enrollments were for 6 months, but in later years they could be extended for up to 2 years. Enrollees first went to army camps for physical conditioning and then were sent to any of about 200 work camps, mainly on public lands in the South, Southwest, or West, to build fire towers, improve trails, cut firebreaks, stock fish, plant trees, and perform other similar tasks. In each camp, a company of up to 200 enrollees worked together on a single project.

> The average enrollee was a 20 year old Caucasian, was equally likely to be from an urban or a rural background, and never held a regular full-time job prior to entering the CCC, came from a household of six children where the father was employed, joined the CCC primarily to help the family financially, had an eighth grade education, performed in the low-normal range on IQ tests . . . and . . . stayed in the CCC 10 months.[7]

Despite the uneasiness of organized labor and the quiet contempt of some of its camps' rural neighbors,[8] the CCC was a considerable political success. It became a very large program, enrolling more than 500,000 men in its peak year.[9] Cumulatively over the 9 years of its operation, it enrolled approximately 3 million young men and comprised more than 4 percent of the federal budget.[10]

In fact, there were three CCCs. The program initially was enacted as a welfare program, at first giving priority, and later exclusive access, to those on the relief rolls. Of the $30 wage it paid each month, the program required that $22 be sent home. This "represented a direct federal assumption of public assistance for needy families . . . [T]here were considerable pressures not to squander this on families who were not already on, or qualified for, local welfare assistance."[11]

Revisions on 1937 modified this policy to make the benefits of the CCC more broadly available to those "who need the employment, the job training, the education and other opportunities offered by the Civilian Conservation Corps."[12] By 1938, a third of the CCC's enrollees would not have qualified under the earlier, more restrictive standards. The program's emphasis also had shifted to place increasing weight on education and training.[13]

At the same time, pressure arose to bend the CCC to serve the nation's growing concerns about military defense. James Lacy has described the results as follows:

> In 1936 a Gallup Poll reported 77 percent in favor of military training in CCC camps; a follow-up poll in 1939 reported 90 percent in favor. . . . In early 1941 the camps began to take a pronounced military flavor. . . . In August, military drills, without weapons, became a camp requirement. . . . At the same time, the nature of camp work shifted. . . . In place of erosion control and reforestation came the building of fortifications and military installations.[14]

By 1942, the changed military situation made the CCC a diversion of labor power from industrial production or military service. As the *Washington Post* commented in a front-page editorial, "The Civilian Conservation Corps today is without function. There is not a boy on its rolls who can't get a job."[15] The CCC did not survive World War II.

The CCC had a younger sibling that is also of interest as a precedent for national service. Established in 1935, the National Youth Administration (NYA), like the CCC, enlisted young persons (at first only youths whose families received public assistance) to work on projects of public value. The NYA provided work for approximately 2.7 million men and women over the course of its 9-year life.[16] Unlike the CCC, the NYA employed youths in their own communities, enlisted women as well as men, offered most enrollees only part-time work, and assigned enrollees to tasks that were much more visible than the conservation work that occupied the CCC. NYA projects included the improvement of grounds around public buildings, maintenance of parks, road construction, and construction of schools and other public buildings. The NYA also preserved food, repaired furniture, and undertook other production for use projects, whose output was distributed through local welfare agencies.[17]

Like the CCC, the NYA was opposed by most of organized labor. Opposition to the NYA was far more intense, however, because NYA workers visibly engaged in work that appeared to compete with the private job market. Operating under local supervision, layered with a substantial bureaucracy, lacking the paramilitary trappings of the CCC, and without the protective cloak of distance, the NYA never generated the public support that the CCC enjoyed.

The political history of recent service programs has exhibited a similar pattern. Remote programs maintain a strong appeal. The most durable program, the Peace Corps, sends small numbers of volunteers overseas. Very small conservation and community service corps now operate in thirteen states, ten of them on a year-round basis.[18] At the federal level, three successive conservation corps were established either as part of the 1960s War on Poverty or under the 1974 Comprehensive Training and Employment Act (CETA). More recently, an American Conservation Corps (ACC), anticipated to enlist 37,000 youths for 1-year terms, was enacted by Congress in 1984. President Ronald Reagan vetoed the ACC, but the congressional action demonstrated the continued appeal of the conservation corps concept.[19] The more visible and controversial CETA urban public employment programs, experimental ACTION programs, and the VISTA program have been eliminated or dramatically cut back.

In short, while the public favors national service in the abstract, almost all the programs that might serve as prototypes have been remote from everyday life. Whether a larger and more pervasive program is enactable, or sustainable, remains doubtful.

Why This Study?

If national service has been discussed since 1910, and if a variety of experiments, federal and state, large and small, have already been undertaken, what is the purpose of this study? Proponents of service might well agree that it is time to grasp the nettle and establish a large-scale program. Opponents might respond that three-quarters of a century of experience demonstrates that, despite opinion polls, comprehensive national service is an idea whose time will never come. Agnostics might simply assert that the remaining questions about national service involve competing values, that no study can resolve such a competition, and therefore that no study is likely to prove useful.

We think, to the contrary, that sustained and dispassionate thinking about national service is very much in order. In our view, the debate about national service, protracted and occasionally passionate though it has been, has been largely cast at a level of generality that has precluded serious analysis of particular forms of service. Further, we think that changes in the nature of U.S. society warrant reconsidering the forms national service might take. Finally, we believe that during the next decade national service may well take a leading place on the national political agenda because of concern about youth unemployment, perceived shortfalls in the voluntary military, or a demand for more public services than the tax system could be used to support. It may be useful to expand briefly on each of these three points.

Deepening the Discussion

One reason why the discussion of national service has been relatively unilluminating is that the object of the discussion has rarely been well specified.[20] As a rule, national service has been treated as an ideal rather than an idea. The particulars of what it would involve rarely are stated clearly. Yet the range of possibilities is great. Would service be voluntary, governmentally encouraged, or mandatory? What incentives would be used to induce service? Would it involve males only or both sexes; youth only or participants of many ages, perhaps especially the elderly? Would participants live at home and work in their own communities or be housed in residential camps? Would participants be compensated modestly, well, or not at all? Would service last for 6 months, 2 years, or as long as the participant liked? Would service involve work that prepared participants for jobs, or on the contrary, could they perform only tasks that did not compete with those undertaken in the job market?

The frequent failure to address these questions is linked to a second, more fundamental, source of confusion: the absence of agreement on the larger values national service should serve. In proposing his army enlisted against nature, William James sought to invigorate pacifism by giving it a positive program. He wanted to reduce the attraction of warfare by giving martial instincts other enemies to attack. That motive has had little relevance to later advocates. For some, in fact, national service is attractive as a means of facilitating military recruitment. For others, as already suggested, current interest in some form of national service seems to spring mainly from a concern to enlarge social programs, to provide jobs for the unemployed, to supplement classroom education, or to have the young pay their dues. As we shall see, these goals are not wholly compatible. Against what purposes, then, should national service, however designed, be judged?

The two deficiencies in most past discussions of national service (lack of specificity as to nature and purpose) have bred a third, lack of empirical reference. It is true that no large-scale system of national service has been tried in the United States, but various partially comparable programs of the 1930s and of the past 20 years, and the social science literature they have spawned, can yield considerably greater insight. We believe they have more to teach us about national service—pro and con—than the largely philosophical discussions that have appeared to date.

In this book, we try to avoid these pitfalls through three devices. First, we adopt a relatively broad definition of national service. Then we define four specific but quite different models of national service that represent the main types of plans that we think fall within the ambit of the definition. Finally, we analyze each model against the full range of considerations that those concerned with national service are likely to value.

In proceeding along these lines we have been conscious that discussion of national service has suffered from having been conducted mainly by enthusiastic supporters or committed opponents of the idea. We count ourselves as neither. We follow the evidence of both costs and benefits to whatever conclusion it seems to lead. This course may frustrate the reader because it leads us to some tentative or ambivalent conclusions. We hope, however, that a balanced and careful discussion that brings new evidence to bear on the issues will focus and deepen the debates that we do not pretend to resolve.

Updating the Discussion

Since World War II the nation's demography has been dramatically altered by the postwar baby boom and its current echo and by the rapid growth in

Americans' life expectancy. Social and economic patterns have been transformed by the radically increased participation of women and teen-agers in the labor force, by rising high school graduation and college attendance rates, by a sharp growth in the number of female-headed households, and by a steady rise in demand for social and environmental services. At the same time, this country has experimented first with peacetime conscription and now with an all-volunteer military of substantial size.

These changes, among others, should affect our thinking about national service, but in our view they have rarely been reflected in debate about the topic. We consider them in the discussion that follows.

The Possible Necessity for Decision

Senator Gary Hart has observed that "compulsory national service may be the biggest issue of the eighties."[21] The same statement might plausibly have been made about almost any postwar decade. National service is an issue whose time seems never to come. Nonetheless, any of three circumstances might intensify debate on this subject and prompt a decision about it over the next decade.

One would be an attempt to compensate for cutbacks in the federal funding of social and environmental programs through the use of what may appear to be inexpensive personnel. National service may seem more attractive than continued deficits as a means of sustaining a higher level of services than the nation is willing to tax itself to support. Second, should the nation slide into another recession or should youth unemployment remain unacceptably high for other reasons, national service may be advanced by those who see in it a solution to the problem of unemployment. The CCC and the NYA of the 1930s might then seem attractive models.

In our view, the contingency most likely to provoke a serious look at national service would involve the armed forces. As we discuss in much greater detail in chapter 4, youth cohorts are now declining and will continue to do so through the early 1990s. By the standards of the last decade, then, the pool from which military personnel must be drawn is unusually small. Should the civilian economy offer more attractive jobs or wages than military service, or should military recruitment goals substantially increase, then the current system of voluntary military service would come into question. A conventional draft would, however, almost certainly prove highly controversial. In such a situation, interest in some form of national service would sharply increase. It would appear to provide a way of sharing the burdens of service more broadly and of permitting youths who resisted military service on conscientious or other grounds to find an acceptable alternative.

The Method of This Study

If an unfocused debate and changing conditions make a fresh look at national service appropriate, they also make it difficult. First of all, we need to set the boundaries of the concept. What do we mean by "national service"?

Given the imprecision with which most discussion of national service has been conducted, any definition is necessarily somewhat arbitrary. But we think it true to the spirit of the long debate to define national service in this way: National service is any federally supported program in which, for a period of time, participants sacrifice some degree of personal advancement, income, or freedom to serve a public interest.

This definition is broad enough to encompass both voluntary and compulsory programs, plans involving only youth and those involving older people, and proposals that would provide no pay or minimal wages to participants. It encompasses activities as diverse as service in the military, work as a hospital orderly or as a teacher corps or conservation corps member, and part-time community service to meet a requirement for high-school graduation.

The definition also excludes. By its terms, for example, employment in the civil service is not national service because it involves no sacrifice of personal advancement, income, or freedom. More important, for the same reason this definition excludes programs whose primary purpose is job training or placement, and which are designed to serve not the nation but their participants. Benefits to society, though they are great when such programs work, are collateral to the effects on the participants.

We realize that many persons look to some form of national service to enhance youth employability.[22] Moreover, some forms of national service may well have such an effect. One of the ways in which we evaluate our alternative forms of national service, therefore, is in terms of their likely consequences for youth employment. We also believe that some job-oriented programs might reasonably be imbedded in a broader system of national service whose main emphasis was something other than employment. One of the forms of service we analyze (model 3) is constructed in just that way.

Given so broad a concept of national service, what particular form or forms of service should we assess, and against what standards should we measure them?

The Models

It is impossible to assess all of the possible national service programs. Instead, we have designed four forms of national service that seem to represent the span of alternatives. Taken together, the four range in their degree of compulsion from voluntary to mandatory; in their inclusion from only nineteen-year-old males who meet the standard of the military draft to all citizens, including the elderly and the handicapped; in their duration from 6 weeks to 2 years; in their control from state and local primacy to highly centralized federal direction; and in their purpose from educating participants and providing social services to assisting the military.

Model 1: School-Based Service

This model treats service primarily as a supplement to schooling, as its purpose is predominantly educational. It offers federal support for programs in which states make 240 hours of service a prerequisite to a high school diploma. At the option of the states or school districts, service could be performed either full-time during summers or part-time during or after school over the course of the student's senior year. Participants would live at home and work without pay in approved charitable or governmental organizations. The option of 3 months in basic military training on a military base also would be open to those who qualified.

Such a program might be appealing because it would be optional to each state, only modestly intrusive on the time of participants, relatively cheap, and locally administered.

Model 2: Draft-Based Service

This model assumes that a military draft requiring 2 years of service is enacted at some future time. Given a draft, it offers all persons actually drafted a 2-year civilian service alternative. It thus establishes for all the equivalent of a conscientious objector program, without requiring conscientious objection. Draft calls would expand to whatever levels were necessary to meet military requirements, given the proportion of conscripts choosing civilian service.

Such a program might be attractive because it would provide the military with any required number of additional recruits, while not compelling military service from those unwilling to undertake it. By expanding the total number of persons serving in either military or civilian capacities, it also might reduce feelings of resentment or inequity among those drafted. We believe that if a peacetime military draft again seemed necessary, proposals of this type would be seriously considered.

Model 3: Voluntary Service

The current wide range of voluntary service might be augmented in a variety of ways. Chapter 7 discusses some of these alternatives and then assesses a model in which existing types of service programs—including the Peace Corps, VISTA, public service employment programs, and conservation programs—would be expanded to provide federal support for a voluntary service program involving approximately 180,000 positions. Such a plan builds on the experience and organizational bases of the past 20 years. It would offer participants of sharply differing needs and abilities the choice of joining, under the unifying theme of national service, whichever program best met their needs and interests.

Model 4: Universal Service

This is by far the most ambitious and most intrusive of the plans. It mandates a year of service and allows essentially no exemptions. It resembles the form of national service that many Americans regularly endorse in national polls. For reasons elaborated in chapter 8, however, the model we have developed provides that the year may be served at any time and that participation is not enforced through criminal sanctions. Rather, a federal income surtax of 5 percent is imposed every year until service is rendered. Military service would continue to be voluntary and, as in each of the models, would count as meeting the service obligation.

Evaluating the Models

Those are the forms of national service we evaluate. How should they be assessed? The only way to compare and evaluate them fairly is to try to apply to each all of the competing values that seem arguably relevant. As a result, we analyze each in terms of five categories of probable effects:

Effects on the provision of public services, including the kind and quality of support it might provide for education, health care, child care, the environment, and other social services;

Impact on the military, including the composition, costs, and probable effectiveness of the armed forces;

Labor market consequences, including likely changes in employment and unemployment rates and labor force participation;

Effects on the participants, including educational, psychological, social, and economic effects;

Public costs and other public consequences, including budgets for each of the programs; the form and size of the agencies required to run them;

effects on relations between federal, state, and local governments; considerations of equity and issues of constitutionality.

Our estimation of those effects is governed, we should note, by two important assumptions. One has to do with job displacement. We assume that no system of national service would be politically tolerable if it assigned its participants to positions in which they displaced current workers or, in expanding services, took places that additional workers would otherwise be hired to fill. We therefore calculate the maximum number of national service positions in a way that does not include such jobs. We specify in the chapters that follow a limited number of potential exceptions to this rule but otherwise observe it absolutely.

The second assumption is that of stability. The world of the late 1980s and 1990s will differ in important respects from that of 1986. Some of the differences, such as shifts in U.S. demography, can be predicted with some confidence, but many cannot. Therefore, except where the text expressly projects changes in social or economic characteristics or in national policy, we assess the effects of national service as though current conditions prevailed. In particular, we assume no new federal programs of relevance to national service and no radical expansion (or contraction) of such programs now in existence.

Notes

1. Within the past 5 years, the concept has been most notably advanced by the Committee for the Study of National Service, sponsored by the Potomac Institute (which published *Youth and the Needs of the Nation*), the National Service Secretariat (founded in 1967), the Youth Policy Institute, and the Roosevelt Centennial Youth Project Commission.

2. Gallup, "Eight in Ten Opinion Leaders Back Compulsory National Service." The most comprehensive discussion of the history of national service programs and proposals is contained in Lacy, "National Service: The Origins and Evolution in Theory and Practice."

3. Ibid.

4. Gallup, "National Service in Exchange for Educational Benefits."

5. In 1979, H.R. 2206, H.R. 3603, H.R. 4040, and S. 2159 covered this span of alternatives.

6. 21 March 1933, *Congressional Record,* 77th Cong., 1st sess., 650–51. The program apparently drew its inspiration from a reforestation program Roosevelt began as governor of New York. On the history of the CCC, see generally, Lacy, "National Service: Origins and Evolution," and Sherraden, *The Civilian Conservation Corps: Effectiveness of the Camps.*

7. Sherraden, *The Civilian Conservation Corps: Effectiveness of the Camps,* 4–5.

8. A contemporaneous account of a farm family's hostility to a North Dakota CCC camp and its occupants is offered in Low, *Dust Bowl Diary,* 221–61.

9. Public/private Ventures ("A Profile of Youth Conservation Corps Programs"), noting a 1934 cost for the CCC of $313 million, calculates this as $2.1 billion in 1983 terms. We note, however, that expenditures reached $593 million in 1936, the program's high point.

10. McEntee, "Final Report of the Director of the Civilian Conservation Corps: April 1933 through June 30, 1942," 92. This was a period in which the total federal budget averaged less than $10 billion a year. Four percent of the fiscal year 1985 budget alone amounts to $37.2 billion, according to data from the Office of Management and Budget, *Midsession Review of the 1985 Budget,* 4.

11. Lacy, "National Service: Origins and Evolution," 20–23.

12. Ibid., 21 (citing CCC, *Annual Report,* 1938, 68).

13. Ibid.

14. Ibid., 22–23.

15. *The Washington Post,* 12 February 1942, A-1.

16. Lacy, "National Service: Origins and Evolution," 15.

17. Ibid., 32–33.

18. For a current listing of year-round and summer state conservation corps currently in operation, as well as other programs in existence, see Human Environment Center, "Conservation Corps Profiles." States having year-round programs as of mid-1985 were Alaska, California, Connecticut, Iowa, Michigan, Minnesota, Ohio, Pennsylvania, Washington, and Wisconsin. Alaska, Iowa, Maine, Maryland, Michigan, and Texas maintained summer programs. For an evaluation of the well-regarded California Conservation Corps, see Bailin, "The California Conservation Corps: A Case Study."

19. H.R. 999 to establish an American Conservation Corps was first introduced into the House by Congressman Siberling (D-Ohio). The House passed it in 1983, but procedural challenges and proposed amendments to the bill kept it from the Senate floor for more than a year. It finally passed the Senate in considerably amended form in October 1984 and was approved by both Houses, with diminished funding, just prior to the closing of the Ninety-eighth Congress. The bill was then vetoed by President Reagan.

20. A distinguished exception is *Youth and the Needs of the Nation,* ed. Landrum.

21. See Rothenberg, *The Neoliberals: Creating the New American Politics,* 210. Besides Hart, Rothenberg identifies Senator Bradley, former Senator Tsongas, and Congressman Panetta as neoliberals interested in national service. Rothenberg argues that national service is "one of the places the neoliberals are leading America," Ibid., 208.

22. See, for example, Foley, Maneker, and Schwartz, *National Service and America's Future,* 1: "Professionals in the field of youth employment claim that a service system would both better prepare young people from all backgrounds for the world

of work and provide a needed range of new opportunities for productivity and tangible contributions by those youth who are severely disadvantaged and chronically unemployed."

Similarly, the Roosevelt Centennial Youth Project "will actively seek broad support for . . . a [nationwide] work and service program complemented by and integrated with a significant educational initiative . . . to serve as a bridge between education and employment in order to help the deterioration of our future work force and in the quality of life which our people enjoy." Roosevelt Centennial Youth Project, *A Policy Blueprint,* 1.

The American Jewish Committee has asserted that a national service program "might more than pay for itself if additional economic benefits such as increased employability of participants and decreased reliance on income transfer are considered." American Jewish Committee, "National Service," 6.

2
Unmet Social Needs

Providing the labor to undertake social and environmental tasks; building character, offering employment, or in some other way strengthening the participants; and more fully or fairly meeting military personnel needs are the three enduring attractions of the ideal of national service. In this chapter, we turn to the first of them, assessing the nature and scale of unmet social needs and offering the bases for our judgments, set out in later chapters, on the degree to which various forms of national service might meet those needs and at what costs.

Some Reservations about Needs

We begin with several caveats. The first is fundamental: "Unmet social needs" is a slippery concept. It presents at least two difficulties. First, how real are needs that society has so far proven unwilling to pay for? Needs currently unmet must, by definition, be needs that neither the marketplace nor our political processes have so far found more pressing than other claims on private or public resources. In the absence of evidence of failure in both the marketplace and in our politics, it can be argued that the net benefit of meeting any such unmet need—that is, the value of meeting it less the costs involved in diverting from their current uses the resources necessary to do so—is presumptively negative. If either our economics or our politics concluded otherwise, the need currently would be met.

The second difficulty is simply that many available calculations of need for additional services in education, health care, child care, environment, and the like have been produced by professionals in those fields, and professionals in every field are understandably predisposed to value their services more highly than does the public at large. Even if legitimate in nature, therefore, the needs may well be exaggerated in scale.

Our response to the second problem has been to impose what we believe to be a realistic limit on the estimate of each social need. In the case of conservation and the environment, for example, the need is limited to work that would prevent measurable degradation from the current state of public lands and waterways and the atmosphere. Need here is thus defined as no more than the maintenance for future generations of the natural settings the current generation inherited. In education, the limit is the number of NSPs that could effectively be supervised by that fraction of the currently projected population of teachers and school administrators who we expect would willingly undertake such supervision. Similar boundaries—each somewhat arbitrary, but each specified and, in our judgment, conservative—are established in other calculations of "need."[1]

To the first objection—that currently unmet needs are not needs that this society values highly enough to pay for—we offer two responses. First, national service may generate multiple benefits. It may build character in its participants as they provide home care for the elderly or clean up urban parks. If so, the costs fairly attributable to providing home care are smaller than if that care were provided more conventionally. Some share of the costs of national service must be attributed to each desirable effect that service may produce.

Second and more fundamentally, needs are not static. Society's allocations of resources constantly change. By opting for national service, Americans may choose to support more social services or to generate more public goods than at present, just as they now provide more services and goods than they did two decades ago. There are plausible objective reasons for making such a decision. For example, between 1963 and 1982, U.S. scholastic aptitude scores dropped by almost 10 percent, and achievement tests administered to representative samples of high school seniors showed similar results.[2] For the first time, a generation of American high school graduates, by debatable but widely accepted measures, was academically less competent than the preceding generation. Similarly, the cost of caring for the ill, aged, and infirm in the United States has now risen, both absolutely and as a proportion of national wealth, to a level that appears unprecedented in human history. Whatever their ultimate merit, therefore, political decisions to apply additional resources to the schools to halt that decline in learning or to health care to slow that increase in cost would represent plausible responses to genuine problems.

The objection nonetheless deserves reflection. The scale of any national service program would involve an implicit judgment as to the extent of unmet social needs, just as the pattern of work assignments within the program would reflect judgments about the nature and relative importance of those needs. Yet it remains true that no consensus now makes legitimate those needs. Any system of national service, moreover, that involved a degree of compulsion would risk weighing these needs excessively and slighting the value of the alternative uses (additional schooling, private employment, recreation, leisure) to which NSPs might otherwise put their time. That danger would be most substantial in the case of a mandatory national service program imposed, by a predominantly older electorate, solely on the young. And any system of national service, voluntary or mandatory, would tend to create a labor force in search of a mission; the amount of public work undertaken would tend to vary with the number of participants rather than with the extent of needs.

A third caveat concerns the displacement of workers. Throughout this book we assume that any system of national service would not be politically tolerable if it assigned its participants to positions in which they displaced current workers or even the normal growth of work forces as a result of increased demand. This assumption constrains the number of NSPs we estimate could appropriately be employed.

This constraint is far easier to apply in theory than to enforce in fact. Existing jobs may be relatively easy to protect: regulations defining the assignments NSPs could be given could (and, as a political matter, surely would) require that no NSP could be assigned to tasks that employees currently fill. Growth in the job market would be considerably harder to protect. Much of the growth in U.S. jobs is projected to occur in service sectors such as care of children and of the elderly and environmental protection, which seem most appropriate as assignment areas for NSPs. This threat of job displacement historically has made organized labor hostile to national service and is one of the reasons why the great majority of past service programs has placed their participants in remote areas and devoted them to environmental conservation, where few jobs exist to be displaced. Even so, organized labor can be expected to oppose much more vigorously a national service program that assigns participants to social service tasks. Such objections should not be regarded simply as the claims of a special interest. The costs of displacement and resulting unemployment, although borne directly by those displaced, would be imposed through welfare and related programs on society in general.

The degree to which displacement limits the value of service or increases political resistance to service will depend as much on political pressures and on day-to-day decisions about the tasks NSPs can be assigned as on the formal rules intended to govern those decisions. For this and other reasons, these displacement effects are hard to predict. Our analysis may understate them and consequently overstate national service opportunities.

A final difficulty concerns training and supervision. The tasks that NSPs might perform are varied and numerous. Some would require prior training; in some (such as the care of elderly persons living alone) unreliable or abusive behavior could endanger the persons being served; others (child care, for example) might be performed willingly and well by NSPs whose temperaments and interests are appropriate for the tasks but might be botched or resisted if that were not the case. In short, the tasks that can be performed effectively will depend not only on the kinds of NSPs a particular form of national service produces but also on the skill with which individual NSPs are matched to particular tasks, the degree to which they are trained, and above all, the care with which they are supervised. None of the discussion that follows assumes what we believe to be unfeasible or cost-ineffective levels of such oversight and administration. We do assume, however, for all the forms of service and each of the tasks we discuss, that appropriate assignment and training policies are adopted and that necessary supervision is provided. Our cost estimates reflect those assumptions.

The Tasks to Be Performed

Caveats noted and assumptions understood, what are the tasks to which a system of national service might address itself? Social commentators and advocates of national service agree on the answer to that question. Adam Yarmolinsky represented that consensus in 1977:

> The greatest unmet needs in the U.S. today are for human services, delivered by relatively untrained but caring people at the local community level. . . . What we lack most are people like home health care aides and classroom aides and playground counselors and helpers in community centers. . . . At the same time public facilities are deteriorating for lack of adequate maintenance, and public use of these facilities is being cut back; there are not enough attendants in public parks or the public libraries.[3]

Over the past 15 years, social critics, labor economists, advocates of national service, and others have attempted to specify more fully the categories of civil tasks to which NSPs might be assigned. Virtually all have identified education, health care (including care of the elderly and infirm), child care, conservation and the environment, and a miscellany of other social services as the principal areas of unmet social needs.[4] Two studies in this period estimated the scale of personnel needs in those areas and yielded roughly consistent results. A 1970 survey conducted by Donald Eberly, a leading advocate of national service, concluded that, over a suitable phasing-in period, more than 4 million NSPs, of whom 2.8 million need not have any college experience, might at any time be matched to those areas of need.[5] The Urban Institute and the American Institutes for Research (UI/AIR), under contract to the Department of Labor in 1977–1978, assessed the opportunities for public sector job creation during a period of high unemployment and concluded that a total of 3.5 million jobs might readily be created, of which approximately 1.2 million require no greater skill than most youthful NSPs could offer.[6]

We approached this problem by asking a number of experts to identify the tasks that NSPs might perform and the number of NSPs those tasks might absorb in the area of their expertise. Their conclusions, consistent with those of the earlier studies, are that in aggregate some 3.5 million person-years of labor by NSPs of varying nonspecialized qualifications could be absorbed each year. We turn now to brief reviews of their findings.

Education

The U.S. school system could use a large number of national service participants. The reasons are several.

First, the system is large. In the late 1980s, some 2.5 million teachers will instruct some 45 million elementary and secondary school students in approximately 80,000 public and 25,000 private schools. The system also operates a well-staffed administrative structure, and it can accurately project future student loads and teaching resources. Therefore, the schools should be able to plan for and administer a large number of NSPs. Moreover, the quality of the school system is very important to society as a whole, and the utility of volunteers in education has often been demonstrated.

The tasks most commonly suggested for NSPs in the schools include teaching assistance in the classroom; tutoring, counseling, and remedial assistance outside the classroom; office and clerical work; and maintenance and repair of school facilities. The UI/AIR study concluded that some 680,000 young people might be usefully employed in tasks of this type. Eberly put the number at approximately 1 million.[7] Relying in part on those estimates, the Potomac Institute's Committee for the Study of National Service recommended the formation of a national tutoring corps, which, with 15 young people in every school district, would absorb some 240,000 national service members.[8]

The Nature of the Tasks

Theodore Sizer's analysis of the implications of our several models of national service differentiated three types of potential NSPs: those who could be depended on to work independently, others who "could be led," and still others who may prove "hostile, apathetic, or untrustworthy." Taking account of these differences, he placed the educational tasks that NSPs might perform into three categories:

> *Mentors; Teaching Auxiliaries* (TAs); and *Management Auxiliaries* (MAs). Though these are familiar labels, they have little usage among school aides and school volunteers—and as such carry little political or historical baggage.
>
> *Mentors* would be high school graduates drawn from the academic top 10% of their class and rated in the "can work autonomously" category. . . . Mentors would have direct teaching responsibility, including some autonomy, while working under the ultimate supervision of a teacher. For example, a Mentor might take five 4th graders who need special tutoring out of their classroom to the library and work with them there. Or a Mentor might visit a sick-at-home sixth grader and explain a set of word problems using percentages that a mathematics teacher might have assigned. Mentors would be expected to make sensible independent judgments and would have to have a solid mastery of the areas in which they tutor and teach.
>
> *Teaching Auxiliaries* (TAs) would be high school graduates from the top 80% of their classes who would assist teachers in a variety of in-classroom but always directly-supervised tasks. They might conduct assigned drills with small groups of students, or run spelling bees, or correct true/false tests, or put galoshes on little children, or organize a finger-painting hour. TAs could be drawn from both "can work autonomously" and "can be led" dependability categories.
>
> *Management Auxiliaries* (MAs) could be drawn from among high school graduates and nongraduates, from any rank-in-class and from both "can work autonomously" and "can be led" dependability categories. Their duties would be to assist school managers—principals, custodians, athletic trainers, groundspeople—in the maintenance of the physical plant and in bureaucratic routine.
>
> Initial placement in one or another category would follow a prospective NSP's preference and the program's selection standards, but NSPs might be reclassified if experience in a school dictated or warranted it. Within each category, a school (or school system, as some NSPs might work in several schools simultaneously, for example as an assistant coach of a city-wide winter track team) could use an NSP as flexibly as needed, with variety of experience a desirable characteristic.[9]

Although in practice the categories of NSPs might well be more loosely defined, with judgments about assignments left to individual schools or teachers, Sizer's categorization appears to span the range of likely tasks.

The Scale of Need

How many NSPs might the schools usefully absorb? Sizer constructs an estimate by first assuming that roughly one-third of U.S. school districts would reject the use of NSPs on grounds of educational philosophy, administrative complexity, or other objections. He then calculates separate ratios of teachers to NSP positions for each of the three categories of school-based tasks, and for elementary and secondary schools. The ratios vary from 10 : 7 for elementary teachers to mentors, to 10 : 1 for secondary school teachers to teaching auxiliaries, to 20 : 1 for elementary or secondary teachers to management auxiliaries. Projecting those ratios against the anticipated number of teachers, Sizer estimates 1.23 million NSP positions in the schools in 1989, the equivalent of one aide position to every two teachers overall.[10]

The Value of NSPs in the Schools

Utilizing national service participants in the schools offers a number of advantages, together with several potential drawbacks. As Sizer has commented:

> In all . . . the schools represent an ideal partner for a National Service program. They are stable, institutionally. The system is large, and thus could absorb many NSPs. The schools are numerous where the population is numerous: there will be few CCC-like relocation problems for NSPs. Educational authorities have a bureaucracy in place to select and supervise participants; some instructors who have trained student teachers from colleges have substantial experience with this sort of supervision. The rewards of labor in the schools are often very visible and heartwarming, quickly attained even by the inexperienced—nice attributes for a National Service program.[11]

There are other advantages. Teaching is a powerful way to learn. NSPs used as mentors or teaching aides are likely to gain greater mastery of the subjects they teach. Those successful at being mentors are also likely to feel needed, and the early experience of young NSPs with teaching may increase the number and enhance the quality of those who later choose teaching as a career. Given the teacher shortage now anticipated for the late 1980s and 1990s,[12] such an effect would have important social value.

It is also true, however, that the high standards Sizer sets for mentors—graduates from the top 10 percent of their classes who are capable of working autonomously—mean that only a small fraction of NSPs could undertake tasks of this character. Correspondingly, much of the work that teaching auxiliaries and management auxiliaries may be assigned (cleaning blackboards, monitoring hallways, helping first graders into their coats) offers little challenge, little enlargement of acquaintanceship, and little experience of being needed. Thus, assignments that most effectively meet societal needs may not serve equally well the personal needs of NSPs, and vice versa. There is no automatic consistency between the requirements of those served and those serving. That tension will reappear in other contexts.

Health Care

Another social service often regarded as able to absorb large numbers of national service participants is health care. We define the field broadly here to include medical research and public health activities, as well as personal medical and nursing care and their supporting services, preventive and curative, in hospitals, clinics, nursing homes, mental health facilities, practitioners' offices, patients' residences, or elsewhere. It includes services not only to persons ill or at risk of illness but also to the disabled and aged.

The system that now provides such services is diverse, very large, and growing. It involves institutions large and small, public and private, nonprofit and profit, custodial and radically interventionist. It includes self-help and voluntary organizations, research units, health planning agencies, consulting organizations, and single practitioners. It involves diagnostic, therapeutic, and rehabilitative services, and it offers levels of care ranging from the casual and backward to the most intense and sophisticated.

The principal elements of the system are more than 7,000 hospitals with 1.1 million hospital beds; some 19,000 nursing homes with more than 1.5 million beds; perhaps 3,000 board and care facilities (community or residential care homes, foster homes, halfway houses, and the like) with between 500,000 and 1.1 million residents; 1,200 hospices; an estimated 400,000 sites in which some form of ambulatory care is provided, as well as the millions of homes in which aged, sick, or disabled persons are cared for or attempt to care for themselves.[13] Approximately 13 million Americans currently suffer degrees of disability that at least preclude normal schooling or occupation and may require assistance with eating, dressing, and hygiene. Between 1.5 and 2 million people live in institutions oriented toward long-term care. Of these, 69 percent live in nursing homes,[14] and 4.9 million living at home require assistance from family, friends, or community social services.[15] Moreover, the aged, who account for a high proportion of those needing home and nursing home care, are the fastest growing age group in the United States. Persons over sixty-five, who accounted for 6 percent of the U.S. population in 1930, are now double that proportion of a much larger population. They will form 21 percent of the population by the year 2030.[16] The oldest old, although a much smaller group, is the fastest growing population segment, and its members almost all require assistance if not institutionalization. In 1950 there were 590,000 Americans aged eight-five or older. There are now more than four times that many, and their number is expected to double again by the year 2000.[17]

Tasks

The health care system—more accurately, the complex of separate and poorly integrated health care systems—provides a large number of sharply differing tasks that might be assigned to national service participants. Many of these tasks, however, present much more challenging problems of supervision and administration than would be the case in the schools. Most users of the health care system are, of course, ill or disabled and isolated. They are particularly vulnerable to incompetent, unreliable, uncaring, or abusive treatment. NSPs must be well supervised when serving patients directly. Moreover, NSPs cannot be utilized in ways that violate licensure or certification requirements; they may have to be insured and, depending on their assignments, may need physical examinations, immunizations, or substantial training. Because health care is a growing field, particular attention must be paid to avoiding the displacement of jobs from the labor market.

What would NSPs do? The analysis of the health service sector conducted for this project by Dr. Phillip Lee and others concluded that tasks would vary greatly, depending on the type of institution to which NSPs were assigned and their own levels of skill, interest, and maturity.[18] In inpatient facilities, for example, NSPs might provide information and referral, transportation, groundskeeping and maintenance, telephone reception, health education, child supervision, and recreation and craft activities. As Lee and his colleagues note, the level of supervision in many inpatient facilities is high, especially in larger hospitals, so a substantial fraction of the less mature and less capable NSPs might provide some of these functions. Nursing homes present a special opportunity because much of their work is performed by service employees rather than by professionals. For the same reason, however, the probable temptation to substitute NSPs for low-wage nursing home employees would have to be offset by firm enforcement of rules against such displacement.

Similar tasks, though in different proportions, might be undertaken in outpatient facilities, which are largely private; in the public health departments of local governments; and in the various alcohol, drug abuse, prenatal, infant care, and outpatient mental health programs that make up the ambulatory care sector of the health system.

Home care presents a different mix of tasks and somewhat more demanding requirements. NSPs might do household chores, deliver meals on wheels, drive the homebound to and from appointments, monitor their health and diet, or simply provide companionship. For most such tasks, little training is required, but since many home care tasks could not be supervised easily and because reliability is crucial to these services, only mature and responsible NSPs could be assigned to them.[19] For the same reasons, these relatively routine tasks might provide NSPs with the experience of being needed and of contributing to the well-being of others.

In voluntary associations and mutual aid groups, most tasks would probably involve clerical, maintenance, escort, or errand services. NSPs who took an interest in the substantive work of such associations also might be assigned to client service, fund raising, or administrative tasks.

The Scale of Need

Lee and his colleagues have estimated the demand for NSPs separately for each element of the health care system and for each of the major categories of institutions and services within them. In larger hospitals, for example, the estimate is based on the judgment that one NSP could be absorbed and supervised for each five current nonprofessional staff members; for small hospitals the ratio is set at 1 : 10. In large nursing homes, a 1 : 5 ratio of NSPs to total staff has been used; for homes of fewer than one hundred beds, a ratio of 1 : 10.[20] These calculations yield, for the late 1980s or early 1990s, the estimate of total demand shown in table 2–1. Although developed quite independently, these figures are roughly consistent with those of Eberly, who estimated that 900,000 NSPs might be assigned to health care positions.[21]

Our own view is that these totals are conservative. Although the estimates are carefully constructed, they assume only programs and facilities that now exist. While we have imposed this assumption on all our projections, it creates particularly artificial limits in the health field. There are convincing cost-effectiveness arguments for substantial continued growth in preventive health and outreach programs, especially for children, teen-agers, and pregnant women. In our view, such programs might create opportunities for 100,000 additional NSPs by 1990, while still allowing for increasing numbers of non-NSP employees.

The Value of NSPs in Health Care

The benefits of NSP assignments would take almost as many forms as there were types of service. Assignments in public health, health education, dietary counseling, and the like should achieve some prevention of disease and disability. In institutions where NSPs supplemented the work of support staff and current volunteers, the quality of care should be improved indirectly and the quality of life, for both patients and staff, might be enhanced. For whatever fraction of the almost 5 million homebound persons who cannot take care of themselves fully and whom NSPs might assist, the quality of life would be more directly and, in some cases, dramatically improved, as it would for the often overburdened relatives, friends, and neighbors who now assist them.[22] NSPs could extend the reach of home care programs now in operation, and their availability also might make feasible kinds and levels of home support that are not now affordable. To the extent that homebound

Table 2–1
Estimated Number of NSP Positions in Health Sector, by Health Setting

Health Care Setting	*Number of NSP Positions*
Inpatient Care	
Hospitals	77,500
Nursing Homes	87,300
Hospices	24,000
Mental Retardation Facilities	2,000
Mental Illness Facilities	2,300
Other Facilities	3,000
Subtotal	196,100
Ambulatory Care	
Outpatient Facilities	12,000
Health Departments	23,000
Alcoholism Treatment	5,500
Drug Abuse	5,000
Community Mental Health	6,000
Subtotal	51,500
Home Care	
Home Health Care	270,000
Meals on Wheels	112,500
Escort and Transportation	56,000
Subtotal	438,500
Other Health Settings	
Voluntary Associations	13,200
Research, Planning, etc.	16,000
Subtotal	29,200
Total	715,300

Source: Adapted from Lee et al., "Study of Service and Social Needs in the Health Sector," 1–50.

persons were able to avoid or defer institutionalization, substantial dollar savings also would result.

Finally, some parts of the health care system, particularly some nursing homes and mental health facilities, are largely hidden from public view. Unobserved services to powerless clients are rarely of admirable quality. The presence of NSPs would open such institutions to wider observation by society. In the first years of national service, this might make little difference, especially if all NSPs were young. But over time, as successive generations of NSPs reacted to the conditions they encountered, and as former NSPs who had experienced such institutions rose to positions of responsibility, their impact might be substantial. Through such a "window effect", if it developed, national service might provide an incentive, as well as a means, to provide higher levels of care.

It is worth repeating that the extent to which any such benefits are achieved will depend entirely on the age, skills, and attitudes of the NSPs associated with the particular forms of national service, on the care with which NSPs are matched to assignments, and on the quality of training and supervision they receive. The health care system, with its vulnerable patients, costly equipment and wide use of prescription and over-the-counter drugs, provides as many opportunities for NSPs to harm as to help.

Child Care

By child care we mean that care of children, from infancy to the sixth grade (roughly age twelve) that takes place outside the school system beginning with kindergarten. From the point of view of national service, the key characteristics of child care in the United States are that it is provided in an extraordinary diversity of settings and that the demand for it is expanding rapidly. The relatively small number of children without families or separated from their families are likely to receive care in child shelters, orphanages, or adoption centers.[23] For the roughly 8.2 million preschool children whose mothers work,[24] child care may take place in public or private nursery schools, preschools, Head Start programs, work site day care centers, cooperative centers, playgrounds, or summer camps. For more than two-thirds of such children, care now is provided either in the child's own home or in the home of relatives, friends, or neighbors.[25] For some school-age children whose parents are not home after school, there is only self-care. Such latchkey children, whose numbers are estimated variously between 2 and 7 million,[26] may return to empty houses, stay with friends, or wander streets or shopping malls.

For both preschool and school-age children, the demand for child care has been increasing dramatically. The reasons are several changes in U.S. social patterns. First is the increasing number of working mothers. In 1947, 19 percent of women with children under eighteen were employed; in 1982, 60 percent were employed. Correspondingly, in 1983, 47 percent of American children under age six had working mothers. By 1990, at least half of all preschool children, or about 11.5 million children, are projected to have working mothers.[27] Moreover, increasing numbers of mothers are now heads of single-parent households. By 1990, nearly one-quarter of American children will live in such households, a doubling of the number in 1970.[28] The problem is compounded, at least for the next 5 years, by the small cohort of American teen-agers. That group, from which a high proportion of informal care givers has traditionally been drawn, will have shrunk by 5 million between 1980 and 1990.[29]

Finally, it is not simply the need to provide supervision for children of working mothers that drives the expansion of child care; parents are becoming aware of the evidence that preschool programs are important developmentally. Indeed, as Kamerman has noted:

> [A] major concern is the possible emergence of a dual system of child care in which children of affluent and well-educated parents attend preschool programs—whether or not their mothers work—and children of low income families use more informal care. As illustration: 53 percent of 3–4 year olds in families with median or higher incomes attended preschool programs in 1982 as contrasted with 29 percent of those in families with lower incomes. Similarly, 72 percent of 4 year olds whose mothers are college graduates were in a preschool program.[30]

Child care has long been regarded as a function to which many NSPs could be assigned.[31] But because it is scattered, unorganized, and based largely in private homes, child care poses difficult problems of administration and supervision. It also poses problems for analysis since, especially with respect to home care, the data are poor. Suzanne Woolsey estimates that up to 90 percent of home care for children is supplied off the books.[32] Thus, as suggested earlier, the report of the House Select Committee on Children, Youth and Families could only estimate the number of self-care school-age children as somewhere between 2 and 7 million.

Tasks

At least in concept, the tasks that NSPs might perform in child care are numerous. In institutions serving children who were separated from their families, NSPs might assist with cooking and serving food, perform clerical services, serve as drivers, or help with maintenance and upkeep. Others, especially the more responsible or imaginative, could work directly with the children, tutoring, supervising play, and reading stories. NSPs also might help serve the great majority of children not cared for in institutions through assignment to day care centers and preschools. In addition, if problems of certification and oversight can be solved, children may also be served by some substantial fraction of the large and growing number of small, unlicensed, for-profit home care sites. In each of these settings, NSPs might care for children directly or assist other providers of care.

Depending on the ages of the children served and on the operating style of the facility, care would range from the monitoring of unstructured play and the maintenance of discipline to tutoring, leading games, coaching sports, and reading or telling stories. These tasks are unlike many other potential national service assignments in that most potential NSPs, including the youngest, have been at least partially prepared for them by experience in large families, school, baby-sitting, and athletics.

The Scale of Need

The U.S. Census Bureau projects that the number of children age twelve or under in the United States will reach 46.4 million in 1990.[33] Through a series of calculations that account for the changing number of children, the increase in employment of mothers, and the differences in demand for child care workers by type of care and by location, Woolsey and Gutchess estimated the total need for child care workers as the equivalent of 5.3 million full-time positions as care givers and some 72,000 positions as cooks, clerical assistants, and semiskilled drivers and custodians.[34]

How many of these positions might be appropriate for NSPs? The question is made difficult by the informal nature and poor state of information about most of the child care industry. Problems of certification, supervision, and potential displacement and the reluctance of some care givers to have strangers in their homes would sharply limit home-based openings. Nonetheless, it seems reasonable to estimate that not fewer than 5 and probably not more than 25 percent of the total number of home-based positions might be assigned to NSPs.

In the much smaller segment of the child care field represented by institutions, NSPs might fill openings of two kinds. One represents excess demand. It is that fraction of positions opened by the growth in numbers of such institutions that cannot be filled by paid workers at prevailing wages. The other would be supplemental positions, created as NSPs were used to reduce current worker-to-child ratios. Again we assume, with Woolsey, that between 5 and 25 percent of the total number of positions in child care institutions could be made available in each category.

The numbers of NSP child care positions for the late 1980s that are yielded by these assumptions are shown in table 2–2.[35]

Even the low end of the range established by these estimates is higher than the estimates offered in partly comparable prior studies. Eberly put the number of day care aide positions at 200,000,[36] and the UI/AIR study projected 139,500 positions.[37] We believe that Woolsey's larger estimates are rea-

Table 2–2
Estimated Number of NSP Positions in Child Care

Source of Demand	*NSPs at 5 Percent*	*NSPs at 25 Percent*
Home Care	170,000	850,000
Center-Based Care	80,000	400,000
Institutional Care	22,000	110,000
Totals	272,000	1,360,000

sonable, given both the sharp increases in demand for child care since the completion of the earlier studies and the likelihood that some proportion of the very large number of children in home care could be served by NSPs. Beyond this, we are impressed by the developing evidence that improving child care from the earliest months of life has an important effect on the cognitive, emotional, and social development of children.[38] As Lisbeth Schorr has commented:

> The gap between this nation's investment and what is needed is probably greater in the area of child care than perhaps any other. To ignore this fact, to assume that public policy will remain constant in the face of evidence of its failure and of shifting public attitudes and to suggest that the demand for child care . . . will remain entirely a function of private purchasing power, the needs of working women and current patterns of public investment seems to me to represent a misjudgement as well as a missed opportunity.[39]

The Value of NSPs in Child Care

If NSPs were used to reduce child-to-staff ratios, the quality of care provided to children should to some degree improve. Particularly for very young children, quite high child-to-staff ratios are important to the quality of care. The federal day care requirements proposed by the Department of Health and Human Services in 1980 to cover federally supported day care centers call for one staff member for every three children under two years of age, and one care giver for every four two-year-olds.[40] But the ratios now common in day care, both at homes and in centers, are far higher.[41] Moreover, older children would probably benefit from exposure to care givers who were diverse in age and sex. As of the mid-1970s, more than 93 percent of care givers were female, and two-thirds were between eighteen and thirty-five years of age.[42] A national service system that placed a significant number of males in child care might therefore yield important developmental benefits.

Also, with an infusion of NSPs, the child care system could be expanded by up to one-quarter if our highest estimates are correct, thus offering services to persons otherwise unable to find or afford them. This would have reverberating effects on adults as well as children. A recent U.S. Census Bureau survey of women who were not in the work force reported that 36 percent of those whose family incomes were under $15,000 said they would seek work if child care were available at "reasonable cost."[43]

Finally, as in health care, NSPs might produce a window effect. They would open up many settings—some of which provide indifferent care and some of which are abusive—to wider observation. The quality of child care might thereby become a question of greater salience to the population at large, and at least the lowest levels of care might be substantially raised.

As in every other sector, however, the benefits to society of the work of NSPs in child care would depend on the degree to which a number of conditions were met. Like the ill and elderly, children are vulnerable. To flourish in day care, they require continuity of care from persons with whom they have stable and affectionate relationships. The younger the child, the more important that requirement. NSP assignments should reflect those needs. In some states, licensing and bonding requirements also would have to be met, which might rule out very young or part-time NSPs on practical or legal grounds. Above all, the difficulties involved in monitoring the use and performance of NSPs in myriad small, unlicensed, poorly supervised home care sites would have to be confronted. Those sites probably offer both the highest risks and the greatest potential gains to be derived from involving NSPs in the U.S. system of child care.

One of the ways in which those risks might be minimized is suggested by the Child Care Food Program currently operated by the Department of Agriculture. That program, which provides partial cash reimbursements for food provided to children in day care centers, also offers reimbursements to family day care homes if they agree to be administered by a nonprofit umbrella organization that provides training and technical assistance and monitors the home.[44] The assignment of NSPs to home-based day care might be made similarly conditional.

Conservation and the Environment

Conservation is the task that most Americans associate with national service. In part this is because, as described in chapter 1, the historical archetype of national service in the United States is the CCC of the 1930s. This also may be because conservation work carries with it the ethic of a toughening grapple with nature, the modern equivalent of settling the frontier. Perhaps most important, very few Americans are employed in conservation, and therefore few feel that their jobs are at risk if NSPs enter the field. This paucity of existing workers does indeed open opportunities, but it also poses problems of supervision that would restrict the absorption of NSPs.

The Tasks to Be Performed

In accordance with current views of environmental needs, we define conservation and the environment more broadly than was the case in the 1930s. We mean to include all efforts to maintain or improve the quality of the nation's physical environment—its land, air, and inland and coastal waters.

The tasks that NSPs might perform are quite numerous. In forestry, they include tree planting, brush control, and the maintenance of logging roads;

in habitat improvement, they include stream clearing, stream-bank stabilization, plantings for food and shelter, and maintenance of hatcheries. Soil and water conservation would involve the construction of sediment traps and of water and wind barriers, the removal of brush, and the planting of trees, shrubs, and grasses. Recreation-related work would include the construction and maintenance of trails, picnic areas, and campgrounds; the maintenance and improvement of urban parks; and the provision of visitor information. In solid waste disposal, NSPs might monitor and survey current disposal practices and organize and staff the separation of solid waste at dumps and landfills. Monitoring and sampling of air and water quality also might be undertaken, focusing, for example, on lakes and streams subject to acid rain, acid mine drainage, or leaching from landfills. In energy conservation, NSPs might survey energy use and heat loss in public and private buildings and perhaps install insulation or take other energy conservation measures. Finally, NSPs might respond to disasters, natural or artificial, including fires, floods, hurricanes, and earthquakes.[45]

While many of these tasks involve strenuous physical activity, a number do not. Energy audits, water and air quality monitoring, and visitor support and information services in parks and forests require little physical effort. Indeed, many visitor information services are now provided by volunteers in U.S. Park Service and U.S. Forest Service programs, and many of the volunteers are retired or semiretired.[46] Some form of environmental work may be suitable for NSPs of a wide range of physical and mental capacities.

Such tasks seem particularly appropriate for national service in a number of respects. Most of them require little skill, but unlike most low-skill tasks, they are not demeaning and may be challenging. They involve little or no contact with vulnerable clients, so the poor or neglectful performance of most conservation tasks would be far less harmful than poor performance in many health or child care assignments. As noted, conservation work also involves relatively little risk of job displacement, since the private job market for all but some energy-related tasks is small. Another advantage is that, unlike most assignments in health, child care, and the schools, most environmental assignments need not be performed regularly or at consistent levels of effort. Most environmental programs could be deferred, accelerated, or adjusted to accommodate budgetary contingencies or fluctuations in the number of NSPs available.

Conservation work does pose logistical and administrative problems, however. Some tasks, such as fish hatchery work and tree planting, are seasonal. More important, a majority of work sites are in rural areas. Perry Hagenstein, our consultant for conservation and the environment, estimates that only about 45 percent of environmental tasks could be performed by NSPs living in communities of 10,000 persons or more.[47] Maintenance and improvement work and various visitor services could be performed in urban parks, and most of the energy conservation and waste disposal assignments would be located in or near cities and towns, as would many coastal zone improvement projects. But more than half the assignments would be far from the centers of population from which most NSPs would be drawn. That fact argues for residential programs similar to the CCC in which groups of NSPs would be housed near their work for extended periods of time. Such arrangements would be dramatically more expensive than those in which NSPs live at home, though, and they would be incompatible with part-time programs and unattractive to older NSPs with spouses or children needing care. It is also true, however, as we note later, that more of the personal needs of the NSPs may be met, or met more fully, in residential than in nonresidential programs.

The Scale of Need

Hagenstein has estimated the potential demand for NSPs in these tasks on the basis of the Five-Year Program for National Forests developed by the U.S. Forest Service, together with a variety of less systematic data pieced together from budgets, surveys, estimates by various state and federal officials, and the assessments of scholars and practitioners of conservation. Admittedly, these are shaky bases, but we believe they define at least a lower bound of need. The numbers that result are conservative in several respects. Tasks are limited to those able to be performed on public lands. If some tasks, such as reforestation, were to be performed on private lands, perhaps under a system of cost reimbursement, the estimates would expand substantially. Similarly, the NSPs we count as needed are limited to those required to restore environmental resources to stable and productive use and to maintain them at that level, but not further improve them. Alternatively, where a dollar remuneration can be shown to be produced by the work—as where the productivity of timber-bearing land is improved through the clearing of undergrowth—the estimates of need are limited to those efforts whose full cost would be offset by the incremental dollar value produced.[48]

Table 2–3 summarizes the Hagenstein calculations. It shows, by category of task, the number of full-time equivalent NSPs that might be absorbed in environmental work.

The conservatism of this approach is suggested by the modesty of the totals. As against the approximately 165,000 positions calculated by Hagenstein, the Eberly study estimated that some 800,000 positions could be created for NSPs in environmental services. The UI/AIR report identified thirty-one categories of environmental work but found data from which to estimate the number of jobs that might be usefully created in only sixteen of those categories. Excluding those related to work on private lands, the UI/AIR estimate for just those sixteen categories was 138,000.[49] We have not

Table 2–3
Estimated Number of NSP Positions for Environmental Sector by Category of Task

Task Category	*Number of NSP Positions*
Fish and Wildlife Conservation	
Habitat Improvement	12,360
Hatcheries	3,600
Surveys	1,320
Forestry	
Planting	3,000
Timber Improvement	1,680
Slush Disposal	2,280
Soil and Water Conservation	
Grazing Land	3,720
Abandoned Mine Lands	1,800
Coastal Zone Protection	360
Parks and Recreation	
Trail Construction and Maintenance	8,040
Facility Rehabilitation	21,600
New Facility Construction	14,400
Maintenance	4,320
Urban Parks	22,680
Water and Air Quality	
Monitoring	1,440
Solid Waste Disposal	
Separation, Collection	21,760
Energy Conservation	
Audits—Low/Moderate Income Housing	7,680
Eliminate Leaks	1,680
Insulate	3,600
Miscellaneous	13,560
Emergency Assistance	13,560
Total	164,440

Source: Adapted from Hagenstein, "National Service: Conservation and Environmental Aspects," 41–42. Hours of service were divided by 40 to yield the number of full-time positions. All estimates include training and program support time calculated at 20 percent of task performance time. Two thousand work hours were taken to equal 1 NSP-year.

troubled much over this differential, however, because of what we take to be the practical and political constraints on employment in this area. Conservation programs assume very large residential components, and as noted, residential components are expensive. Significantly, the largest recent state conservation corps program (California's) involves only 1,800 positions. More typically, Michigan's analogous program offers only 65 year-round and 150 summer positions. Even the CCC at its peak, although it enrolled

520,000 participants, had them for only short periods and, thus, in person-years established fewer than 100,000 positions. Recent bills to establish an American Conservation Corps would have created only 25,000 positions. Significant, too, is the fact that if 165,000 full-time NSPs were assigned the environmental tasks we have cited, they would multiply by seventeen times the paid labor power now devoted to such assignments.[50] In sum, we regard assertions of need beyond 165,000 positions as plausible but probably unrealistic.

The Value of NSPs in Conservation

The principal effect of assigning NSPs to such tasks would be to restore and maintain various aspects of the environment to stable and productive use. Secondarily, the NSPs deployable on short notice against floods, fires, and other disasters could save property and perhaps some lives that might otherwise be lost. But the fact that so relatively modest a number of NSPs would dramatically expand the environmental work now being undertaken on public lands could be said to show that we do not normally place great value on getting this work done. This point is not new. Evaluations of the CETA programs of the mid-1970s noted that while only 2 percent of permanent state and local employees were assigned to parks and recreation work, 8 or 9 percent of CETA public service workers were assigned in those areas. The explanation for those proportions was that "these are activities with a lower claim on local government resources and therefore more readily expanded when extra funds become available."[51] In short, society has placed a relatively low value on additional conservation activity.

But the importance assigned to conservation by the public has grown, perhaps quite dramatically, in recent years. A *New York Times*/CBS News poll conducted in September 1981 and again in April 1983 asked 1,500 respondents whether "protecting the environment is so important that requirements and standards cannot be too high and improvements must be made regardless of cost." Forty-five percent of those polled agreed with this very strong statement in 1981; 58 percent, an increase of almost one-third, agreed with it in 1983.[52] The value that society would place on the work of NSPs in conservation may be considerably greater than the older evidence implies.[12]

Miscellaneous Social Services

A wide variety of social services other than those we have discussed—schooling, health care, child care, and conservation—also could absorb large numbers of NSPs. Among the more promising are criminal justice and public safety, libraries and museums, food distribution, and urban parks and recreation. Here we briefly review the kinds and numbers of tasks that NSPs could perform in the first two of those categories (where the numbers are impressive and the history of volunteer use is extensive), and we offer a very rough estimate of the number of NSPs that might be well employed in all other social service functions combined.

Criminal Justice and Public Safety

The police forces, parole and probation staffs, youth agencies, correctional institutions, public prosecutors and public defenders' offices and courts—federal, state, and local—that make up the U.S. criminal justice and public safety system have long used large numbers of volunteers. The results of a 1981 Gallup survey suggested that 640,000 persons volunteered some of their time to some part of that system.[53] The system's nature—stable, hierarchical, large, and understaffed—suggests that it could effectively assign and supervise considerably larger numbers.

Some NSPs might be used in direct law enforcement. In several cities trained volunteers serve a limited number of shifts as police reserves. In Los Angeles, for example, they are assigned to all types of police work, although in sensitive or potentially dangerous situations they are paired with regular officers. Other NSPs might staff neighborhood civilian patrols modeled on existing neighborhood watch and housing authority volunteer patrols. The New York Housing Authority alone uses 11,000 volunteers in this way.[54] Large numbers of NSPs could be used, as volunteers and civilian clerks are now increasingly used, to assist in the report writing and desk work that otherwise occupy a large fraction of police officers' time.

Crime-related service programs also could absorb limited numbers of appropriately chosen NSPs. These would include victim assistance programs, where NSPs could provide emergency homemaker and child care, help prepare compensation claims, and provide crisis counseling; probationer and parolee support programs, where NSPs (especially older ones) might help with job search or housing arrangements or with applications for training; and diversion programs in which young delinquents are offered friendship matches, recreation, job counseling, and the like.

Finally, many NSPs could work in the nation's prisons, jails, juvenile training schools, and detention centers. Again, older NSPs might be especially useful in filling out short-handed correctional staffs[55] or supplying special services in literacy, recreation, crafts, counseling, vocational training, and the like.

The 1978 UI/AIR study estimated that at least 235,000 new jobs might usefully be created in the criminal justice system.[56] Similarly, the National Manpower Survey of the Criminal Justice System, published in 1978 by the Department of Justice, estimated the number of additional full-time positions necessary to perform then-mandated functions effectively was 220,000.[57] On the basis of those estimates and of the more recent findings of Francine Ra-

Table 2–4
NSP Assignments in Criminal Justice

NSPs (FTE)	*Area of Assignment*
Police Reserve	45,000
Civilian Patrol	50,000
Police Staff Support	75,000
Victim Assistance	5,000
Probation and Patrol Support	3,000
Youth Diversion	5,000
Corrections Staff	67,000
Total	250,000

Source: Estimates are based on the projections detailed in Rabinovitz, "National Service Other Services Study," 21–26, and are limited to totals consistent with the UI/AIR and National Manpower Survey studies cited in chapter 2.

binovitz, our consultant in this field, that considerably greater numbers of NSPs might be used productively in a wider variety of functions,[58] we conclude that 250,000 NSPs might readily be utilized in the criminal justice system. Table 2–4 shows the approximate composition of that total.

Libraries and Museums

Volunteers also have been widely and effectively used in libraries and museums, especially in the past 15 years. Greatly expanded as a result of the federal Library Services Acts of 1956 and 1963, the public library system in the United States currently consists of 8,800 public libraries with 6,150 branches, and it employs about 82,000 persons. But it represents only about one-fourth of the larger system of libraries, which includes those of schools, colleges, and other institutions. Employment in the U.S. library system as a whole totaled approximately 308,000 persons in 1982, of whom just under half were professional librarians.[59]

Especially since the early 1970s, when federally supported library construction coincided with pressure on local staffing budgets, library professionals have come to rely increasingly on volunteers. Volunteers are used to assist with basic library services and to help staff community outreach programs of various kinds. As the American Library Association has noted, the work done by volunteers has included:

> [S]haring of books with children in Head Start and day care groups; preparation of picture files; presenting film programs; making of braille, talking

> books, and tapes; making deliveries to homebound borrowers; storytelling to children in libraries and other locations; teaching in literacy classes; conducting discussion groups inside and outside the library; mending library materials; shelving returned materials; making publicity materials for the library; planning exhibits in the library; preparation of oral history collection; collection of historical and archival materials; preparation of a clipping and vertical file; inspecting and repairing audio-visual materials; manning a circulation desk; manning a book cart in a hospital or home for the aged; and working with outreach programs.[60]

Outreach programs, the current growth area in public library services, might benefit especially from the availability of NSPs. The best established of these programs involve bookmobiles, the maintenance of neighborhood mini-libraries, the provision of reading materials to shut-ins, and talking book programs for the sight-impaired. The more ambitious and newer programs develop exhibits, lectures, film presentations, and classes to fit local interests in subjects such as genealogy, gardening, computers, foreign languages, hobbies, and city planning. They also may make the library a community switchboard, a source of current information and referral about neighborhood activities, jobs, educational or cultural resources, and items for sale. Although the intensity with which volunteers have been used for library functions of all kinds varies widely, we conclude that about 175,000 NSP positions, a little more than one for every two current professional librarians and one for every two library support staff members, might be utilized effectively in public and other nonprofit libraries.[61]

There are about 4,400 nonprofit museums in the United States; more than half of them are museums of history. Science and art museums represent the bulk of the remainder, although children's museums, with hands-on exhibits and lively educational programs, appear to be the fastest-growing category. Here, too, volunteers have been increasingly used in recent years, undertaking clerical tasks and maintenance functions, docent work, outreach activities, and, for those with appropriate skills, research, display development, and repair and conservation work. In 1979, 60 percent of museums of all types reported using part-time volunteers.[62]

NSPs might be assigned roughly similar work, especially in science, history, general, and children's museums, where CETA workers have been used with some success.[63] Calculations made by Rabinovitz on the basis of differing capacities of museums of different sizes suggest that roughly 30,000 full-time NSP positions might be usefully established in museums.[64]

The Remaining Miscellany

It is a feature of U.S. society that the tasks undertaken by volunteers are not only numerous but also wonderfully diverse. They include finding housing for refugees, counting and classifying a city's trees to support a federal program to prevent Dutch elm disease, staffing church-based telephone hotlines for the depressed, feeding the hungry, operating rural fire departments, building sets for local theater groups, assisting family courts in evaluating foster care and child custody issues, and helping host Olympic-type games, to mention only a few activities.[65]

Historically, Americans who volunteer have tended to be well educated, well motivated, of above average ability and income, and maturer than most NSPs would be under many systems of national service.[66] It follows that not many NSPs could take on some tasks that volunteers have typically performed. But any system of national service would produce some NSPs who could undertake virtually any assignment, and, more important, any large system of service would stimulate the development of services that neither paid staff nor volunteers now offer. Programs systematically involving college students in community projects are suggestive. Over the last decade, for example, the Stanford University Action Research Liaison Office has supported student work with city agencies and community groups. Tasks include studying the effectiveness of paramedics, lab-testing procedures, and aid for alcoholics in local programs; designing systems for solar heating of a city swimming pool and for irrigation of a city golf course; writing oral histories of impoverished elderly residents; preparing a promotional film for the chamber of commerce; developing learning materials for the community association for the retarded; designing mailings to promote energy conservation; and writing nutrition guides for teen-age mothers.[67]

In short, it seems reasonable that many systems of national service are likely to offer a more diverse set and a larger number of tasks than we have attempted to account for here. We allow a modest nationwide total of the equivalent of 100,000 full-time NSPs for such unclassifiable functions.

An Estimate of Aggregate Demand

The preceding discussion and estimates suggest that the number of full-time NSP positions that might be utilized in tasks of social value in the late 1980s or early 1990s is just under 3.5 million. The following Table 2–5 summarizes and rounds the composition of that total.

Both within each category and as a total, these numbers are only rough estimates. But we know of no reason to believe they are systematically skewed. Further experience and analysis, we believe, would be as likely to raise as to lower the totals. We conclude, therefore, that the gross implication of those numbers is reliable: For national service programs of even the largest foreseeable kind, the work is there to do. Whether the benefits of programs

Table 2–5
Total Potential NSP Assignments

Field	*NSPs (FTE)*
Education	1,200,000
Health	750,000
Child Care	820,000[a]
Environment	165,000
Miscellaneous Services	
Justice	250,000
Libraries and Museums	200,000
All Other	100,000
Total	3,485,000

[a]This figure represents the approximate midpoint of the range shown in table 2–2.

so large, or of much smaller ones, would exceed their costs is a different question.

Notes

1. Although professional organizations may be inclined to overestimate the need for their services, it does not follow that they tend to overestimate the utility of amateur helpers. They may see the widespread use of NSPs as an impediment to the desired expansion of their profession or of its unions; they also, as professionals, may doubt that anything but menial work can be performed by nonprofessionals, especially young ones.

2. The reasons for the decline are subject to debate. The Advisory Panel on the Scholastic Aptitude Test Score Decline of the College Entrance Examination Board concluded in 1977 that two-thirds to three-quarters of the decline was due to compositional changes in the group of students taking the test. See College Entrance Examination Board, *On Further Examination,* 13–18, 45. Even if correct, that conclusion leaves a substantial fraction of the decline to be explained, and it may not be correct. An analysis of those declines conducted for the Educational Testing Service concluded that shifts in the demographics of test takers were a minor factor contributing to the score decline; and that among the more significant factors were reduced number of hours of homework, reduced proportion of students in academic as against "general" curricula; reduced teaching of science and reduced rating of the quality of schools' instruction, and of schools' reputations in the community—both as perceived by students. See Rock et al., *"Factors Associated With the Test Score Decline,"* 5–9.

3. Yarmolinsky, "National Service Program," 101.

4. See, for example, National Service Secretariat, *A Plan for National Service,* appendix B; Committee for the Study of National Service, *Youth and the Needs of the Nation,* 90–95; and Landrum, ed., *National Youth Service: What's at Stake?,* 87–123.

5. Eberly, "The Estimated Effect of a National Service Program," 8, table A.

6. The Urban Institute, *Counter-Cyclical Job Creation* 1:14–15.

7. Ibid. 2: 42–43, 50.; Eberly, "The Estimated Effect of a National Service Program," 8, table A.

8. Committee for the Study of National Service, *Youth and the Needs of the Nation,* 116.

9. Sizer, "National Service Education Study," 13–15.

10. Ibid., 14–23.

11. Ibid., 5.

12. Ibid., 3. See also, Plisko, ed., *The Condition of Education, 1983,* 173.

13. Lee et al., "Study of Service and Social Needs in the Health Sector," I–1 through I–8.

14. Ibid., I–19.

15. According to data from the Home Care Supplement of the 1979 National Health Interview Study, about 4.9 million adults living in the community needed the help of another person to carry out everyday activities. Of these, 2.8 million were over sixty-five years of age. The need for assistance increases with age. Fewer than one in ten who are sixty-five to seventy-four and not institutionalized need help, compared with four in ten over eighty-five years of age. See Feller, "Americans Needing Help to Function At Home," 1.

16. See U.S. Bureau of the Census, *Population of the United States: 1983–2080,* 41–42.

17. Ibid., 9.

18. Lee et al., "Study of Service and Social Needs in the Health Sector."

19. A particularly vivid and detailed description of the frustration and dependency of home health care patients is presented in Sheehan, *Kate Quinton's Days.*

20. For details of the assumptions as to all types of institutions and for the rationale for each assumption, see Lee et al., "Study of Service and Social Needs in the Health Sector," I–49 through I–69.

21. See Eberly, "The Estimated Effect of a National Service Program," 8, table A. The UI/AIR study provided no estimate for the health care system as a whole on the grounds that suitable data were not available for major elements of it. See The Urban Institute, *Counter-Cyclical Job Creation,* 66–67.

22. According to the Home Care Supplement of the 1979 National Health Interview Survey, 72.6 percent of individuals who required assistance in performing the basic and instrumental activities of daily living were assisted by relatives, friends, or neighbors (informal support network); 2.3 percent of those requiring support had no source of assistance; and 9.2 percent of those requiring assistance received aid from nurses or other health care workers (formal support network). The remaining 15.9 percent received assistance from members of both the formal and informal support networks. See Soldo, "The Elderly Home Care Population," 14.

Soldo also notes that approximately 68.9 percent of the aged do not receive the help they need with mobility; 52.3 percent do not receive the help they need with bathing; 34.8 percent do not receive required help with dressing; 23.2 percent do not receive assistance with toileting or continence; and 13.7 percent do not receive needed assistance with transferring. See ibid., 21, table 8.

23. It is very difficult to estimate the number of such children, but it appears to approximate 400,000. Dr. Penelope L. Maza, "Characteristics of Children in Foster Care," 1, reports that in fiscal year 1982, approximately 425,000 children spent some time in foster care, 259,000 less than in 1977.

24. Bureau of the Census, *Current Population Survey: March 1984 Supplement,* cited in Department of Labor, "Number of Working Mothers Now at Record Levels," table 3.

25. Woolsey, "Child Care Jobs for National Service Participants," 1.

26. House Select Committee on Children, Youth and Families, *Families and Child Care: Improving the Options,* 24.

27. Figures for 1947, 1982, and 1990 come from the prepared statement of Dr. Rachel Tompkins, director of the Children's Defense Fund, before the House Select Committee on Children, Youth and Families, in *Child Care: Beginning a National Initiative,* 33. The figure for 1983 is from the testimony of Dr. Sheila Kamerman in ibid., 10.

28. House Select Committee on Children, Youth and Families, *Families and Child Care: Improving the Options,* iv.

29. Ibid., viii.

30. From the statement by Dr. Kamerman before the House Select Commitee on Children, Youth and Families, *Child Care: Beginning a National Initiative,* 11.

31. See, for example, Committee for the Study of National Service, *Youth and the Needs of the Nation,* 94; and Neugebauer, "Day Care as a Form of National Service," in *National Youth Service: What's at Stake?,* ed. Landrum, 97–101. See also National Service Secretariat, *A Plan for National Service,* 12, table III–1.

32. Woolsey and Gutchess, "Child Care Jobs for National Service Participants," 8.

33. Ibid., 5.

34. Ibid., 10. The calculations can be summarized as follows: An estimate of the ratio of care providers to children for the period of the late 1970s was applied to the number of children under twelve projected for the late 1980s. That number was then adjusted upward to account for the expected increase, by the late 1980s, in the employment of mothers with young children. The total number of hours of required child care produced by those calculations was then distributed among the nine principal types and locations of child care in the same proportions as those types of care now appear to take. The total number of child care workers required for the late 1980s was then estimated by applying differing ratios of workers to children for each of the various settings. According to Woolsey, the nine principal types of child care are provided as follows: in the child's own home by a relative; in the child's home by a nonrelative; in another home by a relative; in another home by a nonrelative; in a nursery or preschool; in a day care center; in a cooperative program; in a school, before or after hours; and in a Head Start program. See ibid., 9.

35. For a full explanation of the derivation of demand, see Woolsey and Gutchess, 4–14, 55–58.

36. Eberly, "The Estimated Effect of a National Service Program," 8.

37. The Urban Institute, "Counter-Cyclical Job Creation," 2:82–85. A lower estimate of 30,000 to 50,000 positions is made by Neugebauer in *National Youth Service: What's at Stake?* ed. Landrum, 98.

38. Zigler and Gordon, *Day Care,* 3–56.

39. Correspondence with the authors, November 1983.

40. National Center for Clinical Infant Programs, "Who Will Mind the Babies?," 9.

41. See generally Johnson & Associates, Inc., "Profile of State Day-Care Licensing Regulations."

42. Woolsey and Gutchess, "Child Care Jobs for National Service Participants," 32, 39.

43. O'Connell and Rogers, *Child Care Arrangements of Working Mothers,* 18, table H.

44. See The Children's Foundation, "Child Care Food Program: Umbrella Sponsorship for Family Day Care Homes"; and "Facts about the Child Care Food Program in Family Day Care."

45. The California Conservation Corps has won much visibility and praise for disaster-response work. It has been estimated that in 1982 members of this corps spent about one-sixth of their time on such work. Bailin, *The California Conservation Corps: A Case Study,* 11.

46. See Hagenstein, "National Service: Conservation and Environmental Aspects," 7.

47. Ibid., 46.

48. For details on the sources of data and basis for estimating each of the various components of need, see ibid., 16–41.

49. See The Urban Institute, Counter-Cyclical Job Creation," 2:53–63; and Eberly, "The Estimated Effect of a National Service Program," 8. Similarly, when the Young Adult Conservation Corps was established in 1977, the Department of Interior identified a backlog estimated at 370,000 work-years of labor needed in national parks and forests. The Department of Agriculture's Forest Service reported a need for 450,000 work-years of labor-intensive tasks to be done in the national forests. Conservation work on state public lands would have added considerably to these totals. These are one-time backlogs, not the amount of effort that would usefully be sustained each year in a multiyear program. See Foley, Maneker, and Schwartz, *National Service and America's Future,* 16.

50. Hagenstein, "National Service: Conservation and Environmental Aspects," 41–42.

51. Mirengoff and Rindler, "CETA: Manpower Programs Under Local Control," 167.

52. "Attitudes on the Environment," *New York Times,* 17 April 1983.

53. Rabinovitz, "National Service Other Services Study," 10.

54. Ibid., 15.

55. One estimate is that to maintain the staff-to-prisoner ratio that was in effect

before the mushrooming of prisoner populations in the 1970s, correctional staffs should be enlarged by 100,000 persons. Ibid., 20.

56. See The Urban Institute "Counter-Cyclical Job Creation," 2:26, 34–35.

57. Rabinovitz, "National Service Other Services Study," 11. (Citing the Department of Justice, *The National Manpower Survey of the Criminal Justice System.*)

58. Ibid., 11–21.

59. Data on the number of libraries and branches come from R.R. Bowker Co., *The Bowker Annual of Library and Book Trade Information,* 347; data on persons employed in libraries, as well as on the proportion of those who are professional librarians, come from Van House, Roderer, and Cooper, "Librarians: A Study of Supply and Demand," 361.

60. American Library Association, "Guidelines for Using Volunteers in Libraries," 2.

61. Rabinovitz, "National Service Other Services Study," 21–26.

62. Ibid., 26.

63. Ibid., 27.

64. Ibid., 26–28.

65. See Gallup Organization, Inc., *Americans Volunteer: 1981,* v.

66. Gallup Survey data from 1981 and 1983 show that college-educated adults tend to volunteer in considerably higher proportions than those at lower education levels; employed adults in higher proportions than unemployed adults; and individuals with household incomes of $30,000 or more in higher proportions than those at lower income levels. Gallup, "The 1983 Gallup Survey on Volunteering," 22.

67. The program is described in *The Stanford Observer,* April 1984, 1. Other innovative possibilities for a less elite group of workers are sketched in Youth Community Service, "Nontraditional Projects and Tasks for Volunteers." For a brief recent survey of college-based programs, see "When Helping Others is Part of Learning," *New York Times Education Supplement,* 6 January 1985.

3
Personal Needs

Probably the most frequently offered argument for national service is the assertion that it would enhance the lives of the persons who serve. This chapter identifies the personal needs that one or another form of national service might meet. It notes, as well, why meeting some of those needs may prove difficult or inconsistent with other goals of national service, such as accomplishing tasks of social value or improving the military. Since some systems of national service, including our models 3 and 4, would permit service to take place in later life, we distinguish in this discussion between the needs of youth and of older persons, both in midlife and after retirement age.

The Needs of Youth

Assertions about the needs of American youth are numerous. They arise from the disciplines of psychology, sociology, history, philosophy, anthropology, and economics. They are amplified by social commentators, educators, and politicians and are made independently by parents and citizens in general. But it is worth noting that no comprehensive statement of such needs is generally accepted. It is widely agreed that young people, like their elders, need occupations, incomes, and satisfying relations with others, but beyond those elemental requirements, assessments of need vary widely. They shift with the training, age, and outlook of the observer, and they are affected by the dominant hopes and anxieties of the time in which they are made. Indeed, it seems fair to say that many assertions about the needs of youth are actually statements about the needs of society with respect to youth. They reflect the concern of society to protect itself against a hostile power (as by toughening science and mathematics requirements after the launching of Sputnik), to socialize a particularly large or rebellious generation (such as that of the late 1960s), or to increase economic productivity, as at present.

A 1974 report of the Panel on Youth of the President's Science Advisory

Committee,[1] though now dated, is probably the most nearly authoritative recent statement on the needs of U.S. youth. The panel, chaired by sociologist James S. Coleman, discussed two general objectives that environments for youth should seek to meet. The first it described as "essentially self-centered . . . and concerning the acquisition of skills that expand the personal resources and thus the opportunities of a young person." The second objective "centered on others rather than self . . . [and concerned] opportunity for responsibilities affecting other persons."[2] The following discussion, although it draws on many sources, is organized in terms of that distinction.

Self-Centered Needs

Work Experience for Students. Many commentators have asserted, as did the Coleman panel, that youth need contact with the world of work prior to the end of formal schooling and that U.S. educational patterns often fail to provide it. Margaret Mead argued that national service would "provide for an interval within our very prolonged educational system in which actual, responsible work experience would precede further educational choices."[3]

Early experience with work might have several beneficial effects. As Mead suggested, such experience might produce maturer and better motivated students who would be able to make their choices of schools and courses more knowledgeably. It also might help students consider their choice of occupations more realistically and perhaps avoid jobs that will later seem unchallenging or unsatisfying. Optimally, it also would develop job-related skills such as familiarity with office procedures, competence with specialized tools, and word-processing experience.

Two reservations about this argument are evaluated in our discussion of the model plans. One is that many of the tasks that might be assigned to NSPs probably would not lead directly to postservice employment or teach skills of direct utility in the job market. If many young men who joined the CCC of the 1930s, for example, benefited greatly from the experience, that was not because it taught them job skills. Few of them later were engaged in reforestation, trail clearing, or fire fighting. As noted earlier, national service is not likely to be politically tolerable if it displaces nonservice employees from their jobs. The tasks found for national service participants, therefore, seem likely to fall outside the existing job market or at its fringes. Many of the skills such tasks develop would not be directly applicable in the job market. Some skills, such as familiarity with hand tools, may have direct employment value, as would the greater maturity and socialization to the discipline of work that could result from service. But those gains may be small in relation to the time invested in service. Other NSPs may be assigned to tasks—for example, developing a computer program to track the health status and service needs of aged persons being cared for in their homes—that would indeed develop skills transferable to the job market. But those cases, we believe, would be relatively rare.

A second reservation is that while a high percentage of those youths who most need employment have the least contact with the world of work as they grow up, many of the youth most likely to participate in national service programs—as opposed to participating in jobs or job-training programs—have considerable experience of work. Nearly 80 percent of American high school seniors have experienced employment.[4] The incidence of their employment grew rapidly in the 1960s and 1970s. It appears still to be growing, and it exceeds by a wide margin the degree of employment experienced by youth in any other industrialized society. The majority of these jobs are low-skill, no-advancement positions at fast-food restaurants, gas stations, small retail establishments, and the like. Still, about 50 percent of the high school seniors who are working report that they find their jobs more interesting than school.[5] Moreover, some of the sales and clerical positions held by those students open possibilities of advancement. Most significantly, all of these jobs provide substantial increments to disposable income (and often important contributions to family income), a sense of the everyday discipline that employment imposes, and a taste of the satisfactions and frustrations of work.[6]

It is not clear, therefore, that national service would add greatly to youth work experience. Indeed, mandatory service surely would preempt the time that many young persons would otherwise spend in jobs.[7]

Jobs for Dropouts and Graduates. It is ironic that despite the very large number of American youth who hold part-time jobs while in high school, the unemployment rate of out-of-school youth in the United States has been persistently high by the standards of industrial societies and savagely high for minority youth, especially in cities.[8] Although this phenomenon is familiar, its scale and inequalities are striking.

In March 1985, 592,000 out-of-school teen-agers, or approximately 1 in 5 of the out-of-school labor force age sixteen to nineteen, were unemployed.[9] Unemployment of out-of-school youth has stood at double to triple the rate of the labor force as a whole throughout the past decade.[10] A 1983 calculation showed that more than 4 in 10 of the 12 million Americans then unemployed were under twenty-five years of age.[11] Aside from the diminishing size of the youth cohort during the late 1980s, no present program or trend is likely to change that relationship.[12] On the contrary, trends in youth unemployment appear worse than those in unemployment generally.

Unemployment rates among minority youth, especially blacks, are far greater than those for whites. Despite substantial recent employment gains made by minority adults, unemployment of out-of-school black youth (like that of all black youth) stood at well over twice the unemployment rate of their white counterparts in early 1985.[13]

This high disparity by race is a relatively new phenomenon. As recently as the early 1950s, the unemployment rates of black teen-agers were only about one-third higher than those of whites. Since then, however, black teen-age unemployment has risen at roughly three times the rate for whites. The result is that during the period 1979–1985, white youth unemployment has ranged from 14 to 20.4 percent, while black youth unemployment has ranged from 33.2 to 44.8 percent.[14] Figures 3–1 and 3–2 show the evolution of this disparity between 1955 and 1983 in terms of employment rates and, more dramatically, in employment-to-population ratios.[15]

Simply by supplying jobs to youth who could not find work in the existing market, national service could provide both income and a record of employment. There is a double irony here. Throughout the nineteenth century, U.S. social policy sought to protect youth against premature employment. Now it might justify national service in part on the basis of a need to enlarge employment opportunities. Second, this is a singular rationale for a service program. "Historically, it has been in response to some shortage of manpower—floods, forest fires, war, oil tankers breaking up and fouling a coastline—that volunteers have come forward. But now the heart of the matter is the exact converse, an excess of manpower over the paid jobs available."[16]

Change: Alternative Settings for Self-Definition

Young people value variety and change. The Minnesota Youth Poll found that the most attractive thing about a proposed national service program in lieu of the senior year of high school was that it would allow them to leave school.[17] A study of 600 New York high school seniors found that:

> Nearly all wanted an escape—most often temporary—from the environment in which they had grown up. A physical change of scene was the primary desire, usually accompanied by the wish for change of "atmosphere." . . . The desire was simply for a diversity of experience and an opportunity for independence."[18]

In arguing for the logic of national service, Morris Janowitz has written, "It is particularly important to have these alternative life chances to overcome the boredom that comes from continuous exposure to classroom instruction."[19]

A related but more fundamental need is for settings other than the home and schoolroom in which a personal identity can be established. Until the early years of this century, as the Coleman report noted, the circumstances of

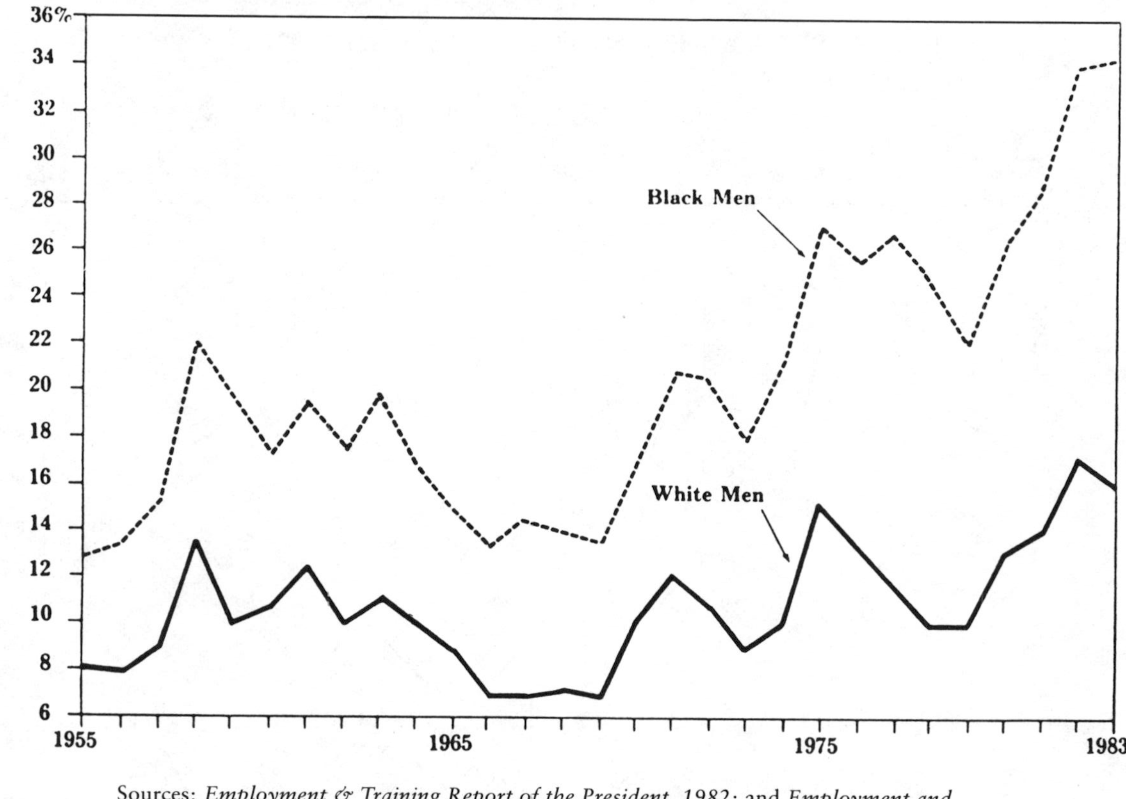

Sources: *Employment & Training Report of the President, 1982;* and *Employment and Earnings*, February 1983–February 1984. Reproduced from Hahn and Lehrman, *What Works in Youth Employment Policy*, 3.

Figure 3–1. Racial Gap in Unemployment Rates of 16–24 Year-Old Men, 1955–1983

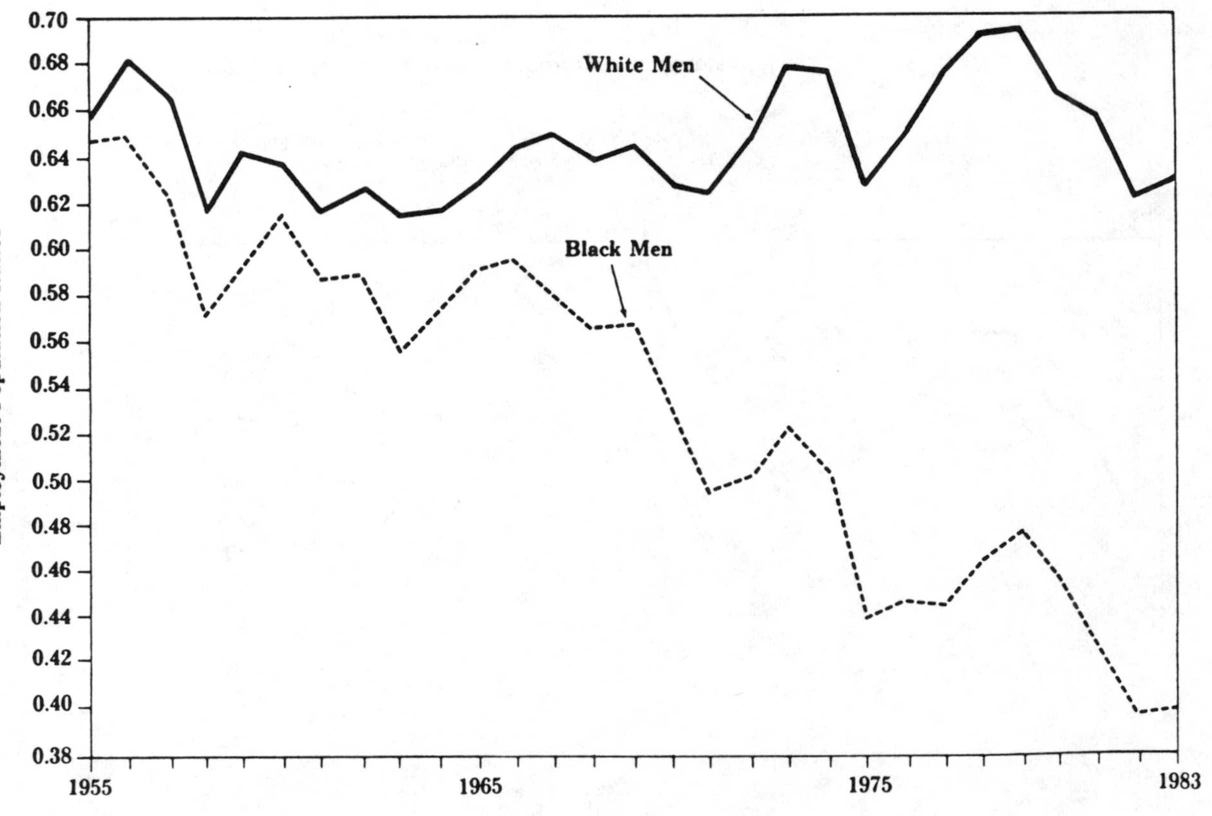

Source: Reproduced from Hahn and Lehrman, *What Works in Youth Employment Policy*, 4.

Figure 3–2. Racial Gap in Employment-to-Population Ratios of 16–24 Year-Old Men, 1955–1983

American youth were typically action rich and education poor; that situation now has been reversed.[20] Janowitz has remarked that:

> [T]he search for personal development and individual identity in a social setting which has a narrow emphasis on individual classroom performance leads all too often to various forms of rebellion and withdrawal. . . . In a democratic society it is particularly dangerous to make school and academic performance the exclusive route to social mobility.[21]

And commenting on the possible utility of national service, Margaret Mead argued that service:

> [W]ould provide an opportunity for young adults to establish an identity and a sense of self-respect and responsibility as individuals before making career choices or establishing homes. At present a very large number go from dependency on their parents into careers that have been chosen for them, or use early marriage as a device to reach pseudo-adult status.[22]

Unfamiliar challenges also may help young people expand their sense of their own capacities. As David Reisman has observed, "being abroad for many [Peace Corps] volunteers . . . liberated them from their earlier definition of what they were capable of."[23] Since more positive self-images are particularly valuable for those whose backgrounds contain broken homes, poverty, frequent moves, and unfinished schooling, the successful handling of out-of-school tasks for such youths may have special value. But such value would not be limited to the deprived. Students who attend college after some prior substantial nonscholastic experience appear to be better motivated and more effective students than those who know only schooling, and the former are less likely to drop out.[24]

Opportunities for Responsibilities Affecting Other Persons

A Broader Range of Acquaintanceship. The Coleman report stressed the importance of enlarging the horizons of young persons through "experience with persons differing in social class, subculture, and in age." The report noted that for some, such experience is obtained in the armed forces or in organizations such as the Peace Corps,[25] but that for most youth, "opportunities for a broad range of experiences with persons from backgrounds other than their own are simply unavailable." The report noted, moreover, that such mixing of class, culture and age appears to have been more common in earlier times, when neighborhoods were less homogeneous, school classes less specialized by age and subject, and jobs and chores put youth into more regular working contact with elders of various social and economic positions.[26]

Margaret Mead identified the same pattern of segregation by class and culture and argued that a properly designed form of national service might ameliorate it:

> Universal national service, if set up in such a way that units were a cross section of the entire society, could compensate for the increasing fragmentation, ignorance, and lack of knowledge of their fellow citizens and the rest of the world which is characteristic of those reared in our economically segregated residential pattern, in which both the poor and the rich, the highly technologically gifted and those with obsolescent skills, the white collar and the blue collar, are each reared in almost total ignorance of the others.[27]

Similarly, Amitai Etzioni has argued that national service provides an opportunity for individuals from diverse backgrounds "to get to know each other on an equal footing while working together at a joint task." He argues further, however, that "the 'total' nature of the situation—being away from home, peers and 'background' communities—and spending time together around the clock," is what promises the sociological impact.[28]

Does contact across class, age, and racial lines enlarge horizons and increase tolerance? Seemingly so. Our consultants, psychologists Michael Maccoby and Cynthia Margolies, have noted that an increase in tolerance and a decline in authoritarianism is reported in studies of several types of service experiences, including work camps, the Peace Corps, VISTA, and the YCC. In a study of 111 urban VISTA volunteers, for example, four-fifths reported more positive attitudes toward the poor and three-quarters more positive attitudes toward blacks and Hispanics. Half reported more negative views of the middle class. Similarly, a survey of 145 YCC camp staff members, administrators, and local community members reported increased tolerance in dealing with people from different racial, ethnic, cultural, economic and religious backgrounds as a benefit of the experience.[29]

But this is not a simple matter. As Maccoby and Margolies note, the attitudinal effects of living and working with other racial or ethnic groups may be different from the effects of serving them.[30] A careful recent assessment of the effect of racial integration in schools has found that the racial attitudes of high school students, strongly affected by the attitudes of their families and closely correlated with their own psychological characteristics, were not significantly affected by the degree of interracial contact the students experienced.[31] It seems reasonable to conclude that to the extent joint effort, shared circumstances, and common goals characterize some national service settings, this would contribute to greater cross-racial and cross-cultural tolerance. But the frequency and extent of such gains is uncertain.

Being Needed. The Coleman panel cited "the experience of having others dependent on one's actions" as a second need centered on others. "It is important," the report argued, "that environments for youth provide opportunities in caring for others who are younger, sick, old, or otherwise dependent, and to engage in activities that are responsible in the sense that they have significant consequences for others. This is a most important apprenticeship for prospective obligations as spouse, parent and citizen."[32]

These opportunities appear more rarely in the United States today than before. As our consultant on schools, Theodore Sizer, has noted, "American social organization seems to compel adolescents to be economic parasites, a condition they bitterly, if inarticulately, resent. There is no honor in adolescence, no reason for self-esteem. The costs of this for society are incalculably high."[33] As a recent set of newspaper articles on youth culture expressed the point, "One could say: Never in the history of the United States has society given a generation so much and asked so little in return. And many young people would respond: that is part of the problem."[34]

A 1985 report sponsored by the Carnegie Foundation for the Advancement of Teaching urged that schools and colleges place more emphasis on service, largely because of a recent "troubling . . . transformation of student attitudes towards their personal responsibilities."[35] Citing annual American Council on Education surveys of college freshmen, the Carnegie report decried what it described as a:

> [F]ifteen year decline in expectation of participation in the political life of the country, in any form of altruism, or of concern for the interests of others . . . The values showing the greatest increases since 1972 are: (1) being very-well off financially, (2) being an authority, (3) having administrative responsibility over others, and (4) obtaining recognition. The values which showed the largest decline are (1) developing a philosophy of life, (2) participating in community affairs, (3) cleaning up the environment, and (4) promoting racial understanding.[36]

The report summarized the survey data as shown in figure 3–3.[37]

The experience of being needed, of being depended upon rather than being dependent, appears to have several kinds of benefits. One of the more consistent gains reported in service programs is an increase in self-confidence. California Conservation Corps participants cited this as one of the three leading benefits of their experience, and VISTA volunteers also cited it with high frequency. A study of American Friends Service Committee Volunteer Work Camps reported participants feeling greater autonomy and less need for aggressive behavior after their work camp experience than before. Similarly, a 3-year study found that Peace Corps volunteers became less concerned with how others viewed them and more capable of accepting others.[38]

In a particularly careful study, similar results were recorded with high school students even though they had been involved in much less intense experiences. Of the students in the sample group, 150 participated in school-

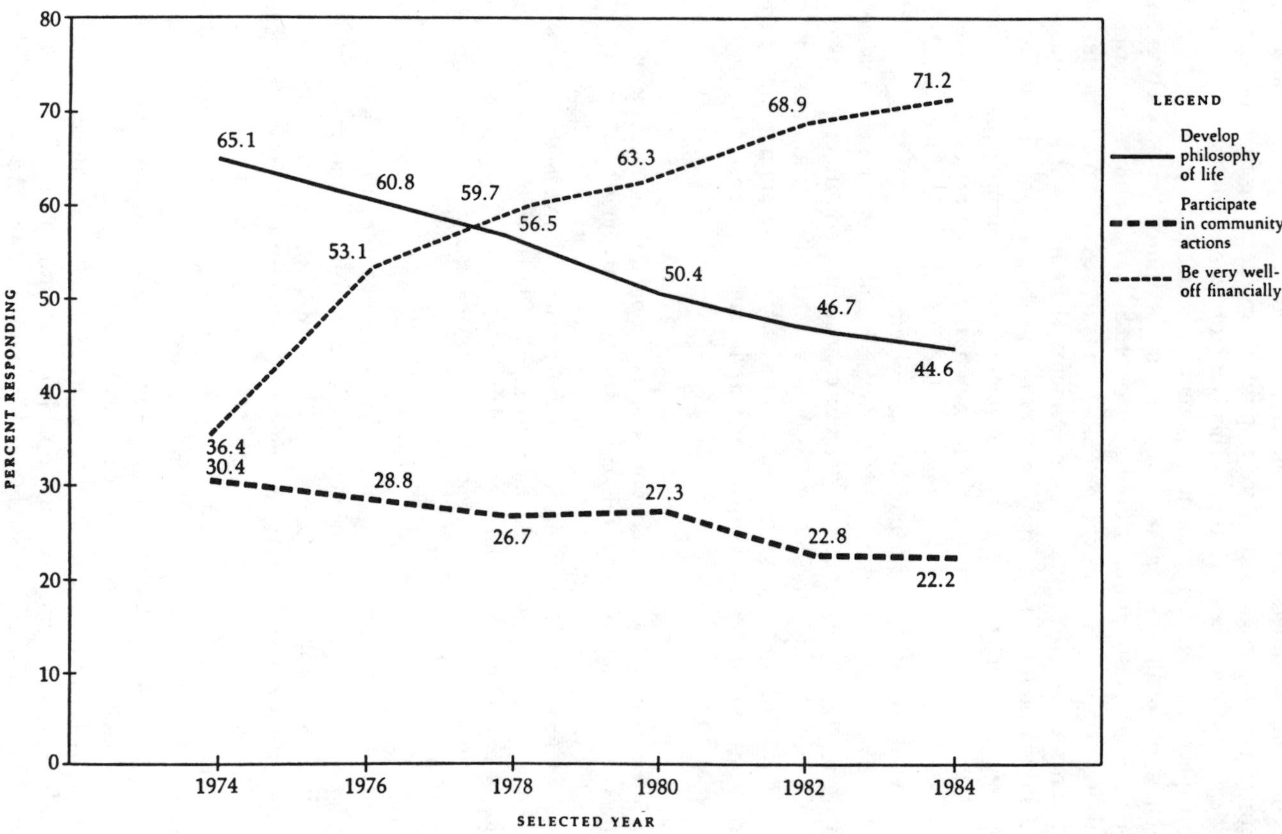

Figure 3–3. Changes in Student Objectives, 1967–1983

sponsored community service projects. They tutored elementary and junior high school students, assisted in nursing homes and hospitals, and helped staff various nonprofit and for-profit service organizations. A control group of equal size and similar charcteristics did not participate. Both groups were tested, through self-report and a variety of objective measures, before and after the service experience. Although the program required only 30 hours of service, the students who engaged in service projects displayed significantly more positive attitudes toward others, a greater sense of efficacy and self-esteem, and larger gains in career planning than those who did not.[39]

Collective Action. Finally, the Coleman panel emphasized the value of involvement in "activities directed toward collective goals, where the outcome for all depends on the coordinated efforts of each."[40] To some extent, of course, this need is met by team sports, whose essence is coordinated effort toward a collective goal. Moreover, many jobs integrate individuals into groups with a common goal or a joint product.

Nevertheless, a system of national service might intensify this experience or make it more common. Margaret Mead argued that young adults need to experience not merely common goals but "the satisfaction of services performed on behalf of the nation and of other fellow citizens—the children, the aged, the deprived," and noted that such service could provide "a paradigm for later social participation not immediately based on the standards of the marketplace."[41] Similarly, one observer speaks of national service as attractive, in part, as a way to "reinforce communitarian values"[42] in the United States. He comments that:

> Neoliberals, and increasingly, mainstream Democrats view community based national service programs as the most effective way to create, or re-create, that missing sense of community in American life. It is closely linked to the same imperative that views worker participation in management, and even worker ownership of business, as an integral part of productivity gains; or that sees cooperation between business, labor and management, or between industry and academy, as a necessary element in national progress.[43]

Earning Adult Status

Many of the asserted needs of youth, personal and interpersonal, can be drawn together under a common theme. Life in the United States tends to insulate and segregate youth, to restrict them to an artificial world where there is little chance to engage in challenging work or realistic training for work, to take responsibility, or to become familiar with the perspectives of other generations, races, classes, or regions.

One of the earlier and more famous of the observations made in this regard underscored a central paradox. In 1949, writing about "Elmtown" in a passage the President's Panel on Youth later called "devastating but accurate,"[44] August Hollingshead commented:

> By segregating [young] people into special institutions such as school, Sunday School, and later into youth organizations such as Boy Scouts and Girl Scouts for a few hours each week, adults apparently hope that the adolescent will be spared the shock of learning the contradictions in the culture. At the same time, they believe that these institutions are building a mysterious something variously called "citizenship," "leadership," or "character." . . . The youth-training institutions provided by the culture are essentially negative in their objectives, for they segregate adolescents from the real world that adults know and function in.[45]

Advocates of national service argue that such insulation from the real business of life produces "the more subtle, subjective states such as apathy, self-hatred, boredom, acute feelings of frustration, loneliness, and meaninglessness."[46] Correspondingly, the ideal of national service appears to draw support from the belief that it might offer a means of entry into adult society, a rite of passage. William James argued that those men who served (he envisioned service only by men):

> [W]ill have paid their blood-tax, done their own part in the immemorial human warfare against nature; they would tread the earth more proudly, the women would value them more highly, they would be better fathers and teachers of the following generation.[47]

Is emptiness and meaninglessness experienced more commonly or more intensely by teen-agers than by others, or more commonly than before? An ad hoc group of twenty-seven Americans, principally educators, argued in a Thanksgiving Day statement in fall 1984 that school activities "should emphasize the theme of service to others" because:

> [T]here has been a long-term rise in many serious forms of youth disorder. . . . Simple statistics put the matter in perspective. Since 1940, the rates of out-of-wedlock births to white females between the ages of 15–19 have increased 800%. The rate of death by homicide for white males, ages 15–24 have increased 315% from 1955 to 1981. The rate of death by suicide for white males, ages 15–24, increased 238% from 1955 to 1981. These measures of youth disorder have increased far more quickly than the similar adult measures.[48]

To illustrate these points, the groups forcefully presented them in graphic form, shown in figure 3–4.

In a similar vein, the 1979 Potomac Institute study urging national service noted the irony that "there are more youth ages 18–24 who are inmates

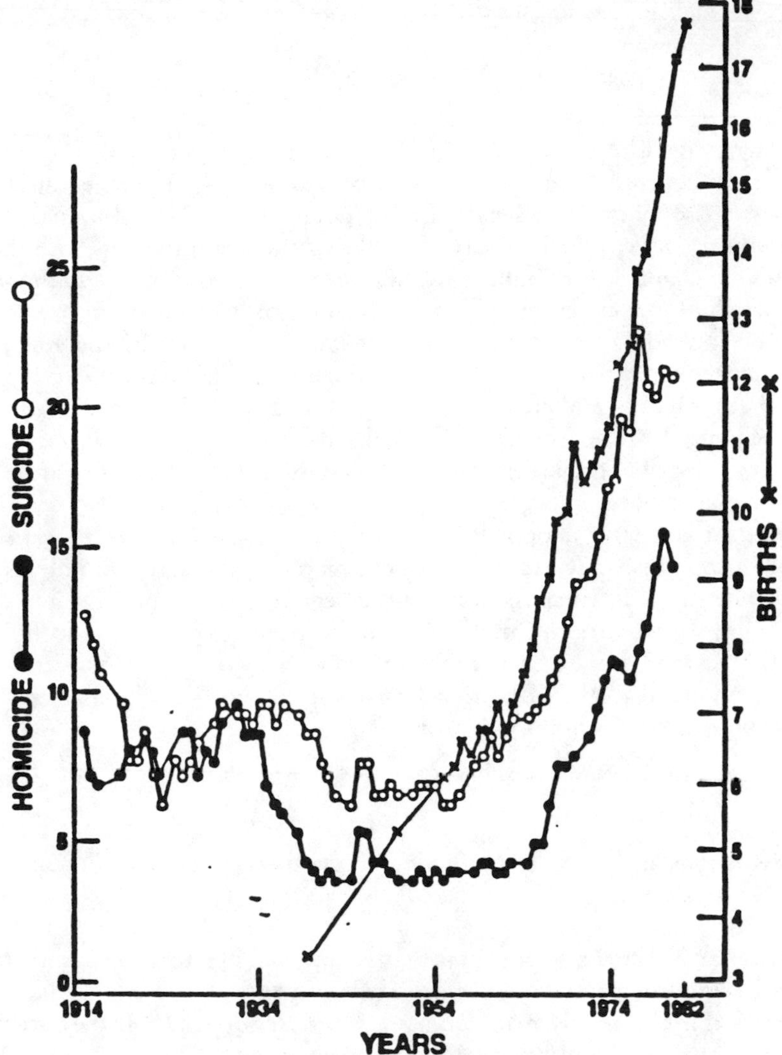

Source: Reprinted from Wynne, ed., Developing Character: Transmitting Knowledge, A Thanksgiving Day Statement by Twenty-Seven Americans. Posen, Illinois: ARL, 1984. Reprinted with permission.

Note: The graph portrays all currently available U.S. Public Health Service data about certain trends in youth conduct. The rates of death by suicide and homicide are for each 100,000 white males, between the ages of 15 and 24, from 1914 through 1981; and the out-of-wedlock births are for each 1,000 white females between the ages of 15 and 19, from 1940 through 1982. There are no comparable statistics for earlier periods. However, the remarkable recent increases, plus the general tendency for each such disorder to be associated with the spread of urbanization, support the contention that the current rates are at the highest point in American history—since 1607.

Figure 3–4. Changes in the Rates of Youth Homicide, Suicide, and Illegitimate Births

of local jails (61,510) than there are in the Jobs Corps or in all the federal service programs added together."[49]

Surveying such evidence, Roger Landrum, writing in the Potomac Institute study, concluded that national service was needed, in part, because "the causes of dropping out, alienation from political processes, drug usage and alcoholism, and criminal activity . . . reflect structural problems with the institutional channels for youth that complicate the transition to adulthood."[50]

We think the evidence as to the alienation of youth is often overstated. The available data on rates of drug and even alcohol use by the young are notoriously uncertain, for example, and the most reliable recent surveys suggest that both drug and alcohol use among high school students actually may be declining.[51] More critically for our discussion, there is no clear evidence that any form of national service would diminish such malaise. The anecdotal evidence does not suggest that drug use is less common among youth who experience collective action through athletic teams. Nor does it seem that alcoholism and suicide are less prevalent among those active in politics and public life. Indeed, when asked to list the negative aspects of participation in the Youth Conservation Corps, respondents listed "exposure to alcohol and drugs at camp" among their top three concerns.[52] One out of every eight people admitted to the California Conservation Corps left prematurely because of drug or alcohol problems.[53]

A Partial Summing Up

These various and partially conflicting observations might be summarized in three propositions.

1. Although there exists no authoritative measure of either the nature or the extent of the psychic and social needs of youth, the needs we have discussed are generally regarded as real and important, and they seem intuitively sound and consistent with experience.
2. Several of these needs appear more pressing now than previously. That is at least arguably true as to employment for out-of-school youth and especially minority youth, as to broader acquaintanceship, as to the experience of being useful to others, and as to visibly earning adult status. These may be more difficult for youth to achieve now than in previous years.
3. Each of the needs might arguably be met to some degree by one or another system of national service.

Some Caveats

In later chapters we will consider how well particular systems of national service seem likely in practice to meet the needs we have thus far described.

Before approaching these particular evaluations, however, some general reservations should be borne in mind.

Needs Differ Sharply. Youth of differing temperaments, ages, abilities, family situations, school histories, locations, sexes, and economic conditions have different, often sharply different, needs. Few farm children are unfamiliar with the discipline of work; severely deprived or alienated youth may be unable to accept that discipline. The needs of an aspiring young pianist do not closely resemble those of an aimless contemporary. The nineteen-year-old male working to support a disabled parent or the eighteen-year-old unmarried mother, although they may experience all the needs we have noted, may feel much more urgently the need to maintain their jobs and income.

The striking effect of the graph presented in table 3–4 illustrates how easily one may lose track of this fundamental point. The data are accurate and seem forceful: Out-of-wedlock births to young white females and suicide rates of young white males have increased dramatically in recent years. Still, illegitimate births involve only 18 of every 1,000 young white females, and suicide is committed by only 21 in 100,000 young white males. Moreover, different subgroups have very different propensities. The suicide rate for young females is less than one-quarter that for males, and the rate for blacks is roughly half that of whites.[54] To what extent should a program intended for a very large population be designed to respond to the problems of so few?

Different Assignments Fulfill Needs Differently. Much would depend on the particular tasks to which NSPs were assigned. Although most service jobs have some basic elements in common (requirements for punctuality, for example), opportunities for learning, interaction with others, and the exercise of independent judgment vary widely. Specific assignments, therefore, would fit the needs of some NSPs far better than others. Some assignments may not effectively meet the needs of any NSPs. Others, although promising in theory, may be frustrating in fact. For example, two-thirds of the volunteers sampled in one Peace Corps study listed helping others as an important motive for their service, but fewer than half felt they had succeeded in doing so.[55]

Needs and Capacities May Not Match. Even a work environment well matched to the needs of some set of young people may be imperfectly adapted to their tolerances or abilities. It might be thought, for example, that residential conservation work programs in national parks would provide a particularly valuable change of scene for urban youths. But contemporaries noted an "allergy" of urban youths to the CCC,[56] and the modern authority on the subject reports that as best as can be told from limited data, nonhonorable discharges from that program "were significantly higher among [those] enrolled from urban areas."[57] This comports with polling data that indicate a significantly lower attraction to jobs in national parks among blacks and Hispanics than among whites.[58] Background factors aside, the California

Conservation Corps, one of the more successful residential programs, retains only 28.8 percent of its entrants for the full 12-month program.[59] Even the Peace Corps loses 27 percent of its entrants before their 2-year term is complete.[60] What young people need and what they will seek, accept, or endure are not always the same.

Quality of Administration Would Be Crucial. Whether any form of national service actually meets its participants needs would depend not merely on its design, or even on the particular tasks it assigns, but on the care and effectiveness of its administration. Something of the significance of even the most mundane administrative skills is suggested by the fact that in the CCC of the 1930s. "[A]n abundance of evidence indicates that camp food was the single most important predictor of enrollee satisfaction."[61]

Much is now known about subtler variables associated with successful service programs. They are characterized by clear objectives, meaningful work, demanding assignments, and careful supervision. Those conditions are not easily met. Organizations such as the California Conservation Corps, which are specifically designed and staffed to utilize volunteers, often provide those conditions. But such organizations are expensive to run. (Annual costs for the California Conservation Corps are roughly $20,000 per participant year, of which participants' stipends amount to about $8,000.) They also tend to be small and, if successful, closely managed by a strong leader and committed staff. One Labor Department veteran put it this way: "Almost anything works if it is administered by inspired, hard-working and competent people; on the other hand, nothing works if it is butchered by its administrators."[62]

If the history of bureaucracies is any guide, large organizations, even if constructed specifically to meet the needs of youth, will tend to be operated in ways that correspond as closely to the desires of their staffs as to the needs of the program beneficiaries. In a national service program where young people were supervised by existing bureaucracies such as hospitals, social service agencies, libraries, and probation offices, whose operating patterns were developed long before national service began, that tendency would be very strong. Volunteers often would find themselves without real jobs or assigned to the tasks that paid staff members find less attractive. This results in part from the natural tendency to use cheap resources carelessly and from the view of many professionals that volunteers are unreliable. It also reflects the understandable desire of permanent staffs to retain the more interesting and satisfying tasks for themselves. Empty, unpleasant, or undemanding jobs are more likely to breed boredom, cynicism, and resentment than to meet any of the needs discussed earlier. A system of national service that participants viewed as a device for having them empty the bedpans of life might create more problems than it solved.

Compared to What? Another caveat is simply that even when achieved, the benefits of a national service program remain to be measured against both their costs and other means of achieving similar results. This point has implications both for analyses of service and for policymaking. Analytically, it suggests that many prior studies are suspect. For example, of the numerous studies referred to here that purport to demonstrate that service accelerates maturation, only one used a control group. To what degree would whatever else the participants might have done with their time have accelerated maturity? We do not know.

Similarly, to demonstrate that national service would have value is not necessarily to demonstrate that it represents enlightened social policy. Its costs may be excessive, or some other set of policies (for example, private sector job creation or training programs narrowly targeted for those who need them) may confer equivalent or greater benefits at lower cost in dollars, dislocation, or dissension.

Needs and Attitudes Are Not Fixed. Finally, we note that there may be dangers in generalizing about the youth of the future from experience with the youth of the 1960s and 1970s. The huge cohort born in the baby boom between 1945 and 1960 hardly was typical. It produced a sudden and dramatic increase in the number of youth to be socialized and employed and similarly expanded the population from which most antisocial behavior of all kinds is produced. Together with the distorting influence of the war in Vietnam, the distinctive characteristics of that generation greatly advanced, if they did not initiate, the development of an autonomous youth culture. As college deans know, generations of youth are apt to differ markedly from their predecessors. The lessons society believes it learned while attempting to absorb and socialize that highly idiosyncratic generation may apply poorly to its successors.

The Needs of Older People

National service need not meet only the personal needs of youth. Some forms of national service, including the voluntary model we discuss in chapter 7 and a universal mandatory system we outline in chapter 8, would utilize participants at every stage of life. It is useful, therefore, to identify the needs of other population groups. We do so briefly here, distinguishing between potential participants in midlife and those at or beyond retirement age.

Midlife Needs

Although midlife (by which we mean the period roughly between ages thirty and fifty-five) covers many years and many circumstances, national service would almost certainly offer less to most persons in those years than it would to youth or to the elderly. We do not attempt to make any comprehensive assessment of the potential value of service in midlife, but it is worth considering several possible benefits from a service option during those years.

A national service option could, for example, provide a chance for a supported, though poorly paid, sabbatical from employment. Surveys consistently show that roughly 20 to 30 percent of employed persons are dissatisfied with their jobs or interested in changing employment.[63] A period of national service might be attractive to such persons either as a break in routine or as a possible transition to some new employment. Service also could be used to fill periods of unemployment in a way that was less corrosive to self-esteem than either inactivity or more conventional government-supported job programs. The record of the New Deal CCC and NYA underscores this potential. At two-thirds the minimum wage, the lowest level proposed in most national service plans, a national service program would provide about three-quarters the level of support of unemployment benefits.[64] At minimum wage, it would exceed those benefits.

For persons in midlife who are not in the labor force and especially for women, national service might offer several benefits. The results of a federally supported work program that offered work opportunities and special supervision for members of disadvantaged groups are suggestive:

> The clearest successes were achieved in projects serving women with dependent children who had long records of welfare dependency. After an average stay in supported work of nine months, welfare mothers worked more and earned higher wage rates than [members of a control group] who had not participated in the program. The reduced dependency outweighed the costs of this government intervention, including day care services, supervision, and peer counselling, by an estimated $8000 per AFDC program participant (1976 dollars) over a twenty-seven month period.[65]

Some component of a national service program might be designed to produce similar effects; the model discussed in chapter 7 provides an illustration. For more advantaged women outside the labor market, a national service option might offer a challenge and sense of purpose at transitional times in life, when the last children had left home or upon divorce or widowhood. For women wishing to find employment after their children were grown, some service assignments also might serve as halfway positions, assisting in socialization or resocialization to the work place.[66]

Needs at or after Retirement

In 1930, persons over sixty-five represented 6 percent of the U.S. population. In 1984, they were 12 percent of a much larger total.[67] In large part for this reason, there has been a rapidly increasing interest in the problems of aging and a growing deference to the political power of the aged. Nonetheless, comprehensive and authoritative assessments of the personal needs of older people are no more readily available than they are for youth. As with our typology of the needs of youth, in discussing the aged we will of necessity rely partly on intuition and everyday observation, while drawing on the work of social scientists to the extent possible. We note four major categories of need.

Income. One in six Americans over sixty-five surveyed in 1981 reported not having enough money to live on as a very serious problem.[68] The same survey showed that 75 percent of persons then working wanted to take paid part-time work after retirement.[69]

The Foster Grandparents Program, one of several ACTION programs involving the elderly, suggests how a service program can justify using even minimally skilled elderly people and paying them for it. Established by the Domestic Volunteer Service Act of 1973,[70] Foster Grandparents offers low-income persons age sixty or over a tax-free stipend of $2 per hour to work with younger people for 20 hours per week. The work takes place in day care centers, schools, illiteracy and runaway programs, foster care homes, programs to prevent child abuse, and the Head Start program.[71] ACTION calculated that in fiscal year 1981, more than 18,000 volunteers with a mean age of seventy-one assisted more than 54,000 children on a given day.[72]

Purpose and Self-Esteem. Extended unemployment aside, retirement produces the most severe loss of status and role that most adults face in their lifetimes. It results, for many, in feelings of purposelessness and loss of self-esteem. While classically this has been true primarily of males, in the future the phenomenon is likely also to be felt by the fast increasing number of women in the work who identify themselves, as fully as men, in terms of their occupations. It is well established that voluntary activity provides for many of the elderly who pursue it a new sense of purpose and a basis for self-esteem. Volunteer work has been characterized by psychiatrist Olga Knopf as "an exquisite form of occupational therpay."[73] Dramatic as it is, the following comment is typical of the assessments offered by elderly volunteers of the impact that volunteering has had on their lives: "Volunteering changed my whole life. I was really as good as dead before but now I feel like I'm alive. . . . I feel like I have some purpose."[74]

There appear to be several closely related but distinguishable ways in which volunteer activity engenders a sense of purpose and strengthens self-esteem. For some elderly people, providing service satisfies a need to repay society for benefits received. The literature on volunteering by the aged is full of citations to persons who take satisfaction in repaying a perceived obligation: "I am an immigrant and I want to help others because of the help given me when I came to this country." Or: "My husband was a veteran and received excellent care in the hospital where I serve now. I am trying to return what was given him."[75]

The second basis for self-esteem is simply the satisfaction derived from finding that one can still meet the needs of others: "It's good to know that I'm still needed in the world." "It is the most rewarding thing when patients ask for you." "I have fourteen grandchildren. They love me. I love them. But they don't need me the way the [Willowbrook Hospital] children do."[76] These, too, are typical comments of elderly volunteers.

Finally, some elderly participants in service programs appear to respond especially well to the opportunity to learn something new. Thus, they feel they are still growing in understanding or in capability.

Morale: The Avoidance of Self-pity. Another source of satisfaction for elderly persons in volunteer activity has been contact with individuals evidently worse off than they are, a contact that diminishes tendencies toward self-absorption and self-pity. "When I come here I see how bad off others are and I feel like I'm pretty lucky." "When I come here I have to do my work and there isn't time to think about all my usual aches and pains."[77] These are typical of the reported comments of elderly volunteers.

Acquaintanceship. Involving the elderly in volunteer activity yields the further benefit of broadening their range of acquaintanceships. Many elderly people feel a growing constriction on their lives, partially resulting from diminished energy and possible ill health, but most powerfully from the departure and death of friends and acquaintances. Thirteen percent of those over sixty-five report that loneliness is a very serious problem.[78] For them, as well as for others who are less severely burdened (or less candid and self-aware), volunteering is an antidote for anonymity. It puts them in contact with new acquaintances of several kinds: those they serve, other volunteers, and professionals and staff members in the institutions in which they work. It also widens the network of supportive social relationships on which they can depend when retirement, death of a spouse, or loss of health imposes further shocks.

The Harris survey carried out for the Council on Aging provides some statistical basis for assessing these needs. The survey asked retirees which attributes of work they missed and which they missed most. Seventy-one percent answered that they missed the income, and 30 percent missed the income most. For 70 and 24 percent, respectively, the answer was the people at work; for 55 and 10 percent, respectively, it was the feeling of being useful.[79]

Volunteering can at least partially meet each of these needs, and its effect on the elderly is powerful and pervasive. The most careful examination of that effect concludes that, as against a control group with identical characteristics, persons over 65 who average 15 hours of voluntary hospital work are "significantly more satisfied with life, have a stronger will to live, [and] report fewer somatic, anxious and depressive symptoms than those who do not engage in volunteer work." Indeed, at least one assessment of the impact of elderly volunteers working with the elderly concludes that the benefits to the volunteers are more striking than those to the clients.[80]

Moreover, existing programs involving the elderly suggest that many persons over sixty can be induced to volunteer significant amounts of time with only modest incentives. ACTION's $2-per-hour Foster Grandparents Program, involving approximately 18,000 elderly workers in 1981, was dwarfed that year by the same agency's Retired Senior Volunteer Program. RSVP enlisted almost 320,000 volunteers that year, contributing, by ACTION's estimate, more than 56 million hours of service. For the average 175 hours secured from each volunteer, ACTION paid nothing, covering only the volunteers' transportation costs and accident and liability insurance. ACTION calculates that 60 percent of these workers were over seventy, and 15 percent were over eighty.[81] Clearly, the desire to volunteer runs well into old age, and volunteering is pursued for reasons beyond financial rewards.[82]

Some Caveats

No less than with youth, the effective involvement of large numbers of elderly in national service programs can be questioned. In voluntary programs, few of the elderly might participate. Although the absolute levels of participation in the ACTION programs and others are impressive, the elderly volunteer less frequently than younger people. Using a broad definition of volunteering, the Gallup organization found in 1983 that 53 to 67 percent of persons in each of several age groupings between eighteen and sixty-four reported having volunteered in the recent past. But only 32 percent of persons sixty-five and older had done so.[83] Applying more demanding definitions, the 1981 survey conducted for the National Council on Aging found that 23 percent of those over sixty-five reported themselves then engaged in volunteer work, with another 10 percent indicating they would like to volunteer.[84] A national service system that called for relatively rigorous or time-intensive service might attract a still smaller fraction of the aged.

A second caveat is that among the elderly, as in all other age categories, the persons who volunteer tend to be disproportionately well educated, financially secure, and deeply rooted in their communities.[85] Thus, a voluntary system of national service would likely disproportionately benefit the relatively well integrated and well-to-do among the elderly who served.

Third, at least one study suggests that the more skilled an occupation a person has known before retirement, the less satisfaction he or she tends to derive from a volunteer assignment that requires little or no skill.[86] Insofar as they have more developed skills, more clearly defined interests, and less flexibility to accommodate new situations, the elderly may prove harder to assign to appropriate tasks than the young. Special efforts to accommodate the elderly might be justified, however, not only by the benefits to them but also by the greater utility of work that many could do and by the fact that elderly volunteers typically remain in their assignments longer than their younger counterparts.[87]

Finally, no coercive system of national service is likely to be imposed on the elderly. Mandatory service for the young might gain public support, perhaps on the theory that young people would benefit more from service, that they have a debt to pay society, or simply that there is already wide acceptance of compulsory education and military service for young persons. For older people, however, coerced service seems far more intrusive. Only a system that encourages voluntary service is likely to involve the elderly as NSPs.

Notes

1. Coleman, et al., *Youth: Transition to Adulthood.*
2. Ibid., 3.
3. Mead, "A National Service System," 108.
4. Steinberg et al., "Effects of Working on Adolescent Development," 385. See the more extended development of this point in chapter 5.
5. Morgan, "Coming of Age in the 80s," *The Washington Post,* 21 December 1984 to 2 January 1982 (reporting on a survey by the National Center for Education Statistics).
6. Raphael, "Youth Employment and its Effects on Performance in High School," 11. See also Lewin-Epstein, *Youth Employment During High School,* 48.
7. Thus, for example, an evaluation of the later experience of fifteen- to eighteen-year-olds who were rejected by the Youth Conservation Corps' summer program found that two-thirds of these unsuccessful applicants had found paying summer jobs anyway. Johnson et al., "The Long-Term Benefits of the Youth Conservation Corps," 45. The majority of these young men and women kept their jobs all summer. See ibid., 47. Those unsuccessful applicants who did not work reported, for the most part, that they spent their summer in travel (31 percent), volunteer work (12 percent), summer school (6 percent), summer camp (5 percent), or other activities (28 percent). Only 18 percent said they stayed at home or did nothing. See ibid., 50.
8. The history of postwar youth labor force participation in the United States has been one of increasing participation for enrolled students and of decreasing participation for dropouts, so participation rates of the former group are approaching those of the latter. See, generally, Reubens, Harrison, and Rupp, *The Youth Labor Force, 1945–1995,* 198–99.
9. Bureau of Labor Statistics, *Employment and Earnings* (*April 1985*), table A–7.

10. Unemployment rates for out-of-school youth over the past decade are based on data from the Bureau of Labor Statistics, *Labor Force Statistics Derived from Current Population Survey,* 755, 759. Unemployment rates for the labor force as a whole over the past decade are from the Bureau of Labor Statistics, *Handbook of Labor Statistics,* table 4.

11. Ford Foundation, "Not Working," 1.

12. As discussed in the next chapter, the youth cohort will diminish over the next half-decade and grow at a relatively slow rate in the early 1990s. This will tend to ameliorate the youth unemployment problem. But other factors seem likely to offset this advantage. These include reductions in the number of low-skill entry-level jobs, high proportions of minority groups in the youth population, potentially substantial immigration, increasing female labor force participation, and increases in the average retirement age.

13. As of March 1985, the unemployment rate of out-of-school sixteen- to nineteen-year-old blacks was 43.1 percent, as opposed to 19 percent for their white counterparts. Bureau of Labor Statistics, *Employment and Earnings (April 1985),* table A–7. At the same time, the unemployment rate for all sixteen- to nineteen-year-old blacks was 39.7 percent, while for whites it was 16.2 percent. Ibid., table A–4.

14. These figures are based on historical data obtained in telephone conversations with analysts at the Bureau of Labor Statistics' Office of Employment and Unemployment Statistics in May 1985. These data refer to all youth ages sixteen to nineteen, not exclusively to out-of-school youth. The point is discussed generally in Ford Foundation, "Not Working," 6ff.

15. Hahn and Lehman, *What Works in Youth Employment Policy,* 3, 4.

16. Dickson, "Reflecting on a Contemporary Taboo," 25. Dr. Dickson is a leading British advocate of national service.

17. Hedin et al., *Minnesota Youth Poll: Youth's View on National Service and the Draft,* 11.

18. This study is cited in Cullinan, "National Service and the American Educational System," 94.

19. Janowitz, "The Logic of National Service," 89.

20. Coleman et al., *Youth: Transition to Adulthood,* 9.

21. Janowitz, "The Logic of National Service," 88.

22. Mead, "A National Service System," 105. More recent research concludes that work experience not only exerts a powerful effect on self-image but that, at least for young men, work that allows for substantial self-direction may be of greater importance than socioeconomic standing for the development of self-esteem. Mortimer and Finch, "The Development of Self-Esteem in the Early Work Career," 20–21.

23. Quoted in "National Service and Education Workshop" in Eberly, ed., *A Report of a Conference,* 223. Given the statement, "I felt more mature than people my age when I came back," 47 percent of a 1975 sample of those who completed 2 years in the Peace Corps agreed, 29 percent agreed somewhat, and only 23 percent disagreed. There was, however, no control group. See Winslow, "Returned Peace Corps Volunteers," 24.

24. Educators and analysts of education informally surveyed by the authors uniformly believed this proposition to be accurate, and it has been asserted to be true by advocates of national service. Nonetheless, there is little systematic evidence directly

regarding this point. In particular, the effects of the greater maturity of older students have not been accounted for in any study we have seen.

25. Asked to choose from a list of factors causing them to enlist in Peace Corps, four out of five returning volunteers cited personal growth and exposure to a different culture. About the same percentage thought their expectations were met in this regard. Winslow, "Returned Peace Corps Volunteers," 14.

26. Coleman et al., *Youth: Transition to Adulthood,* 9–10.

27. Mead, "A National Service System," 105.

28. Etzioni, "National Service for Youth," 13. In *An Immodest Agenda* (159–61), Etzioni briefly summarizes the full range of traditional arguments for the sociological benefits of national service.

29. Maccoby and Margolies, "The Psychological Effects on Youth of National Service," 39–40.

30. Ibid., 40.

31. Patchen, *Black-White Contact in Schools,* 223–28. Interestingly, greater interracial contact (as measured by the racial composition of classes) did produce a greater number of interracial friendships; these, however, did not significantly affect attitudes about the other race as a whole.

32. Coleman et al., *Youth: Transition to Adulthood,* 4–5.

33. Sizer, "National Service Education Study," 7.

34. See the seven-part series, "Coming of Age in the 80s," *Washington Post,* 27 December 1981 to 2 January 1982. The statement quoted appeared in the article of 27 December 1981.

35. Newman, *Higher Education and the American Resurgence,* 36–37. Because the role of adolescents in U.S. society has not changed substantially over these years, one may question the causes, if not the reality, of this transformation. Some have advanced explanations related more to the contemporary political environment than to more basic characteristics of life in the United States. A Carnegie Council on Policy Studies publication, for example, urges universal service for young people as a corrective to the "death of altruism," which is described as the "most serious consequence of the Vietnam/Watergate era." In this period, it is said, "service became a dirty word, associated as it was with a dirty war and a self-serving administration." Levine, *When Dreams and Heroes Die,* 137.

36. Newman, *Higher Education and the American Resurgence,* 37.

37. Ibid., 38. See the graph citing American Council on Education: Cooperative Institutional Research Program, *The American Freshman: National Norms for Fall 1983.*

38. Each of these findings is noted in Maccoby and Margolies, "The Psychological Effects on Youth of National Service," 32–41.

39. Luchs, "Selected Changes in Urban High School Students," 168–82.

40. Coleman et al., *Youth: Transition to Adulthood,* 5.

41. Mead, "A National Service System," 105.

42. Rothenberg, *The Neoliberals: Creating the New American Politics,* 209.

43. Ibid., 210.

44. Coleman et al., *Youth: Transition to Adulthood,* 28.

45. Hollingshead, *Elmtown's Youth,* 149.

46. Bramson, "Social Impact of Voluntary National Service," 107.

47. James, "The Moral Equivalent of War," 14.

48. Wynne, ed., *Developing Character: Transmitting Knowledge,* 7. Ibid., 5.

49. Committee for the Study of National Service, *Youth and the Needs of the Nation,* 77.

50. Ibid., 78.

51. Johnston, O'Malley, and Bachman, *Highlights from Drugs and American High School Students, 1975–83,* 11: "The greater moderation of American young people in their use of illicit drugs is evidenced not only by the fact that fewer are using most types of drugs, but also by the fact that, even among the users of many of these classes, use appears to be less intense." Ibid., 43–44; "[T]o answer a frequently asked question, there is no evidence that the currently observed drop in marijuana use is leading to a concommitant [*sic*] increase in alcohol use. If anything, daily alcohol use has declined."

52. Johnson and Driver, "Final Report of Pilot Study," 11.

53. Bailin and Jaffe, 19.

54. Data from the Bureau of the Census, *Statistical Abstract: 1985,* 75, show that among fifteen- to twenty-four–year–old males, the suicide rate in 1981 was 19.7 per 100,000, while among females of the same age, it was only 4.6 per 100,000. Among young white males, the rate was 21.1 per 100,000, compared with 11.1 per 100,000 for black males; among young white females, the rate was 4.9 per 100,000, as opposed to 2.4 per 100,000 for black females.

55. Winslow, "Returned Peace Corps Volunteers," 15.

56. Sherraden, *The Civilian Conservation Corps: Effectiveness of the Camps,* 138. (Quoting *The New York Times,* 2 May 1936).

57. Ibid., 141. See also Goldberg, *The Noneconomic Impacts of the Job Corps,* 2: "Tough, street-wise youngsters became surprisingly homesick when taken from their debilitating environments for, often, the first time. Job Corps Centers in beautiful national parks and forests were seen as sites of sensory deprivation by city kids. . . . Policymakers were unwittingly placing the young participants in another bastion of middle-class values, where they would fail again. So, centers were opened in cities and participants were permitted to enroll as students."

58. Boris, "Willingness to Work," 589.

59. Unpublished data provided by the California Conservation Corps, Division of Intake and Statistics, Sacramento, California. The program includes a nonresidential component, including about a quarter of its participants.

60. Attrition rate provided by the Peace Corps Public Affairs Office in an unpublished memo to the National Service Study Project, June 1985.

61. Sherraden, *The Civilian Conservation Corps: Effectiveness of the Camps,* 153.

62. Magnum and Walsh, *Employment and Training Programs for Youth: What Works Best for Whom,* 15.

63. See Quinn and Staines, *The 1977 Quality of Employment Survey,* 205–15 (especially table 13.1). The answers depend greatly on the questions asked. Between 85 and 90 percent of the workers questioned in the survey's carefully constructed sample reported themselves either very satisfied or somewhat satisfied with their cur-

rent jobs in each of the 3 years the survey was taken (1969, 1973, 1977). But between 44 and 60 percent of them, if free to go into any type of job they wanted, preferred a job other than the one they had. Perhaps most relevant is the answer to the question, "Knowing what you know, if you had to decide all over again whether to take the job you now have, what would you decide?" Between 63.9 and 70.5 percent would decide without hesitation to take the same job; the remainder would have some second thoughts or decide definitely not to take the job.

64. According to data provided to us by the Department of Labor's Unemployment Insurance Service, the average weekly state unemployment benefit paid in 1983 was $125.55. In comparison, the amount earned in a 40-hour week at two-thirds the minimum wage would be $3.35/hour × ⅔ × 40 hours, or $89.33 per week.

65. Levitan and Johnson, *Beyond the Safety Net,* 126, citing Kemper, Long, and Thornton, *The Supported Work Evaluation: Final Benefit-Cost Analysis.* Both authorities note, as Levitan puts it, that "[A]lthough relatively successful in facilitating the entry of welfare mothers into the labor market, supported work had little effect on the employment and earnings of ex-addicts, ex-offenders, or school dropouts." Levitan and Johnson, *Beyond the Safety Net,* 126.

66. See Appelbaum, *Back to Work: Determinants of Women's Successful Reentry,* 91–94.

67. Data for 1984 derived from Bureau of the Census, *Projection of the Population of the United States: 1983–2080,* 41–42. The data for 1930 were taken from Bureau of the Census, *1930 Population General Report,* 576.

68. Louis Harris and Associates, Inc., *Aging in the Eighties: America in Transition,* 67–69. This was a lower percentage than that for eighteen- to sixty-four–year–olds (22 percent). For elderly blacks and Hispanics, the 1981 figures are 55 and 45 percent, respectively.

69. Ibid., 96s–97.

70. 42 U.S.C. §4992 (1973).

71. ACTION, *Annual Report, 1981,* 5.

72. Ibid., 7.

73. Beverly, "The Double-Barreled Impact of Volunteer Services," 132.

74. Hunter and Linn, "Psycho-Social Differences Between Elderly Volunteers and Non-Volunteers," 212.

75. Community Service Society of the New York, *Proceedings of the Fourth Annual SERVE Volunteer Training Institute,* 41.

76. Ibid., 40–47.

77. Hunter and Linn, "Psycho-Social Differences Between Elderly Volunteers and Non-Volunteers," 211–12.

78. Louis Harris and Associates, Inc., *Aging in the Eighties: America in Transition,* 7.

79. Ibid., 15.

80. See, for example, ACTION, *Senior Companion Program Impact Evaluation: 1980 Summary Report,* 32.

81. ACTION, *Annual Report, 1981,* 4–9.

82. For a description of a wide variety of volunteer programs that use elderly volunteers, see Ventura and Newman, *Voluntary Action and Older Americans: A Catalogue of Program Profiles.*

83. Sec Gallup, "The 1983 Gallup Survey on Volunteering," 21.

84. Louis Harris and Associates, Inc., *Aging in the Eighties: America in Transition,* 29.

85. See Ibid., 29–30, and Monk and Cryns, "Predictors of Voluntaristic Intent Among the Aged," 426–27. These volunteers also are predominantly female. Enrollment in ACTION's elderly volunteer programs, for example, is consistently about 80 percent female. See ACTION, *Annual Report, 1981,* 5.

86. Kaplan, *Role Continuity in the Older Volunteer Role,* 99–100.

87. Comparisons of retention rates were made based on figures provided by Babic, "The Older Volunteer: Expectations and Satisfactions," 87–90; and telephone interviews with the directors of ACTION's Foster Grandparent and Retired Senior Volunteer programs.

4
The Military and National Service

The third of the three primary attractions of national service is that it might enable the nation to meet its military personnel needs more fully and fairly. Just how those needs should be met has been a matter of considerable contemporary dispute. From 1789 to 1945, only during war or on the eve of war were U.S. armed forces made up of conscripts. From 1945 through 1972, however, men were drafted in every year but one. For the past decade, the older pattern has prevailed, as the armed forces have been made up exclusively of volunteers.

Many advocates of a return to a draft find some forms of national service attractive as a framework within which a draft might fit. Many members of Congress and others have shown interest in voluntary national service as a means of buttressing the volunteer force and thus avoiding a draft. As those apparently contradictory impulses suggest, the relationship between military personnel needs and national service is not simple. This chapter outlines the main arguments in the current debate over military manpower and suggests how they might intersect with proposals for national service.

The All-Volunteer Force Debate

Can the all-volunteer force (AVF) indefinitely meet military manpower requirements? Although 1982 to 1984 were banner years for military recruitment, it is generally agreed that military volunteers will be harder to attract in the late 1980s unless the country experiences continued high rates of youth unemployment.[1]

Advocates of the volunteer system assert that as long as military pay is sustained at or near its present relation to civilian wages, the personnel now projected to be required for active duty likely can be drawn from volunteers. They point out that in each year since the AVF was established in 1973, the services have been within 1.2 percent of their targeted strength.[2] Critics respond that in many years this has been only at the cost of a decline in the

Table 4–1
Measures of Quality for Male Army Recruits without Prior Military Service

	Draft-Era		*Early AVF*		*Recent AVF*				
	1960–1964	*1971–1972*	*1974*	*1975*	*1980*	*1981*	*1982*	*1983*	*1984*
Percent Holding High School Diplomas (or More)	64[a]	64	46	54	49	78	85	88[c]	89[d]
Percent in Lowest Acceptable Mental Test Score Category	19[a]	22	19	11	50	32	22	12[c]	12[d]
Percent with Some College	17[b]	21	4	6	3	5	8	—	9[d]

Source: Except where noted, Department of Defense Manpower Data Center Report 0584.

[a]Cooper, *Military Manpower and the All Volunteer Force.*

[b]Unpublished tabulations furnished by the Office of the Assistant Secretary of Defense (Military Manpower and Personnel Policy) and OASD (Comptroller).

[c]U.S. Department of Defense News Release No. 580-83, 23 November 1983.

[d]Defense Manpower Data Center, Report No. 85F931-4.

quality of recruits, and they cite periods of low military aptitude scores and low educational attainment among AVF recruits. Table 4–1 shows some of the fluctuations in recruitment history from 1960 to 1984. Critics fear the recurrence of periods of poor recruitment in the future and point out that the Army Reserve and National Guard generally have been understaffed even in the best of AVF recruiting periods.[3]

AVF advocates make the point that recruitment exclusively through economic and other incentives agrees best with American values of minimal coercion by government. They view the market mechanism as the best means of avoiding the selective compulsion, biases, and abuses of a draft, with its exemptions and deferments. They also note that volunteers have higher morale, serve longer terms, and are much more likely to reenlist than are draftees, with consequent gains in experience and savings in training costs.[4] Further, they argue that a volunteer system drives the military to allocate personnel more efficiently and to treat them more humanely than in a draft system, where recruits are free resources and are valued accordingly.

> I must confess that I like the idea of paying for quality by using bonuses, stripes for skills, educational matching grants and other incentive devices. I like it not only because economically I think it increases the allocational efficiency of society; because psychologically it makes for a more willing soldier; because morally it seems fairer. I like it also because it provides a

> desirable incentive for the military to treat quality as quality and people as valuable resources. Tales of the abuse of quality in the military are probably as old as the military itself. Consider, for example, the historian who repairs tanks, the electrician who paints, the German speaker who is sent to Korea, the college graduate who is woefully underutilized as the company clerk. When resources, be they things or people, come essentially without cost they are treated as though they are without worth, and the waste is horrendous.[5]

Supporters of this system see no principled objection—and many advantages—to a volunteer system of professionals.

Critics regard such gains as offset by the mercenary image of the armed forces conveyed through emphasis on economic incentives and argue that this adversely affects unit cohesion and individual commitment to duty, especially in an emergency.

> Our soldiers are best prepared in a regimented, austere environment. . . . It is not to the best interest of military training to pay a new soldier wages that will support a "pad" in the town nearby, a "hot rod" on the highway or a wife.[6]

Many critics of an AVF also are disturbed by the inability of economic incentives to draw recruits proportionately from among the more privileged classes in the United States. They detect shortfalls in talents and skills, particularly in the Army, and ascribe these to the poor representation of the middle class and the almost entire absence of the college educated in the enlisted ranks.

> College-educated members enriched the skill level and commitment of military units in peace as well as in war. . . . One is struck by the fond reminiscences the older sergeants have of the university graduates who worked under them. These were the kind of soldiers who formed the shadow staffs—as clerks in personnel, supply and operations—which made things run smoothly at company and battalion levels.[7]

The failure of the military to mirror the composition of civilian society also generates political and moral concern about the disproportionate combat risks shouldered by minorities and the poor. As one writer described the situation in 1982:

> [A]bout 33 percent of the Army enlisted ranks are now black (compared to 12 percent during the Vietnam era), and blacks now constitute roughly 22 percent of the Marine Corps enlisted force. When other minority groups (principally Hispanic) are included, the proportions are 41 percent for the Army and 32 percent for the Marine Corps.[8]

Beyond this, some proponents of the draft are concerned that the cumulative effect of relying on the market mechanism in making choices, using economic incentives to induce participation, and accepting the resulting lack of representativeness erodes the sense of public obligation that all citizens ought to share. A leading newspaper put the argument as follows:

> The essential mixture of classes that once characterized the services has largely disappeared. The services are less effective for it. The country is less strong than it should be militarily and, we think, morally. The haves are freed from the obligation of military service, the have-nots are sucked in to fill the vacuum. This is a disturbing state of affairs. More to the point, it is a shameful one.[9]

Finally, in the eyes of some, "[t]he real argument for a draft is that the military will not be respected, and decisions about its use will not be democratically made, unless every class in the nation feels it has a direct stake in its performance."[10]

Despite the strength of these concerns, it is likely that whether or not the United States returns to a draft will hinge on the pragmatic question of whether the AVF can meet future manpower requirements with recruits of reasonable quality. Given entry pay that remains close to the minimum wage, the answer to that question is shaped by two fundamental statistics: the number of young men available for service and the desired size of the armed forces.

In recent years, military recruits have been drawn primarily from a pool of approximately 2 million men and 2 million women who are between the ages of eighteen and nineteen. On the order of 300,000 male and 50,000 female recruits from this pool sustain an active duty force of 2.1 million. Thus, somewhat fewer than 1 in every 10 American youths, or 1 in every 6 males, is drawn into active duty in the military. Another 100,000 youths without active duty experience enter the reserves. By contrast, during the period 1954–1957, when the birth cohort was much smaller, women essentially were excluded, and service strengths were larger, one in every two draft-age males were required to serve.[11]

If anything approaching that ratio were required again, an AVF could not be sustained. No plausible economic incentives consistently could enlist so high a proportion of the population. Conversely, if military requirements dropped sharply—by half, for example—a draft would be difficult to maintain because as long as pay for military recruits remains at or above the minimum wage, requirements can be met fully by volunteers. The contrary position, although arguable, would be difficult to sustain: It would be that a qualified and willing volunteer should be rejected in favor of coercing an unwilling but otherwise identical individual into serving. The AVF recruiting task could be compounded by raising entry standards, but these already eliminate more than a quarter of the population on mental, moral, or physical grounds and mandate that 65 percent of military recruits be high school graduates.

Debate about the AVF occurs when demand and supply fall within an intermediate range where the ratio of the two is low enough to make an AVF sustainable but high enough to make a draft plausible. Cooper notes that historically the movement from conscription to a volunteer system relates

> [T]o some simple population dynamics. . . . Except for the period of the Vietnam conflict, between 1966 and 1970, the number of annual accessions into the military required to man the active duty forces has remained roughly constant since the late 1950s (in fact, it has actually declined modestly . . .). However, beginning in 1954, the number of young men turning 19 increased every year, and dramatically so starting about 1961.[12]

Nelson, Hale and Slackman note the correlation between manpower supply and conscription choices in NATO (North Atlantic Treaty Organization) countries (table 4–2).[13]

This ratio could change on the demand side as a result of a decision to

Table 4–2
Percentages of Eligible Males Required to Man Military Forces in NATO Countries

Country	*Type*	*Percent Required*
France	Conscript	100
Norway	Conscript	97
Netherlands	Conscript	64
Portugal	Conscript	60
West Germany	Conscript	50
Denmark	Conscript	34
United States[a]	Volunteer	17–22
Britain	Volunteer	8
Canada	Volunteer	N/A

Source: Data from Nelson, Hale, and Slackman, "National Service and the Military," unpublished paper, p. I–19a.

Note: The North Atlantic Treaty Assembly publication is not precise about the meaning of "eligibles." It appears that the percentages refer to male recruits entering active duty as a percentage of all physically and mentally qualified youth who, for those countries with conscription, do not obtain status as COs.

[a]U.S. figures show total number of male enlisted recruits without prior military service who entered the military forces in fiscal year 1981 as a percentage of the eligible population of U.S. males. The lower percentage shows active-duty recruits only; the larger one includes reserves. Eligibles were estimated as the total population of males less 10 percent for those not mentally fit (category V) and another 15 percent for those not physically qualified.

expand greatly the size of our military forces.[14] A case readily could be made for such an increase on the basis of present military responsibilities. With approximately 785,800 troops,[15] the all-volunteer Army is far below the Army's pre-Vietnam levels.[16] Expansion of the active duty Army is therefore a possibility even in the current international environment. It would become much more likely if the international situation appeared to grow more dangerous.

Modest personnel additions made slowly, such as an increase of 200,000 (about 10 percent of present strength) over 5 years, perhaps could be handled by the volunteer system. But a large or fast expansion, such as an increase of 500,000 troops (almost 25 percent) over 5 years or of 200,000 in 1 year, probably would swamp the volunteer system. Cooper notes:

> [S]o long as force strengths stay near the present levels . . . the AVF has a reasonable chance. If, on the other hand, manpower requirements increase substantially beyond these levels—say to 2.7 million for the active forces or 1.5 million for the reserves—the AVF will clearly have a very difficult time, unless such force size increases are accompanied by large military pay increases.[17]

Such challenges to the AVF from the demand side are highly uncertain, but if they occur, they probably are unmanageable. Potential problems on the supply side, in contrast, are quite predictable but not likely to prove severe. The declining birth rates of the late 1960s and the 1970s will produce steadily diminishing numbers of youths turning eighteen in the 1980s and early 1990s. In terms of the coming of age of eighteen-year-olds, the peak of the baby boom occurred in 1978. The low point will be reached in 1992. In that year, the eighteen-year old cohort will be almost 25 percent smaller than in 1978.[18] Thereafter, the echo of the baby boom will appear as the first children of the baby boom children are eighteen, and the cohort will increase each year.

In the early 1980s, high unemployment rates in effect offset the diminishing cohort, and a higher proportion of youth found military service attractive. As the number of eighteen-year-olds continues to diminish in the late 1980s and early 1990s, there may be no such offset.[19] Thus, from either supply or demand changes in the years ahead, pressure may grow to abandon the AVF and move to a draft or to some form of national service.

Difficulties with a Draft

Proposals for a draft are likely to encounter three problems, each arising from the fact that except in the event of large-scale military build-up, draft calls would take only a fraction of the 1.6 to 2 million males who would reach draft age in each year. (The fraction would be reduced if women were included.)

First, a draft that inducts only a few is likely to encourage resentment in those who are called. This would undermine that sense of widespread public obligation and shared experience that draft advocates associate with World War II and the Korean War.

Second, although a draft might make the enlisted ranks somewhat more representative of our society, its effects in that regard would not be substantial. So long as volunteers are accepted and a supplemental draft is random, the middle and upper classes will remain dramatically underrepresented. Suppose, for example, that 200,000 male volunteers were accepted and 100,000 male draftees were inducted each year. The volunteers would not include many more middle- and upper-class men than they do now, and in a representative draft only 50,000 of the 100,000 draftees would score above the fiftieth percentile on entrance tests.[20] How substantial an effect would this increment in the quality or representativeness of junior enlisted men, even with all serving 2 years and some reenlisting, have on the more than 2 million member U.S. military? Even with a draft, the racial and economic composition of the military would be dominated by the greater propensity of those from poorer backgrounds to volunteer and reenlist.

The third difficulty likely to face a draft arises from the probable resistance or reluctance of many who would be called to serve. Military personnel officers do not want a truly random sample of able-bodied men and women. The volunteer force provides those who choose to serve. Personnel officers who favor a draft would like to produce men and women who, though not volunteers, would serve willingly once inducted. They do not want to induct that fraction of the population that rebels against military service, produces troublemakers, winds up in brigs, or deserts. The induction of this group is a significant cost of the draft, a cost notably reduced in an all-volunteer system.

The first two of these problems might be circumvented by a system of universal military service. But even at its lowest ebb, and even excluding women, the size of the youth cohort between now and at the end of the century greatly exceeds any probable military demand. In addition, there appears to be no support, least of all in the military, for a near tripling of the armed forces to absorb 2 million people every year for 2-year terms.[21] A draft of this size would distort the military's primary purpose, the nation's defense, to achieve a collateral end: a universal sense of service. Moreover, under such a scheme, military resources would be poorly allocated. Too many dollars would go for training, feeding, clothing, and housing millions of soldiers for whom the Department of Defense, without greatly increased budgets, would not have tanks, planes, transportation, or even guns and ammunition.[22] No likely international situation would warrant, or benefit from, the United States' maintaining and equipping so large a force.[23]

Military Arguments for National Service

Against this backdrop, ideas of compulsory national service—that is, systems of service that would allocate some fraction of the youth cohort to civilian service and some fraction to military service—are appealing to advocates of the draft. At least in the abstract, they offer ways of dealing with each of the three problems mentioned.

First, they would broaden the service obligation, diminishing the inequity of obliging only a few to serve. An expectation of service as a fact of life might thereby become engrained. This was the basis for Robert McNamara's advocacy of national service while he was secretary of defense. In a 1966 speech he said:

> As matters stand our Selective Service System draws on only a minority of eligible men. That is an inequity. It seems to me that we could move toward remedying that inequity by asking every young person in the United States to give two years of service to his country—whether in one of the military services, in the Peace Corps, or in some other volunteer developmental work at home or abroad.[24]

More recently, James Fallows has written, "The problem of capriciousness in a military draft could also be avoided by a generalized system of national service, which is my own preference."[25]

Second, if it were established that all will serve in some capacity, the market available to the military might change markedly. Middle- and upper-class youth could no longer choose between pursuing entirely private ends and enlisting in the military; the choice would be which form of public service, civilian or military, to pursue. Some who have reflected on the matter believe that a substantial number would then choose the military, and fragmentary poll data support that conclusion.[26] If necessary, the system could be weighted to offer greater rewards (principally pay or educational benefits) for military than for civilian service. According to the testimony of Representative Lloyd, "Obviously, we sweeten the deal for those who take the option to go into the military services and once they put in their time will be eligible for the GI bill, which seems to be a major driving force."[27] Some have suggested the imposition of high ability or achievement requirements for military service, while setting no such requirements for civilian service.[28]

Third, a civilian parallel to military service would tend to defuse objections to conscription from those who might tolerate civilian but not military service. It would allow those who would resist military life to avoid it, thus easing problems of military morale, training, and discipline.[29]

As we shall see, each of these advantages carries disadvantages with it. Some of the desired gains are dubious, and some are incompatible with others. But it should be clear from this brief survey why the concept of compulsory national service has a pronounced attraction for advocates of a draft. The most recent and most refined opinion poll data highlight this correlation of views. A 1984 National Opinion Research Center analysis observed that 41.6 percent of adult Americans would favor returning to a military draft and that 44 percent of the adult population favored a compulsory national service program for men and women, even if "such a program made it necessary to increase your taxes by a small amount—for example, 5 percent." The intercorrelation between the two groups was strong. Of those favoring the draft, 58.8 percent favored national service, while only 36 percent opposed it.[30]

It is notable that conceptions of national service and of its consequences are sufficiently diverse as to engage the support of some who favor an AVF. Their view is that if a period of service between high school and a job or college were required or expected of all youth, a higher proportion than now would volunteer for the armed services,[31] and the military would be more likely than now to attract the college-bound and the upwardly mobile. Of course, if a civilian national service plan drew off those who now volunteer for the military without adding at least equivalent numbers to those who serve, it would undermine the AVF. If almost all young people expected to serve, however, that expectation would benefit the AVF.[32] Such an effect might be ensured by conditioning federal student aid at the college level to a period of service[33] or by giving priority for federal employment to those who have served.[34]

The concept of national service thus has special appeal for those who favor conscription but also attracts those committed to the principle of volunteerism. National service, in short, tends to interest all those who are concerned about the staffing of our military, no matter what their preferred solution. In later chapters, we assess how well particular plans for national service are likely to realize these expectations.

Notes

1. On the effects of unemployment on enlistment, see Dale and Gilroy, "Determinants of Enlistments: A Macroeconomic Time Series View," 192–210.
2. See Cooper, "Military Manpower Procurement Policy in the 1980s," 165.
3. Data and a dispassionate summary of the arguments with respect to this and

many of the other issues noted here may be found in Binkin, "Military Manpower Issues in the 1980s: Issues and Choices," 347–74.

4. Cooper, "Military Manpower Procurement Policy in the 1980s," 168. See also Department of Defense, *America's Volunteers: A Report on the All-Volunteer Armed Forces, 65.*

5. Department of Defense, "Remarks of Richard Danzig at the Hoover-Rochester Conference on the All-Volunteer Force."

6. General William Westmoreland, "U.S. Military Readiness Requires the Draft," *The Wall Street Journal,* 26 May 1981.

7. Moskos, "How to Save the All-Volunteer Force," 78.

8. Binkin, "Military Manpower Issues in the 1980s: Issues and Choices," 353. This issue also is discussed at length in Binkin et al., *Blacks and the Military,* also see the references cited there on p. 41, fn. 7. Binkin notes in the latter study that minority enlistments dropped both in proportion and in absolute numbers in fiscal years 1980 and 1981. Ibid. p. 44. The same is true for fiscal years 1982 and 1983. Whether the economy's post-1983 improvement will provoke a return to earlier recruitment patterns remains to be seen.

9. "Army of the Poor," *Los Angeles Times,* 6 April 1981.

10. Fallows, *National Defense,* 173.

11. Nelson, Hale, and Slackman, "National Service and the Military," II–2; and Cooper, *Military Manpower and the All-Volunteer Force,* 44, figure 3.2.

12. Cooper, *Military Manpower and the All-Volunteer Force,* 43–44.

13. Nelson, Hale, and Slackman, "National Service and the Military," I–19a.

14. Early inclinations in this direction by the Reagan administration seem to have moderated in light of fiscal realities and Congressional pressures. The addition of 100,000 persons to the Army would increase personnel costs by about $3 billion per year. Ibid., I–8.

15. Department of Defense, *Defense 84 Almanac,* 24.

16. Department of the Army, *Pocket Data Supplement,* 12, shows that in 1961, 1962, and 1963, the 3 years preceding the Vietnam War, Army active duty strength was at 859,000; 1,066,000; and 976,000, respectively. Thus, in the year immediately preceding U.S. involvement in the war, troop levels were 191,000 higher than at present; 2 years before the war, they were 281,000 higher.

17. Cooper, "Military Manpower Procurement Policy in the 1980s," 171–72.

18. In 1978, there were 4,229,000 eighteen-year-old men and women. The Bureau of the Census projects that there will be 3,199,000 eighteen-year-olds in 1992, 24.4 percent fewer than in 1978. Bureau of the Census, *Projections of the Population of the United States: 1977–2050,* 38; and *Projection of the Population of the United States: 1983–2080, 57.*

19. A recent optimistic assessment of this situation may be found in, U.S. Air Force, *An Analysis of the Effects of Varying Male/Female Force Levels.*

20. These numbers are merely illustrative. In a somewhat more detailed discussion, Bernard Rostker, former director of the Selective Service System, calculated that if the Army drew 50 percent of its labor power requirements from volunteers and 50 percent from conscription, the net effect would be to raise the percentage of accessions in the highest test score groups from 24.3 to 31.6 percent and to lower the percentage

in the lowest acceptable test group from 27.1 to 25.2 percent. He concluded that "the draft would do little to change the profile of today's military accessions." See "How Can the Draft Be Fair," *Washington Post,* 5 August 1981.

Binkin et al., *Blacks and the Military,* undertake a similar analysis and suggest somewhat more positive results. Their chart (p. 146) estimates that the percentage of high school graduates among Army accessions might have increased from 78 to 83 percent, and lowest mental category entrants might have declined from 30 to 18 percent if a 100,000 man expansion of the Army had caused a draft of 51,000 men in fiscal year 1981. Of course, the impact on the total force profile would be substantially smaller than on the profile of accessions.

21. Cooper, "Military Manpower Procurement Policy in the 1980s," 172–75, discusses this alternative and universal military training. His conclusion is the same as ours.

22. In 1984, the Department of Defense estimated that on average it cost $35,000 to pay and maintain a member of the armed forces. *Washington Post,* 20 August 1984, A–16.

23. The Department of Defense has had occasion to address proposals for universal training or universal military service and has repeatedly made these points clear. Flynn, *Lewis B. Hershey, Mr. Selective Service,* 227, 232.

24. In Chambers, *Draftees or Volunteers,* 542.

25. Fallows, *National Defense,* 138.

26. See chapter 6, "Impacts on the Military."

27. House Military Personnel Subcommittee, *Hearings on National Service Legislation,* 96.

28. For an example of this point of view circulating among military officers, see Silver Flash II, "How to Sharpen Uncle Sam's Defense Sword, Increase Home-Front Home Services, Shrink the Government, Cut Taxes, Reduce the Budget and Get America off its Apathy," 99. The Services to America proposal advanced there entails 1 year of conscripted civilian or military service, with no high school dropouts allowed in the military branch.

29. But see, for example, Friends Committee on National Legislation, "National Service—A National Disservice," 2, 4: "Is national service, as it is now being proposed in Congress, just a sugar-coated draft?"; and the comment of Representative Stratton (an advocate of the draft) to Representative Lloyd (an advocate of national service, House Military Personnel Subcommittee, *Hearings on National Service Legislation* 100: "Isn't this really just an attempt, as you said yourself, to sweeten the deal, that you don't want to upset anybody by suggesting that military service would be mandatory. So you put up a facade on it by appearing to indicate that there is some choice, but you put on this a monstrous kind of thing, where you have got perhaps 2 or 3 million people going into all kinds of civilian duties in the hope that maybe you are going to get enough people to fill the military needs. Isn't it like burning down the house in order to get the pig roasted?"

30. Davis, Lauby, and Sheatsley, *Americans View the Military: Public Opinion in 1982,* 23–25. There is a notable segment of the population that would favor a compulsory national service plan but not a military draft. The National Opinion Research Center found that 21.3 percent of the adult American population fell in this

category, a number almost as large as the 25.3 percent who declare themselves in favor both of a draft and of national service. Ibid., 25.

31. "As the idea of voluntary service becomes more widely accepted among the young, the numbers who will choose to serve through the military should increase. Thus the move toward universal National Service should make military recruiting easier, and help restore the tradition of citizen-soldier now giving way to a mercenary system." Committee for the Study of National Service, *Youth and the Needs of the Nation,* 10.

In proposing a voluntary national service plan, the Youth Policy Institute reasoned similarly: "[I]f the need for and value of a period of service to the country is communicated by leaders, institutions and parents to all American youths, and a National [Service] system is put in place, participation [in the military] will be much more contagious than it is under the current system. . . . [Moreover,] service in the armed services carries the traditional status as the premier form of service to one's country. . . . [W]ithin a socially mandated system of voluntary service, military service will be restored to its accustomed status." Foley, Maneker, and Schwartz, *National Service and America's Future,* 24.

32. Moskos, "Making the All-Volunteer Force Work: A National Service Approach," 34. "A growing expectation of voluntary service among youths generally will improve the climate of military recruitment. . . . The grand design is that the ideal of citizenship obligation ought to become part of growing up in America."

In a similar vein, two leading proponents of voluntary national service believe that "if the government expressed its trust in young people by inviting them to serve for a period in voluntary service, before long many young people would come to appreciate the government's trust by enlisting in the military in sufficient numbers to obviate the need for a draft." "A Proposal for National Service For The 1980's," in Sherraden and Eberly, eds., *National Service: Social, Economic and Military Impacts,* 109, citing the testimony of Harris Wofford and Theodore Hesburgh before the Senate Subcommittee on Child and Human Development, *Hearings on Presidential Commission on Volunteerism,* 37–41, 67–70.

33. Moskos, "Making the All-Volunteer Force Work: A National Service Approach," 27.

34. Ibid., 28.

5
School-Based National Service

Having described the three main sources of the conceptual appeal of national service, we consider now how national service might work in practice. In this chapter and in the three that follow, we outline four quite different forms that national service might take and the national service participants (NSPs) that each likely would produce. We then assess each model program against five considerations:

Impact on Social Services: What would be the consequences of this form of national service for child care, criminal justice, education, environmental, and health care services?

Impact on Participants: What would be the likely educational, psychological, and economic effects of the program on its participants?

Impact on the Military: What effect would it have on the composition, cost, and effectiveness of the armed services?

Labor Force Consequences: What risks of the displacement of paid laborers by NSPs would it pose, and what changes in employment and labor force participation rates might it produce?

Cost and Administration: What would such a program cost? What kind and size of government organization would be required to run it? What issues of constitutionality might it raise?

A School-Based Model of Service

One view of national service stresses its potential value to those who would serve. Arguably, national service would broaden the horizons, enrich the skills, and enhance the sense of civic responsibility of its participants. Seen in this way, national service is an adjunct to education.

One approach compatible with this perspective is a national service program operated by high schools and integrated with their curricula. There are several arguments for such an approach. One is clarity of purpose. The mission of schools is to educate. A national service program intended mainly to serve the same goal would seem more likely to do so if operated by schools than if assigned to a bureaucracy unfamiliar with that mission. Moreover, schools are perhaps the most decentralized of U.S. bureaucracies. A national service program administered by some or all of the country's 16,700 public and 2,200 nonpublic high schools would seem least likely to be viewed as an unacceptable intrusion by the federal government and most likely to generate service assignments that fit local needs and values. Further, a school-centered program could profit from the acceptance of education as compulsory and of the wide range of discretion that educational authorities have in establishing prerequisites to a high school diploma. A service requirement established by schools would seem less coercive than any other compulsory system.

A national service program operated by high schools also might provide what a prominent strain in American educational thought has long regarded as the chief missing element in formal education: experience of the everyday world. Tracing their intellectual lineage back to John Dewey, those who seek more experiential education in the U.S. system argue that true learning arises from action. Without experience as "a complement to intellectual activity," Dewey believed, "individuals cannot come either into the full expression of themselves or make a contribution, if they have it in them to make, to the social well-being of others, to the welfare of the whole of which they are a part."[1]

In this vein, the 1974 report of the Panel on Youth of the President's Science Advisory Committee argued:

> At their best, schools [now] equip students with cognitive and noncognitive skills relevant to their occupational futures, with knowledge of some portion of civilization's cultural heritage, and with the taste for acquiring more such skills and knowledge. They do not provide extensive opportunity for managing one's affairs, they seldom encourage intense concentration on a single activity, and they are inappropriate settings for nearly all objectives involving responsibilities that affect others. Insofar as these other objectives are important for the transition to adulthood, and we believe they are, schools act to retard youth in this transition, by monopolizing their time for the narrow objectives that schools have. . . . Our general belief is that environments which provide a significant amount of serious and responsible work experience are much more likely to meet these objectives than are the narrower environments of school that most youth find themselves limited to.[2]

A recent manifestation of this point of view may be found in a private publication released on Thanksgiving Day, 1984, by a group of twenty-seven prominent authorities in the field of education.[3] The statement stressed the importance of "developing good character in the young"[4] and recommended, among other things, that:

> Students, at all grade levels, should more frequently be assigned group responsibilities for academic and school-related activities. . . . The activities should emphasize the theme of service to others. . . . School and community service projects appropriately monitored by adults can be conducted by pupils at all grade levels. . . . States and districts might make such service a requirement for high school graduation.[5]

Whether or not most Americans accept these analyses, the great majority say they favor including a community service option in high school curricula. Asked in a 1978 Gallup poll whether they would like to enable all juniors and seniors in high school to perform some kind of community service for course credit, seven out of eight of those polled responded favorably.[6]

Forms of School-Based Service

A wide range and substantial number of high-school-based service programs already operate in the United States. Since the early 1970s, experience-based career education (EBCE) has been encouraged by the National Institute of Education through a federally funded program in which high school participants spend up to 80 percent of their time over a semester or more in out-of-class work settings. Although EBCE permits private sector assignments, many EBCE positions are located in service agencies. According to the director of the EBCE program at Highland High School in Salt Lake City, Utah, for example, EBCE students in 1984 had internships of their own design in sixty-three sites, forty-two of which were community service or nonprofit organizations. Over a 9-week period, students volunteered in community theaters and city government and at the American Red Cross, the YWCA, historical societies, emergency shelters, archaelogical digs, zoos, and schools. In 1980, EBCE programs operated in 150 communities across the country and involved approximately 20,000 students.[7]

Less intensive programs are more widespread. Perhaps as many as one in every ten U.S. high schools, and some entire local school systems, offer credit, on an optional basis, for service or for classroom reports or other projects related to service.[8] Typically these are 1 hour per day or 1 day per week service course options that last 3 to 4 months. They tend to be justified by reference to their educative value rather than in terms of the social value of the services provided. For example, the Dallas Magnet High School stresses the value of having students "facilitate cultural pluralism" and "take part in service to the community." To this end, sophomores intern in education, child development, or social service positions for 3 hours a week. Juniors volunteer 6 hours a week, and seniors serve 9 hours a week. By their senior year, students seek paid positions, but they volunteer their services until such a position is available. Magnet High School volunteers are reported to work in more than thirty-six social service agencies, interning in halfway houses, neighborhood centers, rehabilitation programs, teen counseling services, and other social programs. Their activities include helping social workers with case loads, counseling troubled teen-agers at homes for runaways, participating in preventive drug abuse training, and planning recreational activities for the elderly.[9]

Officials in at least two states, Maryland and Connecticut,[10] have thought enough of these programs to provide state funding and establish state offices to encourage efforts in this direction.

The state-funded Maryland Community Based Learning Experience program has operated as a demonstration program since 1979. As originally designed, the program invited 9th to 12th grade students at two demonstration schools to join the program 1 day per week for as many semesters as desired. Students obtain a sponsoring faculty member and establish a learning contract with that teacher, including objectives and evaluation strategies. Student volunteers spend an entire class day, 1 day a week, at volunteer placements, with their volunteer time regarded as an excused absence. They make up missed classroom activities on their own time. (Students may submit reports to applicable courses based on their volunteer experiences, but they receive no credit for their community service per se.) At the school whose program we examined, students served as tutors to younger children, assistants to zoo keepers in the local zoo, museum tour guides, and hospital aides. Several students completed a 10-week training program in a local hospice for the elderly and terminally ill.

That the Maryland program has been neither entirely successful nor universally embraced can be inferred from the fact that it has been abandoned at Northwestern High School and operates now only at La Plata High School, the state's rural demonstration site in Charles County.[11]

In 1980, the Utah State Board of Education required high school students to elect one of three options during one semester: 75 hours of paid work, 75 hours of school-supervised service, or an equivalent amount of time in courses in an approved area of concentration relating to a student's career goals.

All these programs share the characteristic that while they encourage service, none requires it. Either they offer service as one among many experimental choices, or they make this type of learning entirely optional. This gives rise to two disadvantages.

First, paid work and course work apparently beat out service in any system of choice. In Utah, approximately 40 percent of the students elected the work option, concentrating in the fast-food industry, and 52 percent enrolled in a cluster of career courses. Only 8 percent chose the service option, most of them working in health care institutions.[12] Because of this and other reasons, the Utah Board of Education elminated the program in 1984.

Second, purely voluntary service programs appear to draw disproportionately from among those already committed to community service,[13] from females,[14] from particular racial and economic groups, and from low and high achievers.[15] This diminishes the possibility that a period of service would be viewed as a universally expected rite of passage; it limits the degree to which services can acquaint NSPs with persons unlike themselves; and of course, voluntary programs allow those disinclined to service to avoid it entirely. Thus, in thinking about national service at the high school level, there is reason to focus on programs that require service.

A number of private schools in the United States, especially parochial schools, have established service requirements as a prerequisite to graduation, and at least one such program now operates in a large, urban public school system, that of Atlanta. The Atlanta Community Service Program, implemented in September 1984, requires students to complete 75 hours of unpaid community service between the 9th and 12th grades as a prerequisite to graduation. The work is done during nonschool hours and in social service agencies approved by the school board. After completion of service, students must write a paper on the experience. Credit for a full-semester course is given on successful completion of the requirement.[16]

Versions of such a program involving more time are easy to conceive but would probably be difficult to implement. After-school programs cut into free time that is highly valued by many adolescents and, in some cases, by their parents. As our education consultant, Ted Sizer, writes:

> American adolescents are very busy people. No age group watches fewer hours of television. The majority have jobs during school time, working an average of fifteen hours per week. . . . Those adolescents who lack jobs and money—usually kids from low-income families pocketed in central cities or devastatingly poor rural areas—nonetheless want them. A relatively autonomous adolescence is increasingly seen by youth as an American entitlement. . . .[17]

Proposals that a semester or year of service should substitute for an equivalent period of school seem even more problematic. The current sentiment among both educators and the public seems to favor more stress on core academic subjects, not less.[18] Further, school systems are tightly geared to established attendance cycles. The pressure from parents, students, and teachers against substituting as much as a semester of service for a semester of school seems to us likely to be overwhelming.

There is a set of possibilities, more modest and flexible than these alternatives but more ambitious than the Atlanta program, that seems worth examining. The particular example of this intermediate category that we choose for analysis is a program in which, in participating states, high school seniors would be required to spend 240 hours (approximately one-fifth of the school year) in a public service activity.[19] States would be free to decide whether this time could be substituted for school time or must be added to it. Although more modest than a semester of service, this requirement demands substantial time, and, under the terms of the program we hypothesize, it would be mandatory where adopted.

Program Particulars

This school-based program (we also refer to it as Program 1) would be enacted by Congress on an entirely permissive basis. The program could operate with any number of states participating. States opting to join would be given great latitude (which they might delegate to localities) in the design and administration of the program, and they might allow school districts to decide independently whether they wished to join the program at all.

To qualify for a federal subsidy under the program (paid on a per capita, per day participation basis) a state would be required to establish a 240-hour public service requirement as a prerequisite for high school graduation. Service would be performed during the 12-month period beginning with the end of the junior year and might be permitted either in lieu of 6 hours per week of classroom attendance or as an afterschool, weekend, or summer activity.[20] States would be obliged to ensure the availability of a range of public service tasks to meet the requirement. Male and female students also would be able to apply to a military component of this program involving 12 to 15 weeks of basic training similar to that now given Army recruits. Those who were accepted could fulfill their service requirement in this way.

Students who participated in the civilian branch of this program would continue to live at home. As with the rest of their educational experience, they would receive no wages for their work. Their on-the-job safety and insurance coverage against accidents would be the responsibility of the state, just as they are when students are in school. Students who opted for and were accepted by the military would be housed in barracks and be subject to military discipline, just like other military trainees. They would not be paid either, but, because they would be away from home and from alternative sources of income, they would receive $20 per week for incidental expenses.

The federal government would assume the full cost of training those accepted in the military portion of the program and would underwrite 75 percent of state operating costs of the nonmilitary portions of the program. As discussed more fully later, these costs would arise mainly from locating service jobs, assigning school students to them, and policing the system to ensure that the jobs were suitable, student attendance and performance were acceptable, and rules against displacement were observed.

Students would be free to select any validated service position that was open in their community and whose particular requirements, if any, they could meet. Positions would be validated by something resembling the following procedure. In each school district, a board would be established that included a school official, a representative of organized labor, and a representative of the county and/or municipal executives. A position would be established by arrangement between this board and employer institutions or as a result of board approval of a project a student proposed on his or her own initiative. Community service positions would be expected to meet each of five criteria.

First, the position should expose the student to problems, settings, or perspectives outside his or her normal experience and thus have educational value.

Second, the position itself, as well as the sponsoring organization, must serve public nonprofit, rather than private profit-making, interests.[21] With one exception, the standards used to make this determination might be those that now determine whether charitable institutions or public associations qualify as recipients of tax deductible charitable contributions under Section 501(c)(3) of the Internal Revenue Code.[22]

Third, the proposed placement must not displace any nonservice workers who, in the judgment of any member of the overseeing board, would otherwise have provided the service. Strikes pose a special problem. We think the 1978 policy developed jointly by the National School Volunteers Program and the National Education Association resolves this issue appropriately, and we would recommend adoption of a similar precept in national service programs. That policy, in regard to the functioning of volunteer programs in the event of strike or other interruptions is as follows:

> The best interest of students is served when volunteers and school staff work cooperatively. In any situation of controversy, the successful relationship between volunteers and teachers can best be maintained if the School Volunteer Program adopts a position of neutrality. In the event of a strike or other interruptions of normal school operations, the School Volunteer Program shall not function in the schools.[23]

Fourth, unless a project has been approved on a one-time basis as a result of the initiative of a particular student, the participating institutions would agree to make a good faith effort to work with any student assigned by the cognizant school officials. Participating institutions would retain the right to dismiss students for cause; the supervisor would then determine whether to grant credit for the experience.

Fifth, the receiving institution must maintain a suitable work environment and provide the student with any training, tools, uniform, or transportation required for job performance.

Program Participants

Program 1 would engage approximately 3.2 million high school NSPs if all states participated now.[24] These NSPs typically would be seventeen or eighteen years of age. Many would be serving involuntarily; all would work for only brief and, in most cases, intermittent periods of time. This would inhibit giving them substantial training. In terms of their capacity to produce work of high social value, therefore, program 1 participants as a group would constitute the least useful national service workers considered in this book. Many service agencies might not wish to accept participants in such school-based programs or would seek to assign them only to simple, repetitious jobs that are hard to reconcile with the educational aims of the program.

The youth of the NSPs would have other limiting effects. Many NSPs would be barred by law or prudent assignment policies from tasks such as driving buses,[25] administering drugs, and maintaining confidential records. More seriously, young people have problems of their own, and often these cause higher than normal absenteeism and other disruptions in the workplace.[26] An evaluation of a Syracuse service project generally involving older participants (sixteen- to twenty-year-olds) noted that "[a] large number of supervisors of inner city projects, including those with successful projects, stated they would be reluctant to sponsor [such a] project again. . . . [Supervisors] felt burdened by responsibilities because of the extensive personal needs of volunteers."[27] Many teen-agers do not have the desire or maturity to assume significant responsibilities. A study of the transition from adolescence to adulthood reports that 65 percent of male high school students apparently preferred jobs where they did not have to take a lot of responsibility, while 5 years later, only 27 percent of the same group adopted that attitude.[28] Similarly, half those of high school age wanted a job that did not make them learn a lot of new things, while only 15 percent had that preference 5 years later.[29] Recognizing these limitations, we turn now to a discussion of the work such NSPs might perform.

Impact on Social and Environmental Services

What might program 1 NSPs do, and what is our estimate of the value of their doing it?

Assignments in the Schools

The school teaching assistant positions described in chapter 2 clearly lend themselves to program 1. The particular tasks assigned to NSPs would be determined by individual teachers, but they could be expected to include instruction (particularly for small groups of students), correction of student work, and assistance in field trips, special projects, and classroom maintenance. Most NSPs should fit relatively easily into these roles. The routines, demands, and physical environments of schools are familiar to NSPs; teachers are used to supervising students; schools are located where the students are, and their terms and times correspond with students' schedules. Moreover, the number of teachers (approximately 2.4 million at work in the country's school systems as of 1984) is so large and so well matched to the number of high school seniors (approximately 2.7 million at present) as to make it possible to absorb all program 1 NSPs within school systems.[30] Even if more than 40 percent of teachers declined to supervise NSPs, a sufficient number would remain to permit teachers to supervise all NSPs, one at a time.

The value of this use of NSPs is hard to measure, but both intuition and empirical evidence suggest that it is significant. Sizer comments:

> Given average [elementary] school class sizes of over twenty, and accepting the fact of human children's glorious variability, the need to break student units into small groups (albeit within the same space) for a variety of purposes is obvious. Few teachers could not benefit from [an NSP] to assist with this process. . . . A reading class of twelve allows more children to recite than a class of twenty-four; a volunteer allows a class to be split. The six arithmetic students who are confused can have fractions effectively explained by a tutor off to one side of the classroom while the teacher moves the rest of the class ahead.[31]

Moreover:

> [E]ach of us learns by making mistakes. We learn to write by trying to write and by having someone point our our errors and suggesting ways to improve. . . . Learning is not a process of group thinking: we learn one by one. A person whom we individually trust and who periodically encourages and helps us is a boon. . . . NSPs can be those sorts of concerned people.[32]

Indeed, student NSPs might be well positioned to win the trust of struggling younger students. As the coordinator of a current school service program comments, "Students with deficiencies are frequently self-conscious and depressed. This problem is sometimes worse around an adult authority figure, but improves around students in the same grade or one or two levels apart."[33]

Many programs of this character have been tried, with generally encouraging results. A program operated by New York's Mobilization for Youth in the late 1960s reported that 4th and 5th grade students who were helped for 4 hours a week over 26 weeks by 10th and 11th grade tutors achieved significantly greater gains than did a control group.[34] Carefully controlled and documented 3- and 5-year experiments in California schools point to similar gains.[35] Although tutees' psychological gains (in discipline, motivation, and so on) are less certain and academic gains vary with tutoring circumstances, the most careful analysis of the extensive literature persuasively concludes that "several different kinds of tutoring programs can effectively improve academic performance of tutees."[36]

Child Care Assignments

Program 1 NSPs also might undertake child care assignments. They would not thereby greatly increase the child care labor force. For the balance of this decade, between 400 million and 500 million hours of child care will be provided in the United States each week by other than members of the nuclear family.[37] Even if 1 million high school students each contributed 6 hours per week to child care and were responsible for two children during that time, the increment would amount to less than 4 percent of the available care. Even if student resources were focused, as we expect they would be, on the small fraction of care administered outside of private homes (typically in nursery and preschools, before- and after-school programs, and coops) the increment would be only 12 to 14 percent of such institutional child care hours.

This contribution, however, might be more valuable than the numbers suggest. NSPs might spend their time consistently with children who need special attention.[38] Some NSPs undertaking child care would be male, and some would be affluent; that alone would be valuable in introducing a broader range of role models into child care settings. At present, 93 percent of all child care workers are females,[39] and affluent workers are rare. NSPs might contribute a valuable variety, energy, and imagination for a significant absolute number—though still a small fraction—of the children requiring day care.

As with assignments in schools, the relative youth of program 1 participants and their limited skills would not be serious disadvantages in child care. Paid child care providers now normally receive no training. Child care assignments for NSPs still in school, moreover, might be combined with courses in child development, now provided in about one-third of U.S. high schools.[40] Ideally, these courses might be established as a prerequisite to a national service child care position and could be used as a screening device to reduce the likelihood that incompetent, uncaring, or potentially abusive NSPs would be assigned to child care.

As compared with school assignments, the transaction costs associated with assigning short-term NSPs to child care would be large. But even if a total of forty day care supervisor hours were devoted to arranging and monitoring each assignment, and even if each of these hours were worth two NSP hours, the net gain still would be 160 hours of service for each NSP who served. We think, in short, that gains would noticeably outweigh debits.

Health Care Assignments

Further along the spectrum of possibilities, but still in the realm where, in our judgment, gains would likely warrant the costs, are assignments in caring for the infirm and elderly. A survey of existing high school service programs concludes that 85 percent of these programs offer assignments in health care, and almost 75 percent participate in companionship programs.[41] Our health consultant writes, "If NSPs are compassionate and caring they may add a great deal to the attention given the aged, mentally ill and disabled. The value of these intangibles cannot be estimated."[42]

The value of NSP services of this type probably would be least substantial for patients in short-term hospital settings, greater for long-term residents of nursing homes, and most substantial where NSPs helped provide companionship, shopping, and basic home hygienic and housekeeping support to some of the roughly 5 million Americans who live at home but "need the help of another person in carrying out everyday activities."[43] Our health consultants estimate that the roughly 300,000 homemakers now available through social service agencies provide 10 to 12 million working hours per week.[44] Five hundred thousand school-based NSPs, each working 6 hours per week, could increase this labor pool by 25 percent. They could thereby provide more varied companionship than is now available,[45] as well as additional support.

The administration of such a program would present difficulties, however. Identifying appropriate persons to be served, matching and transporting students to them, and monitoring the results would be more complicated and more costly than for services NSPs provided in institutional settings. Screening of NSPs for behavioral and health problems would be imperative; physical examinations might be required. In contrast to assignments in schools, child care centers, hospitals, nursing homes, or other institutions, home care services would be provided away from supervisors, other NSPs, and even other recipients. The possibilities for theft, abuse, or simply poor performance are substantial.[46] Quite apart from potential malfeasance, the psychological and occasionally physical costs NSPs might inflict simply by unreliability would be high.[47]

Hoping that we are being clear-eyed in balancing these considerations, our best judgment, like that of our consultants, is that home care and perhaps long-term institutional care are sufficiently promising areas for program 1

NSPs to deserve experimentation, perhaps with health care courses providing a screening, support, and supervision system analogous to that of child development courses for child care NSPs.

Environmental Tasks

Many of the environmental tasks identified in chapter 2 as attractive for national service participants are not well matched to program 1. Many of these tasks are in rural areas, distant from urban participants. Some require the use of power tools or heavy equipment that special licensing requirements or child labor laws forbid to sixteen- and seventeen-year-olds. Some are seasonal only. Others, such as flood relief or fire fighting, may involve greater danger than some states would wish teen-agers exposed to. Some energy conservation tasks require substantial training to perform.

These are important limitations, but as our environmental consultant, Perry Hagenstein, points out, there remain many environmental tasks that, with good supervision, program 1 participants could perform quite effectively. He estimates that a total of 887,000 program 1 NSPs (the equivalent of roughly 88,000 full-time workers) could be utilized while living at home and that 500,000 additional openings would be available if states provided the more expensive option of summer residential programs, most of which would be set in rural areas. In urban areas alone (defined as counties where populations exceed 10,000) 665,000 program 1 NSPs could be utilized while living at home. The majority would be assigned to urban parks (190,000), solid waste disposal (155,000), energy conservation (90,000), or miscellaneous and emergency work (110,000).[48]

Although the precise magnitude of these numbers may be subject to debate, it is plausible that large numbers of high school age volunteers should be able to undertake environmental work effectively. The tasks involved are disparate enough to permit considerable range in their abilities, interests, geographic locations, and service periods. Some functions, such as energy audits and water and air quality monitoring, could be performed by physically handicapped participants. Most environmental tasks demand no more training than could readily be provided on the job. Moreover, in contrast to the relatively high risks of irresponsible performance in many health and child care tasks and in some other social services, there is relatively little risk in the environmental area of great damage being done by antisocial or poorly motivated NSPs. Correspondingly, poor performance would be less sensitive politically.

It is not surprising, therefore, that high school volunteers have in fact been assigned frequently to environmental tasks. In 1980, for example, the Youth Conservation Corps employed 34,000 fifteen- to eighteen-year-olds for 8 weeks of environmental work each summer.[49] The Young Adult Conservation Corps and a variety of U.S. Park Service, U.S. Forest Service, state conservation corps, and private volunteer programs have regularly and successfully placed high school age volunteers in environmental jobs.

Tasks of Other Kinds

NSPs also might be assigned a wide range of other useful work. In many settings, such as state and local government offices, the principal tasks open to program 1 NSPs might be only the most routine and thus barely consistent with the primarily educational purposes of the program. Other institutions might provide settings for useful and educational tasks.

In libraries and museums, for example, school-based NSPs might help staff outreach programs for the ill, confined, and elderly; read to children; prepare displays; and help provide basic reference services. They also might assist curators in children's museums and museums of science or history. (Art museums generally would be less appropriate settings and probably also more resistant to using young NSPs in nonclerical or noncustodial roles.) These are all tasks that could be performed part time with little training and yet yield useful services. If only one-quarter of the roughly 200,000 full-time library and museum positions suitable for NSPs were available to program 1 participants, these alone could absorb half a million school-based NSPs.[50]

The Utility of School-Based NSPs

As we have noted, there are costs and risks associated with all uses of program 1 NSPs, especially in highly personalized contexts. Some NSPs would be immature, unreliable, or incompetent; some may be abusive of the ill, elderly, or young. Screening for behavioral and for health problems would therefore be necessary, especially for assignments such as home care, where supervisors could not always be present.[51] A school-administered program would have three advantages with respect to these costs and risks, however. First, most schools already have the needed background information; typically, in fact, they have more information than they would or could provide to any other agency that might screen national service participants. Second, at least with respect to seniors, the schools have an unusually effective disciplinary mechanism: the threat of nongraduation. Third, and most critical, the 20 percent of the youth cohort that does not reach the senior year of high school is the least able and the least disciplined fraction of their age cohort. Whatever the arguments for drawing the most disadvantaged or most alienated into a national service system, program 1 would not do so.[52] While lowering its value in some respects, that fact improves the program's prospects for delivering social services without imposing excessive costs or risks on the agencies to which NSPs are assigned.

Notwithstanding that fact, program 1, like all other forms of national service, would have to provide alternative assignments to NSPs who seemed poor risks for jobs involving substantial interpersonal contact. As noted, environmental tasks would qualify, as would assistance to maintenance staffs in schools, hospitals, and government agencies.[53]

In short, it seems likely that there would be more useful roles that high school seniors could perform in program 1 than there would be high school seniors to engage them. Assignments in school systems would involve especially low transaction costs. Those costs would rise as students undertook work in other settings, but so, depending on the tasks, might the benefits. Where students were appropriately assigned and effectively supervised, the effects of the program in terms of social work achieved would be notably beneficial. We caution, however, that even if program 1 were widely adopted, the work of NSPs would be too small an increment to the total labor force in any field to effect dramatic change.

Effects on NSPs

The principal justification for program 1 rests not on the social value of the work performed but on the education or maturational benefits it might provide its participants. How substantial would these benefits be? Unfortunately, current knowledge permits no confident judgment on that point. Even the dozen or so serious evaluations of experiential education are of limited utility. Many were conducted without control groups. Others, often conducted by proponents of the experiential approach, tend to focus on exemplary programs. This makes it hard to determine what an average program, under typical circumstances, might achieve. In addition, these studies consider opportunity costs only indirectly, if at all. Consequently, very little in the existing literature assesses what is sacrificed when a high school senior devotes time to community services. We therefore proceed tentatively in gauging the impact of a school-based form of national service on the needs of young NSPs. Our discussion proceeds under headings roughly parallel to those used in the discussion titled "Needs of Youth" in chapter 3.[54]

Contact with the World of Work

As noted in chapter 3, a majority of U.S. high school students now achieve contact with the world of work through paid employment. The data on this point come from several sources, are derived in differing ways, and are striking. In a 1980 Department of Education survey, 63 percent of high school seniors reported that they had worked for pay outside their homes in the previous week.[55] This comports with the most recent census data, which show that of the 18.5 million males and females age fifteen to nineteen, just short of two-thirds reported money income in 1983.[56]

Because older students in the census sample are more likely to work than younger students,[57] because that sample focuses only on 1 year's experience and not on cumulative experience, and because the Department of Education survey asked only about those who had worked in the previous week, we can infer that well over two-thirds of all seniors have had paid work experience. Studying four heterogeneous schools in Southern California, Laurence Steinberg and his colleagues found that "the average working adolescent reported working 20 to 24 hours per week" during the 11th and 12th grades.[58] The authors also note that:

> Today, proportionately more American teenagers are working while attending high school than at any other time in the past quarter-century. Between 1940 (the year that the Bureau of the Census started reporting employment figures separately for in- and out-of-school teenagers) and 1970, the proportion of in-school 16 year-old males employed part-time increased from 4 percent to over 27 percent. For females the same age, the rate of increase was even more dramatic: from 1 percent in 1940 to 16 percent in 1970. . . . By most estimates the 1980 census will reveal a further increase in these figures, and current calculations place the proportion of working 16 year-old high school students at close to 60 percent.[59]

This evidence suggests that if it operated after school or on weekends, program 1 might preempt time at paid work.[60]

Would the special nature of work and supervision in program 1 be so different from paid work as to yield benefits if it had this effect? If paid work remained at present levels, either because program 1 operated in lieu of school time or because seniors sacrificed recreation or other activities to participate in it, would significant benefits derive from this additional exposure to the world of work?

We are inclined to doubt it. The content of most public sector jobs is not much different from that of most private sector jobs. The educational gains from maintenance or clerical work in a school, library, or welfare center are not intrinsically different from those in a local contractor's office or supermarket. A job as a waiter in a neighborhood restaurant or as a camp counselor might teach more, even about altruism and sharing, than a job testing water pollution or filing documents for a public agency. Summarizing recent experience with job programs, an authority writes:

> There has been little success in creating "meaningful" jobs in the sense of new career opportunities for teenagers. There are a broad array of work options available under youth programs, but the preponderance remain entry clerical, maintenance, social service aid and conservation positions. The

> efforts to link jobs to youth aptitudes and aspirations are limited, and evaluators of YEDPA programs have questioned the whole concept because of limitations in available work options and the uncertainty of youth participants about what they want to do until they have gained some work experience.[61]

Would supervisors of school-based NSPs be more likely than private sector employers to create educationally beneficial assignments and stimulating environments with effective supervision? The opportunity to do so clearly exists. The private sector employer is motivated primarily by profit: Fast-food franchises do not purport to design jobs to enhance their workers' self-development.[62] But it is far from clear that the administrators of a day care center, a library, or a police station would regard the development of a part-time NSP much differently. In the 1970s, for example, the Department of Labor mandated that CETA youth work sites provide capable supervision, useful work, and environments that encouraged good work habits. A 1980 General Accounting Office (GAO) survey concluded, however, that only 60 percent of the 5,200 Youth Entitlement Pilot Project sites met these criteria.[63]

Contrasting examples drawn from the GAO report illustrate the range of possibilities. In a favorably reviewed site, "six participants at a Boston high school worked on a general maintenance crew. They worked side-by-side with the regular staff, preparing the school for occupancy in the fall. Their job tasks included washing windows and floors, landscaping, and painting. The supervisor had a schedule of projects to be completed before school began."[64] By contrast, "a large Detroit high school employed twenty-three students in custodial work. The supervisor routinely allowed students to leave after they finished two hours of work, although they were paid for four hours. The site did not have enough work for the youths assigned."[65] The same report noted "a great deal of milling around, little useful work, and no intervention on the part of the supervisors" in a Mississippi school employing 100 youths in custodial functions.[66]

A Youth Community Service program in Syracuse that placed high school age participants in both government and nongovernment nonprofit positions in the late 1970s reported similarly mixed results. Orientation programs for supervisors were neither well-attended nor helpful, and "largely because of other demands on their time, [supervisors] were not able to provide the in-depth counseling and training suggested by the ACTION design."[67]

As a general matter, we know of no empirical basis for believing that exposure to the world of work would be notably enhanced for high school students by jobs in the public sector instead of, or in addition to, work in the private sector. Our judgment is that the primary skills a high school senior learns from work relate to discipline and cooperation. We think that the private sector, in large measure because of its profit motive, is an appropriate place to learn them,[68] and a teen-ager's desire to earn money is a useful prod to doing so.[69] Furthermore, most NSPs will find postservice jobs in the private sector, jobs for which prior experience in that sector is likely to be better preparation than public service tasks. A 1978 analysis of the Job Corps reported that successful applicants who did not choose to join the Job Corps typically had steadier employment records than those who did because they found and maintained work on their own rather than interrupting employment to participate in the program.[70]

What of the minority of youth who have little or no paid work experience because they cannot find work, cannot keep it, or do not seek it? Unfortunately, program 1 would reach a few such youths; it is targeted to high school seniors, while the most problematic unemployed teen-ager is part of the 20 percent of the youth population that does not reach the senior year of high school.

Experience with an Alternative Environment

Students seem to value leaving school. As noted earlier, high proportions of high school students, perhaps especially seniors, appear to want "an escape, most often temporary, from the environment in which they had grown up."[71] Moreover, a 1978 poll of 4,000 high school students who participated in experiential learning programs found that well over 80 percent of them felt they had learned "to get things done and to work with others, to solve problems, to accept the consequences of one's actions, to gather and analyze information, to become more open to new experiences, to feel and act like a useful member of the community, to develop greater self-esteem, to become more self-motivated, and to be more concerned about others."[72] There is presumptively some value in any assignment that exposes a high school student to an unfamiliar setting and special value in a setting that involves a challenge or expands students' interests or skills.

Still, the need to match NSPs with jobs they could reasonably be expected to perform and to minimize the costs of transporting, training, and supervising them would cause many placements to occur in familiar environments. That would be especially true in short-term, school-based programs. Student NSPs serving in schools, libraries, museums, and day care centers would not be likely to find them very novel environments. They would meet and deal with a new set of adults and younger children, but their school experience and prior paid and unpaid jobs (including baby-sitting) would make much of this experience fairly familiar.

Those involved in the more ambitious home care and preventive health programs or the more extended and expensive summer military or environmental programs would experience more unfamiliar settings and tasks and might benefit from them considerably. But expense, matching problems, and supervisor limitations very likely would make these a minority of jobs. Moreover, it should not escape notice that, according to a 1981 survey, more than half of those in the age group that would be affected by this program would have already independently engaged in some form of community service.[73] For many of these students the gain from a school-based service program seems small.

Enhancement of School-Related Skills and Interests

Some service activities may add more than additional schooling would to an understanding of certain subjects taught in school. The empirical work on tutoring by students, for example, suggests that the tutor typically benefits as much as the tutee,[74] a finding consistent with the recognition of most teachers that teaching is an aid to clarifying one's own understanding. Moreover, it seems credible that practical experience can deepen subject matter interests. An interest in history may be aroused by conversations with an elderly home care patient; research skills may be sharpened by service at a library's reference desk; biological processes may be made vivid through work on stream habitats; computational skills may be exercised by a clerical assignment; and some of the realities of organizational life may be learned by service in a museum or library.[75] In general, service assignments may have favorable effects on the learning of academic subjects either by strengthening motivation to learn or by testing the students' theoretical learning against observed realities.[76]

But there is little hard evidence to suggest that most service experiences would improve academic skills more effectively than an equivalent amount of classroom time. NSPs teaching students just below their own level might learn or relearn substantial material, but those teaching students well below their own level[77] or helping children put on galoshes, cleaning classrooms, and correcting papers would gain little in additional skills.[78] Caring for the elderly, the ill, or preschool children, staffing museums or libraries, improving wildlife habitats, and performing many other likely tasks would expand students' horizons and might impart skills and knowledge directly useful in later life. Well-supervised child care assignments might be particularly valuable in this sense. But it remains true that these assignments would not teach substantial academic skills.

The most nearly authoritative evidence on this point comes from the most ambitious of the school-work programs, the EBCE program. That program invested heavily in matching jobs with students' skill levels and career interests. Reading comprehension, arithmetic concepts, and arithmetic application tests taken by participants at the end of the program showed that students would not be academically hurt by being in the program, but for the most part, that no academic or hard skill gains were claimed.[79] Similarly, after reviewing the literature on numerous smaller programs, a recent doctoral dissertation concluded that, "the few studies that were found in the area of intellectual functioning indicated that experiential education programs were rarely successful in raising students' school achievement beyond levels demonstrated in conventional education programs."[80]

A similar conclusion seems appropriate with respect to the military experience program 1 might provide. In 13 weeks of military training, NSPs would be exposed to military discipline and would receive training in basic military skills (including physical training) and perhaps some entry-level training in a military occupational specialty. But because of their limited time commitment, NSPs would tend to be trained in nontechnical and mainly combat-related skills. Typically this training might be for infantry, artillery, armor, food service, or military police positions. More advanced training, including communications, computer, electronic, or medical positions, probably would not be available to program 1 NSPs; if provided, it would necessarily be very brief. As a result—again, putting aside the question of gains in maturity or character—there would be little learning of either academic subjects or skills useful in civilian life.

Responsibility and the Development of Altruism

Intuitively, program 1 seems likely to meet these goals, at least for a fair fraction of NSPs. Many of the jobs we have described require NSPs to undertake substantial responsibilities with co-workers (especially in the military and environmental programs) or dependent individuals (especially in school, child care, and health settings). Indeed, much of the substantial support for peer and cross-age tutoring appears to follow from enthusiasm about its seemingly positive psychological effects on the tutors themselves. For example, Ruth Woodward, director of the Education Cluster in the Human Services Center of Dallas's Magnet High School, testified to the success of her cross-age tutoring program in a conversation with us in November 1984. In that program, 10th graders complete one class unit in tutoring, after which they are assigned as tutors 3 hours per week to a student from the K–3 school located on the premises of the center. During the next 2 years, students work as tutors for 2 or 3 half-days per week in elementary schools (K–6) around the district. Woodward is sold on the program as, she says, are the principals of the elementary schools to which the tutors are assigned. The demand for tutors consistently seems to outpace the supply. Woodward is particularly enthusiastic about the positive effects of the program on the tutors: "Young people blossom out and thrive from some responsibility. They need peer relationships with adults. . . . [W]hat they can do is amazing; these kids are immensely capable. . . . [T]hey develop an air of responsibility, almost professionalism."

Similar enthusiasm was expressed by Dede McGinnis, head of Volunteer Services in Duval County, Florida. Tutoring by students is becoming increasingly common and popular, she says. Secondary school students tutor both elementary school students and their own peers. In grades 7 through 9, students can earn half a credit for tutoring, and in grades 10 through 12, students can gain a full credit. McGinnis points to the gains in self-esteem among tutors.

The Summer Cross-Age Tutoring Program in Detroit's public school system also has met with an enthusiastic response from teachers and administrators. According to one evaluation of that program, 100 percent of teachers wanted to see the program continued following the summer.[81]

Finally, not only peer tutoring but peer helping in general, including companionship and counseling, currently is the object of much enthusiasm among educators. So much so, in fact, that at a national meeting in 1984, it was decided to establish the National Peer Leading Network.[82]

Despite this enthusiasm from some educators, hard evidence on the benefits of peer tutoring is thin. Thus, after a careful review of the literature on tutoring, the leading authorities on the subject noted that "attitudinal and self-concept measures were less regularly obtained than measures of academic progress, and the few reported findings were inconclusive."[83]

In addition, the most ambitious and sophisticated assessments of the effects of service-learning programs arrived at different conclusions. A 1981 study by Conrad and Hedin examined twenty-seven high school experiential learning programs and concluded that they achieved significant gains in the social development of participating students.[84] A thoughtful 1983 report by Newman and Rutter for the National Institute of Education casts doubt on Conrad and Hedin's argument, however.[85] Like Conrad and Hedin, Newmann and Rutter focused on well-established programs, used comparison groups, and administered evaluative tests rather than relying simply on self-report or the impressions of program administrators. They concluded that "no impressive differences [were found] in the amount of positive change between program and comparison students."[86]

One point on which the evidence is clear is that any psychological gains derived from service programs significantly correlate with opportunities for discussion and reflection. Conrad stresses this point, noting the conclusion of one observer that "a combination of contact with old people and instruction about the elderly appeared to positively change adolescents' attitudes towards the aged. No differences were found between the control group and students who had contact with old people but no instruction."[87] Similarly:

> [I]n a cross-age teaching program in which sixth graders tutored mentally retarded children, those who did not have a supervisory seminar developed negative attitudes toward the children and employed more negative strate-

> gies in their teaching. The tutors who participated in a weekly supervision session used more positive teaching techniques and showed increased levels of empathy and learning.[88]

Just as classroom learning can shape the effects of a service experience, so Newmann and Rutter note that classroom learning in and of itself can substantially affect the social development of students. After observing that "neither socioeconomic status, job hours, developmental opportunities in extracurricular activities or in the community-service school classes, have any predictive power of any of the measures of social development," they continue:

> In contrast, developmental opportunities in school classes are positively related to each of the six variables tested to measure social development. Apparently classroom environments that provide opportunities for challenge, student decision making, questioning of values, mutual respect and other developmental opportunities, have a positive impact on sense of social responsibility, competence and participation—independent of socioeconomic status, prior achievement in school or developmental opportunities found elsewhere (e.g., in the family or on the job).[89]

For us, there are several implications from this research. First, it suggests that any psychological benefits derived by students in program 1 might be no greater than if similar effort were directed at orienting classroom teaching to emphasize participation, cooperation, and personal responsibility. Second, the degree of psychological growth achieved probably would depend on the degree of integration between the schools and their service programs. Students in schools that link service to seminars or other opportunities for reflection about the experience would benefit more than their peers elsewhere, and perhaps only they would benefit at all.

Third, even in programs with a reflective component, the magnitude of psychological benefit would be small. This is not surprising. A program of 240 hours would not be likely to have a powerful influence on a character and world view developed over a lifetime in thousands of recurring school,[90] family, and social contexts. Finally, we are struck by the paucity of analysis and the absence of controlled data about these effects. Experimentation and careful evaluation is needed in regard to these questions perhaps more than any others that affect program 1.

Earning Adult Status

Some CCC-like assignments aside, program 1 tasks generally would be too short, too easy, too intermittent, and too distant from public view to be thought of as trials of strength or courage or as high challenges publicly met. In those senses, the program rarely would confer on NSPs the sense that they had completed a rite of passage, but it might nonetheless give many NSPs a sense of earning adult status. Two hundred forty hours is a small fraction of the school experience, but it is no small commitment for a high school senior. Many assignments, perhaps most, should enable NSPs to feel they have undertaken a genuine responsibility and paid at least some dues to society. A number of tasks, especially those involving the environment (planting trees; building trails, shelters, or bridges; restoring urban parks; stabilizing streambanks, and so on) would leave behind satisfying tangible products of the service experience. Summer residential programs also might provide, in some measure, the sense of communal discipline that made service in the CCC of the 1930s so powerful an experience. Physically handicapped participants could perform many functions that might prove particularly rewarding to them. For most NSPs, we believe, the completion of service, together with high school graduation, would make a more satisfying entry into adult life than graduation alone.

Impact on the Military

School-based programs in general, and a 240-hour program in particular, likely would not have significant effects on the military, even if they included an opportunity to enroll (if accepted) in a 3-month military basic training program. Indeed, discussions with military officials persuade us that if the military component of program 1 were to be funded out of the Defense Department budget, the armed services would prefer not to participate in it.

Any estimate of the fraction of participants in model 1 who would apply for military rather than civilian service must, of course, be speculative, a speculation compounded by uncertainty about the number of states that would choose to participate as a whole. In 1979 and 1981, the Gallup Organization asked eighteen- and nineteen-year-olds to choose between hypothetical equivalent 1-year compulsory military and civilian national service programs; roughly 45 percent of the men and 15 percent of the women consistently chose the military program.[91]

If these proportions were to hold for program 1 participants, and if all states participated, then the military would face about 550,000 applications from physically and mentally qualified men and 185,000 applications from qualified women.[92] Smaller numbers of applicants would, of course, result from less than full state participation, from recognition that the military program would demand twice as much time as the civilian program, or from decisions by those interested in military service to choose regular paid military service to begin after high school.[93] Our military consultants believe, however, that it is highly likely that if program 1 were adopted by a substantial number of states, the military would draw many more applicants than it could reasonably accommodate without disproportionately large allocations of money and labor power to expand the training establishment.[94]

For the Army, the service most likely to be assigned those program 1 NSPs who selected military training,[95] training costs would vary from $5,000 per recruit for a small program (around 10,000 trainees) that could utilize current Army training capacity, to $10,000 per recruit for a larger number that would force expansion of the training base. A program for 50,000 participants (in addition to the roughly 230,000 people the Army now trains each year) would entail additional costs of about $540 million per year (less than 1 percent of the Army budget), plus one-time costs of about $40 million to activate training facilities.[96] Such a program would absorb about 1 percent of the Army's career personnel in national service training.

One apparent benefit of the military option in program 1 is that the Army and the NSPs would get a trial run with each other without commitments from either. But the services are now able to discharge unsatisfactory recruits in basic training or later, and recruits can drop out of basic training; approximately 10 percent of them do so.[97]

A more substantial benefit to the Army would be the fact that active duty recruits who had previously taken military training under national service would begin their regular enlistments with 3 months of essentially unpaid training behind them. This would reduce Army training costs and extend their period of useful service,[98] yielding offsetting savings of about $20 million per year.[99]

Reserve recruitment (where about 80,000 new enlistments now occur each year) might benefit most from program 1.[100] One obstacle to reserve recruitment is the 12-week period of initial full-time training, which tends to deter high-quality potential recruits who are unwilling or unable to leave their jobs for so long. If basic training were completed during high school, that hurdle would be lowered or eliminated.[101]

This might be especially important for the Individual Ready Reserve (IRR). IRR members participate in no unit drills or other activities; they simply stand committed to join active units in the event of a national emergency. The current Army shortfall of as many as 240,000 IRR members will be reduced by a 1983 law committing new recruits to an extended time in the IRR after active duty.[102] But if the IRR requirements should rise, as they may, it would be of value to some program 1 participants undertaking IRR commitments. Our military consultants calculate that, as a result of multiyear commitments, approximately 60,000 additional reservists could be added to IRR rolls as the result of an annual participation rate of 50,000 in the military component of program 1.

On balance, however, we believe the military would regard defense dollars as better spent on other means of increasing active or reserve enrollments (as well as for other military purposes altogether) than on a school-based national service program. Those whose military experience consist only of 90 days of individual training without unit experience are only marginally effective soldiers to begin with, and their utility diminishes rapidly as their skills erode with time.

Accordingly, our assessment is that school-based programs similar to program 1 would be unattractive to the military. The military probably would participate in them without objection if doing so were part of a larger national policy, but the services would not propose a military rationale for such a program and probably would resist proposals to fund it through the Defense Department budget. We think that there would be particularly strong resistance to any proposals that the military accept more than about 50,000 NSPs. The military component of program 1, therefore, probably would be a relatively insubstantial part of any large-scale school-based program, involving fewer than 2 percent of potential program 1 participants if a fifty-state program came into existence.

Labor Market Consequences

Assignments in program 1, as in all other programs, would be dependent on a finding that they would not displace paid workers. Since program 1 assignments would be brief and intermittent and the NSPs quite young, temptation on the part of employers to subvert that condition should be far weaker in this than in any other program. The labor force consequences of program 1 similarly should be relatively small.

Nonetheless, some problems might arise. Teachers might feel threatened, either because the time spent out of school by NSPs or the use of some or all of them as teachers' assistants might diminish demand for professional teachers. The teacher shortage projected for the late 1980s and 1990s reduces the chances that current teachers would lose their jobs as a result of the program, but the risk remains that the program might result in less new hiring and heavier teacher loads, which would translate to poorer teacher-student ratios.[103]

To limit such possibilities, a federal program might take special steps to reinforce the third program criterion described previously—that is, to avoid displacement of regular workers by national service participants. The program might require, for example, that in order to qualify for the federal subsidy of the program, participating schools must maintain at least preexisting teacher-pupil ratios. Time freed from obligations to teach seniors could be reallocated to other teaching responsibilities or to administration of the national service program. For teachers receiving national service assistants, the likely result would not be to reduce teaching time but to share classroom burdens and increase the quality of instruction.

Similar situations might occur with respect to home and child care workers. As noted earlier, these are services for which the demand seems certain to grow in the next decades.[104] As in teaching, therefore, the no-displacement rule may have to be enforced by requiring that current (or projected) ratios of nonservice staff to clients be maintained.

Administration and Costs

At the Federal Level

The civilian form of program 1 would assign the federal government two major responsibilities: monitoring the expenditure of the substantial federal financial support and ensuring the consistent application of the principles—especially the rule against displacement—by which jobs were certified as appropriate for NSPs.

Since the financial accounting systems of U.S. school districts are not uniform and those of some districts are rudimentary, the federal government would be obliged to establish minimum accounting standards for all states and districts receiving federal funds under the program and then periodically to review the resulting financial records. Responsibilities concerning the rules on certification would be similar in concept but more difficult in execution and politically far more sensitive. Some federal agency would establish, in far greater detail than we have sketched above, the rules controlling certification and especially those defining job displacement. The same agency then would take responsibility for ensuring the uniform application and enforcement of those rules throughout the participating jurisdictions.

Both those functions would be far simpler if NSPs were confined to assignments within the school system. So, seemingly, would be the decision as to where the federal government should lodge that responsibility. If program 1 were confined to the schools, the Department of Education would seem the clearly appropriate agency. If the program permitted a wider system of NSP assignment, the Department of Labor might be a more appropriate home, given the high sensitivity of the job displacement issue and that department's experience with similar programs. Certainly organized labor would press for that result.

At the State and Local Levels

The breadth of NSP assignments would determine similar issues at the state level. If assignments were limited to schools, most states probably would delegate full responsibility to their school districts, retaining, perhaps, a modest supervisory role for the state department of instruction. School districts then would oversee the processes by which individual schools identified the tasks NSPs should perform, matched students to those tasks, and assigned the teachers or other school staff members necessary to supervise them. Little augmentation of district staffs would be needed.

If a high proportion of NSPs were placed outside the schools, however, both the placement and monitoring of the use of NSPs would become far more time consuming. Indeed, if it placed a high proportion of NSPs outside the schools, program 1, by virtue of the relative immaturity and high turnover of its participants, would require more administration per NSP man-year than any other form of national service we describe. Few school districts are now staffed to undertake such unfamiliar tasks, and we expect that many would resist this work even if given augmented staff. In jurisdictions where schools did not assume this role, it probably would be undertaken at the state level and most likely by state departments of labor. The main business of state labor departments is matching applicants to jobs. Although few of them perform that business impressively, their claim on the program still would be strong if it operated outside the schools. A few states might make their education departments of instruction responsible; others, for administrative or political reasons, might establish special entities reporting directly to the governor.

Program 1 Costs

The costs of administering program 1 would vary with the size and complexity of the administrative system it required, and that would be determined by the number of states and school districts that accepted the program and by the breadth of the NSP assignment pattern. Costs can therefore be projected only in ranges and even then only very crudely. Nonetheless, order of magnitude estimates may be useful.

Direct Federal Costs

The costs of military training aside, federal costs would in any case be modest. Edward Hamilton, our consultant on administration, estimates that approximately 200 additional federal employees might be required to oversee a small program involving 10 percent of the nation's high school seniors, 500 for an intermediate program involving from 40 to 60 percent of those students, and roughly 800 for a nationwide program. These numbers should not vary substantially between in-school and out-of-school programs. At an assumed average annual total personnel cost for professionals and support staff combined of $30,000 per capita, those estimates yield federal costs of $6 million, $15 million, and $24 million, respectively.

As noted earlier, the costs of the military option in program 1, assuming that the supposed maximum of 50,000 NSPs chose and were accepted by the military, would approximate $540 million annually. (We assume that 50,000 NSPs would be accepted into the military program in each of the three sizes of program 1 for which we offer estimates.)

State and Local Costs

These costs would be more variable. For a program limited to in-school assignments, a state of average size (containing roughly 2 percent of the nation's high school seniors), most or all of whose school districts participated in program 1, probably would not need more than 100 additional persons at the state and district levels combined to handle administrative overseeing and financial accounting. At an assumed $25,000 cost per person, totals would approximate $2 million per state. Supervision of the NSPs assigned within the school systems could be performed by the schools without any significant expansion of personnel, given the additional capacity that the NSPs would add. If NSPs were assigned to work in schools other than their own, additional costs would be incurred for transportation, but existing school bus systems might largely meet such needs.

In contrast, we estimate that a program that assigned student NSPs outside of schools would require double that number of persons in senior administration and overseeing positions and, more significantly, one additional state or local employee per fifty NSPs to certify positions, assign NSPs, monitor working conditions, manage reassignments, and perform similar tasks. If all of a cohort of 3.2 million U.S. high school seniors were engaged in out-of-school national service assignments,[105] the incremental costs of the additional 64,000 personnel required, assuming an average cost of $20,000 per person, would be $1.28 billion. Providing these persons with offices, means of transportation, and the like might add an additional 15 percent to that figure. (The costs of insuring students in a wide variety of settings outside school surely would increase, probably substantially, but we present no estimate of that cost.) Correspondingly, for an out-of-school program involving 10 percent of seniors, those costs would amount to approximately $128 million (plus 15 percent) nationwide; if half the population of seniors undertook such assignments, the cost would be roughly $640 million (plus 15 percent).

Table 5–1 summarizes these estimates for a nationwide, a small, and an intermediate-size program. It shows for each the differing costs of in-school and out-of-school assignment patterns. This table suggests that the most modest version of a federal program 1 might operate for about $560 million

Table 5–1
Estimated Costs of Alternative Forms of Program 1
(millions of dollars)

	Large Program (100 Percent of All Seniors)		*Intermediate Program (50 Percent of All Seniors)*		*Small Program (10 Percent of All Seniors)*	
Cost Category	*In-School*	*Out-of-School*	*In-School*	*Out-of-School*	*In-School*	*Out-of-School*
Federal Costs						
Civilian Administration	24	24	15	15	6	6
Military	540	540	540	540	540	540
State and Local Costs (75 Percent Reimbursed)						
Central Administration	125	250	67.5	125	12.5	25
NSP Supervision	0	1,280	0	640	—	128
Supervisor Support	0	192	0	96	—	19.2
Totals	689	2,286	622.5	1,416	558.5	718
Federal Share (Federal Plus 75 Percent State Costs)	657.75	1,855.5	605.6	1,200.75	555.4	674.9
States' Share (25 Percent State Cost)	31.25	430.5	16.9	215.25	3.1	43.1

and the most ambitious version for about $2.3 billion. If the expensive military component were eliminated, then the most modest version of program 1 (involving 10 percent of the nation's seniors receiving only in school assignments) could operate, in our estimation, for less than $20 million. This suggests a possibility for a relatively inexpensive experiment with this program.

Constitutional Considerations

A number of provisions of the U.S. Constitution have been cited by opponents of national service to argue that such service would be unconstitutional or, at least, contrary to the spirit of the Constitution. The Thirteenth Amendment's prohibition of involuntary servitude, the Fifth Amendment's guarantee that one will not be deprived of liberty without due process of law, and the same amendment's assurance that private property will not be taken for public use without just compensation, all provide the basis of arguments that coerced service would represent an unacceptable intrusion of the government upon the individual.[106] It also can be argued that the reach of the federal government is bounded further by the explicit powers delegated to Congress, the executive, and the judiciary under the Constitution and that neither the Congress's power to raise and support armies nor its now broadly read power to regulate commerce validates its establishment of a national service program.[107]

We discuss these arguments in some detail in considering the more extensive and arguably more intrusive versions of national service presented in chapters 6 and 8. Here we think it sufficient to note that the right of the state to mandate a system of compulsory education is established, notwithstanding the Fifth and Ninth Amendments, and that the scope and content of the education the state may require is largely untrammeled. This power, we believe, would readily be held by the courts to permit requiring a program similar to the one we have described.

To elaborate briefly, there can be little doubt about the constitutionality of compulsory education. Challenges to required schooling have been rebuffed whether based simply on an assertion of parental preference for an alternative educational scheme[108] or, more powerfully, on religious objections to continued schooling.[109] We have no doubt that a state appropriately could make community service a requirement for graduation when its justification was the personal development of the student. It is because the state seeks primarily benefit to the student, rather than a benefit from the student's services, that we believe the courts would not hold that program 1 represents an unacceptable taking or deprivation of liberty under the Fifth Amendment or that it forces involuntary servitude as that term is used in the Thirteenth

Amendment. Although there is surprisingly little authority relating directly to this question, all the major Supreme Court decisions that address issues of compulsory education acknowledge the government's right to attempt to develop the character of youthful students through required schooling and required courses. *Wisconsin* v. *Yoder,* a landmark 1972 opinion, provides a good example:

> The State advances two primary arguments in support of its system of compulsory education. It notes, as Thomas Jefferson pointed out early in our history, that some degree of education is necessary to prepare citizens to participate effectively and intelligently in our open political system if we are to preserve freedom and independence. Further, education prepares individuals to be self-reliant and self-sufficient participants in society. We accept these propositions.[110]

This argument could be carried too far. We think there would and should be serious questions about a system that rationalized, on the grounds of education, an extended period of student service that afforded substantial economic benefits to the state. But the relatively short period of service envisaged in program 1 and its clear relation to educational values seem to us to make it most unlikely that the program would be challenged successfully. In the case most closely related to this point, a federal court's assessment of Hawaii's requirement that schoolchildren perform cafeteria duties as a part of their educational requirements, the Court sustained the requirement.[111] We have little doubt that the same conclusion would be reached with respect to program 1.[112]

It may be a source of somewhat greater concern that the program would regulate private as well as public schools.[113] We note, however, that state regulation of private schools is well established, and even Court decisions most adamantly protective of the right of private schools to establish their own curricula concede the right of the states to establish some requirements in the interest of citizenship. In *Pierce* v. *Society of Sisters,* for example, the Supreme Court struck down the Oregon Compulsory Education Act requiring attendance at public schools. The Court went out of its way to note, however, that:

> No question is raised concerning the power of the state to regulate all schools . . . to require that all children of proper age attend some school . . . [and] that certain studies plainly essential to good citizenship must be taught."[114]

Finally, we see no disturbing alteration of the balance of state and federal relations or overreaching by the federal government resulting from program 1. The program would permit state choice and operate largely through state and local school board administration. Against the backdrop of some 100 school programs administered by the U.S. government since the enactment of the Elementary and Secondary Education Act,[115] program 1 would not effect a significant change in federal-state relations.

Conclusion

Our analysis suggests that in several respects valued by national service advocates, program 1 is not likely to show substantial achievements. Our discussion indicates that a school-based program is not likely to help the military and that it would not substantially improve most students' exposure to the working world. We are impressed with the opportunity cost of imposing another demand on the time of high school seniors. We do think, however, that the program could be of value to a student's personal growth and that it could contribute to the accomplishment of some kinds of public service work. Because these gains are potentially significant but uncertain, we think variations of program 1 warrant testing.

Modest experiments would assign all students to tasks within their school systems. Such programs would forego the benefits of exposing NSPs to different types of people in other than familiar settings. To the degree that the school systems are not racially, ethnically, and economically integrated, such programs would not correct for that fact.

Still, they would help instill a sense of service as an important part of education. As Sizer notes, there is a strong argument that "every student should 'work' for his or her own school, just as every child in a wisely conducted home shares the family's chores."[116] By this means, as the President's Panel on Youth put it, "the school becomes a locale for self-centered skill development and learning, but also a place in which young persons engage in constructive activities benefiting younger children."[117]

Such programs should be relatively easy to develop. As noted, many schools and some school systems already operate service programs, most on an elective basis. State or local governments, private foundations, or schools themselves could establish student classroom aid programs with relatively modest funding. We think it would be worthwhile to develop more student-to-student tutoring programs in various settings with diverse populations and then to monitor and evaluate these efforts carefully. The reactions of the students served and serving, of teachers, and of parents could illuminate the costs and benefits of at least this minimal form of program 1.

In more ambitious tests of this program, placements in health and child care facilities, museums, and libraries could be arranged, and some summer environmental programs could be organized. These would yield richer benefits in diversity of experience while posing far greater operational difficulties.

That the added benefits might more than justify the greater difficulty of administration is suggested by the fact that virtually all existing school service programs emphasize service outside the school. We suspect that whether these programs ultimately justified their opportunity costs and political and administrative difficulties would be determined mainly by whether they successfully integrated school and work. We have little doubt that "the ideal program integrates the educational experience and the community improvement effort—for example, a high school course on energy conservation coupled with a housing weatherization project."[118] We are uncertain, however, how widely this ideal can be realized.

On this, as on a number of other central ideas discussed in this book, we think experimentation, coupled with careful evaluation, is warranted. If evaluations are positive, a next step might be to test larger-scale placements modified by the lessons previously learned. If such an expansion were successful, then Congress (or a state or local government) might well consider enacting something like a full-scale program 1.

Notes

1. Winn, ed., *John Dewey: Dictionary of Education,* 39, 123–24. Dewey was greatly influenced by William James, the first prominent American proponent of national service. Daniel Conrad has written that:

> [I]t was William James, the psychologist (and philosopher) who attacked the "spectator theory of knowledge," denied the dualism of thought and experience, and argued that meaningful ideas are those that make concrete differences in real life . . . and it was John Dewey the philosopher (and psychologist, etc.) who extended James' ideas into a more refined theory of experience and suggested their further application to the practice of teaching and the structure and function of schools.

Conrad, "The Differential Impact of Experiential Learning Programs on Secondary School Students," 3.

2. Coleman et al., *Youth: Transition to Adulthood,* 146–47. The checkered history of experiential learning from the time of Dewey up to the 1974 panel cited below is summarized in Conrad, "The Differential Impact of Experiential Learning Programs on Secondary School Students," 2–11. A strong later endorsement of this point of view came from Clark Kerr's *Giving Youth a Better Chance: Options for Education, Work and Service,* a 1979 publication of the Carnegie Council on Policy Studies in Education. Kerr argued in favor of having junior- and senior-year high school students spend only 3 days a week in school, with 2 days devoted to work or community service.

3. Wynne, ed., *Developing Character: Transmitting Knowledge.*

4. Ibid., 5.

5. Ibid., 7. See also Frank Newman's *Higher Education and the American Resurgence,* sponsored by the Carnegie Foundation for the Advancement of Teaching,

which recommends a service requirement for graduation from college or high school in part "to translate the undergraduate experience into a more active learning process" (15).

6. Gallup Organization, Inc., *Americans Volunteer.* There were no significant differences between the responses of public school parents, private school parents, and adults who had no children in school.

7. Data are from Ted Kildegaard, director of the EBCE Dissemination Project, in correspondence with the National Service Study Project, 5 December 1984. For an account of the creation and evolution of EBCE, see Bucknam, "Experience-Based Career Education."

8. A 1979 survey by the National Center for Service Learning (a part of the federal agency ACTION) concluded that approximately 14 percent of all high schools, public and private, had curriculum-related service programs and that almost two-thirds of these awarded academic credit for service. See National Center for Service Learning, *National Survey of High School Student Community Service Programs,* 1. The report notes that "the trend toward credit is relatively new: nearly half of all schools awarding credit for service work (45 percent) have begun doing so since 1974." Ibid.

For some examples of school programs, together with an outline of a service program proposed for general adoption, see Boyer, *High School: A Report on Secondary Education in America,* 202–15. Notable local programs include Adams High School, Adams, Minnesota (work with handicapped children under the supervision of the Mayo Clinic); Champlain Valley Union High School, Hinesburg, Vermont (students undertake individual commitments approved by a faculty advisor for credit); and the Dallas Magnet High School.

9. Correspondence to authors from R. Woodward, Human Services Center, Dallas Independent School District, March 1984.

10. Since 1976, Connecticut has operated a Youth Action program under the auspices of the Governor's Council on Voluntary Action. In 1983, a federal grant was obtained to establish a Young Volunteers in Action program, providing state support for volunteer programs (two of them for credit) at ten high schools. Telephone interview by authors with state education officials, 1984.

11. Unpublished memorandum from D. Hornbeck, State Superintendent of Education, State of Maryland, to State Board of Education, January 25, 1984.

12. These data are from an evaluation of the program issued in September 1981 by the Utah State Office of Education, 3.

13. Analyzing eight established school community service programs, Newmann and Rutter observe that "program students participate more frequently [than control groups] in non-school activities such as church, clubs, Scouts, volunteer work. . . ." Newmann and Rutter, "The Effects of High School Community Service Programs On Students' Social Development," 6.

14. "Program classes contain about 70% women in contrast to comparison classes where women barely exceed 50%." Ibid.

15. Examining programs that operate during school hours, Newmann and Rutter observe that "program students are lower in socioeconomic status, grade point

average, and aspirations for future schooling than their non-participating peers." Ibid. By contrast, after-school programs apparently are more likely to draw college-bound, white middle-income students. Boyer, *High School: A Report on Secondary Education in America,* 207–8.

Discussing the federal vocational educational programs, the President's Panel on Youth noted, "The most conspicuous limitation of these programs is the limitation to terminal education, making the program incompatible with education beyond high school." Coleman et al., *Youth: Transition to Adulthood,* 158.

16. For general information on the Atlanta program, see Atlanta Public Schools' Office of Planning and Expanded Services, "Community Service Requirement: Class of 1988 Duties to the Community." A proposal to establish a 100-hour mandatory after-school service program was put forward by the superintendent of Maryland schools early in 1984, but encountered determined resistance and was withdrawn. The proposal is described in a memorandum from David Hornbeck, superintendent of the Maryland State Board of Education, 25 January 1984.

17. Sizer, "National Service Education Study," 6.

18. See, for example, The National Commission on Excellence in Education, *A Nation At Risk: The Imperative for Educational Reform,* 24, 29: "We recommend that significantly more time be devoted to learning the New Basics. This will require more effective use of the existing school day, a longer school day, or a lengthened school year." Ibid., 29.

Ernest Boyer, though asserting that all high school students should complete a service requirement, simultaneously calls for a more rigorous core curriculum in high schools: "The number of required courses in the core curriculum should be expanded from one-half to two-thirds the total units required for high school graduation." Boyer, *High School: A Report on Secondary Education in America,* 307.

The American public, too, seems to support a fortified academic curriculum. According to one survey of public attitudes, more than 75 percent of all those questioned favor course requirements that "far exceed the strictest high school graduation requirements of any State today, and they also exceed the admission standards of all but a handful of our most selective colleges and universities." National Commission on Excellence in Education, *A Nation at Risk: The Imperative for Educational Reform,* 17.

19. A similar proposal is urged in Menacker and Wynne, "Helping Students to Serve Society," 381–84.

20. A more extended service period would certainly be plausible. Former U.S. Commissioner of Education Ernest Boyer has proposed that all high school students complete a service requirement of not less than 30 hours a year in each of the four high school years. Boyer, *High School: A Report on Secondary Education in America,* 202–15. Service, under Boyer's plan, could take a very wide variety of forms and be accomplished during evenings, weekends, or summers. There would be no corresponding diminution of classroom time. We have advanced different particulars for program 1 in the belief that they would provide a more intensive experience, permit more substantial responsibilities to be assumed, and thus offer both greater educative value to the student and more useful service to the community. In fact, we think there is a strong argument for requiring service over a semester rather than a year. Blackmer

and Irwin, in "A Study of Off-Campus Education" conclude persuasively, after an evaluation of experiential programs, that greater intensity is more valuable than longevity.

21. Essentially this standard is incorporated in Section 421(3) of the Domestic Volunteer Service Act, 42 U.S.C. § 4992 (1973), authorizing federal projects under the aegis of ACTION.

22. Section 501(c)(3) of the Internal Revenue Code describes organizations that are not taxed on their income and enjoy the special privilege of having contributions to them be tax deductible for the donor. To qualify, an organization must be operated for charitable purposes, that is, its earnings may not benefit any private individual or shareholder, and it may not engage in lobbying. See generally Hopkins, *The Law of Tax Exempt Organizations*.

The difficulties associated with determining which organizations are entitled to privileged status under this provision should not be underestimated. "Probably no other one area of the Revenue Code has been more consistently troublesome . . . to administer or proportionately more demanding of the time of senior [Internal Revenue] Service personnel than that of charitable organizations." Houck, "With Charity for All," 1424, quoting the testimony of Mitchell Rogovin at hearings before the Subcommittee on Employment, Manpower and Poverty of the Senate Committee on Labor and Public Welfare, 91st Cong., 2d sess., 141. Houck reports that in 1982 there were 322,000 501(c) exempt organizations and that "even these figures understate the public charities qualified under section 501(c); a single exemption to the United States Catholic Conference, for example, includes over 70,000 subordinate churches and administrative units." Ibid., 1426.

23. Alden, *Volunteers in Education: Future Public Policy,* 139.

24. Plisko, ed., *The Condition of Education, 1984,* 14, 58. The number of high school seniors will grow considerably later in this century. For costing and other calculations, we assume 3.2 million seniors in the program's steady state.

25. Interestingly, seven states (Alabama, Arkansas, North and South Carolina, Iowa, Mississippi, and Virginia) employ large numbers of high school students as school bus drivers. In North Carolina 55 percent and in South Carolina 71 percent of drivers in 1983 were students. "Teenage Bus Drivers: Accident Rate a Worry," *The New York Times,* 24 October 1984.

26. "Annual American Studies since 1973 consistently show 16–19-year-olds with higher percentages of absent workers and aggregate time lost than 20–24-year-olds or 24–54-year-olds; the latter, in turn, have lower rates than young adults." Reubens, Harrison, and Rupp, *The Youth Labor Force 1945–1995,* 25.

27. Gittell, Beardsley, and Weissman, "Final Evaluation Report on Syracuse Youth Community Service," 10.

28. Bachman, O'Malley, and Johnston, *Youth in Transition,* 159, table 8–2.

29. Ibid.

30. Plisko, *The Condition of Education, 1984,* 14, 58.

31. Sizer, "National Service Education Study," 18, 29.

32. Ibid.

33. Telephone interview with DeDe McGinnis, coordinator for Duval County Public Schools, 14 March 1984.

34. Cloward, "Studies in Tutoring," 14–25. The Mobilization for Youth program used disadvantaged youths as tutors.

In 1972, "An Evaluation of the Youth Tutoring Youth Model for In-School Neighborhood Youth Corps," by the National Commission on Resources for Youth, Inc., found that tutees in similar programs in Washington and New York notably improved their reading skills.

35. In the Ontario-Montclair, California, school district, 7th and 8th graders tutored low-achieving 4th to 6th graders three times per week in 35- to 45-minute sessions over a 3-year period. "Results from systematic evaluations showed that both tutors and tutees made academic gains compared to control groups in some of the areas tutored, though results varied from year to year. . . . the strongest positive findings were in the area of academic gains for tutors and tutees." Devin-Sheehan, Feldman, and Allen, "Research on Children Tutoring Children: A Critical Review," 356–57 (citing Ontario-Montclair school district reports).

In a schoolwide program in Pacoima, California, older students tutored younger students. "Data obtained over five years in the area of reading achievement . . . strongly indicated that the program is producing major improvements in the reading achievement of minority students." Ibid., 358.

36. Ibid., 363.

37. Woolsey, "Child Care Jobs for National Service Participants," 8. Note that these are not the number of worker hours but rather of child care hours received. A worker who spends 10 hours caring for five children produces 50 child care hours by this calculation.

38. Some diminution of attention to all children would occur as the energy of regular child care providers was diverted to supervise an NSP. Because, as noted later, NSPs typically would be experienced child care providers, we do not think this diversion would reduce significantly the benefits we describe.

39. Woolsey, "Child Care Jobs for National Service Participants," 37.

40. According to one report, 36 percent of U.S. high schools offer child development courses, with a total of 247,000 students enrolled. See Evaluation Technologies, Inc., "A Trend Study of Offerings and Enrollments," 49.

41. National Center for Service Learning, "National Survey of High School Students Community Service Programs," 5.

42. Lee et al., "Study of Service and Social Needs in the Health Sector," II–9, citing Firman, Gelfand, and Ventura, "Students as Resources to the Aging Network," 18591.

43. Feller, "Americans Needing Help to Function at Home," p. 3.

44. Lee et al., "Study of Service and Social Needs in the Health Sector," I–61.

45. "[M]ost home-maker–home health aides are middle-aged women, although both the young and the elderly work as aides. . . . [O]nly a small number of men currently work as aides, but more are needed, especially to care for elderly men who prefer a male aide." Ibid., I–II.

46. More than 31 percent of high school seniors queried on the point in a recent survey described themselves as having stolen something at least once. See Bachman, Johnston, and O'Malley, *Monitoring the Future: 1982,* 101. Asked the question, "During the last 12 months, how often have you taken something not belonging to

you worth under $50?," 13.9 percent of high school seniors said that they had done so once; 6.9 percent said they had done so twice; 5.4 percent said they had done so three or four times; and 5.2 percent responded that they had done so five or more times.

47. Physical abuse of patients by NSPs is likely to be rare if NSPs are reasonably selected, although even a few instances might endanger the continuance of the program. An illuminatingly detailed description of the difficulties caused by the more mundane problems of unreliable or undesirable home care for the elderly is provided in Sheehan, *Kate Quinton's Days.*

48. Hagenstein, "National Service: Conservation and Environmental Aspects," 46, table I. The numbers of participants are adjusted for a 240-hour program 1 time requirement rather than the 300-hour requirement assumed by Hagenstein in his original calculations (see ibid., 43).

49. U.S. Forest Service, *Youth Conservation Corps: Tenth Anniversary Report,* 45.

50. See chapter 2, "Libraries and Museums."

51. Especially sensitive situations may require more elaborate, perhaps prohibitively expensive, screening. Some mental health programs, for example, require volunteers to take psychological tests. See Lee, "Study of Service and Social Needs in the Health Sector," II–6, citing Levin and Idler, *The Hidden Health Care System: Mediating Structures and Medicine.*

52. One can readily conceive of versions of model 1 that also would target teenagers otherwise likely to drop out of high school. For one example of such an approach, see Senator Kennedy's S. 2397, submitted on March 8, 1984. This bill would assure paid part-time jobs during the school year and full-time jobs during the summer for disadvantaged youths who "sign a written commitment . . . to maintain or resume attendance in a secondary school for the purpose of obtaining a high school diploma." 8 March 1984, *Congressional Record,* (S2397.98 Cong., 2nd Session.S2440. This approach was one of four major programs tested between 1978 and 1981 under the Federal Youth Employment and Demonstration Projects Acts. See generally Diaz, Ball, and Wolfhagen, *Linking School and Work for Disadvantaged Youths.* This program provided private sector as well as public service jobs, but it could be limited to service positions only.

We have not incorporated such an approach in program 1 because we think that it is not compatible with the aims of national service to pay some or all students for service. Here, as elsewhere in considering national service, there is a conflict between what may be desirable in a program specifically targeted for a portion of youth with particular problems and what is desirable and plausible as a program for all youth.

53. Some states or school districts might choose to assign some NSPs who were fully capable of interpersonal responsibility to more routine tasks to avoid the appearance of tracking and to maintain the benefits of NSP contact with a diversity of other NSPs.

54. We have compressed some categories discussed in chapter 3 and added another, effect on academic skills, in proportion to our sense of the significance of these categories for an evaluation of program 1.

55. Epstein, *Youth Employment During High School,* xix.

56. Bureau of the Census, *Money, Income and Poverty Status of Families and Persons in the United States: 1983,* 15, table 10. Of these, 42 percent of the women and 47 percent of the men reported earning at least $2,000.

57. Raphael, "Youth Employment and its Effects on Performance in High School," 11, concludes that seniors are 1½ times as likely to work as sophomores.

58. Steinberg et al., "High School Students in the Labor Force: Some Costs and Benefits to Schooling and Learning," 365.

59. Ibid., 363.

60. See chapter 3, note 7, which indicates the Youth Conservation Corps experience in which two-thirds of the unsuccessful applicants for positions in the program wound up with private sector jobs. Similarly, we are struck by the experience of an Oakland Youth Work program in the 1970s, which carefully structured counseling and job placement activities for delinquents and adjudged potential delinquents between the ages of sixteen and eighteen, and then meticulously compared program achievements with paired individuals not in the program. To the researchers' dismay, they found no significant differences in personal gains such as self-esteem because "analysis revealed that many (75%) of the control cases, while not participating [in the program], did obtain jobs on their own. . . ." It was only when these contaminated cases were discarded that the program could manifest value. See Elliot and Knowles, "Development and Employment: An Evaluation of the Oakland Youth Work Experience Program," 64–73.

61. Taggart, *Vice President's Task Force,* 3.

62. "In an observational study of adolescents at work [in paid jobs] the two activities most frequently observed (regardless of job type) were sweeping floors and carrying objects from place to place." Ruggiero, Greenberger, and Steinberg, "Occupational Deviance Among Adolescent Workers," 426.

63. General Accounting Office, "CETA Demonstration Provides Lessons on Implementing Youth Programs," 10.

64. Ibid., 17.

65. Ibid., 13.

66. Ibid., 18.

67. Gittell, Beardsley and Weissman, 56–59.

68. The limited empirical evidence supports this view. A study of the fast-food industry concluded that:

> For a majority of hourly employees, the fast food job experience helped them become aware of how a business runs. Nine out of ten reported that their job helped them learn the skills associated with dealing with people and working with others (teamwork).

Charner and Fraser, "Fast Food Jobs," 96.

Specifically, this study reported, on the basis of results from more than 4,500 questionnaires, that about three-quarters of fast-food industry workers felt that from their jobs they had learned about taking direction and getting along with co-workers, two-thirds reported learning about finishing assigned tasks and taking responsibility for mistakes, and more than half reported learning about being dependable and on time. Ibid., 63. Charner and Fraser report that employees from lower socioeconomic backgrounds who have completed lower high school grades are likely to benefit more from these jobs than their peers. Ibid., 63–65.

69. To the extent that program 1 preempted time spent working for pay, the loss of earnings also would be an opportunity cost of the program. The Bureau of the Census reported that in 1983, median income for males ages fifteen to nineteen was $1,735, and for females it was $1,675. These numbers included 397,000 male and 310,000 female year-round, full-time workers. Bureau of the Census, *Money, Income and Poverty Status of Families and Persons in the United States, 1983,* 12–13, table 7.

Of students who work for pay, about 10 percent report that they contribute half or more of what they earn to family living expenses, 35 percent say they contribute some or a little to family expenses, and 55 percent contribute nothing to family expenses; 17.5 percent of the sample report allocating half or more of their earnings to savings for future education. Bachman, Johnston, and O'Malley, *Monitoring the Future: 1982,* 193–94.

70. Goldberg, *The Noneconomic Impacts of the Job Corps,* 13, 50.

71. Cullinan, "National Service and the American Educational System," 94.

72. Conrad and Hedin, "Are Experiential Learning Programs Effective?," 102. This study reveals the results of a survey in which 4,000 students were asked to give their responses (agree, disagree, or don't know) to a list of twenty-four items proposed to them as potential gains from their experiential education programs. Only one item—learning to become an effective consumer—was rated by fewer than 50 percent of the students as a benefit of experiential education. All other items had agreement rates ranging from 52 to 93 percent, with twenty of them claimed by 70 percent or more and fourteen of them by 80 percent or more. Ibid., 105. See also our discussion in chapter 3, "Being Needed."

73. Gallup Organization, Inc., *Americans Volunteer,* 12.

74. This is documented in the Ontario-Montclair school system and in the Mobilization for Youth studies discussed earlier in this chapter ("Assignments in the Schools). In the latter case, "tutors showed greater reading gains (3.4 years) than both the control group and tutees." Devin-Sheehan, Feldman, and Allen, "Research on Children Tutoring Children: A Critical Review," 360.

A study by Allen and Feldman directly addressed the question of opportunity cost by comparing tutors with a control group of peers who used what would have been tutoring time to study. Although they experimented with 5th graders tutoring 3rd graders, their observation that tutors improved more than control group members is significant. See Allen and Feldman, "Learning Through Tutoring: Low Achieving Children as Tutors," 2–4.

75. A rich inventory of (primarily British) examples of benefits from this approach is provided in Dickson, "Community Service and the Curriculum." One report shows significantly greater gains in understanding nutrition for 10th graders who participated in a food coop than for those who spent equivalent time studying nutrition in the classroom. Agnew, "Better Education Through Application," 44–48.

76. For a discussion of these two effects, see Conrad and Hedin, "Citizenship Education Through Participation," 139.

77. We find no clear evidence in the literature as to how great the age or competence gap between tutor and tutee may become before the benefit of the tutoring diminishes. Moreover, "it is conceivable that the type of student who benefits from being a tutor—the low-achiever, the child with behavior problems, the unmotivated

child—may in fact be the least beneficial type of teacher for the tutee." Devin-Sheehan, Feldman, and Allen, "Research on Children Tutoring Children: A Critical Review," 367.

78. There has been remarkably little evaluation of the impact on skills or self-esteem of in-school service other than tutoring. For an exception, see Arkell, "Are Student-Helpers Helped?" Arkell concludes that students were neither helped nor hurt by substituting a short period (25 hours) of work as clerks, audio-visual aides, and tutors for classroom time.

79. Bucknam, "Experience-Based Career Education, 36. One school that retested students a year after they had graduated from the EBCE program did report statistically significant gains as opposed to a control group. This led Bucknam to conclude that "students' academic achievement, in the areas tested, is not harmed—and indeed it may be significantly improved with a longer treatment period." Ibid. Steinberg and his colleagues note no gains on a variety of skills tests for students who work after school as against their peers who do not work. They do note some gains on practical knowledge tests (asking, for example, about consumer knowledge of where to go for information, or how to evaluate interest rates). Steinberg et al., "Effects of Working on Adolescent Development," 366, 368. Note that Steinberg's results do not involve situations in which classroom time is sacrificed for work or service time.

80. Luchs, "Selected Changes in Urban High School Students," 169.

81. See Yee, "A Report of The Summer Cross Age Tutoring Program—1980."

82. For a general discussion and list of peer helping programs in the United States, see Sachnoff, *High School Peer Resource Programs: A Director's Perspective.*

83. Devin-Sheehan, Feldman, and Allen, "Research on Children Tutoring Children: A Critical Review," 363. An Israeli study of sixteen-year-olds tutoring fourteen-year-olds carried out in 1982 noted that "the assessment of the effects of cross-age tutoring on the social and psychological attributes of either tutors or tutees has been largely neglected." Yogev and Ronen, "Cross-Age Tutoring: Effects on Tutors' Attributes," 261. With a very limited and self-selected sample, the authors advance some statistical evidence indicating that empathy increased significantly among tutors in a small Israeli program and that "increments in the tutors' scores of altruism, anti-utilitarianism, and self-esteem were also significantly larger than those of the comparison group." Ibid., 266.

Further research with larger, better controlled samples, over longer periods of time, and in a U.S. context would be necessary to assess these conclusions.

84. Conrad and Hedin, "Executive Summary: Experiential Education Evaluation Project," 18.

85. Newmann and Rutter, "The Effects of High School Community Service Programs on Students' Social Development."

86. Ibid., 21. They did note that one scale measuring social competence indicated a possible benefit, although not a statistically significant one, from program participation. Commenting on the differences between their results and the previous study, Newmann and Rutter write:

> In contrast to the present study, Conrad-Hedin found large changes among several variables. . . . Even the most robust findings of Conrad-Hedin, however, do not

generally exceed 3% of a scale's range or average pre-test score. Improving one's score from 1 to 3 items on a 100-item test may be statistically significant (because of sample size) but attaching educational significance to such a small change is problematic. [Ibid., 22]

87. Conrad, "The Differential Impact of Experiential Learning Programs on Secondary School Students," 95, citing Ellington, "The Effects of Three Curriculum Strategies upon High School Seniors' Attitudes Towards the Elderly."

88. Ibid., citing Blum, "A Model of Transition Mainstreaming: A Cross-Cognitive Tutor Program."

89. Newmann and Rutter, "The Effects of High School Community Service Programs on Students' Social Development," 29–30.

90. A student will spend about 15,000 hours in school classrooms before he or she graduates from high school.

91. Gallup first asked, "Would you favor or oppose requiring all young men to give one year of service to the nation—either in the military forces or in non-military work here or abroad, such as VISTA or the Peace Corps?" They then asked, "Suppose all young men were required to give one year of service, which would you prefer—military or non-military?" Similar questions were asked substituting "women" for "men." Gallup Organization, Inc., American Volunteer, 1981, 6.

92. Nelson, Hale, and Slackman calculate those yields from the available high school population.

93. It is also possible that high school students as a group would have different preferences than those in and out of high school who were surveyed by Gallup. Those who preferred military service might be disproportionately unqualified for it. The numbers cited should accordingly be treated as a ceiling.

94. Nelson, Hale, and Slackman calculate that providing basic military training to these personnel would add roughly $2.5 billion a year to costs, plus one-time costs of more than $1 billion to reactivate facilities at about eight existing bases large enough to handle 10,000 students and instructors at one time. Costs could be much higher if many of the program 1 NSPs had to receive training in the summer, creating a peak load problem, or if the government had to purchase land for new bases.

95. Other services could participate in the program. For simplicity, we discuss only the Army.

96. Nelson, Hale, and Slackman, "National Service and the Military."

97. The army projects an attrition rate during basic training of 10.5 percent. Department of Defense, *Military Manpower Training Report, FY 1986,* III–8.

98. Useful service life would be extended only assuming that the Army did not require retraining of program 1 NSPs who elected regular enlistments.

99. Savings would be realized only for those NSPs later entering the Army, since the other services would presumably require retraining. Our consultants estimate that about one-quarter, or roughly 11,000 of the 50,000 program 1 NSPs, would later enter the Army, either on active or reserve duty.

100. Brinkerhoff and Grissmer, *The Reserve Forces in an All-Volunteer Environment,* 7. These are nonprior service enlistments, which do not include former active duty troops who enlist in the Army Reserve.

101. It is difficult to quantify this enhancement. Not only is propensity to enlist in the reserves after program 1 unknown, but there is also no basis for estimating the

diversion of potential reserve recruits into the active force as a result of program 1 or for estimating any mismatch between remaining reserve prospects and unit locations and skill needs.

102. The Army projects that by 1990, the shortage will have diminished to 187,000. Department of Defense, *Manpower Requirements Report, FY 1986,* III–40.

103. See chapter 2, The Value of NSPs in the Schools.

104. See chapter 2, The Tasks to be Performed.

105. The size of the cohort will increase from about 1990 on. We are using 3.2 million as an illustrative number.

106. See, for example, Black, "Constitutional Problems in Compulsory National Service."

107. An unusually well-developed presentation of these arguments may be found in Bobbitt, "National Service: Unwise or Unconstitutional?"

108. See, for example, *Hanson* v. *Cushman* 490 F. Supp. 109 (1980). See also, *State* v. *Bailey* 157 Ind. 324, 61 N.E. 730 (1901); *State* v. *Jackson* 71 N.H. 552, 53A. 1021 (1923); and the often-quoted *Stephens* v. *Bongart* 189 A. 131 (1937), a New Jersey opinion in which the court wrote eloquently:

> If it is within the police power of the state to regulate wages, to legislate respecting housing conditions in crowded cities . . . to compel landlords to place windows in their tenements which will enable their tenants to enjoy the sunshine, it is within the police power of the state to compel every resident of New Jersey so to educate his children that the light of American ideals will permeate his life. [189 A. at 132]

109. The leading case is *Wisconsin* v. *Yoder,* 406 U.S. 205 (1972). For most students, program 1 would be even more defensible because most state laws compel attendance only until age sixteen. See Kotin and Aikman, *Legal Foundations of Compulsory School Attendance,* appendix A. For seventeen-year-old high school seniors in most states, the program would not be compulsory but would operate merely as a condition of continued voluntary pursuit of a high school degree.

110. *Wisconsin* v. *Yoder* 406 U.S. 205, 221 (1972).

111. *Bobilin* v. *Board of Education, State of Hawaii,* 403 F. Supp. 1095 (District Court, Hawaii, 1975).

112. With respect to program 1, we are thus in accord with the judgment of Terrence Cullinan, who wrote 18 years ago:

> The fact that compulsory education has received public approval does not, of course, mean that compulsory national service would be similarly accepted. However, the *legal* bases for both are similar, and the optimum approach to national service thus can be determined without constitutional complications. [Cullinan, "National Service and the American Educational System," 97]

113. The program could be operated exclusively in public schools. This would omit the participation of about 300,000 private school students, or about 9 percent of the pool of high school graduates. See U.S. Department of Education, "A Comparison of Selected Characteristics of Private and Public Schools," table IV.

114. *Pierce* v. *Society of Sisters* 268 U.S. 510, 534 (1925).

115. The act, now codified at 20 U.S.C. Sec. 236, became law in 1965. The estimate of 100 programs was made in Birman and Ginsburg, "The Federal Role in

Elementary and Secondary Education: New Directions and Continuing Concerns," 480.

116. Sizer, "National Service Education Study," 30. See also, Wynne, ed., *Developing Character: Transmitting Knowledge,* 6: "In all Japanese public schools . . . pupils are expected to help keep their school clean and in repair."

117. Coleman, et al., *Youth: Transition to Adulthood,* 147.

118. Michel, "Public Job Creation: A Means to an End," 2.

6
Military Draft-Based Service

A quite different form of national service might arise from the reinstitution of a military draft. We turn here to the possible costs and benefits of such a conjunction of civilian and military service.

A draft might be reinstituted for any of several reasons. Principal among these would be a decision to expand substantially the size of the armed forces, a drop in the number of volunteers meeting required military standards, or some combination of the two. An increase in the demand for military labor power might arise because of a perceived threat to national security. A sharp decrease in the supply of labor power might result from improving civilian youth employment opportunities, an erosion of military pay, or extended involvement in an unpopular war. As detailed in chapter 4, the armed services will be particularly vulnerable to such supply problems in the late 1980s and early 1990s because the youth population will be the smallest since the beginning of the AVF. It is therefore possible that large and recurring recruiting shortfalls would prompt consideration of a peacetime military draft of at least 100,000 people per year. (A draft of fewer than that number is improbable; the number of additional recruits needed would not justify the social and political costs of reimposing a draft. Changes in military pay or bonuses likely would be used to increase enlistment.)

The terms of a draft undoubtedly would be subject to heated debate and the old question of "Who serves when not all serve?" would recur. As our purpose here is to describe a possible national service program, not a military conscription scheme, we have not tried to answer this question. Instead we assume what we think is the preponderant probability: A military draft would operate as it is now defined by statute and regulation. The most significant characteristics of the existing system are these: Only men would be drafted; they would be called within one year after their nineteenth birthdays in order of birth dates selected by a lottery; they would serve for 2 years and receive no educational deferments other than to allow completion of the last year of high school; members of active reserve units would not be inducted; varying proportions (currently roughly 30 percent) of potential conscripts would be rejected for not meeting military mental, moral, or physical standards;[1] volunteers who met those standards would be accepted, and both conscripts and entry-level volunteers would be paid at levels that approximate the minimum wage.

In the event of an apparent need for such a draft, a variety of plans offering a civilian service alternative to the draft might be proposed. Plans of this sort might be attractive principally as a means of granting greater freedom of choice to those subject to conscription. They also would attract support because of the work a civilian service might accomplish. Another possible appeal of such plans would be that, by expanding the number of persons required to serve, they would reduce the inequities associated with the selection of only a few for military service. For its part, the military might see gains from diverting to civilian service those conscripts with a pronounced distaste for military life. Finally, plans of this character might circumvent the need to assess the claims of conscientious objection.

Forms of Draft-Based Service

One such plan was submitted to Congress as the National Service Act of 1970 by Congressman Jonathan Bingham.[2] Bingham's approach was more elaborately developed by the National Service Secretariat, a private organization interested in advancing the concept of national service. In 1979, this more complex version was submitted to Congress by Representative Paul McCloskey.[3] The National Service Secretariat–McCloskey plan would have required all persons, male and female, to register at age seventeen.[4] Literature on civilian and military service opportunities would then be provided to them. On their eighteenth birthdays, male registrants would be invited (though not required) to commit themselves to one of three types of service to be performed before age twenty-three. Service could be either active duty in the military (for 2 or 3 years), membership in a military reserve unit (for 5½ years),[5] or participation in an approved civilian national service activity for 1 year. A registrant who committed to civilian service would be subject to the military draft only after those in his year-of-birth group who had not committed to some form of service. Because a peacetime military draft probably would require only about one in ten men from a year-of-birth group (even a wartime draft would not likely draw all those in a year-of-birth group), this deferment would in practice probably operate as an exemption. In addition, volunteers would receive more substantial educational benefits and wages than those later conscripted into the military.

Although the National Service Secretariat–McCloskey program drew considerable notice in the late 1970s and early 1980s, we do not use it as a model for our analysis of programs of this type. The plan's crucial defect arises, in our view, from the variability of any likely U.S. military draft.

Draft calls will vary according to voluntary recruitment rates and international exigencies. The effects of being conscripted also are quite different in time of war or high tension than in time of peace and tranquility. All plans that permit or encourage civilian national service as an alternative to military conscription are flawed because those coming of age at times of low (or no) draft calls and those not eligible for the draft (including women) would have little incentive to commit themselves to service. By asking for a choice in advance, and by varying the terms and dissociating the times of military and civilian service, the McCloskey plan compounded this drawback. The plan would ask an eighteen-year-old to guess what his probabilities of military conscription would be from ages nineteen to twenty-five.[6] If he thought that probability high, it would invite him to diminish and defer his risk, not by alternative service but rather by a commitment to such service that may be fulfilled over any of the subsequent 5 years. If the risk of conscription later declined or military service became more desirable, the McCloskey program would leave the registrant free to reenter a less threatening draft lottery.

That opportunity could be removed by eliminating the option to reenter the draft pool and making failure to perform civilian service subject to criminal punishment. The opportunities for gaming the system and the likelihood of resulting inequities are not so easily treated by amendment, however, because they are fundamental to the Bingham and National Service Secretariat–McCloskey approaches. Those who opted for civilian service and proved to be right in anticipating low lottery numbers, and therefore a high likelihood of being drafted, would wind up serving a year less than they otherwise would have expected, and at less risk. Those who thought the risk to be higher than it turned out to be and who therefore mistakenly opted for service would serve a year when nothing actually would have been required.

Our sense is that, far from encouraging a spirit of service and affording greater freedom of choice, this plan would be an unattractive exploitation of uncertainty by the government and would leave many young men feeling that they had been induced to make a wrong choice with too little information at too early an age. Moreover, the plan does little to mitigate the problem of conscientious objection. Many men could be expected to contend that although they refused a civilian option at age eighteen, the intervening time and the catalyzing effect of a conscription notice made them conscientious objectors (COs) by the time of induction.[7] These men would claim a right to be excused from military service, but the McCloskey plan would not allow them a right of reversion to civilian service.

The West German Model

Many nations have instituted national service plans of one sort or another. West Germany, France, the Netherlands, and Denmark link national service to a military draft.[8] They use civilian service to provide COs with alternative means of meeting service obligations or to establish additional service opportunities for conscripts too numerous for their military establishments. A number of Third World countries use national service to advance community development, to help integrate minorities into the national culture, or for other reasons.[9] We rely very little on such foreign experience in this study for two reasons. The first is that informative, dispassionate, and reliable examinations of that experience are rare. The second and more fundamental is that the meaning of national service and the nature of its costs and benefits depend so greatly on the characteristics of the society in which it is rendered that lessons lightly drawn from foreign experience seem to us as likely to mislead as to aid Americans' thinking. We make one exception to this rule. The West German system, on which good information is available, poses a useful starting point for developing a model of draft-based national service.

Since the institution of conscription in the Federal Republic of Germany in 1956, a substantial effort has been made to expand the size of the German military forces and to shorten terms so that all eligible males would serve.[10] At the same time, three alternatives to military and paramilitary service have been recognized. From a cohort of some 475,000 eighteen-year-old men in 1979, for example, approximately 17,000 were exempted from the draft in return for a 10-year commitment to unpaid service in the Technical Aid Service, a federally administered civil defense–disaster relief program.[1] Participation requires about 7 hours every other week for 10 months a year, or about 140 hours per year.[2] A smaller number of men (fewer than a thousand) were exempted from military service in return for participation in the German Overseas Development Services. These services are roughly analogous to the Peace Corps but involve long periods of training before assignment abroad, typically when a participant is in his or her late twenties (female volunteers are accepted).

Most significant, 30,000 COs were enlisted in an alternative civilian program principally dedicated to providing social services.[13] Between 1957 and 1977, the percentage of conscripts in a given 1-year age cohort who asserted conscientious objection rose from 1.1 to 13.3 percent and has since stayed at roughly that level.[14]

Within the past decade, this swelling demand for alternative civilian service opportunities has been accompanied by a governmental willingness to grant the opportunities. Two phenomena have combined to produce this effect. First, social service agencies apparently have come to respect and desire alternative service workers, with the result that requests for service workers consistently have outrun their availability, as is evident from figure 6–1. Noting these numbers, one foreign observer of the German experience has concluded that "the social importance of the [COs] is not negligible: in 1977 for instance, 20% of the ancillary personnel in hospitals were [COs], and many non-profit welfare organizations could not operate (survive) without them."[15]

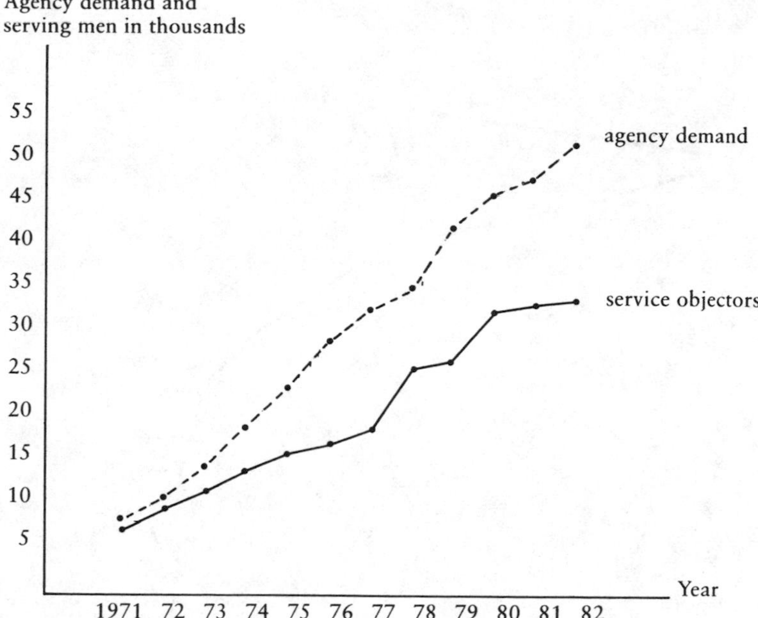

Source: J. Kuhlman, "Linkages Between Military Service and Alternative National Service in West Germany." p. 26.

Figure 6–1. Demand for and Supply of Conscientious Objectors in German Civil Community Services from 1971–1982

Second, perhaps because alternative service increasingly has been accepted as a social service of value, there has been a decreasing inclination to attempt to read the hearts of COs. In recent years, three-quarters of the claims of conscientious objection were sustained by review boards.[16] In 1984, the Bundestag responded to this situation by establishing eligibility for alternative social service on the basis simply of a self-declaration of conscientious objection to military service.[17]

This suggests an interesting possibility for a U.S. draft-based national service program. If a draft were resumed, this country, like Germany, would probably be troubled by the problem of conscientious objection. Figure 6–2 shows a very approximate estimate of the number of COs for the years between 1952 and 1972. The dip at the end of this graph is misleading. By 1972, the draft had been reduced to 15 percent of its 1970 size[18] in anticipation of its termination in 1973, and the Selective Service System, swamped by applications for CO status, apparently stopped processing them. A June 1970 Supreme Court decision expanding the basis for claims of conscientious objection[19] would have increased greatly the number of objectors had the draft been continued at earlier levels.[20]

Figure 6–2. Approximate Numbers of Classified U.S. Conscientious Objectors, 1952–1972

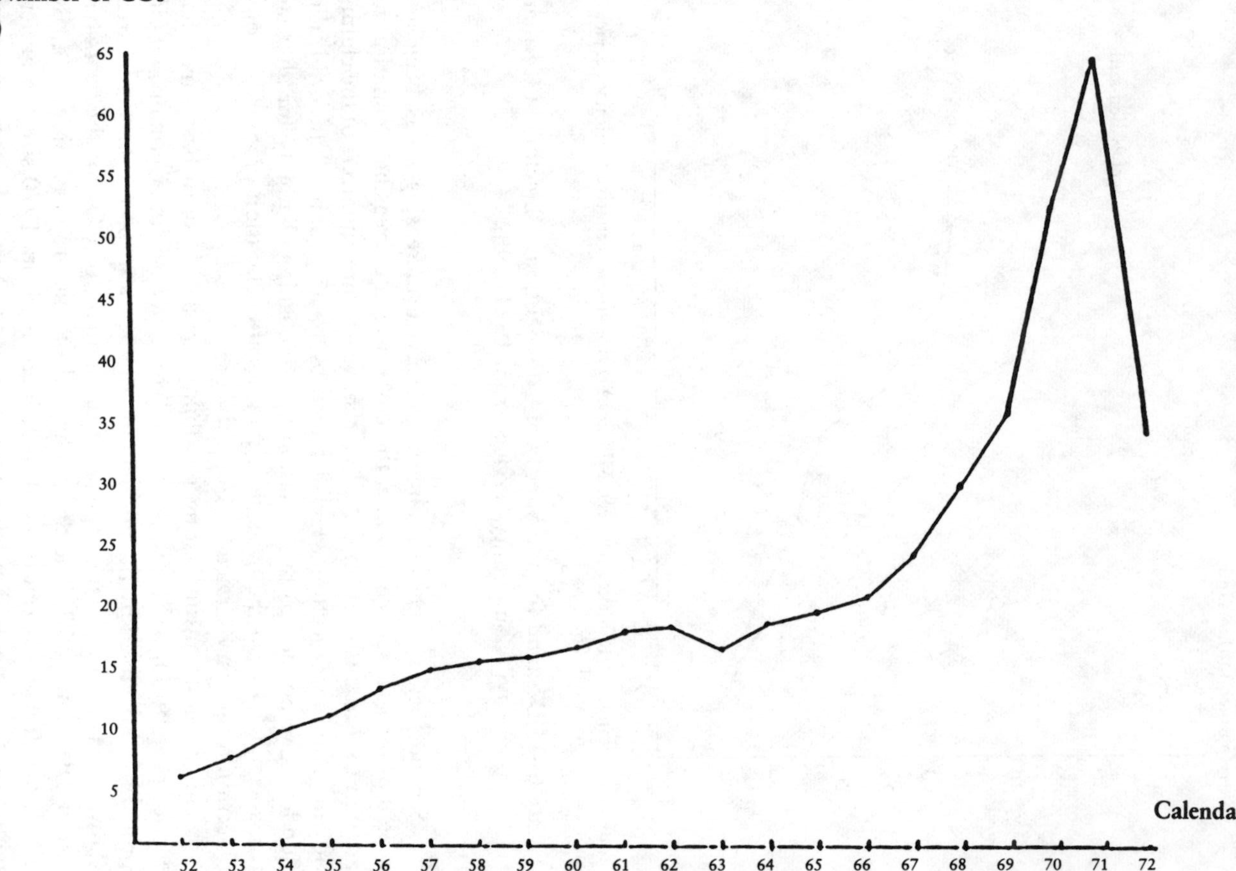

Source: This figure is drawn from Lacy "The Draft," Ch. 7, *passim*. Lacy drew his information from the semiannual reports of the director of the Selective Service System to Congress.

There is remarkable uncertainty about the number of CO applicants and even about the number who achieved this status. The principal data sources are the semiannual reports of the director of Selective Service. From these reports, Baskir and Strauss estimated that there were 171,700 classified COs from among the Vietnam generation of approximately 26.8 million men. Baskir and Strauss, *Chance and Circumstance,* 30, 280. (The Vietnam generation is defined to include those who were between twenty-three and thirty-eight on June 30, 1977, and therefore were theoretically liable to the draft during the period of the Vietnam conflict. Ibid., 276.)

Working with the same sources, Lacy concludes that the number of applicants for CO status cannot be confidently asserted principally because of poor record keeping and the Selective Service System's aversion to showing large numbers of CO classifications. Apparently if CO applicants could be deferred on other grounds, the Selective Service boards typically ignored the CO application and awarded the deferment on this alternative basis. In the later draft years, many of those with high lottery numbers probably did not bother to apply for CO status or were not so classified by the Selective Service System. The figure represents Lacy's best approximation.

The CO issue poses more than a problem of numbers. In the United States as in Germany, success in asserting conscientious objection is strongly correlated to educational attainment and access to counseling, thereby linking it to higher socioeconomic status.[21] In this light, the hard and distasteful process of reading hearts is morally questionable.

If a draft were resumed, many might conclude that the United States should follow the German example and recognize conscientious objection whenever it was asserted and alternative civilian service accepted. But this logic might well lead to something further. If the concept of civilian service commanded public support, a conscript might be afforded a choice between military and equivalently burdensome civilian service without having to assert that he was a CO.

A system of this sort would have attractions beyond those that would derive from circumventing a thicket of CO problems. Such a system might secure many of the same ends as the National Service Secretariat–McCloskey program but without its requirement for gambling on a potential draft liability. A system of free choice on notice of induction might alleviate resistance to a military draft by providing an alternative for those conscripts who found military service especially repugnant. It also would be attractive to the military by filtering out conscripts who were resistant to military life.

Perhaps most significant, an option of this character might appeal to those who wished to make service as nearly universal an experience as possible. Since World War II, it probably has been only during the period between the Korean and Vietnam wars (when about 50 percent of the male cohort served in the military on active or reserve duty) that military service has been viewed as a widely shared rite of passage.[22] With the sharp increase in the size of the male cohort in the late 1960s, offset only partially by later declines, it is likely that only about 20 to 25 percent will serve in the military in the 1980s, without major increases in the size of the armed forces.[23] Even if the military were expanded by a draft of 160,000 men, fewer than 33 percent of all males would serve. Participation of at most one in three men may establish a sense of ill luck and inequity rather than an expectation of service, especially among the 160,000 men (fewer than 10 percent of the cohort) who actually would be drafted. In contrast, poll data described on p. 144 suggest that, with a civilian option at the time of notice of induction, the portion of the male cohort serving would increase to between 40 and 50 percent, with the fraction of those actually drafted doubling to almost 20 percent.

This growth in the numbers of those affected by a draft would render service more acceptable, at least to some, by making it more nearly universal. To the virtue of flexibility, therefore, would be added the virtue of more widespread burden sharing.

Such a program also would generate a substantial civilian service work force and therefore a social work product of potential significance. That product would have some value in and of itself. To some, the placing of civilian and military service on a par would have additional value as a statement of Americans' priorities.

Each of these possible attractions has its countervailing objection. Many would view the increase in the fraction of the cohort serving as an insubstantial gain, since nothing like universal service from those able to serve would be achieved.[24] Others would regard a larger draft as inherently more objectionable than a smaller one, even if it provided the option of civilian service, simply because it subjected a larger number of citizens to governmental compulsion. Some might believe the program's opportunity for alternative civilian service would erode the special significance of military service or the special character of conscientious objection. And the military might suffer more from the frequent choice of civilian service by conscripts from high socioeconomic backgrounds than it would gain from the filtering out of those men who resented military service.

Nonetheless, we believe that a program of this type would be proposed if a perceived need to return to a military draft arose.[25] Accordingly, we have focused on this type of plan as program 2. In the balance of this chapter, we develop its particulars and estimate its probable effects.

Program Particulars

Program 2 assumes a future return to a draft drawing 100,000 to 225,000 men into the military each year. For purposes of analysis, we assume that, on average, 160,000 men will be conscripted into military service annually. Program 2 provides that on receipt of an induction notice, normally between his nineteenth and twentieth birthdays, a conscript may choose to enter either military or civilian service. Evidence presented later suggests that roughly half of those drafted would choose military service.[26] Thus, draft calls likely would have to be issued to about 320,000 youths, yielding 160,000 civilian NSPs along with the 160,000 military inductees. To guard against the possibility, particularly great in times of tension or war, that too few men may opt for military service or that the groups entering the military and civilian programs might be quite different in racial composition or socioeconomic status, the president would be authorized to suspend the program in the interest of national security. More routinely, ratios of military to civilian pay or particulars as to terms and conditions of service might be adjusted administratively to achieve a desired balance.

What might civilian NSPs be paid, and by whom? The traditional U.S. program for COs has provided that private sector employers pay COs as they would any other employee. At the opposite pole, the German government pays those engaged in alternative service an equivalent of the military wage and asks nothing from the private (nonprofit) employer. Taking an intermediate position, Representative Bingham proposed that employers pay the minimum wage, two-thirds of it to the civilian NSPs and the remaining portion to the federal government. This last requirement was intended to diminish the incentive to hire COs merely as cheap labor.[27]

Choices between these and other approaches to this question are highly debatable and reflect differences in underlying goals. Our view is that the most attractive approach would be to pay civilian NSPs at the same rate as entering soldiers (about $600 per month, slightly above the minimum wage) and to divide the obligation for that payment equally between the federal government and the employer. We set pay at this level because we think the burden of conscription should not be compounded by the burden of subminimum wages. We allocated half the cost to the federal government because we would want to encourage nonprofit enterprises to undertake ventures that could not be afforded with full-cost labor power. We allocated the other half to the employer because we value the discipline that spending some of its own money would impose.

We further assume that both military and civilian service draftees would serve for terms of 2 years. But since the military draftee would run the risk of combat and would maintain, as a member of the Individual Ready Reserve (IRR), a 6-year postservice risk of call-up in the event of a military mobilization, we assume that military draftees would enjoy postseparation educational benefits not available to civilian NSPs.[28] We also assume that military benefits would include room, board, and housing (or a housing allowance) for dependents, but that these would not be provided for civilian NSPs.[29]

The civilian option might nonetheless prove so attractive as to require very large draft calls to provide sufficient military recruits. In such an event, the term of civilian service might be extended, perhaps to 3 years. Civilian service also might be rendered less attractive by restricting the choice of civilian assignment or increasing the bonuses or postservice benefits for those choosing the military option. In any event, we believe that, under current conditions, a 2-year term for civilian service, like that for the Peace Corps, would be a reasonable starting point.

Under program 2 as we envision it, those within the military would be subject to discipline and assignment to tasks and locations as they are now. With some modifications, those within the civilian program would operate under rules similar to those that historically have controlled the CO program.[30] The major characteristics of the civilian program would be these:

First, a federal civilian national service agency would be established to certify national service positions. As in program 1, governments, government programs (including VISTA and the Peace Corps), and charitable institutions or public associations meeting the standards of section 501(c)(3) of the Internal Revenue Code would qualify as employers.[31] As in program 1, national service positions could not displace regular salaried jobs and would exclusively involve nonprofit, nonsectarian, and nonpolitical work. Organizations that refused national service applicants, abused or misused NSPs, failed to provide a suitable work environment, or falsely certified work allegedly done by national service workers could be decertified as acceptable places of employment.

Second, because NSPs would be healthy, adult, 2-year employees, half of whose salaries would be paid by the federal government, competition for NSPs—and therefore qualifications for receiving them—would be more demanding than under program 1. Would-be employers would apply for NSPs, and positions would be certified only to the extent that the applications demonstrated realistic plans to use them in effective ways for the public benefit.

Third, lists of approved organizations and jobs would be distributed to local national service offices, and they, in return, would provide them to any eighteen- or nineteen-year-old who requested the information. Prospective NSPs might develop new national service positions by direct contact with qualifying organizations and could submit proposed position descriptions, countersigned by the sponsoring agency, to the national service office for approval.[32]

Many of those who preferred the civilian national service option to the military option probably would arrange placements in advance of induction. The lottery system and the resulting predictable progression through the draft pool would make receipt of an induction notice foreseeable for several weeks in advance of an actual call. Program 2 also would provide for a 21-day delay (subject to presidential waiver for reasons of national security) between a notice to appear for induction and actual induction.

Fourth, on appearing for induction, a conscript would select either civilian or military national service. Those who selected military service would begin service immediately. Those who arranged approved civilian jobs would submit evidence of that fact to the national service office and start those jobs at the beginning of the next civilian pay period. For NSPs who had not arranged approved jobs, the national service office would assign interviews for approved jobs over the next 3 weeks. If no placement were made within this period, the federal government would act as an employer of last resort. Placements in federal facilities in the NSP's community would be preferred, but as an employer of last resort, the federal government could place an NSP in activities outside his or her community to work, for example, in a VA (Veterans Administration) hospital in another city or in a conservation camp similar to those run by the CCC in the 1930s.

Fifth, failure to report for induction would be punishable under the draft laws. (Under current law, punishment could entail fines of up to $10,000 and/or imprisonment for up to 5 years.[33])

Sixth, the federal government would provide health insurance at Medicare levels to civilian NSPs. Employers of civilian NSPs would bear all training and supervisory costs. Under this program, unlike program 1, employers would be permitted to hire NSPs into regular jobs as soon as their terms of national service ended.

Finally, NSPs employed in civilian service would be subject to discipline only by their employers unless excessive absence, misbehavior, or incompetence warranted a complaint to the supervising national service office, in which case that office would review matters. If it determined that the individual was performing satisfactorily, the office would seek to have him continued in the same position, in part by noting the risk of decertification to the employing organization. Alternatively, the office could place the NSP in a new position with credit for his previous service. If his work had not been satisfactory, the office could reassign the NSP but refuse to credit time served or discharge the NSP from the program. Those who did not complete their national service obligation, whether because of discharge or by their own choice, would be subject to induction into the military and prosecution for failure to report for induction.[34]

Should the Program Accept Volunteers?

The question of whether to accept volunteers for the civilian component of program 2 is a difficult one. A volunteer system can be integrated into a conscription system with only minor difficulty, as the military has demonstrated during periods of conscription. As with the military, both men and women could be permitted to volunteer even though only men would be subject to a draft.[35] Volunteers might be limited to nineteen-year-olds who met the mental and moral standards established for military volunteers. Physical standards also could be set, although these likely would be less stringent than military physical standards because of the differences in physical demands associated with civilian jobs.

The arguments for and against accepting volunteers highlight differences in rationales for the program. If the social utility of the work done by a civilian national service corps is taken to be of prime importance, or if the dominant purpose is to provide the experience of service to as large a fraction of youth as possible, then it would be perverse to exclude qualified volunteers for any but budgetary reasons or a lack of qualifying assignments. If the draft continues to be limited by law to males, it is only by permitting volunteers that program 2 could admit women and thus offer national service opportunities to a whole age cohort. Conversely, if program 2 were adopted principally to make a military conscription system more palatable by providing some freedom of choice and circumventing CO issues, accepting those who had not been drafted would only increase costs and blur the character of the program.

We have no strong intuition as to how these conflicting purposes would be resolved if program 2 were enacted. For purposes of discussion, we assume an outcome that we think is plausible and that does not weight our analysis too heavily in either direction. This is that draft-age volunteers (male and female) would be accepted but that their numbers would be capped at about 40,000 per year, or at 20 percent of the average size we would anticipate for the civilian program. Where relevant in the following pages, we will point out the consequences for the overall program of accepting this volunteer component.

Impact on the Military

By hypothesis, program 2 would come into existence only when the nation reinstituted a military draft. Demands for recruits would exceed the supply of volunteers as a result of either a decision to increase the armed forces or a diminution in the number of qualified young men volunteering. In either circumstance, program 2 would appear attractive to the military insofar as it lessened resistance to the draft.

It seems very likely, however, that from a military perspective, the civilian service aspect of program 2 would be best avoided if possible. This would be so for three reasons, none of them individually devastating but all together disadvantageous.

Quantity of Recruits

The least serious disadvantage relates to the most basic question of supply: Would the military reliably get enough conscripts to meet its needs? On designing his program in 1970, Representative Bingham was quite concerned as to whether all young men would decline military and choose civilian service. Without the benefit of empirical evidence, and against the backdrop of the Vietnam War, he concluded that "This would be a very serious problem if the potential draftee were allowed to opt for civilian service *after* being selected for induction."[36]

Although the evidence is only rudimentary, Representative Bingham's conclusion seems to us to be wrong. In 1979 and 1981, the Gallup Organization put to eighteen- and nineteen-year-old males the following question: "Suppose all young men were required to give one year of service, which would you prefer—military or nonmilitary?" VISTA and the Peace Corps were given as examples of nonmilitary service. In 1982, Gallup put a similar

Table 6–1
Youth Preferences As Between Military and Nonmilitary Service

Gallup Survey	*Age*	*Sample Size*	*Choice*	*Percent*
March 1979	18–19	49	Military	47
			Nonmilitary	49
			No Opinion	4
June 1981	18–19	88	Military	44
			Nonmilitary	42
			No Opinion	14
December 1982	16–18	131	Military	47
			Nonmilitary	53
April–June 1984	16–18	125 (?)[a]	Military	49
			Nonmilitary	46

[a]The published data on this poll reflect a sample of 504 thirteen- to eighteen-year-old males and females. Gallup's report implies that one-quarter of this sample were males, ages sixteen to eighteen. There are no separate data on choice of service for this subset of males, but Gallup notes no differences appeared by age in the type of service preferred. A greater uncertainty in interpreting these data is introduced by the fact that apparently only the 60 percent of males who indicated that they favored national service were asked which branch of service they would prefer. Gallup, "Majority of Teens Favors National Youth Service."

question to sixteen- to eighteen-year-old males but included help for the elderly and work in hospitals as examples of civilian service. In 1984, this question was put to thirteen- to eighteen-year-olds. The responses were rather consistent across the four samples. As seen in table 6–1, they suggest an approximately even split between military and civilian service among those at or approaching draft age.[37]

These numbers suggest that to draw 160,000 men into the military in any given year, induction orders would have to be issued to roughly 320,000 qualified men, about half of whom probably would select civilian service and half military service.

This is hardly conclusive evidence. The sample sizes are small, and some of the information is dated. Even much larger and more current surveys would not be conclusive. Not until a specific program was adopted would it be clear how the nineteen-year-olds of that time would act.

It remains true, however, that the youth cohort is so large relative to any likely military demand in peacetime that even if four out of five conscripts chose civilian service (a highly unlikely ratio),[38] 160,000 military conscripts still could be obtained each year from among eligible men turning nineteen. Further, as long as the president retained the power to suspend the system, the risk of obtaining too low a military participation rate seems to us to be negligible.

Quality of Recruits

A more substantial difficulty arises not from the number of conscripts electing civilian service but rather from their character. One of the criticisms of the present all-volunteer military is that it tends not to draw a representative share of the most educated and the most privileged of the nation's youth. To the extent that a draft operated randomly, it would produce an evenly distributed population of military recruits. If those who scored in the lowest 20 percent on the Armed Forces Qualification Test were disqualified, for example, one in eight of those conscripted would score in the top 10 percent and half would score above 60 percent.

The option of civilian as opposed to military service introduces a sorting that would not be random. One of the advantages of program 2 would arise from its tendency to filter those with a distaste for the military out of the pool of military entrants. But if the highest test scorers and the best educated members of the cohort predominantly selected civilian service, and the lowest scorers and the least educated selected military service, then program 2 would yield less able military recruits than would a traditional military draft.

The very fragmentary polling evidence reinforces this concern. In the 1984 Gallup survey, "those from blue-collar backgrounds were . . . more likely to express preference for military service (43 percent vs. 31 percent of teens from white collar households)."[39] More seriously, of the eighteen- to nineteen-year-old men who chose military over civilian service in the Gallup surveys, only 47 percent were high school graduates. By comparison, roughly 68 percent of that cohort now graduates from high school,[40] and the draft in two representative years (1964 and 1971) yielded a military recruit population of which 69 and 68 percent, respectively, were high school graduates.[41]

This information comports with what is known from surveys conducted for the Department of Defense of the propensity of sixteen- to twenty-year-old males to enlist in the military. Defining a positive propensity as an interviewee's statement that he will definitely or probably be serving in at least one of the active duty services in the next few years, a 1982 survey contrasts positive and negative propensity groups as shown in table 6–2.

These data are indicative[42] of a problem. The problem could be addressed by manipulating civilian and military entrance criteria or incentives. But this manipulation, it should be noted, has its costs. As it is, conscription standards eliminate roughly 30 percent of any male year-of-birth group; higher standards might exempt a distressingly large proportion of the population or create perverse incentives. (If high school graduation were a prerequisite to conscription, for example, graduation rates might decline.) The use of incentives such as higher pay and educational aid to choose military rather than civilian service would be more practical, but it also would be expensive.

Table 6–2
Demographic Analysis of Males with Positive and Negative Propensities for Military Service

	Percent of the Positive Propensity Group	*Percent of the Negative Propensity Group*
Race/Ethnicity		
White[a]	66.1	82.5
Black[a]	20.3	8.1
Hispanic[a]	11.1	6.9
Other	2.4	2.5
Employment Status		
Employed fulltime[a]	19.3	33.8
Employed parttime	25.9	27.5
Not employed, looking for a job[a]	41.2	21.7
Not employed, not looking for a job[a]	13.6	17
Ever Employed Fulltime		
Yes[a]	57.3	67.4
No[a]	42.7	32.6
Educational Level Completed		
Less than 10th grade[a]	12	4.9
10th grade[a]	25.2	13.8
11th grade[a]	29.2	19.9
12th grade[a]	26.9	42.7
Some college or vocational school[a]	6.7	18.8
Mean number of years of school completed[a]	10.89	11.59
Age (Mean Value)[a]	18.18	18.81
Educational Status		
Student[a]	60.8	56
Nonstudent[a]	39.2	44
Type of High School Curriculum		
Vocational	50.9	36.3
Business/Commercial	15.5	16.1
College Preparatory[a]	31.9	45.4
Did Not Attend/Did Not Know	1.7	2.3

Source: The data in this table were taken from Market Facts, Inc., "Youth Attitude Tracking Study, Fall 1982," 14. More recent comparable data have been published in Research Triangle Institute, "Youth Attitude Tracking Study II, Fall 1983," 41. This report yields fundamentally the same results, though not all the categories are precisely the same.

[a]Difference between the two groups is significant at the 95 percent level of confidence.

Volunteers

The third difficulty with program 2 from the Pentagon's perspective arises from the fact that the military would almost certainly continue to seek volunteers even under a draft regime. In drafts since World War II, conscription has been used almost exclusively for the Army. The Air Force, Navy, and Marine Corps have been almost entirely manned by volunteers. Even the Army has used conscription only to obtain about half of its enlisted recruits; officers' positions and jobs requiring longer training normally were restricted to volunteers. Volunteers are important to the military both because conscription is unpopular and therefore to be avoided as much as possible and because volunteers normally obligate themselves to serve 3 or more years, while peacetime conscripts typically serve 2 years.

But program 2 impedes volunteering. This is because the men it draws into civilian service would be available as potential soldiers either in a purely voluntary system or under conscription. By contrast, program 2 would pay them a soldier's wage not to be soldiers. Since these men had not volunteered and, as conscripts, chose civilian rather than military service, one may infer that they had a relatively low propensity for military service and that only a minority might have been successfully recruited. But if only one in eight of the civilian NSPs had been recruited successfully into the military, this would still amount to 20,000 volunteers. Thus, 20,000 volunteers would be lost to civilian national service.[43]

In sum, although program 2 might be attractive to a draft proponent for political reasons, its practical consequences for the military would be undesirable. Military conscription could work with a civilian alternative, but it would not work as well as it would without that alternative. The civilian component would introduce challenges and expenses that otherwise could be avoided. If the AVF were failing, conscription with a civilian option might seem a price worth paying to achieve any conscription at all. But the Pentagon probably would prefer conscription without national service.

Program Participants

Program 2 would produce a civilian national service work force with three limiting characteristics. First, although a small fraction of women and other age groups would participate as volunteers, for the most part (given the numerical limits we have imposed) program 2 NSPs would be nineteen- or twenty-year-old males. The range of skills available for service work would therefore be more limited than in programs 3 and 4, which would draw from other segments of the population. Doctors, nurses, trained teachers, and experienced organizers, for example, would not be represented significantly in a pool of nineteen-year-old men. Second, the number of civilian program 2 participants is likely to fluctuate as both military draft calls and preferences between the military and civilian forms of service vary. Third, even if the number of NSPs remained constant, their geographic locations, skills, and interests would vary over time. That might make it difficult to rely on NSPs as the sole source of labor power for given assignments. It also would make preparations for replacing NSPs as they moved out of jobs more important. This phase-out is of particular concern because there is very little history of successful dealing with such problems.[44]

Still, individual program 2 NSPs in some respects would be unusually attractive potential employees. Having met draft criteria, they would be competent, healthy young adults without serious criminal records, available for 2-year assignments, with half their salaries paid by the federal government. They would be subject to criminal discipline for incomplete or grossly unsatisfactory job performance.[45] And their selection of civilian service, and in many instances their choice of a particular job, would create for some a psychological commitment similar to that of traditional volunteers. At a minimum, then, program 2 NSPs would have many of the attributes that characterize good paraprofessionals. Which forms of public work are most likely to utilize such NSPs effectively? And to what extent would social gains thereby be accomplished?

Impact on Social and Environmental Services

As is true for the other programs we discuss, it is exceedingly difficult to assess the social value of the services that would be rendered by program 2 NSPs. Given that there is no accepted calculus for computing the value of libraries, environmental improvements, schools, or child care, there can be little confidence in an estimate of the incremental value of contributions to them by NSPs. Further, given the substantial freedom of choice between public service assignments that we assume for program 2, it is difficult to predict how these NSPs would distribute themselves and therefore whether they would undertake particularly high value assignments. This section provides some insight into the likely impact of the program by hypothesizing a plausible pattern of assignments and assessing the increase in services that would result from it.

Assignments in Schools

Schools appear to be a natural arena for NSPs in the school-based program 1, but that setting is less attractive for program 2 participants. This is true despite the fact that, as our education consultant notes, "schools have much

Vietnam era experience with [CO] 'war dodgers,' and much is favorable."[46] Vietnam-era COs served for the most part when the military draft called twenty-six-year-olds first and eighteen-year-olds last. In consequence, although we find no data on the point, it appears that COs who served in schools typically were in their twenties and college educated. Paid at regular teachers' wages, they were given regular teaching jobs. As a result of the later restructuring of the draft to call nineteen- and twenty-year-olds first, program 2 NSPs would be younger and less educated than their alternative-service predecessors. In the main, they would not be college graduates, nor would they be likely to be so mature as to warrant giving them unsupervised responsibility for groups of students. This suggests that program 2 NSPs would be used mainly in support roles as teachers' aides, tutors, athletic instructors, and administrative or maintenance personnel.

These are the positions that we thought program 1 NSPs might fill, but we doubt the social utility of assigning program 2 NSPs to such roles. Program 1 would provide very young workers for a few hours at a time over a short period; using them in familiar settings where they were already obliged to be would have obvious advantages. The older program 2 participants would serve for 2 years on a full-time basis. They could be better used for more demanding jobs. Moreover, many, we believe, would be underutilized in tutoring and would prefer settings less familiar than schools.[47] As a consequence, we do not believe that many NSPs would or should pursue school assignments under this program.

Assignments in Child Care

Assignments in child care seem to us to be modestly promising. The relatively small number of program 2 participants ensures that, as in the case of program 1, program 2 would produce no large-scale impact on child care. Child care might seem familiar and insufficiently demanding and challenging to the NSPs and to the public asked to equate it with military service. Nonetheless, some NSPs might be put to good use in this context. Although still young, program 2 NSPs would be emotionally and physically more mature than program 1 NSPs. They would therefore require somewhat less supervision, a substantial advantage in child care settings outside of relatively well-staffed and well-administered child care centers. Their 2-year service period would justify as much training as a child care center's practice or state licensing requirements made necessary, and it would permit NSPs, toward the end of their terms of service, to supervise newer NSPs or other young providers of child care. The children cared for by program 2 participants would be likely to benefit from contact with these NSPs, some of whom, unlike the very large majority of current child care workers,[48] would be male and middle class.

As would be true of all young NSPs assigned to child care, there would be some benefit, difficult to measure but possibly substantial in degree, to the children the NSPs later reared. The education for parentage that national service might provide NSPs would be particularly intense in program 2, since its longer term of service would justify training in child development and would in any event give NSPs extended experience with a variety of children, often in increasingly responsible roles.

Health Care Assignments

Health care might provide especially appropriate settings for the assignment of these NSPs. The opportunities that are most striking to us are in home health care and preventive programs. As noted in chapter 2, both areas face a shortage of workers and are unlikely (at present prices) to satisfy a strong demand for services through the balance of this century. Whereas program 1 NSPs assigned to home care likely would be limited to providing companionship and simple shopping and housework aid, program 2 NSPs could be expected to do more. The age, good health, full-time commitment, and 2-year term of service of these NSPs would justify both the initial investments in training them and the administrative costs of matching participants with patients and monitoring and supervising their performance.

The home care activities of these NSPs might include rudimentary medical work (checking pulse, respiration, and temperature; changing dressings; assisting with and recording consumption of medication) and physical therapy (helping with prescribed exercises and walks; assisting with braces, artificial limbs, and hydraulic lifts). Basic personal support activities (shopping, cooking, bathing, cleaning, transporting the person to the hospital or doctors' offices) also might be undertaken, as might tasks such as assistance with medical paperwork and representation required to ensure insurance benefits or coverage by various social service programs.

As our health consultants write:

> [H]omemaker-health service[s] . . . are among the fastest growing type of health care services, increasing from 60,000 personnel in 1974 to 300,000 in 1982. Their growth is mainly due to increased federal funding . . . through Medicare, Medicaid, and Title XX (Social Services) of the Social Security Act.[49]

At least four beneficial effects might result from the assignment of program 2 NSPs to home care.

First, in cases that are especially difficult or have been plagued (as many are) by a high turnover of home care workers, NSPs may prove far more effective than relatively transient hourly workers.[50] Second, most program 2 NSPs would be men; this would broaden the repertoire of program administrators whose pool of workers now is overwhelmingly female.[51] In some instances, young men may be especially valued because of their strength; in others, they may be less embarrassing providers of care or better able than women to provide psychological support. Under any conditions, variety in home care providers would be a gain. Observers of the German program have commented that this experience demonstrates that young men can care effectively for aged persons and that both the served and the serving often derive strong satisfaction from the experience.

Third, the increase in the absolute numbers of home care workers could be far more significant than would be the case either in schools or in child care. If 1 out of every 4 conscripted NSPs in a 160,000-NSP annual program were to enter home health care, the effect would be to increase the number of providers by almost 25 percent. Another 10 percent gain might be achieved if 1 in 3 of the hypothesized 40,000 volunteer NSPs chose this type of work. Moreover, because of the federal subsidy of half their wages, these workers would cost the providing agency only half of what a regular worker would cost. Of course, such an increase also could be accomplished without establishing a national service system by a grant system or by authorizing Medicare funds. Apparently, there is no current willingness to make such expenditures; thus, national service might indirectly generate more home health care than society is now willing to pay for directly. One will approve or disapprove of this result according to whether one believes—as our health consultants and we do—that present mechanisms underfund home care.

Fourth, we expect that exposing healthy young people to the world of the incapacitated would have a subtler long-term benefit. As relatively uncalloused providers while they serve, potential documenters of what they observe, and in a variety of roles later in life, some NSPs would be likely to draw society's attention to needs and abuses that otherwise are easily overlooked, much as VISTA volunteers of the 1960s called attention to black lung disease and the then inadequate means of either preventing or compensating for it.[52]

Environmental Tasks

As discussed in chapter 5, there are many constraints on the assignment of part-time, school-based NSPs in program 1 to environmental tasks. None of these constraints applies to program 2 NSPs. The participants produced by a draft-based program would serve long enough to justify their transportation to and lodging in remote rural areas; they are old enough to be licensed to use any necessary equipment; and having been draftable, they are, by definition, not too young to be exposed to the dangers of responding to fires or floods.

In short, program 2 NSPs seem ideally suited to environmental tasks:

young, healthy, physically fit, and likely to respond well to the sharp change of setting that, for most of them, environmental work in remote areas would involve. In these respects, program 2 NSPs resemble the young men who flocked to the CCC in the 1930s.

Program 2 NSPs could undertake not only the limited range of largely urban environmental tasks described in chapter 5 but also the full range of work in forestry (tree planting, brush control, maintenance of logging roads); habitat improvement (stream clearing, stream bank stabilization, maintenance of hatcheries); soil and water conservation (construction of sediment traps and water and wind barriers; removal of brush; planting of trees, shrubs, and grasses); recreation (construction and maintenance of trails and campgrounds); and response to fires, floods, storms, and human disasters. These tasks are particularly appropriate for national service because although they require little skill, they are not regarded as demeaning, can be physically challenging, and can leave behind satisfyingly tangible results.

In addition to these advantages to the participants, there are advantages to society in environmental assignments of NSPs. One is that, as noted earlier, they are low-risk assignments. Poor or neglectful performance in most environmental tasks would create far less risk of lasting damage than correspondingly poor performance in health, child care, or even school assignments. Second, conservation tasks involve comparatively little risk of substantial displacement of paid workers. The concern is still there, as union resistance to recent proposals for an American Conservation Corps remind us. But the current market for environmental workers is small, and the use of NSPs in environmental tasks might enlarge it by creating a new demand for NSP supervisors and leaders. In addition, unlike health care, child care, and school-based tasks, most environmental tasks need not be performed on a regular basis or at consistent levels of effort over time. That fact neutralizes one of the potential difficulties with program 2—namely, that changes in draft calls or in the propensity of draftees to choose military versus civilian service would make the maintenace of consistent levels of effort in program 2 very difficult.

Finally, the relatively small size of the conservation sector in the U.S. economy means that the assignment of any substantial fraction of even the relatively small number of program 2 NSPs to environmental tasks might reduce greatly the backlog of those tasks. Our hypothesized program 2 would involve about 200,000 new civilian NSPs per year, each serving for 2 years. As detailed in chapter 2, our environmental consultant, Perry Hagenstein, concludes that about 165,000 full-time environmental tasks would be appropriate for assignment to NSPs. If even one-fifth of the 400,000 NSPs serving in program 2 after the first year undertook environmental tasks, they could perform nearly half of those assignments. This would multiply the number of full-time persons now assigned to such tasks by a factor of eight or nine.[53]

A difficulty may arise from the length of service in program 2. Especially for conscripted service in remote places and in barrackslike quarters, 2 years is a long time. The CCC sought enlistments initially for only 6 months, later extendable to 1 year. Yet despite the powerful economic attraction of the program in the depths of the Depression, the average length of service in the CCC has been estimated at only 9 weeks. Similarly, the current California Conservation Corps has an attrition rate of approximately 71 percent over the length of its 1-year program.[54]

These are warning signs for program 2. Its conscripts, of course, would be performing civilian services as an alternative to a military draft, so attrition would be diminished by threat of induction. It also is true that what is being asked of the program's NSPs is no more than is asked of many military draftees: service in remote places under spartan conditions. At a minimum, however, the morale problems foreseeably associated with these assignments suggest costs (for supervision, recreation, housing, and away-from-site rest and relaxation) that would diminish the program's net benefits.[55]

Other Social Services

Program 2 participants also might prove useful in a variety of other social services. In the realm of criminal justice and public safety, for example, NSPs might be used to assist in the report writing and record keeping that loom large in routine police work. They also might be assigned to victim assistance programs, to drug abuse prevention or minor offender friendship programs, to tutoring prison inmates in basic skills, or to work in recreation or job development programs for minor offenders.

As in the case of program 1, program 2 NSPs might be used in libraries and museums, both to assist in providing basic services and to help the staff in various community outreach programs. Unlike program 1 NSPs, program 2 participants would be present on such assignments long enough to justify training and to merit substantial advancements in responsibility over the period of their service. After a brief initial period of formal or on-the-job training, program 2 NSPs could be used for tasks requiring a fairly high degree of responsibility, such as the operation of neighborhood minilibraries, the selection and delivery of reading materials to shut-ins, or the development of exhibits or courses. In general, NSPs probably would be asked to undertake more routine assignments: shelving and cataloguing books, staffing circulation desks, and the like. All in all, however, these contributions could be significant to the library system. If 15 percent of the 400,000 NSPs available each year under program 2 chose to serve in libraries, they would augment total U.S. library staffs by roughly one-fifth. Even where their assignments involved relatively routine tasks, their presence could serve to free a substantial number of professional librarians to undertake more imaginative or more productive tasks.

Similarly, in museums, program 2 NSPs might perform the relatively routine clerical and maintenance functions likely to be assigned to program 1 participants, but they also could be trained to undertake research, docent work, the repair and maintenance of exhibits, and other curatorial assignments.

Finally, we expect that, faced with 2-year assignments, program 2 NSPs would exercise considerable initiative and ingenuity in identifying, from the almost infinite number of possible assignments that a society as diverse as ours might provide, tasks that not only met the requirements of the program, but that the NSPs considered to be of particular interest or value. While these assignments are impossible to catalogue or assess, it seems reasonable to consider that as many as 10 percent of NSPs would seek them and that a high proportion of those assignments, because they fully engaged the interests of the NSPs assigned to them, would prove particularly productive.

The Utility of Program 2 NSPs: A Summary

As we describe in the section titled "Administration and Costs," program 2 would involve far higher dollar costs than program 1, but its participants would produce substantially greater social value than those of program 1. The two reasons for this are simple but powerful: The nineteen- to twenty-two-year-old program 2 NSPs would be more mature than the seventeen- to eighteen-year-old participants in program 1, and the term of their service would be 100 weeks rather than 6. Their greater maturity would enable program 2 NSPs to undertake virtually any assignment suitable to young adults. Their far longer term of service would mean that, depending on the nature of their assignments, training periods of up to 3 or 4 months might be justified economically. In addition, participants could remain in assignments long enough to become far more proficient than school-based NSPs and perhaps to advance to supervisory roles.[56]

Prospective employers, in turn, would view these NSPs as far more significant assets and would take greater care in their assignment and supervision as well as in their training. Correspondingly, the NSPs would tend to take their assignments more seriously, choosing them with greater attention to the skills they might wish to acquire, the career fields they might want to explore, or perhaps simply the tasks they believed they would most enjoy. The net result of these differences should be, on average, a far higher standard of NSP performance in more demanding assignments. Although the impact of program 2 on the NSPs might be substantial (we discuss this in the section titled "Effects on NSPs"), the program would be most significant for its contribution to society in general.

Thus while program 1, consistent with its educational rationale, would serve mainly its participants, program 2, consistent with its service rationale, would serve mainly society. Depending on the skill and seriousness with which it was operated and within the limits imposed by the small size of its civilian component (involving perhaps 5 percent of the age cohort), its participants might greatly improve some aspects of health care, child care, or environmental protection in the United States.

Labor Market Consequences

Program 2, if it came to pass, would probably be brought about either by an expansion in the demand for military labor power or by a diminution in the supply of military volunteers. A dramatic expansion of the armed forces probably would be accompanied by an increase in military budgets and production. If the armed forces, at their present size, failed to draw the required numbers of volunteers, this probably would be because the civilian economy was offering attractive job alternatives.[57] Either circumstance would imply low levels of unemployment. Therefore, one concern might be that program 2's redirection of approximately 160,000 conscripted men and 40,000 volunteers per year to civilian national service could intensify labor power shortages. But the national labor force is now so large (more than 100 million workers) that the effect of withdrawing of redirecting 200,000 workers per year, 400,000 workers at any one time, would be insubstantial. Although unemployment rates for men in the particular age group drafted would diminish by perhaps one-twelfth, the net effect would be to reduce total unemployment by between three-quarters and nine-tenths of 1 percent of the then existing rate.[58] (For example, a 7 percent unemployment rate would be reduced to about 6.94 percent.)

The labor displacement effects of program 2 warrant more attention. In this regard, there are two seemingly contradictory precedents. On the one hand, the CO program of the Viet Nam era apparently had no significant labor market effects, perhaps because there were not a great many COs and they were paid at normal wage rates. In only rare instances—for example, as school teachers in New York in the later 1960s—were they so concentrated as to be noticeable in the labor market. Under these circumstances, their major effect seems to have been a greater than normal turnover in entry-level jobs because, presumably, they left their jobs in greater than normal numbers after their 2-year obligation was fulfilled.[59]

On the other hand, no-substitution rules were a major source of controversy and contention in the CETA public employment programs of the 1970s, and there were numerous charges of layoffs of regular workers in order to hire cheaper CETA workers.[60] Further, an analyst of youth employment programs has calculated that approximately one-third of the work performed by CETA program participants would have been performed by regular workers if the program had not existed and another third would have been partially performed.[61] We infer, as others have done, that about one-half of CETA work displaced work that would have been done by regular employees, the other half being new work.[62] This provides only the roughest estimate of job preemption, but it legitimately may raise fears that as many as 50 percent of program 2 NSPs would displace regular workers.

We think that job displacement would be a significant problem in the administration of program 2. NSPs in the program might be as much as ten times more numerous than COs working during the Vietnam years,[63] and unlike those COs, they would cost their employers only one-half the minimum wage. That generally would be less than half the cost of employees of comparable quality. More significant, program 2 NSPs would be more able, more disciplined, and committed for longer terms than their counterparts under previous government-sponsored employment programs. While the no-displacement requirement for participation in the program might be enforced vigorously enough to prevent many instances of visible substitution, preemptions of new hiring would be far harder to prevent and would occur, we believe, in substantial numbers.

Conversely, program 2 is a federally subsidized job creation program. Notwithstanding the fact that unlike most of its predecessors, it would draw persons who were readily employable, its primary effect would be to create jobs. The program would conscript otherwise employable young men (and would accept 40,000 volunteers) out of the labor force and into civilian national service. It seems reasonable to estimate that about one-half of the entrants into civilian national service would leave open jobs they would otherwise have filled. (The other half would have attended school.) Although the calculation is very crude, it seems a reasonable assessment that in its gross labor market effects, the program would be roughly a wash, freeing jobs and preempting jobs in roughly equal numbers.

Effects on NSPs[64]

In assessing the potential effects of program 2 on the NSPs who would participate in it, we examined three precedents that seem analogous: the experience of COs assigned to civilian service, the consequences of service for military veterans, and the effects of service on Peace Corps returnees.

Unfortunately, the data from these experiences are remarkably limited, the difficulties of properly using that data are substantial, and (not surprisingly) some contradictions appear in the inferences that are drawn from the studies that have been done. There is no useful study of the effects of service as a CO.[65] Of two studies on the Peace Corps, one never progressed from a draft version to a final report.[66] The more numerous military studies rarely address psychological variables and disagree even on basics such as whether veterans are economically advantaged by their military service.

Our observations about the impact of program 2 on its participants are therefore constrained and cautious. We comment here on essentially the same categories of effect discussed in the previous chapter but (reflecting the paucity of evidence) do so under three headings that are somewhat broader than those used previously: effects on future work opportunities and income, effects on attitudes and self-definition, and effects as a potential rite of passage into adult status.

Future Work Opportunities and Income

It is sometimes assumed or asserted that national service might improve the future employment prospects of many of those who serve. There is some disagreement, but to us the weight of the evidence suggests an opposite conclusion. In 1969, a presidential commission charged with recommending whether or not to establish an all-volunteer military commissioned David Kassing, an authority on military labor power, to assess military experience as a determinant of veterans' earnings. After reviewing studies and presenting his own analysis, Kassing summarized their results:

> The thrust of these studies' conclusions is clear and is the same: military service cannot be said to increase the earnings of veterans relative to what these same men would have earned if they had remained in civilian life. The claim that military service "is good for you" is not confirmed by an economic consideration. . . . Rather military service experience has little or no effect on a veteran's attitude or income.[67]

Kassing based his judgment in part on his observations that the military afforded very little training of specific relevance to jobs typically held by veterans in civilian life. He calculated that although approximately 80 percent of those who entered the military received some training relevant to certain civilian occupations, only between one-third and about one-half of the men who left the military looked for a job in the area in which they had been trained; only about two-thirds of those found such a job; and only about three-quarters of them then took the job they found. As a result, only between 15 and about 30 percent of all veterans (the percentage varied by service) ultimately used their military training in civilian jobs. As Kassing observed:

> Men who serve in the military get experience in the military, those who remain civilians get experience in the civilian labor market. This latter experience is generally more relevant for civilian employers than military experience.[68]

The data on relative incomes reviewed by Kassing bear this out. When data were adjusted to control for education, Kassing found that nonveterans earned more than veterans. To the same effect, he noted, a University of Chicago study concluded that "neither military occupation nor length of service has anything to contribute to the income of veterans."[69]

Although less extensive and less carefully analyzed, Peace Corps data point to the same conclusion. A 1969 Louis Harris and Associates study reported the result of interviews with three groups of approximately 300 volunteers, each of whom had completed 2-year terms, and compared them with approximately 400 early terminees and 300 contemporaneous applicants who had declined invitations to join the Peace Corps.[70] In 1978, a second study of similar design was undertaken.[71]

The Harris study concluded that about 16 percent of the returned Peace Corps volunteers and 21 percent of the early terminees switched career plans to enter service-oriented areas,[72] but acknowledged:

> What is most striking about the . . . results is the similarity between the returned Peace Corps Volunteers and [those who declined to enter the corps] in their current jobs. It suggests that the impact of the Peace Corps does not significantly alter the types of job choices volunteers make. Accepting that returned Peace Corps volunteers and [those who declined to enter] started with basically the same set of goals, the fact that they end up in the same kinds of jobs implies that other factors than the Peace Corps influenced their choice.[73]

In numbers roughly analogous to their military counterparts, only about a third of the volunteers, whether early terminees or those who served full term, reported that they had "learned any technical or vocational skills in the Peace Corps which helped them on the job."[74] Most notably, the Harris data showed that "the Peace Corps experience has postponed income growth for the returned Peace Corps volunteers, and consequently, their current income lags behind [the declines, i.e., those who were admitted, but declined to enter the Peace Corps]."[75] The study concluded:

> [T]here can be no question that, in the short run, Peace Corps service puts the two-year volunteer at a disadvantage. A 1966 returned Peace Corps volunteer is earning a median of $6,720, while a 1966 decline is earning a median of $8,875; a 1964 returned Peace Corps volunteer is earning a median of $8,200 while a 1964 decline is earning $9,580.[76]

Just how long the short run would be—indeed, whether it might last over a whole career—is not clear. The passage just quoted shows the gap diminishing over time. As the 1978 study observed, "[V]olunteers who have returned relatively recently tend to earn considerably less than people much like themselves who had declined Peace Corps invitations, [but] this inequity may be corrected as the length of time since the end of service increases."[77] Nonetheless, the study noted that "even among the 1968 returnees, there were fewer individuals with incomes over $20,000 than the national average for family income at the time of the survey."[78]

We would not overstate the significance of this loss. For many returned Peace Corps volunteers and military veterans, the years immediately after service are disadvantaged because of short-term readjustment problems, seniority lag, and time spent catching up within the educational system.[79] In the long term, economic benefits may equalize.

Two recent studies of military veterans support this line of thought. Little and Fredlund focused on men a quarter of a century or so after they had served. They report:

> Depending on the form of the equation and the definition of earnings, white veterans are shown to have earnings 5 to 10% higher than non-veterans, given age, schooling and job tenure. Non-white and black veterans show even larger benefits . . . in the neighborhood of 13 to 15%.[80]

Little and Fredlund comment that they cannot calculate whether this later advantage compensates for the accumulated penalties others have observed earlier in veterans' careers. But some indication along this line is provided by Segal and Segal, in a study on veterans of all ages in Detroit. Taking the entire population of veterans then in the labor force, they found that "there was no significant difference between the veteran and non-veteran groups in either occupation or family income."[81]

In sum, the literature on the economic effects of service supports a skeptical position with respect to arguments that service is notably economically advantageous or disadvantageous. Judging from the precedents, for most, on average, it seems most likely to be neither. In phrasing our conclusion this way, however, we offer an important qualification. Any judgment about effects on average tends to mask different effects that might be experienced by NSPs with different backgrounds and ability levels. There has been intense debate, for example, about whether Hispanics and blacks benefit more from military service than whites.[82] It may be that for some, and particularly for the disadvantaged, a system of service would provide general training (even if not job-specific skills) and a useful bridging mechanism to mainstream jobs. This would not make a strong case for program 2, which conscripts a sample of the whole population and therefore few of the disadvantaged. But as will be seen in the next chapter, it is relevant to discussion of voluntary programs that attempt to be more narrowly targeted at those who would benefit from service.

Attitudes and Self-Definition

The 1969 Harris study of returned Peace Corps volunteers found that "a majority of volunteers see their Peace Corps experience as benefitting them in more general and personal ways rather than helping them along a specific career path."[83] This observation, consistent with earlier studies,[84] was repeated in the 1978 Peace Corps study:

> The Peace Corps experience has an important effect on the returnees' attitudes and plans. The majority said it had "definitely":
> —Broadened their perspective on international affairs (87%);
> —Made them more tolerant of others' conditions, religious beliefs, etc. (69%);
> —Broadened their perspective on national politics (58%); and
> —Made them more mature than other people [their] own age who stayed in the United States (61%).[85]

The same study stressed that "a substantial number of returned volunteers make major commitments of their time to passing along their knowledge about development to other Americans. . . . Most volunteers also become actively involved in community groups, . . . nearly half work with volunteer organizations."[86] This comports with what returned Peace Corps veterans often say. As one recently wrote, "the service ethic in Peace Corps circles is almost Biblical in power."[87]

When the Peace Corps studies moved from measuring former volunteers' views of themselves to assessing their activities in comparison with their peers who had declined invitations to join the Peace Corps, they found, in the words of the later study, that "the decliner group had higher participation in each of the four types of [volunteer, altruistic] organizations in which substantial percentages of returned Peace Corps Volunteers participated."[88]

Both studies reasonably inferred that one cause of this differential might be a lag in participation in society after returning, akin to the lag experienced in the job market. A comparison of returned volunteers with decliners who were 2 years younger showed roughly equal participation rates.[89] This is not, however, a very positive conclusion.

We have no similar data on the activities or the self-reported effects of service for veterans. The President's Commission on the All-Volunteer Military did sponsor an examination of service experience as a determinant of veterans' attitudes,[90] but the authors found that all other socioeconomic variables were more significant than whether a respondent had been a veteran. The paper concluded:

> [T]he evidence examined here is persuasive that there are no significant attitudinal differences that can be traced to military experience. . . . Whatever qualities veterans bring to their communities—informed judgement or ignorance, self-discipline or personal disarray, community participation and leadership or apathy and withdrawal, "dovishness or hawkishness"—are characteristics that probably would have existed among these individuals in the absence of military experience.[91]

Several years later, this conclusion was echoed by Segal and Segal in their study of Detroit veterans. Assessing trust in government and isolationism-interventionism, these authors reported that "when veterans and nonveterans were compared, the most striking finding was the absence of differences between the two groups."[92]

The Peace Corps and veterans' studies are, at most, suggestive. They do not address what seems to us to be the plausible hypothesis that the comparative value of service experience is not necessarily great in the short term but rises with time. In the short term, 2 years in a regular job may be as maturing as 2 years in the military or the Peace Corps. But over a lifetime, the comparison is between 40 years in the standard work force on the one hand and 38 years in that work force and 2 years in a service program on the other. The latter career pattern may prove more rewarding in terms of personal development, if for no other reason than its diversity. The marginal psychological growth from 5 percent more time in the work force likely would not be as great as the increment from spending those years in a different environment.

We can conclude only that the case for many possible psychological benefits of national service is neither made nor disproved in the existing literature. Further research would certainly be warranted.[93]

Service as a Rite of Passage

Often it has been argued that the military draft of the 1940s and 1950s served as a rite of passage for the nation's young males. Assertedly, military experience tended to unify each generation by providing a shared experience, and it gave each participant a certain pride in the recognition that he had come of age and earned citizenship through this assumption of responsibility. Might program 2 produce a similar effect?

We doubt it. As noted earlier, the arithmetic of service is fundamentally different now. Service in the military was the norm for healthy young men in the mid-1950s; half the total cohort, roughly 60 percent of those eligible to serve, served. But only about 40 percent of the cohort would be engaged in national service under program 2. This would expand significantly the 30 percent of the male cohort who would serve in the AVF as supplemented by our hypothesized draft. It does not appear to be a large enough fraction to make service a normal expectation and a unifying influence among young men coming of age.

Moreover, the nation's definition of the relevant cohort appears to have evolved to encompass women. As long as a military draft remains sex biased—as we expect it will be for a long time to come—it and any national service program tied to it will not be likely to unify a generation of men and women.

Further, a clearly dominant factor in past experience was the presence of a galvanizing task—to win a war—and an immediate enemy threat. The Vietnam war suggests that when no challenge or threat is widely accepted, the unifying effects of service are undercut. Certainly, civil challenges can be unifying, but their impact seems to us likely to be small except where especially difficult, dangerous, or important tasks were performed. Almost by definition, these would be rare.

Finally, we note that there is a dark side even to the psychological effects of cohesion and validation that many people associate with the mid-century draft. This is the exclusion of roughly 30 percent of the male cohort from service on physical, mental, or moral grounds.[94] This exclusion probably is useful, and perhaps essential, to the esteem and bonding of those not excluded. But the exclusion creates one outcast for every two or three members.

In sum, it seems to us that any program of national service that formed an adjunct to military service would be defective as a unifying experience because of the relatively small fraction of the cohort needed to meet military requirements, the exclusion of women and ineligible men, and the probable absence of a galvanizing mission.

Administration and Costs

As with each of the forms of national service we consider, the costs and, to a lesser extent, the administrative structure of program 2 would vary with the program's size. For the reasons reviewed earlier,[95] a draft-based system of national service would be unlikely to produce fewer than 100,000 or more than 300,000 new NSPs each year. We will analyze such a system on these alternative premises.

Administration

We anticipate that program 2 would be administered by a federal headquarters in Washington, D.C., and field offices throughout the country. A revitalized Selective Service System (presumably renamed the National Service System) would be the logical home for the program. This is because the principal concerns of the program's national headquarters would be twofold: establishing the procedures for conscripts to choose between military and civilian service (including adjusting the terms of service to encourage the appropriate mix of military and civilian choices), and establishing the procedures for ensuring that commitments to civilian service actually were fulfilled and that military draft assignments or prosecution for avoiding conscription followed if they were not.

Alternatively, the civilian program might be lodged with other federal volunteer or service-oriented organizations. As the government currently is configured, this would make it part of ACTION, the agency encompassing VISTA, the Retired Senior Volunteer Program, and the National Center for Service Learning, among other entities. An argument also could be made that the program should be placed within the Department of Labor, principally on grounds that the program's politically most sensitive and hence most important task is to ensure enforcement of the rule against worker displacement and that subordination to the Labor Department would best ensure that result. Indeed, that subordination might be a condition to the program's political acceptability.

Finally, the program might be made a freestanding entity, as is (after a period of submergence within ACTION) the Peace Corps. Freestanding status might be justified by the need to give autonomy and visibility to a significant new program and provide it with a direct reporting relationship to the president.

Any of these placements could be justified and made to work. The alternative homes for the program underscore, however, the number of interests affected and bureaucratic tensions likely to be aroused by what is proposed.

The field offices would have four principal functions. They would evaluate proposed positions in public and private nonprofit organizations for their suitability for the assignment of NSPs (following guidelines established by national office); assist prospective NSPs in choosing among available positions; monitor the conditions of employment of NSPs to ensure conformance with the rules of the program, particularly the condition of nondisplacement; and review and act upon allegations of absence or inadequate performance on the part of NSPs.

These are substantial responsibilities that are not easily administered. The processes of assignment and of discipline probably would prove contentious. Would an NSP be fairly treated if he were dismissed from civilian service and made to undertake a full military term? Would assignments be biased by impermissible racial or sex-based considerations? Would some jobs be refused or endorsed because of impermissible political considerations? These and a host of other questions would arise and in some fraction of cases would be litigated. They would produce in the national service system many of the procedural tangles, tensions, delays, and costs that were associated with the draft.

Issues associated with job placement may be particularly difficult. Several hundred thousand young people who meet military standards and are available to work at the minimum wage for 2 years would represent a substantial national asset. Like any other national asset, they would be quarreled over. As with the VISTA and CETA programs, mayors, governors, city councils, labor unions, and nonprofit organizations all could be expected to compete with each other in seeking influence over the assignment process. Instances of waste, corruption, and abuse in that assignment system predictably would occur. These considerations, in turn, would increase the tendency toward the bureaucratization of the system. Accounting controls, audits, and inspections would absorb labor power; dossiers on jobs would be developed; counseling and disciplinary systems for NSPs would evolve.

None of this is unnatural, and it does not suggest a compelling objection to program 2. It underscores, however, that hopes of a lean bureaucracy supporting willing volunteers engaged in altruistic activity are not likely to be realized.

Costs

The costs of program 2 would depend principally on the number of NSPs involved, on the proportion employed by the federal government, and to a much lesser extent, on the size of the program's administrative operation.

We assume that a total of 200,000 youths—160,000 who chose civilian over military service and another 40,000 volunteers—would enter the program each year. If each served for 2 years, approximately 400,000 NSP man-years would be served in each calendar year after the first. Program 2 NSPs would be paid the equivalent of the minimum wage, currently about $7,000 per year, half to come from the federal government and half from the NSP's employer. We assume that at least 75 percent of the NSPs would be employed by qualifying organizations other than the federal government. With respect to about 300,000 NSP man-years per year, the federal government would pay only half of the $7,000 salaries, or a total of $1.05 billion. For the remaining 100,000 NSPs, for whom the federal government was the chosen employer or the employer of last resort, salary costs would total some about $700 million. In addition, the federal government would cover the medical insurance for all NSPs; at roughly $500 per year per NSP, this would come to $150 million. Training costs for the 100,000 NSPs employed by the federal government might average $500 per NSP, or an additional increment of $50 million. Finally, we estimate that perhaps 10 percent of program 2 NSPs would be devoted to conservation and environmental work and live in residential camps. The costs of their food and lodging would be deducted from their wages, but incremental costs for transportation and uniforms might amount to another $400 per NSP per year, or roughly $16 million. In total, the costs attributable to NSPs themselves and payable by the federal government would total nearly $2 billion.

Administrative costs would be far smaller. On the basis of an amalgam of the costs of the administrative structures of several partially comparable programs, we estimate that, for a program in which 400,000 NSPs served each year, approximately 2,000 administrative and support personnel would be required in Washington, D.C., as well as about 5,000 persons in perhaps 1,000 field offices around the country. Average annual salaries of $30,000 for each of these administrative personnel, together with an additional $2,000 per person to cover travel and staff training, would bring the cost of program administration to approximately $170 million. Total costs for the hypothesized program of 200,000 entrants per year would therefore come to more than $2.1 billion. Since administrative costs would not be substantially different for programs of 100,000 or 300,000, the similarly projected costs for programs of 100,000 and 300,000 entrants would total about $1.1 billion and $4.2 billion, respectively.

Constitutional Considerations

Program 2 raises three serious constitutional questions. These are whether the program would contravene the prohibition of involuntary servitude expressed in the Thirteenth Amendment, whether the program would exceed the congressional powers to raise and support armies and to regulate commerce, and whether the program's conscription of men and not women would violate the Constitution's equal protection guarantees. Although the program is more vulnerable to constitutional challenges than program 1, we conclude that none of these grounds poses a debilitating constitutional impediment.

By most common-sense definitions, conscripted military service is involuntary servitude, and conscripted civilian service as an adjunct to such a system would be at least equally objectionable. At the end of World War I, however, the Supreme Court held that conscripted military service was not meant to be encompassed within the Thirteenth Amendment's prohibitions. To the contrary, the court concluded that to argue that "the exaction by government from the citizen of the performance of his supreme and noble duty of contributing to the defense of the rights of this nation" was prohibited by the amendment "is refuted by its mere statement."[96] The Court's conclusion was merely an assertion, devoid of any supporting logic and predicated on a view of military service that not all share.[97] One can hardly doubt, however, that the Supreme Court would reach the same conclusion today and that the vast majority of Americans would regard that conclusion as correct. For better or worse, the constitutionality of military conscription is now well established in this country.

The constitutionality of requiring alternative civilian service from those who do not enter the military also is well established. Conscientious objection has not been held to be a constitutional right,[98] rather it has been legislatively created. Given its constitutional power both to conscript to military service and to exempt or to withhold exemption from that service, it is persuasive that Congress also should have the power, constitutionally, to make that exemption conditional on a requirement of alternative service. Congress has done this for more than four decades now, and every Court of Appeals that has considered the matter has rejected the Thirteenth Amendment challenge to this condition. As the Ninth Circuit Court of Appeals put the matter in 1959:

> Compulsory civilian labor does not stand alone, but is the alternative to compulsory military service. It is not a punishment, but is instead a means for preserving discipline and morale in the armed forces. The power of Congress to raise armies, and to take effective measures to preserve their efficiency, is not limited by either the Thirteenth Amendment, or the absence of a military emergency.[99]

In this light, it seems highly unlikely that a Thirteenth Amendment objection to program 2 would or should prevail in the courts.

In a thoughtful essay on this subject, Professor Philip Bobbitt has advanced a second, subtler argument against plans like program 2. He observes that the Ninth and Tenth Amendments, which reserve to the people and to the states rights not otherwise explicitly delegated to Congress, establish that Congress is not omnipotent: It must justify any requirement of national service by reference to a power explicitly delegated to it by the Constitution. But:

> There is no explicit authority empowering Congress to coerce large scale labor, in contrast to the explicit authority for Congress to provide for the punishment of counterfeiters or to suppress insurrections or to establish post offices. . . . The power . . . to draft a civilian work force . . . is not one delegated to the United States by the Constitution.[100]

Only two specific provisions of the Constitution arguably empower Congress to establish national service: the Article I, Section 8 authority to regulate commerce among the states and the same section's provision authorizing Congress to raise and support armies. In Professor Bobbitt's view, "once we put the question plainly" as to whether national service could be established as a means of regulating commerce, the question:

> [W]ould seem to be a simple one. Its answer is "No." I doubt that many persons would think of such a law as the regulation of commerce; and, if they did, I submit that everything and anything is a regulation of Commerce and then we are back to an omnicompetent Congress—which the Constitution says we do not have.[101]

Professor Bobbitt concedes that it may be constitutionally sound to establish national service on the basis of the congressional authority to raise and support armies. He argues, however, that if Congress acts predominantly because of a desire to establish civilian national service rather than because of a desire to improve a military draft, its reliance on its responsibility to raise and support armies would be a sham and should therefore be unconstitutional.[102]

We do not believe that these arguments would or should render program 2 unconstitutional. A congressional endorsement of this program could, in our view, properly rest on a judgment that the program was a means of raising an army in an equitable and acceptable fashion.[103] Not only is this likely to be the primary motivation of a program like this one, but also the Supreme Court repeatedly has shown itself unwilling to look behind an assertion of a proper congressional motivation to see whether an improper motivation also is at play.[104]

The most serious constitutional objection to program 2 is that its conscription of only men and not women would contravene both the spirit and the letter of the constitutional guarantee of equal protection under the laws.[105] This objection might be pressed by men who felt disproportionately burdened by the plan or by women who felt that the program foreclosed opportunities or denigrated the status of women by affording nearly all civilian national service opportunities only to men.

As noted earlier, this sex bias in program 2 is a consequence of the sex bias in the laws that now regulate the military draft. Although the Carter administration proposed the registration of women as well as men, Congress restricted registration—as it historically has been restricted—to men.[106] This position promptly was challenged in the courts, and the Supreme Court held in 1981 that a single-sex registration for a military draft was not unconstitutional.[107]

The Court reached this conclusion by deferring to the reasoning of those in Congress who regarded the exclusion of women from combat as an appropriate policy and the registration system as a means, principally, of securing combat soldiers.[108] The large number of noncombat roles in the military causes us to question this rationale for a single-sex military draft. Clearly there are many roles that women could fill in the modern military, and it therefore seems that the constitutional mandate would best be honored by drafting women as well as men, at least to the extent that there were vacancies in positions available for women.[109] Certainly the addition of a civilian service component to a military draft would strengthen this argument. Not only would women be qualified to fill at least 12 percent of the positions in the military,[110] they also would be qualified to undertake virtually 100 percent of the jobs in civilian national service. If, as we have estimated, the number of civilian service conscripts equaled the number of military conscripts,[111] women would be qualified for more than half the total number of jobs for which people were conscripted.

Would Congress be persuaded by these considerations? If it were not, would the Supreme Court hold that women also must be conscripted to meet the constitutional mandate of equal protection under the laws? On balance, we think that constitutionally, the wiser course would be to conscript women as well as men. Our best guess, however, is that Congress would not take this course and that the Supreme Court, as it did in evaluating all-male registration, would give Congress considerable leeway in this matter and uphold its actions.[112]

Conclusion

We think that program 2 might improve the equity and the political palatability of a military draft if one were resumed. Others may debate whether it would be worth its costs in this context and also, of course, whether a military draft would be desirable. But in this chapter, we have focused instead on the three criteria that we suggested at the outset might warrant a system of national service. On these grounds alone—that is, putting aside its effects in facilitating acceptance of a military draft—we do not believe that a strong case can be made for program 2. The program would accomplish a substantial amount of useful social work, but when all the costs are considered, nothing suggests that it would accomplish this work more efficiently or effectively than could be accomplished through direct hiring. To the contrary, the costs of obtaining, screening, assigning, training, supervising, and disciplining draftees for terms of 2 years seem likely to exceed those associated with hiring workers through the regular labor market.

We also are unimpressed with the evidence that the benefits of service to the draftees warrant such a program. Experience with analogous situations suggests that NSPs would at best catch up with their peers in career development and earning power after a period of disadvantage caused by their service. There may be positive psychological effects from service in terms of maturation, empathy, breadth of experience, and even development of altruism, but those effects have not been convincingly demonstrated in analogous prior programs.

We also are struck by the fact that if national service, through plans like program 2, is to be justified primarily by reference to the benefits it yields the participants themselves, there is a strong argument that the program should focus not on the young men who pass but on those who fail to meet military entrance standards. Members of the latter group more than of the former need jobs, a change of scene, discipline, and a sense of mission. To encompass this group would be to revise the program entirely: to make it universal (at least for men—and then why not women?), to shift some of its focus to remediation rather than services, and to disconnect its rationale from the military draft. We return to a discussion of universal compulsory programs in chapter 8. For the moment, we note only that its absence of universality, and especially its slighting of the less fit, is a notable weakness of program 2.

Finally, we think program 2 would be more likely to hinder than to help meet military manpower requirements in the event of a draft. This is because the program is likely to bleed especially qualified men out of the military and into the civilian branch of service. This tendency could be offset by making military service more financially attractive or by extending the required period of civilian service. As noted also, a civilian program might facilitate acceptance of a military draft. But this is only to argue that, from a military perspective, civilian national service might be a price worth paying to achieve a draft and that it is a price that could be minimized. Political acceptability aside, program 2 would more likely worsen than alleviate military manpower problems.

In sum, program 2 may be warranted as a means of broadening the choice for those who are drafted. It also might permit large-scale experimentation with national service and thus help resolve the many questions and uncertainties that have rendered this issue so difficult for so long. These may be sufficient justifications for the program, but in terms of the primary and traditional arguments for national service, in our view, present evidence does not warrant the program.

Notes

1. About 9 percent of the Army's recruits are now excluded for mental reasons, 16 percent for physical causes, and 4 percent for moral reasons. Department of

the Army, U.S. Army Recruiting Command, "Fact Sheet: Prime Market Calculation," March 8, 1984.

2. H.R. 18025, *National Service Act of 1970,* 91st Congress, 2nd session, June 1970. "A Bill to Create a New National Service Agency to Fill Military Manpower Requirements, to Create a Voluntary Civilian Service as an Alternative to Military Service, and for Other Purposes." The history of Bingham's bill and his arguments for it are sketched in Bingham, "Replacing the Draft."

3. H.R. 2206, *The National Service Act of 1979,* "A Bill to Establish a National Service System Under Which the Young People of the United States Have the Choice of Either Entering Voluntary Military or Civilian Service or Being Subject to Induction into Military Service by Random Selection." 96th Congress, 1st session, February, 1979. A committee of the New York County Lawyer's Association is preparing a revision of the bill for resubmission.

4. A later addition to the bill stipulated that failure to register would be punishable by up to 2 years in prison. See ibid., section 112.

5. This would require 6 initial months of full-time training and then attendance at drills for 1 weekend a month and 2 weeks each summer.

6. The bill speaks of 6 years of draft liability, but it does not make clear whether it would revert to the old system of calling oldest first or whether it would follow the 1970s practice of calling those turning twenty in that calendar year first.

7. The McCloskey plan recognizes a right of conscientious objection to any form of service.

8. Landrum, "National Service in West Germany and France," is the best available source in English on the French and the West German programs.

9. Pinkau, *Services For Development,* though now dated, is the most nearly authoritative study of Third World programs.

10. Sohlberg, "Defense Manpower Policies in Seven Northern and Central European NATO Countries: Part II," 52–53. About 20 percent of the eligible male cohort is excluded from military service for physical, or social reasons. Landrum, "National Service in West Germany and France," 74.

11. See ibid., table 5.1. Kuhlmann notes that the number of draft-deferred openings in this program is negotiated between the Ministry of Interior (which runs the program) and the Ministery of Defense. Kuhlmann, "Linkages Between Military Service and Alternative National Service in West Germany," 30.

12. Kuhlmann describes the terms of service in ibid., 8–9.

13. The right of conscientious objection derives from the guarantee in Article IV of the Federal Republic of Germany's Basic Law that "no one may be forced to bear arms against his will."

14. Kuhlmann, 22. Landrum, "National Service in West Germany and France," 75–76, presents somewhat different numbers; the difference is immaterial for our purposes.

15. Colombatto, "Foreign Evidence Relevant to the Proposed Nationwide Social Service in the United Kingdom," 7.

16. Kuhlmann, "Linkages Between Military Service and Alternative National Service in West Germany," 25.

17. Ibid., 18. In 1977, the Bundestag passed a law to the same effect, but the Federal Constitutional Court declared this law unconstitutional. The court held that

the government could not permit a lighter civilian burden without independent verification that the registrant's motive stemmed from conscience rather than convenience. This concern apparently was met, however, by increasing the requirement of civilian service to longer than active military duty.

18. In fiscal year 1972, there were 27,000 inductions, as against 207,000 in fiscal year 1970. Cooper, *Military Manpower and the All-Volunteer Force,* 20.

19. *Welsh* v. *United States,* 398 U.S. 333 (1970). While in Germany the right of conscientious objection is constitutionally guaranteed, in the United States it is statutorily based. Section 6(j) of the Selective Service Act, 50 U.S.C. App. 456(j), provides that "[N]othing contained in this title . . . shall be construed to require any person to be subject to combatant trainiang and service in the armed forces of the United States who, by reason of religious training and belief, is conscientiously opposed to participation in war in any form." In *Welsh,* the court concluded that an applicant with a moral or ethical opposition to war "held with the strength of traditional religious convictions" met the standard of section 6(j).

20. Commenting on *Welsh* and two other 1970 decisions in their book *Chance and Circumstance,* Baskir and Strauss write:

> Coming at a time when the war and the draft were beginning to wind down, the decisions destroyed much of whatever enthusiasm remained for enforcing the [draft] law. . . . In Milwaukee, for example, prosecutors trimmed their five-hundred-case backlog to just one hundred immediately following the 1970 Supreme Court decisions. . . . Prosecutors in New York City, San Diego, El Paso, New Orleans, and Miami dropped more than 95 percent of their cases. The national average was 89 percent. [Ibid., 78–81]

It has been reported that "during the month after *Welsh,* Selective Service recorded 100,000 applications for exemption." Seeley, "Three Hundred Years: The Struggle for Conscience in America."

21. Kuhlmann notes that two-thirds of those achieving CO status in Germany have 2 or more years of college, while only 20 percent of the age group achieves that level of education.

> Higher intelligence and an extensive vocabulary would be the requirements to convince the testing boards about their . . . arguments. . . . They would be able to convince the testing boards more easily not only because of their eloquence but because they had more frequent and longer opportunities than those of their own age group with less education to come to terms with the conscientious objection Basic Law and to reach their own opinion. [Kuhlmann, "Linkages Between Military Service and Alternative National Service in West Germany," 33]

22. Cooper, *Military Manpower and the All-Volunteer Force,* 44.

23. See chapter 4, The All-Volunteer Force Debate.

24. As discussed in the concluding section of this chapter, a broader male conscription system might be created by drawing those rejected for military service into service or remediation programs. Efforts in this direction were made through an early 1960s program offering all Selective Service rejects counseling from the Department of Labor and in Project 100,000, a late 1960s program that admitted to the military low-scoring men who normally would have been rejected.

25. The 1982 report of the Military Manpower Task Force, a U.S. government interagency group set up to review the all-volunteer force and alternatives to it, in-

cluded a consultant paper by James Lacy on national service. Lacy, an advocate of the draft, concluded that a program of this type is:

> [P]robably the only feasible device for dealing with the legal issues concerning conscientious objection in any resumed draft. The Congress could try to rewrite the CO law to make it usable in practice as well as conforming to Supreme Court opinion, but this was attempted in the late 1960s without success. Draft excusal for COs could be abolished entirely (the special CO status is not constitutionally required), but this would be a radical departure from some 300 years of public policy. (Abolishing the status would also result in the disagreeable chore of having to imprison fervent, traditional pacifists). Unlike the other compulsory national service options, [this option] proceeds from considerations of practical necessity . . . [Lacy, "National Service as an Alternative or Complement to an All-Volunteer Force," 22]

26. See table 6–1 and the related discussion of the Gallup youth surveys.

27. Bingham, "Replacing the Draft."

28. For those now entering military service and completing at least 3 years of service, the new GI Bill provides basic educational benefits of as much as $300 a month for 36 months. To be eligible, recruits must contribute $100 a month of their pay during their first 12 months in the military. Additional benefits may be available, without further contribution, for those with designated skills who remain in the military beyond their first term of service.

29. A civilian NSP receiving room and board would have his salary reduced to pay for these benefits.

30. In 1984, the Selective Service System CO program has been reviewed, and modern regulations have been promulgated. See 32 C.F.R. §1656 (July 1984). The differences between these regulations and those that have historically applied are not material for our purposes.

31. Under existing regulations for alternative civilian service for COs, "the Director will determine in accordance with the Selective Service Law which employment programs or activities are appropriate for alternative service work" and will certify those jobs. 32 C.F.R. §1656.5(a) (revised as of July 1984).

32. Under existing alternative service regulations for COs, 32 C.F.R. §1656.5(g), the sponsoring agency submits the position descriptions for approval. We are impressed, however, with the experience of ACTION public service projects, which indicates that having the participant write the description increased the assurance that he would understand and be committed to his job. See ACTION, "National Youth Service Demonstrations," 10.

33. 50 U.S.C., App. §462(1948).

34. This is the case under the existing regulation for COs who fail to perform alternative service. 32 C.F.R. §1656.14(c)(1983).

35. Men conscripted while serving as volunteers could be permitted to elect the national service option and continue in their jobs with credit for time already served. The period of postconscription service would then be made subject to the disciplinary procedures and sanctions that applied for draftees.

36. Bingham, "Replacing the Draft," 17. The emphasis is in the original.

37. The 1979 and 1982 polls also reported results for males eighteen to twenty-four. The 1979 results showed a pronounced preference for civilian service in this older group (39 percent preferred military service, 56 percent preferred nonmilitary

service, and 5 percent indicated no opinion, with 201 in the total sample). The 1981 results showed no significant difference between the twenty- to twenty-four-year-olds and the eighteen- to nineteen-year-olds. Data for 1982 were provided in a memo from the Gallup Organization Inc., to the National Service Project; 1979 and 1981 data are based on unpublished computer data provided by the Roper Center in Storrs, Connecticut.

38. Surveys of sixteen- to twenty-year-old men, conducted for the Department of Defense from 1975 to 1982, at their lowest showed 29.4 percent of the respondents definitely or probably inclined to enter a military service. A high of 35.8 percent expressed this propensity in 1982, and in the most recent (1984) survey, 29.9 percent of the respondents exhibited a positive propensity to join the military. See Laurence and Bridges, *Youth Attitude Tracking Survey: Historical Evolution and Characteristics*, 20, table 4.

39. Memo to the National Service Study Project from the Gallup Organization, Inc., 2. There also may be problems of representativeness by race. The combined Gallup data from 1979, 1981, and 1982 suggested that, on average, 75 percent of the military entrants would be white, while 85 percent of the population is white, according to data from the Bureau of the Census, *Estimates of the Population of the United States by Age, Sex and Race: 1980–83*, 13, table 2. On the other hand, the draft, in 1964 and 1971, produced a population of recruits that was 89 and 85 percent white, respectively. Nelson, Hale, and Slackman, "National Service and the Military," tables IV–3 and A–IV–2.

40. Data from 1983 show that 67.9 percent of eighteen- to nineteen-year-old males held high school diplomas in that year. Bureau of the Census, *School Enrollment—Social and Economic Characteristics of Students: October 1983 Advanced Report*, 9.

41. This observation is tempered by the fact that the recruit cohort in these years included women and older men. If older men (20 to 24 years old) in the Gallup survey are considered, the percentage of those disposed to military service who are high school graduates rises to 75 percent. Nelson, Hale, and Slackman, "National Service and the Military," table IV–3.

42. The data are only indicative because those with a present negative propensity to serve in the military might prefer military to civilian national service if conscription gave them only that choice. Conversely, those with a propensity for the military might prefer civilian service, although this fact is not apparent now because the civilian alternative is not available.

43. It follows from this that military reservations about program 2 would be compounded if the program included a volunteer component. As noted in our discussion of purely voluntary national service (program 3, discussed in chapter 7), paid volunteer work competes directly with the military volunteer effort.

44. See, for example, VISTA, "VISTA Volunteer Sponsor Survey," 59: "Generally . . . a paucity of information, understanding, and activity was apparent in the phase-out of VISTA activities."

45. "If the military is a guide, attrition might run above 15 percent. For male enlisted personnel who joined the Army in fiscal years 1971 and 1972—the final years of the draft—the attrition rate during the first two years of military service was about 21 percent: 14.4 percent for failure to meet minimum behavioral or performance

criteria; 3.3 percent for medical reasons; 1 percent for dependency or hardship; 0.3 percent died; and 2 percent for other reasons." Office of Naval Research, *First-Term Enlisted Attrition, Volume I: Papers,* 15.

46. Sizer, "National Service Education Study," 38.

47. We also note that schools as work settings for program 2 NSPs might raise equity problems. The relatively short school day and 9-month school year with extensive vacations might be seen by many as far easier than military service, even if NSPs were given supplementary tasks. If so, such a disparity probably would be less acceptable than when alternative service was limited to those demonstrating conscientious objection.

48. See chapter 5. Child Care Assignments.

49. Lee et al., "Study of Service and Social Needs in the Health Sector," I-9.

50. The costs of turnover are skillfully illuminated in Sheehan, *Kate Quinton's Days*.

51. See chapter 5. Health Care Assignments.

52. The achievement is celebrated in *VISTA,* 28, published by VISTA in 1980 on its fifteenth anniversary.

53. Hagenstein, "National Service: Conservational and Environmental Aspects," 41–44.

54. See chapter 3, note 62.

55. A possible method of dealing with this problem would be to permit NSPs who chose environmental assignments in remote areas to limit those assignments to 1 year (or 6 months) and subsequently to take different assignments to complete their 2-year terms.

56. Peace Corps volunteers offer an analogy. Even before being sworn in for their 2-year terms, they receive 8 to 14 weeks (on average, 11.4 weeks) of training. About 2 percent of Peace Corps volunteers become volunteer leaders, most of them after extending their terms of service to 3 years.

57. If undervolunteering were due to an erosion in military wages, we assume that Congress's most likely response would be to raise military pay.

58. Ashenfelter and Oaxaca, "Potential Labor Market Effects of National Service Programs," 25–26, tables 2.1–2.6.

59. As with many other matters relating to the CO program, no data are available on this point.

60. Mirengoff and Rindler, "CETA: Manpower Programs Under Local Control," 173–76.

61. Zimmerman and Masters, "A Pilot Study of the Value of Output of Youth Employment Programs"; and Zimmerman, "A Study of the Value of Output of Participants in the Summer Youth Employment Program," 61.

62. Hahn and Lehrman, *What Works in Youth Employment Policy?,* 75.

63. Baskir and Strauss, *Chance and Circumstance,* 30, estimate that only 96,200 of the 171,700 men classified as COs between 1963 and 1972 completed their alternative service. Even given a heavily disproportionate concentration of CO service later in the Vietnam years, accounting for 2 years of service by those who completed, and recognizing that some COs rendered service for less than a full term, a very rough calculation suggests that it was unlikely that more than 30,000 to 35,000 COs would have been performing alternative service at any one time.

64. This section focuses exclusively on the effects of program 2 on the men who would be drafted under it. We anticipate that the program's effects on the 40,000 individuals who volunteered for civilian national service would be very much like the effects on program 3 volunteers, described in the next chapter.

65. There is no significant scholarly literature or data on the experience of COs after World War II. The limited literature on the war period tells little about the work done in service and less about its effects on COs. It focuses, understandably, on church-run work camps that were very different from settings envisioned for program 2. The most useful sources are Selective Service System, *Conscientious Objection;* and Sibley, Milford, and Jacobs, *Conscription of Conscience: The American State and the Conscientious Objector.*

66. Smith, Hunter, and Zildjian, "The Impact of Peace Corps and VISTA Service on Former Volunteers and American Society." We refer to the draft text, as this report was never finalized or officially released by ACTION. In 1979, ACTION's Office of Policy and Planning published its own report, "A Survey of Former Peace Corps and VISTA Volunteers," noting in its foreword that "the delay in producing this report since the data were collected in 1978 is due to the failure of the contractor to produce a final report which met the needs of the agency." Where relevant, we will quote from this ACTION report as well as from the draft document.

67. Kassing, "Military Experience as a Determinant of Veterans' Earnings," III-8-19.

68. Ibid., III-8-4.

69. Ibid., III-8-17.

70. Louis Harris and Associates, Inc., "A Survey of Returned Peace Corps Volunteers."

71. Smith, Hunter, and Zildjian, "The Impact of Peace Corps and VISTA Service on Former Volunteers and American Society."

72. Louis Harris and Asociates, Inc., "A Survey of Returned Peace Corps Volunteers," 21. See also Cullinan, *Attitudes of Returning Peace Corps Volunteers Concerning Impact of Peace Corps Interlude on Subsequent Academic Work.*

73. Louis Harris and Associates, Inc., "A Survey of Returned Peace Corps Volunteers," 47.

The 1978 Peace Corps study arrived at the same observation as its predecessor: "It may be inferred . . . that Peace Corps service has not had a major impact on the broad areas of work chosen after service." ACTION, "A Survey of Former Peace Corps and VISTA Volunteers," 12. In general, the report noted that:

> [T]here is no evidence that Peace Corps service results in major shifts in career. . . . [T]he salaries of former volunteers seem to be about what they would have been had they entered the job market two years earlier. In addition to losing two years of income, volunteers frequently seem to have to start employment at entry level positions. [Ibid]

74. Louis Harris and Associates, Inc., "A Survey of Returned Peace Corps Volunteers," 52.

75. Ibid., 53. This fact emphasizes the importance of acquiring actual evidence about experience in service programs rather than relying on the reported expectations or feelings of volunteers. The 1969 report recorded that "only a small minority (9 percent) [of volunteers] feel their time overseas has slowed them down in their career,

a clear tribute to the perceived value of Peace Corps service." Ibid., 24. See also ibid., 22, which reports that 59 percent of the volunteers felt that the Peace Corps helped their career advancement.

76. Ibid., 54.

77. ACTION, "A Survey of Former Peace Corps and VISTA Volunteers," 13.

78. Ibid., 8. This result almost certainly would have been compounded if the comparison had matched Peace Corps returnees with contemporaries similarly educated rather than with the whole population.

79. Ibid., 4: "The integration of former volunteers into the work force is a slow process. Very few work during the first three months after they return. . . . [T]he majority of volunteers returned to school after service." The same report notes that 63 percent of the volunteers continued traveling during their first 3 months after service. Ibid.

80. Little and Fredlund, "Veteran Status Earnings and Race," 256–57.

81. Segal and Segal, "The Impact of Military Service on Trust in Government," 209.

82. Compare Browning, Lopreato, and Poston ("Income and Veteran Status: Variations Among Mexican Americans, Blacks and Anglos"), who show positive effects for Hispanics and blacks, with Cutright ("The Civilian Earnings of White and Black Draftees and Non Veterans"). Cutright criticizes the first study on the basis of considerations such as small sample size and failure to control for age, reaching the opposite conclusion on the basis of a Selective Service sample.

83. Louis Harris and Associates, Inc., "A Survey of Returned Peace Corps Volunteers," 24.

84. See Stein, *Volunteers for Peace*. The studies and the literature in general are conveniently summarized in Smith, "The Impact of Voluntary Action Upon the Volunteer/Participant," 191ff.

85. ACTION, "A Survey of Former Peace Corps and VISTA Volunteers," 9. For similar data, see Louis Harris and Associates, Inc., "A Survey of Returned Peace Corps Volunteers," 137.

86. ACTION, "A Survey of Former Peace Corps and VISTA Volunteers," 2.

87. Landrum, "National Service: A Grass Roots Expansion" 24.

88. Ibid., 32. See also Harris and Associates, Inc., "A Survey of Returned Peace Corps Volunteers," 57: "Compared to the control group of decliners, volunteers (particularly the duty terminees) are less likely to belong to any organizations."

89. ACTION, "A Survey of Former Peace Corps and VISTA Volunteers," 33. See also ibid., 36, noting that "slightly more 1976 early terminees than former PCVs participated in voluntary groups after service"; and Louis Harris and Associates, Inc., "A Survey of Returned Peace Corps Volunteers," 60: "The . . . results suggest that the rate of voluntarism is pretty much the same for volunteers and decliners yet decliners have had more time to become involved in volunteer work."

90. Wilson and Hoack, "Military Experience as a Determinant of Veterans' Attitudes," III-7-2. This study focused on predominantly political attitudes, but to a modest extent also measured personal commitment and knowledge of world affairs. Because we doubt the adequacy of military experience as an indicator of attitudinal changes, we do not give it much weight.

91. Ibid., III-7-16.

92. Segal and Segal, "The Impact of Military Service on Trust in Government," 210.

93. As with income effects, one focus of research might be on the differential psychological effects of service on those from different backgrounds. The average results reported in the studies now available may mask differences of considerable interest. A program that is not universal and random could generate greater benefits than one structured like program 2. We shall have more to say about this in chapter 7.

Further research on the psychological effects of service also might attend to negative as well as positive effects. Our psychological consultants, Maccoby and Margolies, comment: "It is well known that morale problems are significant in both the Peace Corps and VISTA. In fact, the pattern is so common in the Peace Corps that there is a graph of predicted ups and downs. Stein's Peace Corps study found that volunteers' sense of well-being declined while abroad, and their anxiety rose." Maccoby and Margolies, "The Psychological Effects on Youth of National Service," 43.

Commenting on the military experience, Maccoby and Margolies noted that "in France, where military service is compulsory, many young men feel their 12 months are wasted. Roger Landrum found some Frenchmen thought the year was spent cleaning floors with a razor blade! There have been demonstrations by conscript soldiers and the goal seems to be unionization. The negative effect of reluctant nonmilitary recruits might be even worse." Ibid., 95. Maccoby and Margolies conclude: "Our view is that in [program 2] it is likely that the two years of service would do damage." Ibid., 97.

In this regard, we note that more than 40 percent of the junior three ranks in the volunteer military described themselves in a recent survey as at the lowest two levels of satisfaction on a given point scale asking them to evaluate military life. More than one in four respondents gave the military experience the lowest ranking, very dissatisfied. Dorring and Hutzler, *Description of Officers and Enlisted Personnel in the U.S. Armed Forces,* 591, table 499.

94. See note 1 of this chapter.

95. See Chapter 4, The All-Volunteer Force Debate.

96. *Selective Draft Law Cases* 245 U.S. 366, 390 (1918).

97. For a trenchant criticism, see Friedman, "Conscription and the Constitution: The Original Understanding."

98. *U.S.* v. *MacIntosh* 283 U.S. 605, 623 (1931). It is conceivable that a right to conscientious objection could be derived from the First Amendment's guarantees of free exercise of religion or even free speech. Even then, however, it seems probable that the practice of making alternative service a condition of exercising this right would be continued.

99. *Howze* v. *U.S.,* 272 F.2d 146, 148 (9th Circuit Court of Appeals, 1959). This passage is quoted with approval in *U.S.* v. *Holmes,* 387 F.2d 781, 784 (7th Circuit Court of Appeals, 1968), *cert. denied* 391 U.S. 936 (1960). See also *Heflin* v. *Sanford,* 142 F.2d 798, 800 (5th Circuit Court of Appeals, 1944):

> There can be no doubt whatever that Congress has the constitutional power to require appellant, an able-bodied man, to serve in the army, or in lieu of such

> service to perform other work of national importance. The Thirteenth Amendment abolished slavery and involuntary servitude, except as a punishment for crime, but was never intended to limit the war powers of government or its right to exact by law public service from all to meet the public need.

Heflin also notes a line of cases in which public service obligations such as jury duty and compelled labor for road repair withstood challenge under the Thirteenth Amendment. We comment on these cases in regard to program 4 in chapter 8.

100. Bobbitt, "National Service: Unwise or Unconstitutional?," 311–12.

101. Ibid., 315.

102. Ibid., 313.

103. We believe that a national service program also would be defended as within congressional power under the commerce clause, but this argument is not fundamental to defending program 2. We return to it in our discussion of program 4, which is not intertwined with a military draft.

104. As Professor Bobbitt acknowledges, *U.S.* v. *O'Brien,* 391 U.S. 367 (1968), provides a relevant instance of just such an attitude. There the court upheld a congressional penalty on draft card burning on the grounds that the power to forbid this destruction was a relevant corollary to the power to raise armies, even though there were strong indications that a dominant congressional motive was a constitutionally impermissible desire to punish dissenters.

105. This guarantee appears in the Fourteenth Amendment as a limitation on the power of the states but has been implied by a reading of the Fifth Amendment to limit the federal government as well.

106. See 126 *Cong. Rec.* 8601-02, 8620, 13876-13898 (1980).

107. *Rostker* v. *Goldberg,* 453 U.S. 57 (1981).

108. Ibid., 76–77.

109. This argument is developed in "If the Draft Is Resumed: Issues for a New Selective Service Law," *Record of the Association of the Bar of the City of New York,* 1981.

110. Congress and the Supreme Court evaluated the all-male registration system in light of emergency mobilization needs, which were estimated to permit women to fill only one in eight of the jobs for which registrants would be drafted. *Rostker* v. *Goldberg,* 453 U.S. 57, 100 (dissent of Justice Marshall) (1981). This is approximately the percentage of women in the peacetime military.

111. Conscripting women under program 2 probably would increase the percentage of conscripts who preferred civilian to military service. (The 1984 Gallup poll reported more than two-thirds of female respondents had this preference.) This would intensify the argument in the text, although it also gives rise to the objection that including women as conscripts would increase the cost of the program. Gallup, "Most Teens Favor National Youth Service," 3 October 1984.

112. Justice Rehnquist wrote for the majority in *Rostker* v. *Godlberg,* 453 U.S. 57, 64–65: "The case arises in the context of Congress' authority over national defense and military affairs, and perhaps in no other area has the Court accorded Congress greater deference."

7
Voluntary Service

Many supporters of national service prefer a voluntary system of service, one that induces participation rather than compels it through school requirements (program 1), a draft (program 2), or economic or criminal sanctions (program 4, described in chapter 8).

There are strong arguments for volunteerism.[1] If national service is justified by reference to the value of service to the NSPs, then a voluntary model is appealing because it is consistent with the principle that adults are the best judges of what is good for them. If service is justified by reference to the social utility of the work accomplished, it seems fairest to compensate those who produce that utility, setting a wage or other incentive high enough to draw a willing work force. As the Thirteenth Amendment (prohibiting involuntary servitude) reminds us, our society requires not only compensation for work but also, generally, a free choice as to whether to exchange the work for the compensation. A compulsory system raises fears of totalitarianism or at least of an overbearing state. A voluntary system greatly diminishes those concerns.

A volunteerist approach also reduces the chances that national service might become a self-perpetuating folly and an administrative burden. A compulsory program might outlive its usefulness; a voluntary one must at least repeatedly meet the market test of recruitment. Further, a compulsory program must inflict punishment on those who do not serve and thereby encounter the complexities of due process and issues of exemption. Moreover, at least some coerced participants would be more resentful, unwilling, and uncooperative than volunteers, and a compulsory program would make it more difficult to screen out the disruptive or irresponsible. Conversely, because most compulsory programs would take in everyone of a certain age who met minimal qualifications, it is also more difficult to target these programs to those who might profit most from them. Finally, there is at least a paradox and perhaps a contradiction in attempting to induce a sense of altruism and caring through coerced rather than freely given service. As one critic has argued, "Service is freely given; if it is compulsory, it is no longer service. . . . The involuntary aspect is better expressed by the word servitude."[2]

Unfortunately, however, a system of voluntary national service must confront its own paradoxes and difficulties. To begin with, a great deal of volunteer work now is conducted without government involvement. Indeed, the norm of volunteering appears to be stronger in the United States than in any other nation, with the possible exception of Great Britain.[3] In 1983, an estimated 92 million Americans served as volunteers in churches, schools, hospitals, political action groups, and a vast range of civic organizations.[4] A 1974 study concluded that the United States had about 40,000 voluntary organizations directly or indirectly involved with environmental problems alone.[5] If volunteer work were recognized and perhaps rewarded through a system of national service, should similar service that is now provided also be recognized? If so, a now commendably decentralized and private system may become at least monitored, if not administered and paid for, by the state.[6] If not, then an ambitious effort to stimulate national service work may displace at least some of the other voluntary work that is a traditional and attractive aspect of life in the United States.

How could service be encouraged in a voluntary national service system? As the Potomac Institute's Committee for the Study of National Service noted:

> There are grounds for considerable skepticism about the achievement [of broad-based participation in national service] to any reasonable extent through a voluntary scheme, whatever the incentives and sanctions. Why, for example, would youth from wealthy backgrounds with either an open route through professional school or a life of ease choose to spend a year in National Service? Why would youth from families that struggle for economic survival serve for a period of time at subsistence wages? And why would academically gifted youth from all backgrounds interrupt rigorous training in physics or the fine arts for a period of National Service? Parallel questions can also be asked about other subgroups of the general youth population—young women who are homemakers, young apprentices in blue collar trades, youth from minority groups. And yet if all types of young people do not participate, the idea of National Service loses some force.[7]

It is difficult to identify an appropriate incentive for a voluntary program. If the government imposed sanctions such as those in programs 1 and 2, the program would not be voluntary. A program encouraging service through substantial pay may be difficult to distinguish from an employment or training program and probably would draw mainly participants who valued pay highly and service less. Analyzing national service plans in 1980, the Congressional Budget Office concluded that a program offering only about two-thirds of the minimum wage for civilian service would attract anywhere between

730,000 and 1.4 million potential volunteers who found the income preferable to their present employment status.[8] A program dominated by such applicants would fall far short of the vision of NSPs from different social classes and races jointly serving their society.

One response to these problems would be to leave the encouragement of voluntary service to the private sector. As it is, churches, schools, civic organizations, fraternal organizations, volunteer groups, and innumerable individual and family activities shape the spirit and practice of service in the United States. Public discussion and private example could generate more or less of this activity in the years to come, quite apart from any position taken or program established by the government. We are especially impressed with the potential that three institutions in society, not normally associated with service, have for increasing volunteering. These are businesses, professions, and colleges.

Businesses could increase service activity significantly by encouraging paid, or even unpaid, time off from work for service activities by giving preference in hiring or promotion to those who have served or by associating corporate charitable contributions with employee service. Notable instances of such efforts already exist. A 1979 survey identified forty major corporations, including IBM, Xerox, and Wells Fargo, that granted paid full-time leaves of up to a year for selected employees to devote themselves to public service projects.[9]

Levi Strauss provides a particularly imaginative example of the potential for corporate encouragement of service. Employees are encouraged to form Community Involvement Teams (CITs), typically consisting of between five and fifty persons, to assist local service agencies in defined projects. Once a CIT commits itself to a project, the associated agency becomes eligible for funds from the Levi Strauss Foundation. In 1982, CITs were operating in fifty-six communities in fifteen states, working especially on problems of domestic violence, parent education, employment, and aging.[10] Levi Strauss also donates funds to nonprofit service-oriented organizations in which individual company employees or retirees actively participate.[11] By these means, the corporation reports, roughly 20 percent of its work force has been drawn into public service work.[12]

Despite such examples and the effort of some nonprofit agencies to encourage corporate volunteerism,[13] the record of business support for service is lackluster. The leading study concludes that in the corporate world "for the most part volunteer employee programs are not taken seriously, are given relatively low priority and do not have the resources needed to be successful."[14] Chief executive officers, public opinion leaders, and foundations that favor voluntary public service could put more effort into encouraging corporate service programs.[15]

A similar effort could profitably be made to establish service expectations as a part of licensing or granting credentials for doctors, lawyers, architects, social workers, skilled artisans, and others. Typically, licensing bodies and professional associations now encourage but do not require the donation of time for unpaid service. In 1979, the American Bar Association (ABA) considered requiring its members to perform 40 hours of *pro bono* work each year. In the face of intense opposition, this proposal was revised to require lawyers to perform some *pro bono* work, without specifying a required number of hours. That formulation also was rejected, so current ABA guidelines only commend public service work.[16] In practice, a 1985 ABA poll shows that only half of all lawyers performed any *pro bono* work within the previous year and the median time they devoted to this work was 28.3 hours.[17] In the professions, as in business, enthusiasm for national service first might be directed to achieving a group commitment to service before attempting to enact a federal program.

In the same vein, we think that universities and colleges could provide powerful incentives to increased service by youth in the United States. If respected public and private colleges were to join, for example, in giving admissions preference (akin to the preference for alumni children) to applicants who had participated in community service,[18] the effects on their prospective students might prove profound. Programs like our school-based program 1 would become attractions rather than distractions for the most competitive college-oriented high school students. Some school systems might seek to advance their students' chances of college admission by implementing programs of this type. Similarly, graduate and professional school admission or scholarship preferences for those with service experience would encourage college graduates interested in further training to spend time in public service. A British proponent of national service has eloquently put the matter this way:

> Why should it be evil if say [a medical school] were to say [to an applicant] . . . It's clear that you're academically gifted—but to what social purpose have you ever put your intelligence? . . . Are you even sure of your vocation to be a doctor? Come back in a year's time with evidence of your having done something to alleviate distress—and then we'll be happy to accept you.[19]

Colleges and graduate schools also might influence those they had already admitted by establishing requirements for the application of classroom knowledge to service projects in surrounding communities.[20] Finally, as has recently been urged by a Carnegie Foundation study,[21] they might allocate student work-study funds to support community service work instead of (as now) using them to pay for work performed on campus.

Similar ideas are being discussed and, to a limited degree, implemented.

Recently, seventy-five universities formed a coalition to encourage their students to undertake service activities.[22] Brown University, a leader in this field, offers National Service Fellowship stipends of $1,000 to $1,500 to both incoming and already-enrolled students who have performed at least 1 year of voluntary public service.[23] The university complements this incentive with a wide range of service internships and community outreach programs. As a result, Brown estimates that approximately 25 percent of its undergraduates currently are participating in public service activities.[24]

Nonetheless, most colleges and universities support no such public service programs. A 1968 survey by the American Council on Education and the National Service Secretariat is broadly indicative, though dated. This survey queried 2,100 colleges and universities on their support for student public service activities. Of the 623 institutions that responded, 93 percent claimed to "give moral support to the value of service experiences," but in only 28 percent of the schools was someone paid to identify these opportunities. In addition, only 23 percent of the institutions responding said that they "offer financial support to permit students to undertake service experiences," and only 13 percent awarded credit for this activity.[25]

Whether these activities should be developed more fully seems to us a question to be decided by the universities and colleges themselves. Some proponents of national service have suggested that the government might foster such activities by making federal scholarship money conditional on an applicant's having undertaken some period of service. Some precedent for this may be found in the federally operated National Health Service Corps (NHSC). This program offers graduate school scholarships for students in the health professions in exchange for a commitment that for each year of financial aid received, the student will serve 1 year after training in an officially designated health manpower shortage area.[26] For reasons described in chapter 8, we do not believe that adding service scholarships to the existing pool of federal aid would have a significant effect on encouraging service, nor do we favor reallocating existing federal undergraduate aid so as to tie its award to service. As we explain in chapter 8, the effects of such a step seem to us to be biased toward certain income groups; we doubt that it would prove a very powerful incentive; and we think it would encourage resentment. If access to higher education is to be used as an inducement to public service, we think the appropriate sources of that inducement should be the colleges and universities themselves.

This leaves open the question of what steps the federal government might take to encourage voluntary national service. Taking account of the difficulties already discussed, there are a number of possibilities.

One alternative would grant to private voluntary organizations and government agencies a subsidy of perhaps $500 or $1,000 for each unpaid volunteer such organizations utilized per year.[27] Such subsidies would be intended to create the incentive and to provide the resources for organizations to solicit, train, and supervise volunteer labor.[28] The presumption of such a plan is that the main constraint on volunteering is neither a shortage of work to do nor an unwillingness of additional citizens to volunteer but the limited ability of service organizations to bear the costs of effectively finding, training, placing, and supervising additional volunteers.

If this premise is right, such a program might stimulate increases in volunteering while leaving its character unchanged. On balance, however, we conclude that the growth in numbers of volunteers would not justify the cost and degree of bureaucratization that such a plan would generate. We believe that the psychological, political, and economic costs would be likely to outweigh the gains in participation and service.

Volunteer plans of the type repeatedly proposed by institutions advocating national service, such as the National Service Secretariat, the Potomac Institute, the Youth Policy Institute, the Roosevelt Centennial Youth Project, and the National Council on Employment Policy, are of greater interest.[29] Although these proposals diverge in many particulars and are silent on some key points, common to them is the concept that a system of national service should be created by reviving or expanding a group of service programs that are thought to have proved themselves already and by integrating these efforts into a larger and more visible national service system. Such a system, encompassing the Peace Corps, VISTA, one or more conservation corps, local community service programs, and other components,[30] might draw more volunteers than the various components could attract operating independently and might utilize incentives and rewards in addition to modest in-service pay or allowances. These might include priority for educational grants and loans, preference for federal jobs, or (in the event of a military draft) draft deferment. Further, the hope of proponents of these programs is that not all such benefits would be provided by the government. Participation in such a program might be recognized by businesses in hiring decisions and by colleges and universities in admissions decisions. In these ways, society could place value on the experience and reinforce the concept of service as an obligation of citizenship.[31]

Program Particulars

How might such a program work? We think it might most feasibly be designed as follows.

A national service organization (NSO) would be created as a federal agency charged with coordinating national service activities. The agency would operate no programs. Instead, it would publicize opportunities for various forms of national service, refer applicants for service positions to approved programs, allocate federal matching funds to approved state programs, monitor program grantees to ensure compliance with grant conditions, and evaluate program experience with respect to the goals of national service. The NSO would take a number of steps to foster a sense that national service is truly national. It would aim to balance its grants of matching funds to achieve geographic diversity and an overall program in which the ratio of participation of high school graduates and nongraduates approximated the national average. It also would design a standardized credential to be awarded on completion of service and would encourage private and public institutions to give preference in hiring, training, and education to persons who had earned it.

The three major components of program 3 would be federal military, federal civilian, and state civilian programs.

Military Programs

As is the case now, advertising, recruitment, and selection for military service would be the exclusive responsibility of the Department of Defense. Insofar as the NSO's advertising and recruitment efforts yielded candidates for military service, the NSO would refer these men and women to the armed services. The Pentagon would, as now, pay whatever wage was required to enlist the numbers and types of men and women that were desired from the standpoint of national security. In addition, however, completion of a full term of active-service military duty (typically 2 to 4 years) or a full term of part-time reserve duty (typically 4 to 6 years) would be acknowledged as a national service contribution. A soldier, marine, sailor, or airman with an honorable discharge would earn a certificate of completion of national service.

Federal Civilian National Service

This branch of national service might provide approximately 55,000 positions, 40,000 of them for 1-year terms and 15,000 (in the Peace Corps) for individuals serving 2 years. As in the state portions of the national service system, all members of the federal civilian national service would be paid a subsistence allowance equivalent to two-thirds of the minimum wage while in service, with a completion payment equal to one-third of the minimum wage. The program would incorporate the Peace Corps, VISTA, and a federal conservation corps.[32]

Peace Corps. Since its establishment in 1961, the Peace Corps has been the flagship of federal service programs. Created by President John F. Kennedy, the program is closely associated with ideals of citizen service. Further, its college-educated volunteers give the Peace Corps prestige and a well-placed alumni constituency.[33]

The program always has been small, and in recent years, it has grown even smaller. From a peak of 15,000 volunteers in service in 1967, the program has fallen to a total of fewer than 5,500 in each of the years 1981–1984.[34] For proponents of national service plans like program 3, this illustrates how service opportunities are now unduly constricted and could be expanded in programs already in operation.[35]

Quite apart from interest in national service, many Peace Corps proponents have urged an expansion on its own terms. In 1980, the program's director set an enrollment target of 15,000 volunteers by 1985.[36] More recently, in the absence of progress toward that goal, Representative Jim Leach of Iowa introduced legislation mandating an increase to 10,000 positions.[37]

As with any other program, the size of the Peace Corps is a consequence of the supply of volunteers, the demand for volunteers (in this instance from foreign countries), and the extent of support provided by Congress through the appropriations process. If program 3 were enacted, it seems plausible that all three variables could be adjusted to return the Peace Corps to its historical peak enrollment of 15,000. On the supply side, about 15,000 applicants were screened in 1985, yielding 2,500 new trainees to be placed abroad.[38] We think that pool could be expanded simply by enlarging the Peace Corp's restricted advertising budget of $250,000. Indicative of the potential pool of applicants are 1973 and 1974 numbers of 35,000 and 30,000 applicants, respectively.[39]

Arguably, foreign demand for volunteers may not warrant a tripling of the program. In recent years, 65 to 75 percent of foreign requests have been filled,[40] implying a potential for at most a 50 percent growth. Furthermore, some requests probably should not be filled for diplomatic reasons or because of inadequate working conditions. Nonetheless, foreign demand is affected partially by the supply of qualified volunteers. We conclude, therefore, that a steady state of 15,000 volunteers is achievable.

It is worth noting that the Peace Corps is expensive. The 1984 appropriation of $115 million for just under 5,500 volunteers yielded an average cost per volunteer of about $20,900.[41] This sum covers administration, training (typically 2 to 4 months), medical care, operating expenses, a subsistence allowance intended to permit volunteers to live at the level of host-country co-workers, and a readjustment allowance, paid on completion of service, of $175 for every month in the corps. Maintaining this expenditure pattern but assuming some economies of scale, an expansion of the corps to 15,000 members would require an appropriation in the range of $300 to $325 million.[42] The failure of Representative Leach's bill to date suggests a political unwillingness to make these expenditures. As a part of program 3, however, we will assume that appropriations at this level were offered and the Peace Corps brought back to an enrollment level of 15,000. At the present attrition rate of roughly 27 percent,[43] the Peace Corps would then take in approximately 9,000 members per year, with 6,500 remaining for their second year of service. Experience suggests that a negligible percentage of the accepted volunteers would be under twenty-one, more than half would be between twenty-one and twenty-five, and another quarter would be between twenty-six and thirty-one.[44]

Volunteers in Service to America (VISTA). VISTA was conceived in the early 1960s as a national service program. In fact, it was almost named the Volunteer National Service Corps.[45] Speaking on behalf of the program, Secretary of Labor Willard Wirtz was concerned about distinguishing it from proposals whose aim was to help the unemployed:

> [T]he Youth Employment Act . . . [was] designed to give actual employment to 50,000 to 60,000 youths . . . a year.
>
> This [VISTA] is an entirely different program involving the recruitment . . . of something in the neighborhood of a thousand who would go out to do service work with respect to groups of one sort or another. The other is an employment program; this is a service program.[46]

Enacted in 1964 and modeled on the Peace Corps, the program enlists volunteers for a year of antipoverty service in public and charitable (including church-operated) agencies. Typical assignments include organizing or working in local literacy drives, food distribution projects, and alcohol, drug and employment counseling programs. Workers are provided living costs during training and are paid a subsistence allowance after training that varies with the cost of living in their places of assignment.[47] Subsistence allowances averaged $424 per month in fiscal year 1985.[48] Further, as in the Peace Corps, volunteers accumulate a readjustment allowance (in this instance, $75 per month beginning after training) payable on completion of a full term of service. In sum, assuming a 40-hour week, the typical VISTA volunteer ultimately receives approximately the minimum wage.[49]

VISTA enrollments, never large, have declined even more dramatically than those in the Peace Corps. From a high of 4,580 volunteer-service-years in fiscal year 1975, budget cutbacks forced enrollments down to 3,982 service-years in fiscal year 1980 and to 1,728 in 1983. Projections for fiscal year 1985 put the figure at about 2,200.[50] In large measure, this decline can be attributed to the political controversy generated by VISTA, which is itself instructive about the sources of resistance to national service as realized by programs like program 3. Whereas Peace Corps volunteers operate with low visibility, VISTA volunteers often have come into conflict with established interests. Tenant unions, agricultural cooperatives, legal aid activists, publicists of black lung disease, and Hispanic and black lobbying groups all have used VISTA volunteers—or have been used by them—to work for controversial goals. The resulting political criticism has limited VISTA budgets.[51]

Despite that phenomenon, we assume that VISTA would be expanded to the anticipated size of the Peace Corps—that is, to about 15,000 volunteers in service at any one time. These volunteers would serve for 1 year.

If historical patterns hold, the characteristics of these volunteers would be different from their Peace Corps equivalents. In the late 1970s and thereafter, while the Peace Corps increasingly sought individuals with technical skills, VISTA moved in the opposite direction toward employing volunteers from among the populations that would be served by VISTA programs. In 1983, 11 percent of VISTA's volunteers had less than a high school education, and 29 percent reported completing only high school. Only 23 percent (in comparison with the Peace Corps' 78 percent) held college degrees.[52] As with the Peace Corps, however, most participants would be substantially older than program 2 participants. In 1978, the median age of VISTA volunteers was twenty-seven; in 1983 it was thirty-five.[53]

The American Conservation Corps. The notion of a federal conservation corps derives from Franklin Roosevelt's CCC, which itself drew inspiration from a reforestation program Roosevelt began as governor of New York.[54] In the 1930s, the CCC was regarded as a success, and that popularity has continued. A poll in 1936 reported that 82 percent of the public favored the CCC and 78 percent wanted to make the program permanent.[55] A quarter of a century later, Senator Hubert Humphrey commented, "[T]he CCC left no bad taste. Even the bitterest opponent of the New Deal has to admit that the CCC was a sound investment in both people and land."[56]

Given the favorable recollections of the CCC, it is not surprising that when the War on Poverty turned its attention to disadvantaged youth in the mid-1960s, the resulting Job Corps established a number of rural residential centers where sixteen- to twenty-one-year-olds would undertake conservation work. Under Department of Interior and Department of Agriculture supervision, the Job Corps maintained thirty centers engaged in conservation activities through the 1970s and early 1980s. Between 1971 and 1982, this program was supplemented with a summer Youth Conservation Corps (YCC), which reached a peak of 30,000 positions in 1980. Between 1978 and 1982, these two agencies operated a third program,[57] a year-round Young Adult Conservation Corps (YACC) providing about 25,000 positions for unemployed sixteen- to twenty-three-year-olds.[58] Both the YCC and the YACC offered residential and live-at-home job opportunities.

By the end of 1982, the YCC and YACC had been scaled back through budget cuts. The YACC was eliminated when CETA (under which it had been authorized) was replaced by the Job Training Partnership Act,[59] which did not provide for a conservation corps. The YCC has continued with a greatly reduced annual budget of $10 million (down from $60 million) divided between the U.S. Forest, Park, and Fish and Wildlife services. In summer 1984, each of these bureaus had 2,000 youths under the YCC.

In 1984, Congress voted by a wide margin in both chambers to establish a CCC-like American Conservation Corps. The bill was vetoed by President Reagan on the grounds that it generated unnecessary public sector employment instead of more desirable private sector jobs. A similar bill was introduced into both houses early in 1985,[60] evidence of the fact that there remains substantial support for programs of this type.[61]

Against this backdrop, we have included in program 3 an American Conservation Corps (ACC) offering 25,000 full-time jobs mainly in residential settings on federal lands for men and women between the ages of eighteen and twenty-three.[62] Because we see the ACC as a service rather than an employment program, admission would not be restricted to the unemployed as in the early CCC and in the YACC.

Participants in the YACC were paid a minimum wage for a 40-hour week, and legislation establishing the ACC similarly would provide for a full minimum wage. Such provisions may be necessary in the face of union opposition to lower wages. For our analysis, we assume, as has typically been proposed by national service advocates, that two-thirds of the minimum wage would be paid to federal conservation corps participants, with a separation allowance bringing this to the equivalent of a full minimum wage upon completion of a 1-year term. As in the YACC, a nominal amount ($3 per day in the YACC) would be deducted for the room and board of participants in residential programs.

The likely demographics of the resulting program may be roughly inferred from the experience of the YACC. Over the 5 years we analyzed (1978–1982), approximately 60 percent of that program's participants were high school graduates, roughly two-thirds were male, two-thirds were white, and one-third were disadvantaged.[63]

State and Local Programs

We think that the components of program 3 described above would be appropriately sponsored and operated by the federal government. The armed services and Peace Corps involve national defense or foreign policy issues that are clearly best left to the federal government. The ACC would work primarily on federal lands, and it seems desirable to have a national program like VISTA to give volunteers an opportunity to serve outside their own states.

But many national service programs could be run by state and local governments. State programs would offer opportunities to work on state and local problems, including state parks and forest conservation, road beautification, city service needs, and disaster-related work. Locally controlled programs also could enhance program variety and moderate the objection that national service would expand undesirably the role of the federal government.

State and local programs would diminish prospects of welding the nation's youth together in a common experience, but because they would be localized, they could enhance their participants' sense of common service to their own community. Further, by including selected state and local programs in national service and by having the NSO create a common recognition for all service activity, some synergy and sense of unity could be created among state programs and between state and federal programs. We would have the NSO endorse and subsidize half the costs of two kinds of local programs, conservation corps and community service programs.[64]

State and Local Conservation Corps. Approximately one-third of the dollars allocated to the YCC and the YACC were designated for state and local conservation corps programs. The loss of this support, however, has hardly terminated state interest in such projects. As noted in chapter 1, year-round programs, mainly oriented toward environmental work and administered by state departments of natural resources, are operating in ten states, while several other states have experimented with summer programs or were drafting conservation corps plans as of mid-1985. Among these are a notable county program begun in Marin County, California, in 1982 and a city program started in San Francisco in 1983.

State and local conservation programs are strikingly small, ranging from 65 year-round positions in Marin County to about 300 positions in programs in Ohio and Wisconsin and 1,900 positions in the eight-year-old California Conservation Corps, by far the largest. Even if federal funding produced expansion in these programs, they would remain relatively small. This, we think, is an attractive feature, encouraging experimentation and facilitating detailed evaluation.

Program 3 would provide for a federal subsidy of half the cost of year-round state conservation corps programs up to a limit of 25,000 positions across the nation, or about three times the number of state positions that existed under the YACC at its peak.

Local Community Service Programs. In the late 1960s and at dramatically expanded levels in the 1970s, the federal government experimented with substantial public sector programs for unemployed adults. Unlike the Peace Corps and VISTA conceptions of the early 1960s, these were large programs designed to counter enduring (that is, structural) or cyclical unemployment rather than to provide service opportunities. The centerpiece of these efforts was the Comprehensive Employment and Training Act of CETA 1974.[65]

CETA workers were employed by state and local governments or by private nonprofit agencies. This employment bore some resemblance to national service. Projects to which workers were assigned had to meet additional community needs beyond those already being met by the hiring agency. Although CETA workers acquired the reputation of being low skilled and unemployable, this image derived primarily from the characteristics of participants in the Title I training programs for those most in need. In the mid-1970s, "seventy-five percent of the CETA participants filling public service jobs had at least a high school education. Many had college degrees. Unpublished data . . . shows 16 percent of all CETA participants in public employment had 4 or more years of education after high school."[66] The average worker stayed in the program for 8 months.[67]

These programs provide a plausible model for another form of adult national service. As the experience of CETA indicates, however, employment programs, even when they embody elements of service, do not enjoy political support proportionate to their substantial expense. Moreover, the massive numbers of those who need jobs necessarily drives such programs to accept many who are less than fully qualified and to reject others who appear employable. Finally, nothing about these jobs distinguishes them from normal employment. They are taken for pay, are performed individually, and provide no sense of a cohort of workers pursuing a common aim.

More attractive as a model for national service have been the several very small and experimental programs that hired small numbers of younger people for periods of community service.[68] Between 1973 and 1977, the Program for Local Service (PLS), established first in Seattle and then throughout Washington state, demonstrated possibilities through this approach with an enrollment of 300 to 400.[69] In 1978, a Youth Community Service (YCS) program in Syracuse, New York, and surrounding areas took the same tack, reaching enrollments of 2,000.[70] In the 1980s, a number of such programs have flowered as a result of local initiatives. Of these, the most visible example is in New York City, which has established the City Volunteer Corps (CVC) operated by the municipally funded National Service Corporation and designed to put about 1,000 eighteen-year-olds to work, in teams, on a variety of human service and environmental tasks.

Under program 3, we anticipate federal sponsorship of approximately 100,000 positions in locally run community service programs. Although a limited number of programs might be supported at higher enrollment levels to test the greater administrative complexities and the possible economies of scale in larger programs, as a general rule the NSO would fund programs of fewer than 2,000 positions. In this way, available funds would be distributed through many jurisdictions and larger, more heavily bureaucratic operations would be discouraged. This level of funding would imply federal support for about 100 programs across the country.

Criteria for Funding State and Local Programs

We envision the following twelve criteria for state and local programs eligible for funding by the federal NSO under program 3:

1. Programs could be operated by state, city, or county agencies or, as in the YCS and New York City programs, by separately incorporated organizations with their own boards of directors. Funding for approved programs would flow from the federal NSO through the states to local governments or the independent corporations designated by local governments.
2. Local programs could establish admissions criteria or targeted recruitment efforts according to their own priorities as long as at least half of their participants were under the age of twenty-three. This requirement is intended to ensure that the community service programs join with the other components of program 3 to provide a substantial array of service opportunities for each cohort of young people.

   Conversely, the requirement permits experimentation with including older persons,[71] and it does not require targeting only those of a given economic status, such as the unemployed. We anticipate that many programs would target the unemployed, and most, whether targeted or not, would draw heavily from that group. We would like to avoid characterizing the national program in this way, however, and we would value the information that some states and cities might provide about the rewards of programs that recruited more broadly. Some localities even might be encouraged to follow the Peace Corps and Teachers Service Corps models by targeting the educated and advantaged segments of the population.
3. State and local authorities could mix residential and nonresidential positions as desired.
4. Initial and in-service training periods could vary at the discretion of the program operators.
5. Supplemental educational efforts (as in New York City, which requires classroom work several nights per week) could be required or offered at the discretion of the local program.
6. Terms of service could be 6, 9, or 12 months and would be determined by the local program.
7. NSP compensation would be set at two-thirds of the minimum wage while in service, with a readjustment allowance equal to at least the remaining third of the minimum wage on satisfactory completion of a full term of service.[72]
8. Projects could be undertaken for qualified governmental agencies and nonprofit entities as in programs 1 and 2. (The experience of the PLS and

YCS programs was that project sponsors tended to be about evenly divided between the public sector and private agencies; neither program experienced any shortage of willing sponsors.) Acceptable projects would be limited to those that did not violate the labor displacement rule, as discussed in chapter 2.

9. Funding preference would be given to programs that caused participants to see their work as part of a larger pattern of service. This perspective might be encouraged, for example, by involving participants in responses to community emergencies, by collateral activities such as donating blood or tutoring, by organizing participants into work teams, and by emphasizing service goals during selection and training.
10. Funding preference would be given to programs that provided substantial supervision. Youth, and especially disadvantaged youth, would probably warrant a ratio of supervisor-to-enrollee hours of better than one to twelve.
11. Supervision might be provided by program employees or by the agencies for which the NSPs were working. The NSO would distribute funds to test whether either method consistently was preferable and whether efforts (such as those in New York City) to maintain NSP crew or team cohesion would warrant their costs.
12. All costs of the program other than those met by sponsor contributions would be paid equally by the NSO and the local government.

Program Participants

The components of program 3 add up to a total civilian national service program of about 180,000 positions, as shown in table 7–1. Because of the high attrition rates (discussed in the next section) experienced by virtually all analogous programs, the number of NSPs entering the program each year would be at least one-third larger than this number of positions, bringing total civilian participation in any year to about 240,000 young men and women. When military recruits were added to this number, the total would exceed 600,000. Put another way, under program 3, roughly one in every six youths would serve in one capacity or another.[73] Because men have more opportunities in the military and apply in greater numbers than women for several components of the program, as many as one in four men may serve, while as few as one in eight women may participate. Table 7–2 summarizes our estimates (based on experience with analogous programs in previous years) of the principal characteristics of the likely NSPs. It suggests that, apart from the underrepresentation of women, program 3 as a whole is likely to be broadly representative of youth, although each of its components probably would draw disproportionately from different parts of the youth population.

Table 7–1
Civilian Program 3 Positions

Component	*Positions*
Peace Corps	15,000
VISTA	15,000
American Conservation Corps	25,000
State and Local Conservation Corps	25,000
Local Community Service Programs	100,000
Total	180,000

Impact on Social and Environmental Services

In considering the impact of program 1, we noted that its NSPs would be young and inexperienced and typically would serve in short periods for a relatively small number of hours. From this we inferred that the net worth of the social services performed would be relatively low (though not insignificant). Because program 2 NSPs would be drawn only from the ablest portions of the population, would be older, and would serve 2-year terms, we concluded that the value of their activity would be considerably higher. Apart from administrative costs, we concluded that a program 2 work force would be more productive than a hired adult minimum wage work force of the same size.

Program 3 falls between these two levels in the relative value of its workers and, under most conditions, in its likely impact on social services. Program 3 participants could undertake the same kinds of work as those of program 2. They could serve, as noted, in conservation corps, in the Peace Corps, and in urban projects, including health preventive and patient care work, day care and recreational assistance, teaching, and property rehabilitation. Several factors would limit the impact of these activities, however. Most critically, program 3 participants typically would serve only 1-year terms. This would create an inefficiently rapid personnel turnover and would limit the time that could be profitably spent in training. Even worse, because it would be voluntary, program 3 predictably would suffer from substantial attrition among its recruits. Preliminary figures on the experience of the New York City Volunteer Corps, for example, show attrition of 46 percent after 6 months and of 59 percent after 9.2 months.[74] High rates of attrition and the related problem of absenteeism make for inefficiency and reinforce the argument against substantial investments in training.[75] Finally, while program 2 would draw its recruits only from those who met military entrance stan-

Table 7–2
Estimated Demographics of Program 3 Annual Entrants

Entrant Characteristics	*Military*[a]	*Peace Corps*[b]	*VISTA*[c]	*ACC*[d]	*State Conservation Corps*[d]	*Local Community Service*[e]	*All Components*
Number per Year	520,000	9,000	20,000	33,000	33,000	133,000	768,000
Median Age	19	24	35	19	19	19	19
Percent High School Diploma[f]	90	100	70	50	40	25	76
Percent Minority	25	5	40	25	50	85	38
Percent Male	88	55[f]	30[f]	65	65	50	77

[a]Including all non-prior service entrants to active-duty and the reserve and guard. Estimates based on 1986 discussions with Office of the Assistant Security of Defense for Force Management and Personnel.

[b]Estimates based on 1983 data obtained from the Peace Corps Public Affairs Office, see "Peace Corps," chapter 7.

[c]Estimates based on present program information from VISTA. See "VISTA," chapter 7.

[d]Estimates based on data drawn from YACC Annual Reports, 1978–1982; 1985 interviews with Staff members of Public/Private Ventures; and evaluation of several conservation corps programs.

[e]Estimates drawn from 1985 interviews with staff of Public/Private Ventures and review of demographics of analgous community service programs.

[f]Based on data from ACTION, *Annual Report, 1981*.

[g]Includes those with GED.

dards, program 3 is designed to draw from the full range of the population. This probably would lower the average productivity of the volunteers. In sum, it seems clear that the work performed through program 3 would be less extensive and lower in quality than that of program 2, but higher than that of program 1.

It is difficult to proceed from this generality to a more informative estimate of program 3's net worth. Conceptually, there is much dispute over how to measure the benefit of service programs. A Public/Private Ventures study notes at least seven plausible methods of assessing program value and persuasively concludes that each has fundamental conceptual difficulties as well as problems in execution.[76] Moreover, the range of work in program 3 would be so broad, its members so diverse, and the characteristics of program supervisors and administrators so varied that program performance would be very difficult to predict. An indication of this problem is that in an existing program, when sponsors were asked to evaluate projects, they reported values ranging from thirty-five times project costs to one-eighteenth of those costs.[77]

Nonetheless, the question of average work value may be better addressed for program 3 than for any other program because analyses are available of results of several programs on which program 3 is modeled. In addition, since the returns from program 3 are likely to fall between those from programs 1 and 2, an empirically informed estimate helps establish an upper bound on the rewards from program 1 and a lower bound on the rewards from program 2, both of which have less precedent.

In a series of careful studies, David Zimmerman and his colleagues at Mathematica estimated the value of the work performed by participants in a number of federally sponsored public service work programs. Zimmerman's analysis of the value of work in five upstate New York programs is illustrative of his methodology and his results.[78] The participants in those programs were not precisely like the members of program 3 because they did not include any middle-age or elderly workers and did include a significant number of students still in high school, part-time workers, and summer workers.[79] Nonetheless, the work (including land and building maintenance, recreation assistance, clerical support, teacher assistance, and day care),[80] the work sites (public and nonprofit agencies),[81] and the participants (predominantly eighteen- and nineteen-year-olds, with a mix of high school graduates and nongraduates)[82] were similar enough to the mainstream of program 3[83] to make Zimmerman's results useful in assessing the likely product of this program.[84]

Observing eighty-eight public service work projects, Zimmerman and his colleagues calculated that "an alternative supplier would have charged $3.23 to produce the goods and services produced by participants . . . during each hour that they were engaged in output producing activities in these programs."[85] Since the minimum wage was then $3.10 per hour, this result appears highly encouraging.

These results should not be exaggerated, however. The alternative supplier price would have included fringe benefits, overhead costs, and a profit factor. A local community service program in program 3 would not have a profit and might involve low fringe benefits, but because of a need for close supervision of a fluctuating and inexperienced work force, its overhead costs would be substantial. Putting these costs aside and comparing workers' productivity directly, Zimmerman observed that "we can be 95 percent confident, in a statistical sense" that each hour's work by participants in the program was "between 67 and 79 percent as productive" as the employee of a private sector contractor would have been at doing the same work.[86] To this less favorable estimate must be added the fact that, as Zimmerman acknowledges,[87] program participants would not be likely to devote as many hours in a 40-hour service week to work as would regular employees.

In the most tentative and controversial portion of his report, Zimmerman estimates not simply the cost of supplying the services offered by the program participants but also the value of those services—that is, what society would pay for them if normal demand factors applied. He and his colleagues used a variety of indicators (such as waiting lists for services, the value of time freed for permanent agency personnel, and agency willingness to subsidize program costs) to assess the output value of program projects. Discarding those evaluations in which they did not have substantial confidence, the evaluators recorded 20 percent of the projects as having intermediate value, 40 percent as below that level, and 40 percent above it. They then discounted the dollar cost of obtaining private sector labor to produce these projects by factors of from 0 to 100 percent depending on project ratings. (The most highly valued projects received no discount, while poorly valued projects were highly discounted.) Reviewing only cases in which they had substantial confidence, the evaluators thus arrived at an adjusted estimate suggesting that the labor in these programs produced goods and services that would be valued at, on average, $1.86 per hour,[88] or 60 percent of the then prevailing minimum wage.

Like others, we would differ with some of Zimmerman's methods. The fact that these observations were quantified and calculated should not obscure their debatable and subjective basis. The method displays no evident bias, however, and appears as refined as the subject permits. The results, moreover, comport with our separately developed sense of the likely average productivity of NSPs in program 3. We conclude that, because of the lower productivity of short-term and inexperienced workers, the value of program 3 services[89] probably would be between one-half and three-quarters of the minimum wage for the hours in which work actually was performed.[90]

These very crude estimates are hardly dispositive. Even if Zimmerman's findings and our inferences from them were indisputable, community service programs could improve their productivity by, for example, engaging older and more skilled workers as NSPs or by improved supervision and training. In fact, program 3's funding criteria encourage such steps. It also is possible that larger programs established for longer terms could achieve economies of scale not possible in the small, short-term programs that Zimmerman evaluated.

More fundamentally, one could argue on either of two grounds for investment in program 3 even if it returned only half the wages paid. First, to the extent that participants in program 3 would have been underemployed or unemployed outside the program, the program might produce net social gain through the combination of the work accomplished and the avoidance of the social and financial costs of unemployment.

Second, it may be unreasonable to expect the program to pay its own way in work produced. If it paid half its costs in this way, the remaining half may be justified by the program's effects on its participants.

Effects on NSPs

The variety of the program's participants, of their activities, and of the terms and circumstances of their service makes it difficult to assess its likely effects on NSPs. The program would include Peace Corps volunteers, often with college backgrounds, predominantly in their mid-twenties and sometimes much older, living in foreign countries, frequently apart from other volunteers as well as their families for 2-year terms; it would include community service program participants, typically eighteen or nineteen years old but sometimes much older, many of whom did not receive high school diplomas, performing social service work for 1 year in urban areas while living in their own homes; and it would include conservation corps members spending a year in predominantly rural settings, living in barracks, and doing work that would involve them more substantially with other volunteers than with service recipients.

The difficulty of assessing effects on the NSPs is compounded, moreover, by the absence of reliable analyses of the effects of conservation corps and community service corps experiences on their participants.[91] As with the Peace Corps studies discussed in chapter 6, the available reviews typically suffer from a reliance on self-report, form an exclusive focus on short-term effects, from response bias (the tendency for a disproportionate number of those with favorable views to respond to questionnaires), from design bias (questions inherently likely to elicit only positive answers), and above all, from a failure to focus on opportunity costs (to use a control group to gain some insight into what would have happened to enrollees without the program).

Taking these caveats into account, our discussion proceeds under the three headings used in chapter 6: effects on work opportunities and income, effects on attitudes and self-definition, and effects as a rite of passage.

Work Opportunities and Income

Our discussion of program 2 already has summarized what is known about the effects of service in the Peace Corps.[92] In short, it appears that service causes a delay in entry into the career work force and a consequent lag in earnings and advancement. This lag is most pronounced on return but is still in evidence several years later. There is no direct evidence as to whether it eventually disappears or perhaps even reverses itself later in volunteers' working lives, although one military study suggests such a reversal.[93]

In one respect, we believe that the Peace Corps experience will be indicative. As a general rule, community service and conservation corps are not likely to provide specific skills that will lead directly to private sector jobs. In an early report, the California Conservation Corps offered an optimistic view of the match between tasks its members undertook while in service and jobs they might hold after service. For example, it noted:

> Seed-cone collection provides a unique training opportunity because the preferred method of collection involves tree-climbing. During 1978 about 100 corps members were trained in safe tree-climbing; 72 received certificates and are now qualified to work for utility companies as linemen or to enter the tree service field, where there is a lack of experienced climbers.[94]

Most tasks associated with conservation work do not generate highly salable special skills. The same report acknowledges, for example, that while "selected corps members gained valuable mapping and photo-interpretation skills [while working on irrigation and water conservation projects], most of the work in this category consisted of cleaning out and repairing water ditches."[95]

In this respect, the model that often dominates thinking about national service, the Roosevelt administration's CCC, is misleading. The economic benefit to participants in the CCC arose primarily from the income it provided when jobs were scarce. The CCC was not an effective career development or job placement program. As the most comprehensive study of the program observed:

> [T]he CCC did not do all things well. . . . [E]ducation and training received little emphasis. It is widely acknowledged that the CCC had limited success in meeting these secondary goals. . . .
>
> In a survey of enrollees from the first enrollment period (summer, 1933)

> a Federal Emergency Relief Administration study finds that of those enrollees who left *during* the enrollment term, 24.7% were employed several months later; of enrollees who completed the first enrollment term, however, only 14.8% were employed several months later.[96]

Similarly, community service corps programs have not built an encouraging track record of postservice employment success. Although we have found no quantitative data on the point, it is notable that a reason given for abandoning the Seattle Program for Local Service (PLS) after 3 years of operation was that "state officials feel that the experience has been costly and has not appreciably reduced the youth unemployment rate."[97]

Nonetheless, there is some basis for believing that program 3 could aid the employment prospects of its participants. Although service programs would teach few specific skills, private sector employees do not normally expect these skills from the youths they hire. Rather they value socialization to the world of work, as is manifested by traits such as punctuality, reliability, and the capacity to follow directions. For NSPs able to obtain and maintain private sector jobs, a national service program would add little to the ability to acquire and demonstrate these skills. The relatively privileged Peace Corps volunteers are, for the most part, in this position. But for those who had not acquired those skills independently, a service program would offer a means of socialization to the workplace.

Would this socialization be accomplished? Experience suggests that it can be in programs with substantial supervision, strong discipline, and high morale. Substantial supervision is costly but imperative. As one program evaluator put it, "[O]verseeing a group of three hundred you're not likely to see who's late; supervising a group of thirty you can't see who's slacking off; supervising a group of six, you can set and maintain standards that matter." The stress we place on supervision in program 3 stems from this and similar observations.

The case for program 3 in this regard is strengthened by the fact that service programs lend themselves especially well to high morale and strong discipline. Conservation corps value skills in fire-fighting and other emergencies in large measure because they underscore vividly the need for discipline and team cohesion while raising the participant's sense of self-worth. According to a similar theory, New York's urban community service corps organizes its participants in teams, brings them together regularly, and emphasizes targeted, visible projects.

This approach has intuitive appeal. Its benefits, however, have not been documented and may be more substantial in theory than in practice, a circumstance that strengthens the case for experimentation with program 3. Similarly, there is some basis for the argument that these programs create effective incentives for academic progress when traditional schooling has not done so. Several conservation and community service programs are now experimenting with required evening classes in basic math and language literacy (2 nights per week in the New York City Volunteer Corps), with daily writing assignments (keeping a diary in the California Conservation Corps), and with self-paced instruction. By establishing these requirements, these programs may strengthen basic academic skills. Also, if service assignments reinforce these skills and demonstrate their importance, this can have positive consequences. The results of this melding of course work and job work in the Job Corps are very encouraging. Gains of more than two months in reading and arithmetic have been reported for every month in which programs mixed remedial classroom with vocational training on approximately a 50-50 basis.[98]

The variation between components of program 3 would permit some choice about where such remediation activity would be warranted and where it would not. Peace Corps participants, for example, would not be likely to justify such an effort. Conversely, we think that an NSO would be wise to encourage such efforts for disadvantaged members of community service corps. As one group of observers has concluded:

> [S]imply put, the evidence is that work experience programs that are not connected to remediation services and post-program vocational opportunities are unlikely to produce the same results as "enhanced" work experience programs.[99]

NSPs under program 3 also would benefit from the validation that program completion would provide. Again, this gain would be marginal for advantaged NSPs with previous certifications from school degrees and job completion. But for those without such credentials, the qualifications could improve their employability considerably. By placing all its components under one rubric, that of National Service, program 3 might enhance the prestige of conservation and community service completion. A credential otherwise viewed with skepticism might become more valuable. In this way, national service might create a civilian means of making it for disadvantaged youth analogous to the route long available through the military. Because the community corps could (and probably would) accept those who were less accomplished than military recruits, this might be an important increment in the opportunities available to the least advantaged segment of the youth cohort.

In sum, the evidence suggests skepticism about the economic effects of service on privileged participants in program 3 but some reason for believing that the effects on underprivileged participants would be positive. Much would depend on the skill with which remediation activities were integrated with service activities, on whether supervision and discipline were tight, and on whether the public image of the value of program completion was maintained. These variables are as hard to predict as they are critical.

Attitudes and Self-Definition

Roughly three in five of the Peace Corps veterans surveyed on the matter believed that they were maturer than their peers.[100] Our own intuition, educated by discussions with Peace Corps alumni, is that the experience is psychologically enriching for the three-quarters of the Peace Corps volunteers who complete the program. In the short term, we believe the enrichment is probably not unlike that derived from satisfactory completion of college or work: Skills, interests, and self-esteem all are enhanced by immersion in a new environment and by meeting its challenges. In the longer term, however, gains are achieved because a Peace Corps veteran has enjoyed a more diverse experience than a peer whose whole adult career has been confined to the U.S. work force.

In program 2, this benefit had to be compared with the costs associated with compelled service. About that program we asked whether the personal benefits of service would warrant preempting the other activities that normally would have occurred during that time. We concluded that the available evidence was not strong enough to make a persuasive case for conscription on the grounds of benefit to the individual NSP. In a voluntary program like program 3, the situation would be different. Volunteers would apply because they anticipated that the personal gains from service would exceed the personal costs. Assuming that this is a sound judgment, the question remains whether those gains warrant the general public's paying the costs of the program. Taken without regard to the value of the Peace Corps to U.S. foreign policy or to recipients of its services, we do not believe that the effects on the participants justify much of that program's cost of more than $20,000 annually per volunteer. We base our assessment on two considerations. First, there is no evidence that Peace Corps volunteers contribute more to U.S. public life after their service than they would have done without their service. As discussed in chapter 6, the evidence suggests the contrary. Whatever the personal gains from service, they do not appear to produce a public benefit. Second, the personal gains to Peace Corps recruits are gains to the more privileged members of society. As noted, well over 90 percent of Peace Corps members have completed at least 1 year of college. Although the personal development of any citizen is to be valued, the case for a subsidy is weak when the cost is high, the public reward small, and the recipient not disadvantaged.

Conservation and community service corps programs would be less expensive, and most expenditures from these programs would be expected to be directed to the less advantaged members of the youth cohort. Almost half the members of the California Conservation Corps, for example, have neither a high school diploma nor a General Education Diploma[101]; two-fifths of them worked at or below the minimum wage before entering the program[102]; and in the words of one assessment, "70 percent of the entering corps members were at-risk in the labor market because of either economic or educational disadvantage."[103] Similarly, more than half the members of the Syracuse Youth Community Service Program had not graduated from high school,[104] and more than two-thirds of the participants in the Seattle Program for Local Service were unemployed and looking for work.[105]

Although the evidence is impressionistic,[106] program 3 seems likely to provide significant psychological advantages for many of its participants. Psychological gains would be likely to accrue from the visible value of the work accomplished, from the teamwork regularly called for in environmental and some social service projects, from the positive, all-enveloping environment often created in residential camps, and simply from the experience of helping others.[107] But we know of no evidence that would indicate that these programs would build self-esteem more substantially than progressing in school, building a family, or securing a job in the private sector. Accordingly, the psychological benefits of the program would help to justify it predominantly for those least integrated into the mainstream of U.S. society: those who probably would not progress in school, build a family, or secure a private sector job during the same period in their lives.

If the psychological benefits parallel the economic benefits in this respect, why not target program 3 exclusively to unemployed or otherwise disadvantaged youth? It is very unlikely that any form of program 3 would have the resources to involve more than a fraction of the almost 5 million sixteen- to twenty-four-year-olds who are not in school but have not earned a high school diploma.[108] Why permit expensive positions to be filled by high school graduates when this less achieving group probably would benefit more substantially from the program? As two respected observers have written, one of the more essential but often slighted responsibilities of policymakers planning employment programs is to recognize their limited resources and "to identify an actionable universe of need, establish priorities among the groups within the universe, and design overall programs that . . . are realistic in labor market terms."[109]

This is a recurring and critical issue for national service programs like program 3.[110] Most similar proposals seek the aura of service by aiming to involve at least a significant fraction of privileged participants. One could argue for this by asserting that the higher achievers would repay society by making a larger social contribution later in life as a result of their participation in the program. But we find little evidence to support this proposition,[111] and, as noted, the Peace Corps evidence suggests the opposite.[112]

One also could argue that the value of social services rendered by privileged participants would more than repay the costs of their participation. If a skilled NSP wished to work in a voluntary program for minimum wage, why refuse him or her? Although this argument is plausible, it is not supported by the existing evidence. As sketched earlier, program 3 would be likely to involve too much turbulence and administrative and supervisory cost to produce bargain services.

Probably the most compelling rationale for the participation of the more advantaged is that they would enrich the program for the less advantaged. This proposition lies at the core of the appeal of national service, but again we find no empirical evidence to support it. It may be that the presence of more successful young men and women would validate the program. It may also be, however, that the better opportunities and rewards within this program would tend to go to those from more successful backgrounds and that the result would be further self-depreciation by the less privileged. This seems a particularly plausible hypothesis for a plan like program 3 that would take a portfolio approach, drawing different types of NSPs into different activities rather than mixing them all in a single pot.

A 1978–1979 test that mixed low-income and higher-income participants in forty-three job training programs reported "that, in most sites, test managers, counselors, participants or all three . . . felt [that mixing incomes] made a difference and . . . was more useful than not mixing."[113] However, the quantitative data on attitudinal change, skills acquisition, and postservice experience point to no such effects. The evaluators concluded:

> In general, the results . . . are inconclusive. . . . [A]t this time, taken as an aggregate, it is difficult to accept the test hypothesis that mixed income grouping (heterogeneous) will result in greater gain for income eligible youngsters than for non mixed income groupings (homogeneous).[114]

This "inconclusiveness" is hardly surprising. The programs evaluated typically ran for only 3 to 6 months and at most for a year. They had heavy classroom components, limited success in creating a sense of cohesion among program participants, and apparently drew the near-poor rather than the well-off as representatives of higher-income groups.[115] The value of mixing income groups remains unclear.

Equally troublesome, and equally basic to the evaluation of all national service programs like program 3, is the question of whether, for disadvantaged participants, the anticipated psychological gains from having accomplished service are more valuable than the economic gains that might be achieved by more narrowly focused job training. In the Job Corps, for example, there is very little pretense that participants accomplish useful service work; the program is mainly a narrowly targeted, well-focused effort to provide remedial training. It is reasonably clear that this benefits its participants economically. For at least 4 years after the program, graduates enjoy about 4 weeks per year more employment and 15 percent more earnings than their peers.[116] No such case can now be made for any service program. At present, accordingly, someone counseling a disadvantaged person purely from the standpoint of economic welfare could not reasonably urge them to enter a service program rather than the Job Corps.

Rite of Passage

For those who completed a full term in the program, the experience might provide a successful rite of passage. It likely would generate the sense of having met challenges and made a worthwhile contribution, both as an individual and part of a group. The California Conservation Corps illustrates, however, how this feeling of accomplishment is established in part by setting tough standards, holding all those who enroll to them, and then, of necessity, dropping from the program those who do not meet them. One result is that almost four out of five participants in this program leave it prematurely.[117] As previously noted, attrition rates in all service programs are high: more than 25 percent in an elite program like the Peace Corps and typically from 40 to 60 percent for other programs.[118] We have assumed an overall attrition rate of 33 percent in program 3. If even this fairly optimistic estimate were to be realized, the adverse consequences for the one-third who dropped out could not be ignored. A 1978 study of the Job Corps found only one statistically significant consequence of the program in regard to job-related attitudes. This was a negative impact on men who dropped out. The authors hypothesized "that a failure to complete . . . (or even to last more than 3 months) was one more failure to these young men, and that such a premature termination may have a substantial negative impact on attitudes."[119]

Impact on the Military

Uniquely among the programs described in this book, program 3 would have at least small negative effects on the AVF. This is because the program offers 180,000 paid positions to men and women, many of whom would be in the age group that the military seeks to recruit. The program thus would compete with the AVF and predictably would tend to diminish military recruitment. We anticipate that this effect would be noticeable though not debilitating.

The critical variable in this regard is the program's effect on the ability of the AVF to recruit male high school graduates who score above the bottom one-third of the population on standardized tests. Neither officers, who are mostly college graduates, nor female enlistees, who are limited in number, are expected to be in short supply over the next decade.[121]

Several components of program 3 probably would have divergent effects on this core group. Neither the Peace Corps nor VISTA would likely have notable consequences on recruitment of military enlistees. Peace Corps volunteers are a mixture of recent college graduates and older professionals, technicians, and craftspeople. The median age of the volunteer is twenty-five. VISTA volunteers, with a median age of thirty-five, are even less likely to be drawn from a military-eligible population.

Potential competition for military recruitment would come from the ACC, state and local conservation corps, and local community service programs. The conservation corps, in particular, would draw from the primary market for military recruiting. Because the corps offer residential programs of disciplined service on federal lands or other government sites, they have attributes in common with military service. The demographic data in table 7–2 indicate our estimate that about 20,000 male high school graduates could enter the program every year out of total conservation corps entrants of about 67,000.

Local community service programs, while large, are expected to consist primarily of youths who have not completed high school. Participants would tend to serve in their communities and live at home. But if these programs drew 25 percent high school graduates, as suggested in table 7–2, and half of these were male, this could provide some drain from the pool of those the military wished to recruit.

How much these programs would in fact affect military recruitment depends to a great extent on whether national service and military enlistment, from the viewpoint of participants, would be substitutes or complements. If substitutes, national service programs would appeal to those most strongly attracted to the military and hence provide competition. If complements, NSPs would tend to participate both in national service and military programs. While many male high school graduates could be expected to consider both civilian and military national service, significant differences between civilian and military service likely would be apparent to this group. Military enlistees would serve at roughly 50 percent higher pay levels than NSPs, would serve substantially longer periods of time (3- to 6-year terms are the norm), and after a period of formal and on-the-job training, would qualify to work in some military occupational specialties. Because of these differences, there is no reason to believe that those otherwise attracted to the military would choose instead to serve in the ACC or state and local community service or conservation corps. Nevertheless, one could expect some degree of competition to occur, perhaps principally from those who otherwise would select the military because they had no apparent civilian alternative. In the absence of compelling evidence, we speculate that program 3 work would tend, to a minor degree, to draw potential recruits away from military service.

If our estimates in table 7–2 are correct, about 36,000 young male high school graduates would enter the civilian components of program 3 each year. This would be slightly above 13 percent of the current number of male military enlistees with a high school diploma and around 4 percent of the present annual total of male high school graduates. We doubt that even a quarter of these otherwise would have enlisted in the military; that is, we estimate that the military loss probably would be in the range of 10,000 male high school graduates, or about 3 percent of present entrants of this type.

The consequence of this loss to the military would depend on prevailing recruiting conditions. Our analysis of the prospects for the AVF shows a high likelihood of success where the size of the military force remained constant and economic growth rates fell into the moderate range. In these cases, the loss of 10,000 or even more enlistees to national service programs would reduce high school graduate percentages but not below the level recently set in law as the congressionally desired minimum percentages for male high school graduates.[122] If military forces were growing or economic growth was especially rapid, losses of recruits could be especially painful and might require steps such as higher pay, bonuses, or more vigorous (and expensive) recruiting programs.

Proponents of plans like program 3 would argue that this line of reasoning overlooks a potentially important change in attitudes. The Committee for the Study of National Service, for example, has noted:

> As the idea of service becomes more widely accepted among the young, the numbers who will choose to serve through the military should increase. Thus the move toward universal National Service should make military recruiting easier, and help restore the tradition of the citizen-soldier now giving way to a mercenary system.[123]

This view may be right, but in the context of program 3, it should be apparent why we doubt it. This program and alternatively plausible voluntary systems of service are almost certainly too small to affect the attitudes of the youth cohort as a whole. We believe that the propensity to serve in the volunteer military would correlate, as is the case now, with alternative employment prospects, military wages, views of the international situation, and military recruitment efforts. As against these, the attitudes induced by a program like program 3 seem to us likely to prove insignificant or at least incapable of offsetting the losses to the military caused by its employment effects.

We conclude, then, that program 3 would produce a greater degree of competition in the market for military recruits but that these effects would be small and that any loss of recruits could be remedied, if necessary, with higher pay and bonuses for military recruits or with more intensive recruiting efforts.

Labor Market Consequences

The size of the program would make its employment effects small, though favorable. Some measure of the effect is suggested by the fact that in 1980, CETA programs drew some 2,000,000 new enrollees,[124] while leaving unemployment rates generally, and youth unemployment rates in particular, at the discouragingly high levels described in chapter 3's section on "Jobs for Drop-outs and Graduates." In a national labor market of well over 100 million jobs, with 3.5 to 4 million people becoming eighteen each year, a civilian job program of 180,000 added to an already existing 400,000-person military recruitment process would have relatively little impact. Moreover, any program of this type would draw a significant fraction of its participants from those who did not previously participate in the labor force either as job holders or job seekers. They also would mitigate its effects on unemployment as we normally measure it.

Labor substitution effects also probably would be small. As noted in chapter 6, some fraction of the work accomplished in a program of this character would substitute for work that would otherwise have been performed by those hired through the regular labor market. Rules against labor displacement would limit direct job loss as a result of this substitution, but growth in the affected labor force would likely be somewhat retarded whatever the rules. Our best guess is that something on the order of one-quarter to one-third of the new positions established under this program would be offset by the preemption of jobs that would have been created had the program not been established.

The program's net effect, taking account of these points, likely would diminish the number of those unemployed by less than 100,000. At present levels of unemployment, this means the program would provide jobs for about 1 of every 100 unemployed people now looking for work. If all program jobs went to the young, it would help about 4 of every 100 unemployed young people looking for work.[124]

Administration and Costs

Since programs already in existence provide the core of program 3, its administrative structure and, to a lesser degree, its costs can be outlined with greater confidence than was the case for programs 1 and 2.

Administration

As noted earlier, supervisory responsibility for program 3 would be lodged in a small NSO. ACTION, an independent federal agency whose mandate is to "mobilize Americans for voluntary service," operates VISTA, one of the three federal civilian components of program 3. ACTION formerly had responsibility for the Peace Corps as well. ACTION might simply be retitled the NSO and given that office's additional responsibilities. If the president wanted to emphasize the priority his or her administration gave to volunteering and to national service or wished to symbolize a close association with the new program, the NSO (either a new entity or ACTION with a new name and broadened mission) might be made part of the executive office, as was the Office of Economic Opportunity in the early years of the War on Poverty. Either arrangement would be adequate to permit the NSO to carry out its function: not directly to administer the program but to publicize the advantages and opportunities for service, refer applicants to the appropriate operating programs, allocate federal funds to qualifying state programs, monitor the performance of the numerous and disparate elements of the program, help formulate and defend their budget requests both within the executive branch and before Congress, and attempt to provide the semiautonomous entities it supervised with as strong a common rationale and sense of unity as the facts permitted. We estimate that, wherever placed, the NSO would require a staff of only about 200.

Actual operation of the federal elements of program 3 would fall to the augmented staffs of VISTA and the Peace Corps (since 1981, as before 1969, an independent agency) and to the new staff responsible for the ACC. Preferably the ACC also would take the form of an independent agency operating, like ACTION and the Peace Corps, under the coordinating supervision of the NSO.

Local programs would be operated by whatever agencies the participating local jurisdictions chose. We expect that, as is now the case, conservation programs normally would be based in departments of natural resources or of the environment. Most public service programs would probably be administered by departments of employment. Some programs of both types would be operated, like the Wisconsin Conservation Corps and the New York City Volunteer Corps, by independent units governed by boards appointed by governors or mayors.

Costs

The costs of the NSO should not exceed $10 million. The significant costs of program 3 would be incurred by its constituent elements.

As noted earlier, the Peace Corps, enlarged to comprise 15,000 volunteers, would require appropriations in the range of $300 million to $325 million, assuming modest economies of scale. That range represents an increment of approximately $200 million over the Peace Corps' fiscal year 1984 appropriation of $115 million. Bringing VISTA to the same level of 15,000 volunteers, assuming that proved politically feasible, would be less expensive. Since VISTA volunteers receive less training and require fewer supporting services and no long-distance transportation, the total average cost per volunteer approximated $8,500 in fiscal year 1985.[125] The incremental cost of an expansion of VISTA from its current level of 2,200 to 15,000 volunteers would total about $110 million.

The costs per position of the ACC would, we estimate, approach those of the Peace Corps, although their composition would be different. We assume that living conditions (largely in barracks on federal lands) would be spartan in the ACC. Nonetheless, we believe that the standards of close supervision, suitable equipment, and competent staff support established by the California Conservation Corps likely would be taken as an appropriate model[126]; if so, ACC average costs would approximate $20,000 per position. A 25,000-person ACC would therefore require appropriations of about $500 million annually. Total costs for all three federal programs, plus the NSO, might approximate $925 million.

Additional federal as well as state and local costs would result from the conservation and public service programs operated by localities. The costs of conservation programs obviously would depend on the quality and number of the staffs employed, the degree of training and equipment provided, the attrition rates experienced, and especially the proportion of residential to nonresidential programs. The current year-round state conservation corps appear to be predominantly nonresidential.[127] We anticipate that, despite the 50 percent federal subsidy available to qualifying state and local conservation programs under program 3, that pattern would endure. We therefore assume that, of the 25,000 total state and local positions contemplated by the program, about 15,000 would be nonresidential. We have found little cost information on current nonresidential local conservation projects, but it seems reasonable to assume that, if total compensation equaled the minimum wage, or approximately $7,500 annually, the total cost per enrollee would approximate $14,000. Total costs for the 15,000 nonresidential NSPs would amount to $210 million. We believe that local residential programs would adopt essentially the same standards of training and support, on average, as the federal ACC; indeed, because of the federal subsidy, costs may exceed the ACC's $20,000 average. Assuming that average, the 10,000 state and local NSPs in residential conservation programs would produce costs totaling another $200 million.

The tasks set for NSPs in the community service programs would vary more widely than would the environmental tasks of the conservation programs. Similarly, the amount of training offered, the degree of supervision provided, and the attrition experienced probably would range across a broad spectrum. Hence, average costs would differ, perhaps sharply. Nonetheless, these would all be nonresidential programs paying participants who completed the program the equivalent (counting subsistence-level wages and completion allowances) of the minimum wage and meeting the minimum standards of both the NSO and the sponsors who must contribute on-the-job supervision. Those characteristics would place an implicit floor under costs and suggest that average costs should approximate those in the nonresidential conservation programs, or $14,000 per position. The sponsoring agencies would bear part of this cost, however, by providing some supervision. If the average total cost of the sponsor supervisors approximated $40,000 per year and one such supervisor-supplemented program employed supervisors for every twenty NSPs, then $2,000 of the total $14,000 average cost per NSP would be borne indirectly by the sponsors. (The NSO and the state or local corps would divide the remainder evenly.) Thus, the total costs of the public service program, with 100,000 participants, would total about $1.4 billion in 1985 dollars, of which $600 million would be borne by the NSO, $600 million by the jurisdiction establishing the service corps, and the remaining $200 million by the sponsoring agencies, some public and some private.

Total costs for all elements of program 3 would therefore approximate $2.6 billion annually, of which the federal government would be responsible for roughly $1.2 billion.[128] Table 7–3 summarizes these calculations.

Constitutional Considerations

Program 3 poses no serious constitutional problems. It has no adverse effects on personal freedoms because it is entirely voluntary. It raises no contentious new issues concerning federal-state relationships because it follows well-established precedents. Whatever the novelty of the CCC, the Peace Corps, or federal CETA programs when first established, nobody would seriously doubt their constitutionality now.

Conclusion

We believe that program 3 would be attractive but for modest reasons. We anticipate that the civilian program would have beneficial economic and psychological effects on approximately 120,000 participants. This is the number we estimate would join and complete the program, while an equal number could be expected to drop out without completing it.[129]

Would these benefits justify the expenditure of some $2.6 billion? We

Table 7–3
Costs of Program 3
(millions of dollars)

Program Element	*Total Costs*	*Federal Costs*	*State/Local Costs*	*Sponsor Costs*
NSO	10	10	—	—
Peace Corps	200[a]	200[a]	—	—
VISTA	110[a]	110[a]	—	—
ACC	500	500	—	—
Local Conservation Corps	410	205	205	—
Local Service Corps	1,400	600	600	200
Totals	2,630	1,625	805	200

[a]Increments over existing programs.

think that depends in some measure on whether the program concentrated its expenditures on the disadvantaged. If it did, one must ask whether its return for this group would be greater than more focused, Jobs Corps–type training. If it did not, one must ask what special benefit would derive from the participation of the advantaged and whether that benefit would be worth its costs. We do not think these questions can be answered from the knowledge now available. This makes a modest case for setting up program 3 as an experiment. If properly conducted, it should afford the necessary insight into whether targeted or broad-based service programs would afford special rewards as compared with more clearly focused job training programs.

In our view, not much can be expected of program 3 beyond this. Such a program would be too small and too varied in its functions, its enrollment, its locations, and its administrative components either to provide very substantial social services or to shape the attitudes of youth toward service. A bigger program of the same type might have a greater effect, but we doubt that it could be created. If it were created, a larger voluntary program would be representative of the nation's youth. If enrollments were expanded at minimum wages, recruits would be drawn for the most part from among the most disadvantaged. As it is, our calculations suggest that approximately 80 percent of the participants in the civilian component of program 3 would not be high school graduates. Only by including the military would the total program be made roughly representative of the youth population.

We also doubt that higher wages could be used to enhance recruitment, partly because of budget constraints, but even more fundamentally because higher wages would undermine the character of the program as a service program. We believe that a bigger program also would be less likely to achieve the special commitment, even elite status, that has been associated with the California Conservation Corps and that may be attained in other local programs.

This size limit on program 3 logically limits its impact. Indeed, we think that no voluntary program is ever likely to be big enough to make a substantial difference in the character of life in the United States. A small volunteer program may be warranted even if it did not meet that standard. But if advocates of national service are to realize their most ambitious aspirations, we think they will have to come to grips with the issue of compulsion.

Notes

1. A well-developed discussion of the pros and cons may be found in the Committee for the Study of National Service, *Youth and the Needs of the Nation,* 103–14.

2. Bird, "The Case for Voluntary Service," 485–86.

3. The propensity for voluntary activity in the United States has been noted at least since de Tocqueville called this a "nation of joiners." de Tocqueville, *Democracy in America,* 130.

4. Gallup, "The 1983 Gallup Survey on Volunteering," 20. See also the President's Task Force on Private Sector Initiatives, "Volunteers: A Valuable Resource"; and Morgan, Dye, and Hybels, "Results from Two National Surveys of Philanthropic Activity."

5. Smith and Baldwin, "Voluntary Associations and Volunteering in the United States," 286.

6. This is a problem particularly in the United States, although volunteerism is "by no means unique" to America. See ibid., 277. In nations that have seriously considered or established national service systems, voluntary organizations apparently accept state supervision more readily than in the United States.

7. Committee for the Study of National Service, *Youth and the Needs of the Nation,* 110.

8. The lower estimate assumed that a vast majority of participants would be economically motivated. The larger estimate assumed that a substantial but unpredictable number of volunteers would be motivated not economically but by the desire to serve. These numbers were projected for 1982, the assumed starting point of the programs under consideration in the study. It was further projected that the civilian labor power supply available to a national service program would drop over the following 5 years, pushing the number of economically motivated volunteers down to

400,000 in the broad-based case and 220,000 in the small-scale case by 1986. Congressional Budget Office, *Costs of the National Service Act (H.R. 2206),"* 16–17.

9. See Allen et al., *Volunteers from the Workplace,* 18–19. One should not assume that this survey provides an authoritative measure of the current level of private sector involvement in volunteerism. Only 3,500 corporations, including virtually no small businesses, received the survey, and only 364 responded. Nonetheless, the survey is the best source of baseline data on the topic. It is supplemented by Mutual Benefit Life, "Report II: Small Business Commitment to Volunteerism and Community Involvement," based on a 1984 survey of small businesses.

10. Levi Strauss Foundation, *1982 Annual Report,* 6. A 1978 survey identified 207 companies in which employees were involved in group projects. Allen et al., *Volunteers from the Workplace,* 18.

11. The 1978 study identified 125 companies that practice this form of support for service. Allen et al., Volunteers from the Workplace, 18.

12. This is a very rough estimate provided by the Department of Community Relations of Levi Strauss, Inc., in San Francisco.

13. Approximately 150 local United Way organizations operate Management Assistance Programs (MAPs). These serve as liaisons between private sector employees interested in volunteering and nonprofit organizations in need of various types of expertise. United Way of America, *Management Assistance Programs: A Closer Look,* 1.

Even more ambitious is VOLUNTEER's Workplace in the Community project, a venture largely underwritten by the Levi Strauss Foundation, CBS, Honeywell, and the Aetna Life and Casualty Foundation. This 2-year project operates in cooperation with roughly 380 volunteer centers around the country to stimulate and support corporations in the establishment of volunteer programs and to induce social service agencies to put the volunteers to use. In Dallas, for example, the volunteer center created the Business Volunteer Council, which reports it has placed more than 20,000 volunteers in community service activities in its first 3 years of operation. VOLUNTEER, *The Workplace in the Community:* Fact Sheet.

14. Allen et al., *Volunteers from the Workplace,* 21. The study goes on to point out that just 6 percent of the companies interviewed had full-time staff assigned to their volunteer programs; very few if any companies kept records on the number of employees who volunteered or the amount of time they gave; and "few companies have well-articulated goals for their programs and even fewer can describe criteria through which they will be evaluated." Ibid.

The Mutual Benefit Life study of small businesses reports that "even though a majority of top executives are themselves involved in voluntarism, only a third encourage employees, and few companies have a formal program of either encouragement or recognition." Mutual Benefit Life, "Report II: Small Business Commitment to Volunteerism and Community Involvement," 4.

15. The President's Task Force on Private Sector Initiatives, established in 1981, is an example of a government effort in this direction.

16. American Bar Association, *Code of Ethics,* Section 6.1.

17. Reskin, "Law Poll," 42.

18. The views of several admissions officers in this regard are reported in ACTION, "Candid Admissions."

19. Dickson, "Youth Call: The Real Questions," 9. Numerous instances of just

such an approach at the graduate level could be cited. Dr. William Bakewell, admissions chairman for the medical school at the University of North Carolina at Chapel Hill has noted that "some form of medical service experience has become so routine that we might make it a requirement on the application." ACTION, "Candid Admissions," 5. Similarly, according to an official at the University of Rochester, the medical school there "is actively seeking individuals with a strong interest in community service." Ibid.

Other types of graduate institutions place considerable importance on service as well. For example, the director of admissions at the University of Chicago's School of Social Service Administration states that "the desire to serve without rewards of money or academic credit remains strongly appreciated here." The dean of the law school at the University of Texas, Austin, says that "community service and leadership experience are very important. . . . [T]his law school is looking for students with compassion." Ibid.

20. These activities are common in some areas of study, particularly in the health sciences. The Vanderbilt Center for Health Services, for example, provides stipends of $150 per week for up to fifty undergraduates to spend 10 weeks during the summer assisting in the provision of health care to rural areas. See generally *Streams of Idealism and Health Care Innovation: An Assessment of Service-Learning and Community Mobilization.* At the graduate level, the medical school at the University of Illinois' Rockford campus requires students to work in a community health center during their second through fourth years.

21. Newman, *Higher Education and the American Resurgence,* 85–7.

22. "New College Presidents' Group to Promote Public and Community Service by Students," *The Chronicle of Higher Education,* 23 October 1985, 27; "Universities Take Lead in New Volunteer Efforts," *The New York Times,* 17 October 1985, A–116. The June 1985 *Bulletin of the American Association for Higher Education* presents several articles describing and arguing for these developments.

23. See "The C.V. Starr National Service Fellowship Program at Brown University," a prospectus published by the university.

24. Telephone interview of Susan Stroud, Office of the President, 1985.

25. This and other information on college programs is provided in Eberly, "Service Experience and Educational Growth." Some of the programs developed since Eberly's article are described in Kelley, "Many College Students Show an Inclination to Get Involved"; Gilinsky, "When Helping Others Is Part of Learning," 23–24; and Meyer, "More Students Finding Time to Give the Needy a Hand," 20.

26. This program, however, has been in constant decline since 1980. In fiscal year 1981, NHSC awards were restricted for the first time to students with exceptional financial need. The number of participants began to decline dramatically, as did the program's budget. Funds appropriated for the program dropped from a high of $79.5 million in 1980 to just under $5.7 million in 1984; the number of individuals covered by HNSC awards fell from 3,150 in 1978–1979 to 320 in 1984–1985. These figures were calculated on the basis of information provided to the National Service Project by Dr. Helen Hanlon, chief of the Operations and Analysis Branch of the Division of Health Services Scholarships, in a memo dated 3 April 1985.

27. There is some precedent for this type of plan. For example, ACTION's Young Volunteers in Action, established in 1981, provides about $1 million in grants averaging $20,000 each to support the efforts of private charitable agencies and local

governments in soliciting volunteers between the ages of fourteen and twenty-two. To qualify, prospective grantee organizations are asked to present plans for soliciting at least 8 hours per month from volunteers and on average to secure at least 10,000 hours of service from about 200 volunteers. We have found no evaluation of this modest forerunner of some types of program 3 plans. A description of grant priorities for this program may be found in 47 *Federal Register* 35018 (August 12, 1982).

28. Under a plan of this type, NSPs could secure a subsidy for only one employer organization each year and not for an organization that otherwise paid them. To activate a grant, NSPs would have to volunteer some minimum number of hours—say, 150 or 200 hours per year.

29. For more information on the proposals of these institutions, see, respectively, Eberly, *National Service: A Report of a Conference,* appendix A (an updated version of this plan may be found in Eberly, "A National Service Model Based on Experience and Resaerch"); Committee for the Study of National Service, *Youth and the Needs of the Nation,* 97–142; Foley, Maneker, and Schwartz, *National Service and America's Future,* 22–28; Roosevelt Centennial Youth Project, *A Policy Blueprint,* 9–15; National Council on Employment Policy, "Investing in America's Future," 32–38.

30. A number of programs might be cited as precedents for a national service program besides those mentioned in the text. We also note Project Hope (a health careers program for in-school youth); the Teacher Corps (scholarship aid for teachers who commit to later public school service); Youth Community Conservation and Improvement Projects (community economic development projects for unemployed sixteen- to nineteen-year-olds); Youth Incentive Entitlement Pilot Projects (part-time and summer work for low-income youth on the condition that they remain in school); and Ventures in Community Improvement (construction apprentice experience for out-of-school youth).

31. Committee for the Study of National Service, *Youth and the Needs of the Nation,* 4.

32. The model we describe is built around administrative entities such as the Peace Corps and VISTA. It also might be organized around tasks. For example, corps for child literacy, maternal health, and home care might be organized, and each could be used to unite what might otherwise be perceived as disparate efforts around the country. Corps of this type also might benefit from clearly stated goals and public appreciation of those goals.

33. A September 1984 memorandum to this project from the Peace Corps Public Affairs Office reports that 93 percent of Peace Corps volunteers then in service had completed at least 1 year of college or received a degree from a professional or technical school, while 78 percent held undergraduate college degrees or higher.

34. The figures for 1981–1984 were provided in 1985 by the Peace Corps Public Affairs Office. Data on the number of Peace Corps volunteers in 1967 come from Foley, Freeman, and Schwartz, *The Peace Corps: More Today Than Twenty Years Ago,* 5.

35. See, for example, ibid.; and Carp, "The Organization of National Service: The Peace Corps Today," 319.

36. Foley, Freeman and Schwartz, *The Peace Corps: More Today Than Twenty Years Ago,* 37.

37. H.R. 1121. Similarly, the Returned Peace Corps Volunteers of Washington, D.C., has urged the Peace Corps to "set a goal of having 10,000 Volunteers in service overseas by 1988." Returned Peace Corps Volunteers of Washington, D.C., "Peace Corps 1985: Meeting the Challenge," 3.

38. *Peace Corps Congressional Presentation,* Fiscal Year 1985, 13.

39. Peace Corps Public Affairs Office.

40. Writing in 1981, Foley, Freeman, and Schwartz estimated that between 65 and 70 percent of foreign requests were filled. *The Peace Corps: More Today Than Twenty Years Ago,* 20. However, the Peace Corps Public Affairs Office provided a more recent figure, estimating that in fiscal year 1984, 74 percent of foreign requests actually were filled.

41. These figures are based on data provided by the Peace Corps Public Affairs Office in 1985.

42. Our calculations assume, as stated, a return to roughly 1983 unit costs.

43. This figure was provided by the Peace Corps Public Affairs Office.

44. Ibid., based on the age distribution of 1983 volunteers.

45. VISTA, *VISTA,* 25. Among the people instrument in developing VISTA were advocates of national service such as David Hackett, Willard Wirtz, and Adam Yarmolinsky.

46. House Committee on Education and Labor, Special Subcommittee on Labor, *Hearings on H.R. 5625, A Bill to Provide for a National Service Corps to Strengthen Community Service Programs in the U.S.,* 43.

47. VISTA, *Volunteer Handbook,* 25.

48. This information was provided in a May 1985 telephone interview with Diana London, VISTA branch chief in Washington, D.C.

49. See calculations in chapter 3, note 54. It is shown there that two-thirds of the minimum wage for a 40-hour week yields $89.33 per week. That would amount to $357.32 monthly.

50. Information provided by VISTA in a May 1985 telephone interview with Diana London, VISTA branch chief in Washington D.C.

51. See ACTION, *Annual Report, 1981,* 21: "The fact is that in the last administration VISTA rapidly became a tax-supported tool in the hands of political activists."

52. Data provided by ACTION/VISTA office in a 1985 memo to the National Service Study Project.

53. Ibid.

54. See our discussion of this program in chapter 1, "Precedents."

55. Gallup and Robinson, "American Institute of Public Opinion—Survey, 1935–38," 373.

56. Senate Committee on Labor and Public Welfare, *Youth Conservation Corps and Youth Public Service,* 9.

57. "These [two] Departments are operating three distinct, yet overlapping youth programs and are the *largest* federal youth employment agencies in terms of *direct* services to youth." Butler and Darr, *Lessons From Experience: An Interim Review of the Youth Employment and Demonstration Projects Act,* 26 (emphasis in the original).

58. Because the average YACC participant stayed in the program for only

about 4 months, there were two to three times as many participants in the program as there were slots during these years.

59. *Job Training Partnership Act,* Pub. L. No. 97-300, 96 Stat. 2631 (1982).

60. H.R. 99, *The American Conservation Corps Act of 1985.*

61. See generally Human Environment Center, "Youth Conservation Jobs and Service—A New National Corps?" The Human Environment Center estimated in a 1985 communication to this project that The *American Conservation Corps Act of 1984* (H.R. 999) would have provided full-time positions for about 18,500 youths in its first year of operation, 27,700 in the second year, and 37,000 in the third year. The 1985 legislation would employ between 28,100 and 29,400 youths in each of the first 3 years. The smaller number assumes a state matching requirement of 15 percent, as proposed in the Senate version of the bill, while the larger number assumes a state matching requirement of 25 percent, as in the House bill.

62. A small number of nonresidential positions may be established for those living near work sites.

63. Based on data drawn from Young Adult Conservation Corps, *Annual Reports, 1978–82.*

64. A similar system of federal subsidies for state and local youth service programs has been proposed by Representative Leon Panetta (D-California) and introduced into the House of Representatives. See H.R. 888, *Voluntary Youth Service Act.*

65. Title II of CETA, following some earlier examples, authorized federally funded public sector hiring in regions with unemployment rates above 6.5 percent. Later in 1974, the severity of the year's recession prompted the enactment of a Supplemental Title VI, which authorized $2.5 billion for a short-term countercyclical public service employment program. By June 1975, 275,000 people were employed under these titles. Three years later, that number reached 525,000, and by the end of the Carter administration, 725,000 public service jobs were being funded under these two titles.

66. Mirengoff and Rindler, "CETA: Manpower Programs Under Local Control", 169. The authors also note that less-qualified CETA candidates often were put in Title I training programs, leaving the more qualified for public service. Ibid., 171.

67. Ibid., 173.

68. The history is well summarized in ibid., 158.

69. Donald Eberly, executive director of the National Service Secretariat, notes that "Community Service paired with Environmental Service [in his National Service plan] is modeled after PLS." Eberly, "A National Service Model Based on Experience and Research," 7.

70. See generally Gittell, Beardsley, and Weissman, "Final Evaluation Report on Syracuse Youth Community Service."

71. As the Program for Local Service (PLS) did in Washington.

72. There is an argument for varying wages according to varying costs of living in different areas. Experimentation also may be desirable with varying readjustment allowances, perhaps providing, as in the New York program, a greater allowance as a tuition credit than could be received in cash. Our cost analysis assumes that total compensation would equal the minimum wage, although the NSO might permit experimentation on this point.

73. A somewhat larger program might be established, but we regard much more ambitious notions of the potential size of a plan like program 3 as unfounded. Eberly, for example, says that the growth of civilian service under his plan would be gradual, but he projects "an expected 100,000 in service at the end of the first year; 300,000 at the end of the second year; and 1,000,000, expected to be the plateau level, at the end of the third year." Eberly, "A National Service Model Based on Experience and Research," 10. We doubt that such levels could be reached while maintaining a representative sample of high school graduates.

74. Communication to the authors from Carl Weisbrod, New York CVC executive director, September 1985.

75. Training, particularly short initial training, may however, be especially desirable as a screening device when attrition rates would be likely to be high.

76. Public/Private Ventures, forthcoming (1986). There is also a very lucid introductory discussion of the problems of analysis in this context in Hovey, *The Costs and Benefits of Universal and National Service Programs,* 46–65.

77. Public/Private Ventures, forthcoming (1986).

78. Zimmerman, Egan, and Ross, "A Study of the Value of Output of Participants in Youth Demonstrations and CETA Programs in New York State." The programs were the Syracuse Youth Community Service Program (described earlier as one of the models for program 3), the Youth Employment and Training Program, the Youth Community Conservation and Improvement Project, the Summer Youth Employment Program, and the Youth Incentive Entitlement Pilot Project.

79. Ibid., 38, 36.

80. Ibid., 29.

81. Ibid., 13–16.

82. Ibid., 38–40.

83. Unfortunately, we cannot compare the additional, important variable of supervisor qualities and ratios. If program 3 improved on Zimmerman's examples in this respect, productivity probably would improve similarly.

84. We have no method for assessing the value of the work done by Peace Corps participants. We assume that their 2-year terms, age, and prior educational accomplishments would cause them to perform more like the average program 2 NSPs than like the participants described in the following discussion. Nor does Zimmerman's work cast light on the value of conservation corps. Public/Private Ventures is undertaking an assessment of the value of conservation corps work that promises to add to our understanding of that subject when it is completed in late 1986.

85. Zimmerman, Egan, and Ross, "A Study of the Value of Output of Participants in Youth Demonstrations and CETA Programs in New York State," 113.

86. Ibid., 68.

87. Ibid., 48.

88. Ibid., 101, fn. 1.

89. Although we cannot validate the point, we assume that the value of the efforts of Peace Corps volunteers abroad would be rated at least equal to the minimum wage and would therefore raise the program's rate of return. On the other hand, the administrative costs of the program, described later, would depress further the cost-benefit ratio of the services delivered by the program.

90. If this calculation suggests a ceiling for the reward from NSP work, it does

not establish a floor. The value of an NSP service-year would in turn be diminished by the time devoted to activities other than work.

91. Public/Private Ventures, forthcoming, 1986, 49, may be helpful in this respect.

92. See chapter 6, Future Work Opportunities and Income.

93. *Ibid.*

94. California Conservation Corps, *1976–79 Report to the Legislature,* 34–35.

95. Ibid., 36.

96. Sherraden, *The Civilian Conservation Corps: Effectiveness of the Camps,* 7, 170. We also note that the evaluators of the Job Corps, focusing on the economic value of training for the disadvantaged, concluded that "civilian conservation centers were not worth their costs as compared with centers that established more structured learning environments less oriented to hands-on outdoor work." Maller et al., *Evaluation of the Economic Impact of the Job Corps Program,* 21.

97. ACTION, "Two Demonstrations of National Service," 7.

98. Levitan and Johnston, *The Job Corps,* 84–85.

99. Hahn and Lehman, *What Works in Youth Employment Policy,* 81.

100. See Chapter 6, "Attitudes and Self-Definition."

101. Public/Private Ventures, "The California Conservation Corps: An Analysis of Participant Characteristics," 9.

102. Ibid., 13.

103. Ibid., Ex-2.

104. Gittell, Beardsley, and Weissman, "Final Evaluation Report on Syracuse Youth Community Service," 2.

105. ACTION, "Two Demonstrations of National Service," 16.

106. Bailin, *The California Conservation Corps: A Case Study,* 27.

107. Sherraden reached the same conclusion in his study of the Roosevelt CCC, "although there is little substantial evidence to verify this perspective." Sherraden, *The Civilian Conservation Corps: Effectiveness of the Camps,* 158.

Commenting on the nonresidential YCS program, Gittell concludes: "Significant benefits of the YCS program cannot be quantified. The ethnographic research performed for this evaluation revealed that, for many volunteers, YCS provided an opportunity to improve work habits and practices and increase self-esteem through community service." Gittell, Beardsley, and Weissman, "Final Evaluation Report on Syracuse Youth Community Service," 11.

Carl Weisbrod, director of the New York CVC program, remarks that participants are unmistakably more confident than simple maturation would explain and that they attribute this especially to being able to help others. Communication to the authors, September 1985.

108. The Roosevelt Centennial Youth Program estimated in September 1985 that there were 4 to 9 million Americans in this situation.

109. Magnum and Walsh, *Employment and Training Programs for Youth: What Works Best for Whom?,* 14.

110. Thus, for example, the Nixon administration argued against the YCC and in favor of targeted manpower training (see Nye, *The History of the Youth Conser-*

vation Corps, 29), and a decade later, the Youth Policy Institute decried the absence of Labor Department evaluations assessing the YACC's performance as compared with more narrowly targeted training programs. "Youth Service and Conservation," 24ff.

111. A 1982 study of the Youth Conservation Corps suggests some tendencies in this direction on the basis of a comparison of 87 YCC members and 205 of their peers who were sampled in a national survey. The authors found that only a negligible percentage (0.5 percent) of the youth in the national sample reported participating in community affairs or voluntary work almost every day, and only about half (54 percent) reported participating at all. But 5.6 percent of the YCC alumni reported participating almost every day and more than four out of five of the total group participated at least occasionally. Johnson, Lynn, and Driver, "Final Report of Pilot Study," 17.

112. See chapter 6, "Attitudes and Self-Definition."

113. Mark Battle and Associates, Inc., "Local Mixed Income Testing," III–4.

114. Ibid., III-3. See also Mark Battle and Associates, Inc., "The Mixed Income Experiment, Report III," VII-1ff., for more detailed findings to this effect.

115. See generally the program sketches in Mark Battle and Associates, Inc., "Local Mixed Income Testing," III-10ff., and the detailed analysis of five sites in idem., "The Mixed Income Experiment, Report III." A second 1981 report ("Mixed Income Experiment, Phase III, Report II) summarizes participant development 8 months after the programs were completed.

116. Taggart, *A Fisherman's Guide*, 332–33.

> . . . the taxpayers' benefits do not exceed costs under most assumptions. There is no doubt that the Job Corps provides a unique opportunity which results in substantial gains for those who complete. But participation does not assure self-sufficiency. Even though the proportion of 1977 participants who were taxpayers in the next two years was a fourth above the proportion among like nonparticipants, and even though the proportion who were welfare recipients declined by half, a fourth of Corpsmembers were still outside the labor force two years after termination. . .
>
> Two years after termination, less than three of ten second-half 1975 trainees had annual earnings of over $6,000—or roughly the 1977 poverty level of a nonfarm family of four—and two-fifths of these were persons who had earnings above $4,000 in the year before entry . . .
>
> Are these reasonable batting averages? The answer depends on perspective. For instance . . . for white males, four years of college is associated with between one-third and two-fifths higher earnings than for high school graduates, and one to three years of college is associated with between 5 and 10 percent higher earnings.

117. Bailin reports that only 22 percent of California Conservation Corps participants graduate from the program. Of those who leave, he notes positive terminations for 9 percent who leave for jobs or military service and for 3 percent who leave for school. Bailin, *The California Conservation Corps: A Case Study*, 19.

118. See generally Lacy and Kleindienst, "NYC National Service Demonstration Project—Attrition: Projects and Implications," unpublished memorandum, 5 April 1984, A-8.

119. Goldberg, *The Noneconomic Impacts of the Job Corps*, 31.

120. Because the program would not provide a draft deferment, its impact on a

conscripted military would be negligible. Its impact would arise only from the tendency of the program to reduce military volunteering and therefore to increase marginally the size of draft calls.

121. Exceptions may occur for technically trained officers with degrees in science or engineering and for physicians.

122. The worst case would occur if all losses were felt in the Army, where recruiting targets are more difficult to achieve. We have no a priori reason (except Murphy's law) to expect this to occur.

123. Committee for the Study of National Service, *Youth and the Needs of the Nation,* 10.

124. Levitan and Magnum, *The "T" in CETA,* 11.

125. These figures are calculated on the basis of the 8.4 million Americans reported unemployed by the Bureau of Labor Statistics in July 1985, of whom 39 percent or 3,276,000, were under age twenty-five.

126. VISTA's Public Affairs Office in Washington, D.C., reports total fiscal year 1985 VISTA costs of $17 million, which when divided by VISTA service-years (2,200) yield an average cost of $7,727 per service-year. That figure omits some overhead functions that are funded through the ACTION budget. Our estimate of $8,500 per service-year attempts to allow for those functions.

127. As of 1981–1982, some 25 percent of the California Conservation Corps budget was spent on staff support and 35 percent on facilities and equipment. Bailin, *The California Conservation Corps: A Case Study,* 6. According to the California Conservation Corps Office of Public Information in Sacramento, the ratio of total staff to corps members in 1985 stands at about one to five.

128. See Human Environment Center, "Conservation Corps Profiles."

129. Program 3 could diminish slightly the average income of those of its participants who otherwise would have been employed. This would translate into a loss of tax revenue for both federal and local governments. Given the low effective tax rates applicable to most program 3 participants, that effect could be expected to be quite small. Moreover, it would be at least partially offset by the reduction in unemployment that we project program 3 to cause. In any event, our calculations do not take account of such possible tax losses (or gains).

130. Although it cannot be said that all who drop out would receive no benefit and all who stay would gain from the experience, we think it is a fair rule of thumb to presume that the exceptions in each group would balance each other.

8
Universal Service

The characteristics of programs 1 through 3 range from compulsion to volunteerism, from paid to unpaid work, from full-time to part-time service, and from participation by teen-agers only to participation open to all age groups. But each program is relatively modest, and any of them might become a way station to another or to a more ambitious program. In short, any or all of these programs would permit the nation to experiment with the idea of national service at significant, but not enormous, social and economic costs. Many advocates of national service have in mind a much broader program; critics of national service also often assume a more ambitious plan than any so far described. Accordingly, program 4 is an attempt to cast in its most feasible and useful form the type of program most commonly associated with the concept of national service: universal service for a period of 1 year.

Such a program seems to us politically implausible at least for the near future. Moreover, its novelty and sweep inhibit inference from existing precedents and thus make difficult the type of detailed analysis we have attempted in discussing the preceding models. For both these reasons, we sketch program 4 and its likely consequences in less detail than was presented for its predecessors. The sketch should still be of interest because the ideal of universal service evokes strong views, pro and con. These views, in turn, color reactions to the programs we have already described, perhaps because those programs are feared or welcomed as precedents that may lead to universal service.

The Form Chosen

In thinking about large-scale programs of service, there is a tendency, perhaps unconscious, to begin from premises resembling those that shaped the Selective Service System in past years. Compulsory national service is therefore imagined to require all men—and perhaps women—to serve at or around age nineteen unless they qualified for defined exemptions. Those who refused to serve, but were not exempt, would be criminally prosecuted.[1]

After some reflection, we have taken quite a different tack in the definition of program 4. We would establish a civil rather than criminal penalty for nonparticipation in the program, allow service to be performed at any point over the course of a lifetime, and concomitant with these liberalizations, permit no exemptions from service.

Specifically, we would impose a 5 percent surcharge on the tax paid each year by all income taxpayers, but we would forgive that charge to anyone who had previously performed 1 year of national service. Service might be undertaken as early as age eighteen,[2] after college or graduate school, before the beginning of a career, in middle age, around retirement, many years after retirement, or not at all. The only prod to service would be the surcharge. In this sense, program 4 might best be described as coerced, rather than compulsory, service.

In this system, individuals claiming conscientious objection, hardship, school or occupational imperatives, or physical or mental deficiencies would receive no exemption. They could, however, self-exempt by accepting the tax penalty until their circumstances permitted service or for their entire lives if they so desired.

Program 4 departs radically from the model of the military Selective Service System. It is not imposed exclusively on men, on the fit, or on the young; nor is it imposed on pain of prosecution. We believe that the flexibility gained from these relatively novel program characteristics yields many benefits, including the following.

Reduced Opportunity Costs

Choice as to when to serve would reduce the intrusion, disruption, and opportunity costs national service otherwise would impose on participants. As noted in the preceding chapters, a problem in designing programs for large groups is that what is easy or desirable for some is difficult or inappropriate for others. For an unemployed, out-of-school eighteen-year-old, an immediate year of service may be attractive or at least useful; for a college-bound contemporary, the intrusion may be resented and counterproductive; for a young mother or a worker supporting an infirm parent, national service may be intolerable. Conversely, service that might cause resentment at one time might be attractive at another. A student pursuing a medical career might see service before medical school as a detour but after medical school as a fulfillment. A worker might resent having to leave a job to serve but might be eager to serve when unemployed. Many might prefer to serve before retirement, but some might find service after retirement particularly attractive. Moreover, freed from a once-and-for-all choice of whether to participate, individuals could watch the program develop and allow their own attitudes to evolve before making a decision about whether to serve.[3]

Diversity of Age and Experience

Choice as to time of service would yield the social benefit of a diversity of skills and ages at the time of service. In a military draft, younger people are arguably more attractive than older ones because they are better qualified for the physical demands of the tasks they must undertake. In a national service program, many jobs would be better performed by older, more skilled, maturer individuals. A national service program involving older people also would reduce supervisory burdens, both because those who are maturer and more skilled generally need less supervision and because they may themselves supervise other NSPs. As noted in chapter 7, both the Peace Corps and VISTA have tended in recent years to seek older volunteers for just these reasons. This effect is particularly important because while the armed services can assimilate recruits through a 3- to 6-month training period and provide oversight from a 1-million-man career force, a national service program would have no such assets.

Ease of Program Start-up

Providing choice of time of service would result in only a fraction of the cohort participating immediately. This would reduce the size of the program in its early years while experience was gained with problems of supervision, discipline, job identification, administration, and so forth. Disruptive effects on society as a whole, particularly on college attendance, also would be far smaller than if service were required of all in their teens or early twenties.

Automatic Adjustment to the Labor Market

Flexibility as to time of service should enable the program's labor market effects to fit in better with shifting national needs. In times of high unemployment, either a rigid or a flexible program probably would draw participants out of the private sector labor market. During periods of labor power scarcity, a rigid program would do the same thing, thereby intensifying the scarcity. A flexible program, in contrast, would experience declining participation as a result of competition from attractive alternative job opportunities and would accordingly avoid overheating the economy.

Avoidance of the Need for Criminal Penalties

This form of coerced universal service would avoid the financial, psychological, and political costs of prosecution. Some number of persons, for philosophical or personal reasons, would not participate in any program no matter how minimal or generally accepted. Although not registering for the military draft is a felony punishable by 5 years in prison and a $10,000 fine,[4] 7 to 9 percent of the eighteen-year-old male population has failed to do so,[5] even though registration now entails no obligation to serve. No matter what the sanction, the inducement, or the popularity of a plausible national service program, it seems imprudent to design the program on the premise that noncompliance could be reduced to less than half that rate.[6] With a cohort of more than 3.5 million young people required to participate, even one-quarter of that rate, or a 2 percent rate of nonparticipation, would generate 70,000 potential prosecutions per year, or approximately three-quarters of a million in the first 10 years of the program. This is a highly unappealing and probably unworkable prospect.[7] Many would feel that the program embodied, as Kingman Brewster said about the draft, "a cops and robbers view of national obligation."[8] By contrast, when failure to serve merely incurs a tax surcharge, most enforcement is reduced to bookkeeping, the enforcement process expands public revenues rather than expending them, and the personal anguish and political divisiveness that accompany criminal trials is avoided.

A Means of Dealing with Dropouts

There are corresponding gains in dealing with the less obvious but even more difficult problems posed by those who begin service but then leave in midstream or who perform so unacceptably that they must be discharged. As we noted in chapter 7, attrition rates in public service programs have ranged from 25 to 60 percent, and there is little basis for believing that a national service program would do dramatically better. Yet it seems highly undesirable to prosecute those who prematurely leave program 4. Not only would the number of prosecutions likely be disturbingly large, but also dropping out often would be reasonable in terms of personal needs (such as family dependencies)[9] or opportunities (such as obtaining a private sector job, reentering school, or family moving to another part of the country). Moreover, the attrition of reluctant NSPs would make discipline and high levels of performance easier to maintain. Finally, absenteeism,[10] misconduct, indifference, and incompetence would be significant problems in any program. They would be especially difficult to control in broadly inclusive programs unless, in addition to more limited forms of punishment, discharge from the program were a realistic possibility. Supervisors would be far more likely to remove a nonperforming or misbehaving NSP from the program if only economic consequences followed than if criminal sanctions were the result.[11]

Constitutionality

The case for the constitutionality of a universal compulsory national service program would be stronger when benefits were predicated on program participation than when the criminal process was used to achieve the same ends. As discussed in the section titled "Constitutional Considerations," the Thirteenth Amendment proscription of involuntary servitude is a potential barrier to any universal national service program. Criminal penalties for failure to render national service might well be unconstitutional. A threatened deprivation of benefits also could be viewed as unconstitutionally coercive, but we believe that program 4 would pass constitutional muster if, avoiding criminal penalties, it posed a voluntary, economic choice.

Inclusiveness

A criminal sanction would require reading the hearts of those who assert a conscientious objection, examining the bodies and minds of those who claim to be physically or mentally incapable, and assessing the circumstances of those who claim that they support dependents. In contrast, program 4 could maintain its universal character, allow no exemptions, and administer no evaluations of individual circumstance, but instead simply allow those who chose not to serve to pay an economic price for their decision.

Arguments to the Contrary

There are, of course, weighty opposing considerations. Those who value the sense of an entire cohort together experiencing a rite of passage may be particularly critical of program 4. Its freedom of choice as to time of service would raise uncertainties about whether individuals who had not served actually intended to serve. A sanction as mild and attenuated as a modest tax surcharge could prove insufficient to encourage widespread participation, to achieve adequate retention among those who enrolled in the program, or to make the system representative of different sexes,[12] socioeconomic levels, backgrounds,[13] races,[14] or even regions.[15]

Although the substantial progressivity of tax rates would nominally increase individuals' incentives to serve in rough proportion to their earnings, both the wealthiest and the poorest members of the cohort might be especially accepting of an income tax surcharge, the former because they could readily bear its costs and the latter because it would be small or nonexistent. A national service program that relied on economic sanctions would thus risk echoing the moral deficiencies of the Civil War conscription system that permitted the hiring of substitutes.

Economic sanctions also would be complicated by the effects of marriage. As we envision it, program 4 would subject joint tax returns to the average surcharge that would be assessed on a husband and wife together—that is, 5 percent if neither had served, 2.5 percent if one had served, and nothing if both had served. This decision obviously makes an individual's income taxes dependent not only on his or her own activities but also on his or her spouse's participation in national service. We think that such an effect is not alien to the intention or practice of the present system, where joint tax returns are normal and where, in another context, a survivor draws social security benefits in proportion to a deceased spouse's earnings. Moreover, this decision enhances the propensity of economic sanctions to draw women as well as men into program 4.

A program that depends for enforcement on the income tax system also poses risks to that system. The principle that taxes vary only with present income and not with status or past achievement is important; it has been preserved despite contentions that the work of veterans, firefighters, teachers, and others warrants a tax exemption.[16] Furthermore, there are troublesome interactive effects between a tax surcharge and an individual's propensity to work, to make productive investments, and to report income honestly. A tax surcharge itself ultimately would rest on the sanction of criminal prosecution for failure to pay.

Finally, a tax penalty would highlight questions of intergenerational equity. If those who turned eighteen after the program was enacted must pay a surcharge unless they served, why not ask all—or perhaps all who were not yet sixty-five—to serve and impose the tax on those who chose not to serve regardless of age? Were the service requirement to be enforced by criminal sanctions, this question, we believe, would be much less likely to arise; middle-age and elderly citizens could hardly be imprisoned for failure to serve in a system that had been established after their youth. The use of a tax penalty, however, would create a serious problem of how to treat those who were already middle-age and elderly at the time of enactment.

There are three ways to get around this problem: impose the program only on those who turned eighteen after it was enacted; impose the tax on their elders but not permit service by this group; or impose the tax on the whole adult population and permit service as an alternative to payment by anyone affected.

The first alternative is somewhat illusory. In its first decades, the program's cost would be considerably higher than the surtax revenues from those who came of age but did not serve.[17] These costs must then be taken from the general federal revenues, which in large measure would be paid by mature wage earners—just as in alternative two, but less explicitly. This cost should be made explicit, however, since it is likely to make for more focused debate about the desirability of national service. A recent poll showed, for example, that while 72.8 percent of the adult population favored national service, support declined to 44 percent if the program caused a 5 percent increase in their taxes.[18]

The third alternative—permitting anyone to serve in lieu of paying the tax—is conceptually attractive but poses an operational problem of unmanageable proportions. If many of the 150 million Americans now over eighteen actually sought to serve, they would swamp the system. Moreover, those most likely to serve would be those whose alternative opportunities were least attractive. By and large, they would be the persons least skilled and most difficult to absorb into national service.

Further, if service were permitted for the entire population when the system began and many did not serve, that choice likely would be demoralizing. The sanction is prompted by a desire to encourage participation, not to collect taxes. The tax surcharge is intended to function as an annual reminder that those paying it have not given service while others have. The effectiveness of this reminder would be diminished if the vast bulk of the population chose to pay rather than serve. We would rather focus the choice on those most likely to accept it by opening it only to generations now coming of age.

The middle alternative, taxing the entire population but permitting only the young to serve in lieu of the tax, also has its drawbacks. It clearly discriminates against the older generation by refusing them the choice between service and tax. It also deprives the national service corps in its early years of the important benefit of the services of older people. We believe, however, that these disadvantages would be more tolerable than the alternatives. If program 4 were implemented, the form of the surtax we consider least problematic would apply to the entire population but be forgiven for those born after a given birthdate who chose to serve.[19] The following section underscores some of the serious moral and practical questions that any coercive national service program would confront and proposes some solutions to those problems.

Alternative Forms of the Program

Perhaps problems could be avoided through the use of civil sanctions other than taxes. We considered two penalties that illustrate the range of alternatives. Under one plan, we envisioned predicating full social security retirement benefits on 4 quarters of national service, just as full benefits are now awarded only after 40 quarters of regularly paid employment. Benefits might be reduced by perhaps one-fifth for those reaching retirement without having served. Such a sanction might be attractive in principle because it would make the national commitment to supporting the elderly partially conditional on their willingness to serve the nation at an earlier age. The effects of a social security sanction probably would be quite remote, however. Eighteen-year-olds would be asked to act now in the expectation of some gain secured (or penalty avoided) a half-century later. Time discounts and speculation that either the national service system, the social security system, or both would change before that date make this, in our judgment, a poor lever to motivate behavior.[20] Moreover, we fear that connecting national service with the social security system would make both systems so politically contentious that both would suffer.[21]

A more frequently suggested sanction (some would call it an incentive) would predicate postsecondary federal educational benefits on a period of service.[22] This approach has a strong intuitive appeal. Under the G.I. Bill, the nation has awarded more than $57.1 billion of educational support to the 18.2 million veterans who served between 1944 and 1976.[23] This has been a widely applauded program. Without any requirement of service, the federal government now provides more than 10 billion a year to more than 5 million individuals attending postsecondary schools.[24] Some have called this "the G.I. Bill without the G.I."[25] Why not require service as a precondition for this benefit?[26]

First, it is worth noting that the G.I. Bill was not designed as an incentive to serve in the military. Rather it was intended to compensate conscripts whose lives had been disrupted by the draft (though it applied to volunteers as well) and who needed or deserved help in reintegrating themselves into civilian society. It also was seen as a means to mitigate the high levels of unemployment that large-scale demobilization was expected to produce. Thus, the experience of World War II, Korean War, and Vietnam War veterans does not demonstrate that educational incentives are an effective mechanism for inducing service. To the contrary, after the establishment of the AVF, secretaries of defense have consistently taken the position that substantial educational funds are not a cost-effective incentive to service.[27]

Moreover, the effects of the G.I. Bill in the quarter century after World War II were quite different from the effects that such a program would have today. Part of the attraction of the G.I. Bill was that, when first established, it provided the only substantial source of financial aid for higher education. In contrast, proponents of predicating federal scholarship aid on service must urge either the replacement of the existing $10 billion system of federal aid with their new system or the addition of the new system as an increment to the existing system. In either event, there are strong reasons to reject the idea.

First, we note its distorted distributional effects. Only about one-third of any given age cohort, or about 1.25 million young people, receive federal educational aid, and most youths do not go on to postsecondary education.[28] For this group, the promise of aid for further schooling is no incentive to serve, and if they do serve, the distribution of this aid represents a reward for their co-workers but not for them. Some, of course, who otherwise could not continue their education would do so if the funding were available, but in a system of universal service, a sizable percentage, perhaps as many as 40 percent, of the participants would not actually benefit from support for postsecondary schooling.[29]

Among the fewer than 50 percent who normally undertake postsecondary education, only about three-fifths receive aid. Even for this group, the threat of making school benefits conditional on a year of service would loom larger for the least affluent students. Economically disadvantaged students receive a disproportionate share of the aid currently given,[30] their expenses typically already exceed their income,[31] and as compared with more affluent students, they have few alternative resources to fall back on.

Thus, a deprivation of educational benefits may be a strong prod to service for upwardly mobile students from poorer families, but it would be a weak one for nonstudents and for students from wealthier families.

The most careful analysis of what students would do without federal grants supports these observations. Studying the Basic Educational Opportunity Grant (BEOG) program (now known as the Pell Grant program), Manski and Wise calculated that:

> [A]wards to upper- and middle-income youth have very little effect on their enrollment patterns, whereas awards to low-income students have a substantial effect on their postsecondary school enrollment. . . . Total enrollment was 21 percent higher with BEOGs than it would have been without them, according to these estimates: 60 percent higher among low-income students, 12 percent higher among middle-income students, and 3 percent higher among upper-income students.[32]

In sum, using the 1979 Pell Grant program as an indicator, if service were a condition of a grant, more than 37 out of 100 low-income students would find providing service to be a practical prerequisite to continuing their education past high school, while only 10 out of every 100 middle-income students and fewer than 3 out of every 100 upper-income students would confront the same requirement.[33] Manski and Wise bluntly conclude that "only the behavior of low-income students is sensitive to the existence of the BEOG program."[34] We believe that the same would be true of a national service program induced by educational grants.

Second, we doubt that confining educational benefits to those who serve or establishing a special additional pool of benefits for participants would cause many to serve, even among the poor. Present and foreseeable federal educational benefits work at the margin of students' choices between school, service, and work. For most young people who are qualified for college and want to attend, pursuit of the present typical aid package, a $900 grant and a $2,200 loan at 9 percent (interest-free during school)[32] in each of 4 years, would not justify a year's delay and an interruption of schooling. We believe that most would take more part-time jobs, obtain more state or private aid,[36] borrow more from their families and other sources, or attend cheaper colleges. Thus a Congressional Budget Office (CBO) study of this issue concluded that the data

> [D]o not support the hypothesis that cuts in student aid would discourage large numbers of youths from attending college [and thus encourage them to enlist in military service, the subject of the CBO report]. Rather, the cuts would be more likely to affect the type and extent of college attendance (for example, shifting attendance from four-year private to four-year public institutions).[37]

Manski and Wise reached the same conclusion. They say that "the awards have virtually no effect on enrollment in four-year colleges for any income group, according to our estimates."[38] Where the awards do have an impact, according to these economists, is at the bottom of the educational ladder: "The effect of the awards is to increase enrollment by low-income students in two-year colleges and in vocational-technical schools."[39] Perhaps 40 percent of these students now receiving aid would respond like their B.A.-bound contemporaries and substitute part-time work, other sources of income, or cheaper schools for the loss of aid. For the other 60 percent, three options would be open: national service followed by school on scholarship; market-wage work followed by school on savings; abandonment of school plans. The mix between these choices would depend on the level of awards, wages, and school costs and cannot be predicted with any confidence. We are not optimistic, however.

> [F]or many low-income youth the awards seem to tip the balance in favor of junior colleges and vocational schools versus full-time employment. . . . It seems plausible . . . that two-year schools, vocational schools, and work are much closer substitutes for one another than four-year colleges are for any of these three.[40]

On current evidence, we conclude that if federal educational benefits could be procured only by national service, the gain in the numbers and mix of those undertaking national service would be outweighed by the adverse pressures on students to downgrade to cheaper schools, to take on more substantial financial burdens and part-time work, or particularly in the case of vocational and 2-year college students, to abandon or defer educational plans. If national service scholarships were merely an increment to the present system of aid, these adverse consequences would disappear but so, in our view, would effective incentives to service.

As a smaller but still significant consideration, we note that providing educational benefits as an incentive for service poses substantial problems for the military. In other components of a national service program, the postservice occupational choices of those who complete a year of service would not affect the success of the program. But the armed services depend on reenlisting a substantial percentage of their first-term recruits. An educational bonus for service functions as a negative reenlistment bonus: It rewards those who leave the military and must be sacrificed (or at least deferred) by those who reenlist.[41] From the military standpoint, it is a less desirable incentive than cash or waiving of a tax surcharge.[42]

Finally, as our previous discussion indicates, we value the flexibility that permits different individuals to serve at different points in their lives. Educational incentives would be aimed essentially at the young. Their capacity to draw older and more skilled NSPs into service would be small.[43]

Thus, although waiver of a tax surcharge would by no means be a perfect incentive to participation in national service, we think that, compared to the alternatives of a criminal sanction, a social security penalty, or the gain or loss of educational benefits, it appears the least problematic means of establishing a program in which participation is strongly encouraged as a duty of U.S. citizenship. We turn now to the specifics of program 4.

Program Particulars

All citizens of both sexes and of all ages and physical and mental conditions would be affected by the program. Those eighteen or under at the time of passage of the legislation would either serve or incur the tax surcharge for nonservice. Those over eighteen would pay the surcharge. An NSP's year of service might commence at any time after age eighteen or graduation from high school, whichever came first. It would have to be continuous and involve at least 40 hours per week. Service could be rendered either as a civilian or as a member of the military. The military alternative would be voluntary; standards for entrance, terms of service, and pay and benefits would be established as necessary for recruiting the numbers and kinds of volunteers needed. Service in military reserve units over a 4-year period would be acceptable as a fulfillment of the obligation.[44] Civilian service opportunities would be established and supervised by national service boards according to the same criteria and for the same types of work as in program 2. Also as in program 2, the federal government would be the employer of last resort.

NSPs engaged in civilian service in program 4 would, like their counterparts in programs 2 and 3, be given a subsistence allowance equivalent to two-thirds of the minimum wage and a service completion payment equivalent to the remaining third. As previously discussed, the program also would impose a 5 percent surcharge on the income tax paid by all taxpayers each year after the program was enacted and would forgive that surcharge to eligible NSPs who served for a year.[45] Proceeds from the surcharge would be applied first to the expenses of operating program 4, but to the extent that there was a surplus or deficit, the program would contribute to or draw on general revenue.

The surcharge would not be a 5 percent additional tax on income but rather a 5 percent increment in taxes paid. For a taxpayer paying an average 20 percent tax on his or her total taxable income, a 5 percent additional tax on income would bring the average tax to 25 percent; a 5 percent increment in the tax would bring the average rate to 21 percent. A surtax on income, moreover, would be a flat rate tax. A surtax on tax would be progressive, just as the tax system is progressive.

The impact of this surcharge on taxpayers with varying gross incomes in 1981 would have been as shown in table 8–1.

The effects of this surcharge would be modest for low-income taxpayers. Had it been in effect in 1981, persons whose gross reported income was under $5,000 would have paid an average surcharge of only $7.05; those with incomes between $5,000 and $9,999, $26.75; and those with incomes between $10,000 and $14,000, an average of $61.55. Taxpayers reporting around the median family income would pay a surcharge of around $170 per year.[46] For taxpayers in higher brackets, the costs become progressively more pronounced, reaching, for example, $1,145 as the average surcharge for those with incomes between $75,000 and $100,000.

The surcharge would have five useful attributes. First, it would enhance the economic attraction of national service for those with high wage expectations, while retaining identical compensation for all participants. The compensation alone would draw large proportions of the unemployed and underemployed into national service. Waiver of the surcharge would introduce an incentive for the more privileged.[47] Second, the surcharge would make service more equitable because it would award tax advantages in proportion to future earnings and thus in proportion to the opportunity costs associated with the year of private sector income that was foregone.

Third, the surcharge would present a recurring reward to those who had served and an annual prod to those who had not. Fourth, since avoidance of the surcharge is based on satisfactory completion of service, it would serve to discourage attrition. Finally—though for our purposes this is a collateral point—the surcharge would raise revenue and thus offset some of the costs of program 4. In 1981, for example, the surcharge would have raised about

Table 8–1
Hypothesized National Service Surcharge by Gross Income, 1981

Average Size Income	*Number of Returns*	*Average Tax*	*At 5 Percent*
$1,000 under $2,000	175,173	$85	$4.25
$2,000 under $3,000	174,743	166	8.30
$3,000 under $4,000	1,857,034	65	3.25
$4,000 under $5,000	2,439,688	160	8.00
$5,000 under $6,000	2,444,811	287	14.35
$6,000 under $7,000	2,472,332	425	21.25
$7,000 under $8,000	2,851,669	529	26.45
$8,000 under $9,000	2,922,204	611	30.55
$9,000 under $10,000	3,105,488	753	37.65
$10,000 under $11,000	3,059,017	916	45.80
$11,000 under $12,000	2,902,523	1,086	54.30
$12,000 under $13,000	2,717,660	1,240	62.00
$13,000 under $14,000	2,638,170	1,432	71.60
$14,000 under $15,000	2,441,101	1,573	78.65
$15,000 under $16,000	2,350,975	1,751	87.55
$16,000 under $17,000	2,201,494	1,922	96.10
$17,000 under $18,000	2,192,035	2,078	103.90
$18,000 under $19,000	2,043,463	2,289	114.45
$19,000 under $20,000	2,036,360	2,449	122.45
$20,000 under $25,000	9,024,551	3,012	150.60
$25,000 under $30,000	7,175,004	3,975	198.75
$30,000 under $40,000	9,162,812	5,654	282.20
$40,000 under $50,000	4,162,941	8,370	418.50
$50,000 under $75,000	2,805,962	13,068	653.40
$75,000 under $100,000	647,420	22,902	1,145.10
$100,000 under $200,000	522,552	41,838	2,091.90
$200,000 under $500,000	120,631	108,540	5,427.00
$500,000 under $1,000,000	16,280	280,106	14,005.30
$1,000,000 or more	5,507	914,033	45,701.65
Total Taxable Returns	76,682,212	3,720	186.40

Source: Columns 1 to 3 are drawn from Internal Revenue Service, *Statistics of Income Bulletin,* 2, 7. Taxable returns with adjusted gross incomes under $1,000 are omitted here, though included in the bottom line total. There also were 18,602,601 nontaxable returns in 1981. *Statistics of Income Bulletin,* 2.

$15 billion, or approximately three-quarters of the first-year costs of the program. Over the later life of the program, as an increasing fraction of taxpayers were excused from the surcharge because of having given their national service, the revenue-raising advantages of the surcharge would diminish.

Effects of the Program

Our assessments of the likely results of programs 1 through 3 involve projections, guesses, and assumptions, many of which are inevitably debatable. Nonetheless, the overall pattern of operation and effects of each of those programs can be estimated because, in key respects, each one resembles prior or current programs—existing school service plans, CO programs, VISTA, the Peace Corps, and conservation corps—on whose experience we can draw. Program 4, by contrast, is essentially without a precedent. This country has never attempted to draw everyone above a certain age—male and female; able and handicapped; independent, dependent, and depended-upon; wealthy and poor; upwardly mobile, downwardly mobile, and (to stretch the term) immobile—into service. The likely results of such a program are far more difficult to project. We therefore assess program 4 more tentatively and more generally than the others, and do so predominantly by comparison with what we have said about the programs already described. This is consistent with our sense, already noted, that while any of the first three programs might be considered seriously within the next decade, program 4 is not likely to be politically plausible in that period. If it ever became plausible, it would likely be because of experience with programs like those we have already described.

Program Participants

The flexibility designed into program 4 makes it particularly difficult to predict how many people, at what skill levels, would participate in the program at different times. It is even more difficult to estimate the probable times of service by socioeconomic level, race, sex, or region. We have found no relevant survey data, and even if such data existed, they probably would be poor predictors. Attitudes could be expected to vary as, among other things, evidence accumulated about how national service actually worked and as employment conditions changed. Periods of high labor demand surely would lower propensities to enter national service, while periods of high unemployment would prompt greater participation.

Despite these uncertainties, some estimate of national service participation must be made as a basis for gauging the possible costs and benefits of

Table 8–2
Estimated Typical Pattern of a Birth Cohort's National Service Participation
(in thousands)

Beginning Age	*High School Nongraduates*	*High School Graduates*	*Total*
To Military Service[a]			
18–23	90	375	465
To Civilian Service	720	1,625	2,345
18–19	350	450	800
20–21	75	200	275
22–23	60	250	310
24–25	25	200	225
26–30	50	100	150
31–64	135	340	475
65 +	25	85	110
No Service	190	1,000	1,190
Total	1,000	3,000	4,000

[a]Including reserves.

program 4. Moreover, some tendencies can be predicted. The greater benefits from disposing of the tax surcharge early, coupled with the relative freedom of the young from commitments that would impede service, would tend to provoke enrollment at an early age. However, because the 5 percent surcharge would have little effect during school years when a student's income is low, many would be expected to defer service until after completing their education.

Child rearing can be expected to diminish female participation in the program during the first decade (ages eighteen to twenty-seven) in which a cohort would be eligible for participation,[48] but female participation should increase afterward, in part because it would provide a means for women to reenter the work force when their children reached school age. Members of the one-third or so of the cohort that obtained steady full-time work prior to age eighteen probably would enter the program when they experienced their first period of unemployment or as a means of effecting a career transition.[49] These and other considerations lead us to estimate cohort participation very roughly (table 8–2.).

As an uncertain but plausible pattern of participation in program 4, table 8–2 suggests both the way a given cohort (for example, all those born in 1970) might react to national service and also what a program 4 work force might look like at any given moment. Viewed as an indication of cohort response, the chart indicates our guess that the raw numbers of those recruited to military service would be about as they were in the early 1980s and are projected to be (without the program) in the latter part of the decade;

that about 20 percent of those who did not graduate from high school and slightly more than 25 percent of high school graduates would not participate in the program at all; that the peak period of civilian service would be at ages eighteen and nineteen, with approximately one-half of those who were going to engage in civilian service likely to do so within their first 5 years of eligibility. But as the table also suggests, half of those who would serve would do so over the following 40 years. Our estimate is that after the age of thirty, about 1 percent of those who had not served would enter the national service program each year. They would do so principally as a means of reentering the labor force (especially for women), as a method of dealing with unemployment, or as an interlude in an otherwise conventional employment history. We estimate that even after age sixty-five, about 8 percent of those who had not served would do so, the poorer among them principally for the income gained and the wealthier mainly as a means of continuing to feel useful.

Viewed as a snapshot of those who would be serving at any one time, the table displays our guess that in program 4's steady state, roughly half the civilian national service work force would be under and half over age twenty-three. The table also indicates our guess that in program 4's first and second years, its civilian component could be expected to be between relatively modest enrollments of 400,000 and 800,000, with the program then doubling over its next 5 years of operation to the level of 1.5 million entrants per year. At a favorable 30 percent attrition rate, this would put program enrollment in a given month at this stage at about 1.2 million. (At that attrition rate, only 1.05 million of the 1.5 million entrants would "graduate" from the program.) In its first 2 years, the proportion of high school graduates to nongraduates among entrants might be about 3 to 2. During the subsequent 5 years of substantial growth, this proportion would be enriched to 2 to 1, and toward the end of the program's first decade, perhaps 25 percent of its participants would be college graduates.

As the program gradually grew by another 50 percent over the next 4 decades, the proportion of high school graduates to nongraduates would remain about the same, but the proportion of college graduates could be expected to rise modestly. More significantly, the program would gain from the introduction of older participants. Thus, in its later years, the program 4 work force would be maturer and more skilled than previously. If military service and prior civilian programs are any guide,[50] the attrition rate of high school graduate, college graduate, and older enrollees would be lower than that of younger enrollees and those who did not graduate from high school. This, too, would contribute to improvements in the stability and quality mix of program participants over the years. These demographic changes would cause program 4 to encounter notably different challenges, costs, and benefits at different stages of its operation.

Impact on Social and Environmental Services

The Early Years

In its early years, program 4 would make available for social and environmental tasks a cadre of NSPs who, like those in program 2, would be primarily between eighteen and twenty years old. Unlike program 2, which would be selective because of the physical, mental, and moral requirements established by a draft, program 4 would include the bottom quartile of less able youths with less successful school or social histories. Moreover, these youths would be subject only to an economic sanction for improper performance or dropping out, as contrasted with the criminal sanction for desertion in program 2. Again unlike the NSPs of program 2, those in program 4 would serve only 1 year and would include a far higher proportion of young women. By far the most significant factor concerning the impact of the program is that even in its opening years, program 4 would yield far greater numbers of NSPs than any other system we have outlined.

In its first years, program 4 would afford opportunities for accomplishment similar to those of program 2, though at a greater cost. More numerous workers, available for half the time, with a less impressive quality mix and less compulsion to stay on the job would entail more transaction costs to achieve an appropriate placement, require more supervision, warrant less training once placed, and produce quality work for a shorter period of time before they left.

This suggests to us that in the early years, before older and more skilled NSPs were available, the mix of settings in which program 4 operated would be weighted toward those that required little training, provided relatively close supervision, and would not be severely affected by high attrition rates. If so, the program would be an even less attractive source of classroom teachers in those years than program 2; it probably would not be a good source of home health care services, where patients are especially vulnerable and dependent or where a sophisticated service needs to be provided; and it would not be a likely source of new and innovative programs operating outside traditional structures. Conversely, during these years, the program should provide labor power that could be used wherever cheap semiskilled labor might be employed. Settings that seem plausible include CCC-like environmental programs (we estimate 105,000 positions), child care facilities (820,000 jobs), hospitals (75,000 jobs), home care visits that provide housekeeping rather than medical services (440,000 jobs), libraries (175,000 jobs), and city environmental and maintenance work (85,000 jobs).

As with program 3, we are unimpressed with suggestions that this work force would be unusually cost effective. To the contrary, as our discussion of the preceding programs suggests, we believe that the relatively youthful and modestly skilled workers in the early years of program 4, serving for short terms, would produce work of less value than the wages they were paid. Further, because of the special administrative costs associated with the program (discussed later), we anticipate that program 4 would give society a poorer return than a simple federal wage subsidy for state and local government to hire the unemployed or the young into relevant jobs.

Later Years

Program 4 would grow far larger as it matured, reaching, by our estimates, 1.5 million entrants in its seventh year of operation, 1.75 million by its twelfth year, and 2.5 million entrants by about its fortieth year. This growth would make national service a major force in the accomplishment of a wide range of public tasks.

Just as significant as its growth, however, would be the change in the composition of the program's NSPs. Later years would see an increasing fraction of maturer and better educated NSPs. If our estimates of ages of participation in table 8–2 are correct, then in its steady state, one in every three of program 4's NSPs should be above the age of twenty-three and one in every five would be thirty-one or older. The presence of these participants should have at least four important effects.

First, the larger number of mature adults, and especially the presence of trained professionals or semiprofessionals, should lessen the demands on supervisors; in some situations, NSPs would supervise. In the 1930s CCC, for example, "about 5 percent of enrollees were skilled craftsmen who acted as foremen on work projects."[51] At least in its later years, program 4 could be expected to draw a far higher percentage of potential supervisors.

Second, the availability of NSPs with mature judgment and developed skills would open to national service many jobs that would be difficult or impossible to fill in other programs. In the criminal justice arena, for example, older NSPs might staff probation offices, supervise work crews of delinquents, provide victim assistance, and undertake traffic and crowd control tasks. In some such assignments, the availability of NSPs able to make experienced and independent judgments might make a substantial difference. In 1983, to offer one example, each of the roughly 15,000 probation officers, in the United States was responsible, on average, for some ninety-nine cases.[52] The result was that in most jurisdictions, no effective supervision was maintained. If 7 of every 1,000 NSPs were of sufficient maturity and temperament to be assigned to this system, the program would in its steady state double probation labor power and drive case loads toward the professionally recommended level of fifty cases per officer.[53]

An increase in the number of mature NSPs also could complement the use of less mature NSPs in program 4. Probation and parole officers, to continue the example, now have little help in providing tutoring, vocational training, and job search for the persons they supervise. Although younger NSPs from programs 1, 2, and 3 might in theory provide some of these services, parole officers under present circumstances would find it difficult to oversee the NSPs properly. The older NSPs in program 4 might make it possible to establish teams of, for example, two tutors (younger NSPs), two vocational trainers, and a job development specialist (older NSPs) to work with 50 or 100 probationers. Similar opportunities for mixing the work of older and younger NSPs abound within all the fields discussed in this book.

Third, professionals and semiprofessionals might undertake projects outside the framework of established public institutions. The possibilities here are uncertain, but the potential is great. Professionals in a number of fields might develop programs staffed on a rotating basis by regular staff members doing their year of national service. NSPs who were doctors, nurses, and medical technicians might undertake forms of preventive medicine that no community agency in their locality provided. Screening for lead poisoning, new-baby care among the poor, preschool immunizations, and early testing for vision, hearing, and other defects are examples of such possibilities. Psychologists and social workers might offer education and therapy to reduce smoking and the use of drugs and alcohol. Businesses and labor unions could staff training programs with members performing their national service.

The fourth effect maturer NSPs might have is related to the other three. As we have noted earlier, some public bureaucracies and nonprofit institutions in which NSPs might serve follow routines better adapted to the interests and capacities of those who operate them than to the needs of those they serve. By definition, large bureaucracies are low-change institutions, resistant to innovation and accomplished at housebreaking newcomers. Many older NSPs would be no more successful at infusing those institutions with greater energy, imagination, or empathy for those served than would younger NSPs. But it remains true that more experienced NSPs would be more likely, on average, to have confidence enough in their judgment to question standard operating procedures that seemed uncaring or ineffective. They also would be likely to understand better how (and how not) to try to introduce innovation. They probably, therefore, would become more effective agents of institutional innovation and reform.

We should not exaggerate these possible gains. The number of NSPs able to operate effectively outside of existing institutions would be small and might well be smaller than the number who attempted it and performed badly. Similarly, the assumption by NSPs of more responsible (and thus, in general, more desirable) tasks, and their challenge to familiar ways of doing business, would be likely to meet powerful resistance. While successes in such efforts would have great social utility, the number of failures would be substantial, and the conflict and frustration they produced would be high. Yet over the long term, after mature NSPs had been available for several decades and after NSPs who had served while young achieved senior positions in society, the balance might shift. Legislators, donors, and persons assigning NSPs to jobs all might come to expect that institutions using NSPs should use them productively. Institutions might then be forced to adapt to the energy and skills of its NSPs rather than the other way around.

Whether or not such transformations occurred, it is clear that program 4 could, after its early years, produce some work that was higher in quality than that produced in any other scheme we have described. Program 4 also would be vastly larger in scale than any other program we have described. The significance of these two points is that, alone among the four programs, program 4 might change the tenor of American life, producing some or all of the favorable effects projected by advocates of service. To a degree impossible in the other programs, social services might be improved, social cohesion enhanced, the military democratized, and so forth. But the dangers and difficulties would be correspondingly great.

Impact on the Military

Both the active-duty and reserve components of the armed forces would benefit significantly from program 4. It is true that, as with program 3, paid civilian national service opportunities would compete with AVF recruitment. But in program 4, this disadvantage would be more than offset by the imposition of a tax penalty on those who undertook no service. The resulting attraction of some form of service would be likely to outstrip substantially the recruitment loss to the civilian branch of program 4. To estimate the gain in military recruits, we reasoned that the program would have the effect of confronting a potential recruit with a $6,000 to $12,000 present-value penalty for failure to serve. Recent interview data suggest that a bonus of that magnitude would increase the military enlistment application rate by more than 40 percent from roughly 9.3 percent of the men in a given age cohort to 13.3 percent of that cohort.[54]

Bonuses at this level probably would maintain the peak 9-to-1 ratio of high school to nongraduate graduate recruits that the services achieved in 1983. This seems likely even if civilian unemployment, a key variable affecting propensity to enlist, were to fall to 6 percent after 1987, as is projected by the Congressional Budget Office in its high growth scenario.[55]

If unemployment remained high or military recruitment continued to be strong for other reasons, the active forces could exploit the recruiting advantages of program 4 in other ways. They might, for example, lessen first-term pay while increasing career pay on the theory that with an adequate supply of recruits, the best course would be to increase reenlistment rates, especially for the ablest soldiers. Our military consultants conclude that a one-third reduction in entry pay would be possible under program 4 if that were an end to which the program's military recruitment gains were allocated. This could save as much as two billion dollars per year.[56] Alternatively, first-term enlistment periods might be extended beyond the present norm of 3 years. Three-year terms now place a stiff demand on potential recruits, but under program 4, recruits might think of the requirement not as a 3-year obligation but as a 2-year incremental commitment. An extension of the term of service would keep the most experienced soldiers on duty, increase the ratio of useful service to training time, and lower recruitment needs. Alternatively, program 4 would offer the option of substantially expanding force size while maintaining a volunteer system of recruitment.

With respect to the military reserves, the effects would be similarly favorable. A 4-year reserve commitment would require only slightly more than the number of working days in a full year of continuous civilian national service, while probably appealing to many as a minimally intrusive manner of performing that service. If present comparative pay rates were sustained, we estimate that waiting lists for reserve units would result, permitting improvements in the quality of reserve recruits comparable to those that could be effected for the active force. Reserve recruitment of college students might become common again.

This is not to say, however, that improvements in military recruitment prospects would sustain a case for program 4. By definition, what would be achieved by program 4 could be achieved largely by direct bonuses to military recruits. Bonuses would be more familiar recruiting tools with more predictable effects and, because young men have very high time discounts,[57] bonuses would have a higher impact than a recurring tax deduction of nominally equal value. Perhaps most significant, bonuses could be targeted more precisely to high-quality prospective recruits than could the broader brush incentives associated with a national service program. The active duty Army, for example, now recruits only about 130,000 people per year, and of these only 55,000 are male high school graduates in the upper half of the population according to test scores. To increase the proportion of high-quality graduates to the Army's goal, only 10,000 more of these quality recruits need to be drawn.[58] The Army now gives bonuses to about 26,000 recruits per year. Its estimate is that by a further use of bonuses, it could reach its accession goals at a total incremental cost of about $200 million per year, even given a substantial diminution in unemployment rates.[59]

Taking account of reserve recruitment and of some complex interservice interactive effects, our estimate is that the gains to the military associated with program 4 probably could be achieved by bonuses at a steady state cost of about $350 million.[60] Conversely, economic analysis may not capture the full measure of potentially positive consequences of program 4 for the military. The program employs a tax sanction for its psychological as well as economic effects. If service comes to be expected and accepted as a matter of course—and program 4 might achieve this—the military's draw from upper-class and highly educated young men and women might be expanded, and the standing of the military in society might be enhanced. Such gains are highly uncertain, but they would be significant if they occurred.

Labor Market Consequences

An NSP labor force of 800,000 in the late 1980s (the hypothesized work force in the early years of the program) would enroll between one-half and three-quarters of a percent of the nation's workers. A force of 2.5 million members in the first decade of the next century probably would enroll between 1 and 2 percent of the total work force. Accordingly, even in the short term, and more pronounced over the long term, the program would have much more significant labor market effects than any of the plans we have discussed previously.

An estimate of these effects is complicated by the program's desirable tendency to swell or contract in response to the opposite tendencies in the labor market. Further, the labor market effects of program 4 would vary depending on the types of NSPs it drew, and this in turn would vary with the overall employment rates and with unemployment rates among different subsets of the U.S. population. In different mixes under different employment situations, the program would draw some workers from employment, others from unemployment, and still others from among nonparticipants in the work force. Conversely, because the program would create a significant number of jobs, it would affect unemployment rates. The mediating mechanism, causing changes in unemployment to affect the program's size and causing the program to affect employment and labor force participation rates, is the program's flexibility as to when service occurred and the resulting likelihood that NSPs would choose to serve at times that minimized their opportunity costs.

Weighing the large number of variables, our labor consultants, Ashenfelter and Oaxaca, estimate that aggregate unemployment could be reduced by as much as a fifth, or about 2 percentage points, if a full-sized program 4 operated at a time of high (9 to 11 percent) unemployment. At full employment (4 percent unemployment), the proportionate reduction in unemployment rates would be smaller and the absolute reduction in the number of unemployed would be smaller still, with unemployment falling to about 3.4 percent. In such a circumstance, the program might contribute to an overheating of the economy.[61]

Turning to its differential effects on subgroups, program 4 seems likely to increase the labor force participation of white females of all ages and dramatically reduce the unemployment rates of eighteen- to twenty-year-old males. In periods of low unemployment, Ashenfelter and Oaxaca estimate that as a result of program 4, rates of unemployment for eighteen- to nineteen-year-old men would drop by about 15 percent, for twenty- to twenty-four-year-old men by 25 to 30 percent, and for middle-age men by 25 to 30 percent. (The lower percentage reductions would be experienced by blacks; higher reductions would be achieved by whites.)[62] In periods of high unemployment, gains would be in the range of one-tenth less unemployment for eighteen- to nineteen-year-old white males and would be negligible for nonwhite men of the same age. Twenty- to twenty-four-year-old men would benefit by reductions of one-fifth to one quarter in their unemployment rates, and middle-age men would experience reductions of between one-fifth (for blacks) and one-third (for whites).[63]

Effects on NSPs

NSPs who joined the program in their late teens could be expected to react to the experience in much the same way as described in our discussion of earlier programs. Thus, in its early years, program 4 could be expected to have effects similar to those of programs 2 and 3, but it would affect larger numbers and a wider range of participants.

Because of its size and diversity, we anticipate that the program would provide less supervision and training for its disadvantaged participants than would program 3. We are therefore skeptical about its efficiency as a bridge for these people into better paying, more rewarding jobs. The special questions about program 4 relate to its effects in later years, when it would engage older people. Unfortunately, it is precisely for that segment of the population that we are most lacking in predictive information. Optimistically viewed, the possibilities for beneficial effects are numerous. As we have noted earlier, a housewife interested in returning to the labor force could use her national service to effect a reentry into the paid work force. An unemployed worker could undertake service in lieu of receiving unemployment benefits or after those benefits had run out. The spouse of an intermittently employed worker might turn to national service as a means of achieving some income stability during a difficult year. Mature workers might use national service as a way of freeing themselves from the binding patterns of an established career. Geographic moves for all segments of the population might be facilitated by the assurance that if private sector jobs were not available, national service employment would be a possibility.

On the other hand, an income limited to two-thirds of the minimum wage would impose a year of a very low standard of living, a significant indebtedness, or a drain on savings that the completion allowance would in many cases only partially relieve. Longer term economic costs probably would accrue for many NSPs from the loss of a year's experience and seniority in the private sector.

Perhaps the greatest imponderable would be the effects of program participants on each other. Program 4 in its mature years could bring NSPs of diverse backgrounds together in a common experience. It might awaken different segments of the population to the needs and qualities of other segments in a manner that would contribute powerfully to a sense of national fellowship. The participation of many who could be working at regular jobs might make the program a valued credential.

But there also are negative possibilities. As great numbers of people became NSPs, served, and left (many prematurely), great demands would be placed on the administering bureaucracy. When the military conscripted soldiers, it failed to meet such demands with much sensitivity to individvual skills or difficulties. Would those administering a national service do much better? The variability in mental, physical, and emotional capacities of program 4 participants would far exceed that of armed services recruits. Appropriate work assignments might be more difficult to discern and work teams more difficult to integrate. The result might be a de facto mainstreaming in which NSPs tended to be assigned to projects with others of similar age, skills, and background and in which there were no opportunities to change stereotypes about capacities because the opportunities for performance in other than stereotyped roles were few or fleeting. This situation might only reinforce prejudices and promote a sense of alienation from the assigning bureaucracy and the government it represented.

Although they would not encompass the full range of NSP characteristics described here, program 3 and to a lesser extent program 2 could cast some light on the likely character of these effects in program 4. Moreover, if program 4 were to appear on the national agenda after some experience with program 3, it would be plausible to expand the third program as a way station on the road to the fourth. Program 3 could, for example, place special emphasis on mixing ages and classes within a program. The nation could then assess the desirability of universal service on the basis of better evidence than now exists.

Administration and Costs

In its first year, if our projections are roughly correct, program 4 would involve approximately twice the number of NSPs that the draft-based program

2 would produce or that might join the various nonmilitary components of the voluntary program 3. By the fifth year, program 4 would be inducting, training, and assigning more than seven times the number of NSPs of programs 2 and 3. That disparity in scale would only increase as program 4 gradually reached its full dimensions over the following several decades.

What dominates the questions of administration and cost, then, as it dominates the effects of program 4, is simply its scale, which is far greater than that of any peacetime program of any kind in U.S. history. The significance of size lies not merely in the numbers but in the diversity those numbers would embody. A system that permitted service at any age after eighteen and granted exemptions to no one would draw, in substantial proportions, the severely handicapped and disabled, the rebellious, the irresponsible, and the inept. It must seek to train, assign, and supervise them all and to give each a reasonable opportunity to contribute. That is not only a large task but one largely without precedent. We therefore do not attempt any fine-grained examination of the numerous and complex administrative procedures the system would require or of the many cost elements it would entail. We attempt only to identify some of the major issues of administration and to sketch in the probable range of costs.

Administration

A threshold question is whether program 4 should be administered by a federal agency or whether the federal role should be limited to the financial support and policy oversight of a network of state and local entities.

Two arguments might be made for federal administration. The first is essentially symbolic: This is a program whose origin, scope, funding, and title would be national. It is intended, among other objectives, to provide a common bonding experience to all citizens of the nation. It would be fitting, then, that the program be operated by an agency that represented the nation. The second argument is practical: A program as large as this, involving as many difficult decisions as to assignment, definition of acceptable performance, discipline, and the like, would raise substantial questions of interregional equity if practices were substantially looser in some parts of the country than in others. Operation by a federal agency, under a single set of regulations, would be more likely to avoid such questions than would the inevitably divergent practices (if not policies) of fifty state agencies.

On balance, however, the argument for state (and local) administration seems to us to be stronger. The key to the success of program 4—for its participants and for society generally—is in developing assignments that match real social needs with appropriately chosen and effectively trained and supervised NSPs. This is more likely to be achieved by local than by federal agencies, principally because a high proportion of NSPs probably would be assigned to state, county, or municipal agencies[64] or to private nonprofit organizations that, like hospitals and day care centers, are licensed and overseen by state agencies.

Under local administration, federal responsibilities still would be substantial. As in the school-based and locally administered program 1, the federal government would retain responsibility for ensuring the consistent application of the principles governing local administration. For example, it would need to ensure that only appropriate job assignments were certified for the tax credit and that consistent and fair rules regulated the grounds for dismissal of NSPs from the program. It also would be concerned with the legitimacy of the expenditure of the very substantial (and wholly federal) funds paid to cover the costs of training, assignment, monitoring, and general local administration, as well as the wages paid the NSPs.

Enforcing a rough consistency in the administration of the program would be difficult, given the range of administrative issues likely to arise from the extreme diversity in the nature, capacities, and circumstances of the NSPs. For example, should persons employed in local government or nonprofit institutions before their period of service be encouraged, permitted, or forbidden to perform their national service by remaining in their positions and simply accepting, for 1 year, the low rate of pay for NSPs? Should persons with severe physical or mental handicaps be encouraged, permitted, required, or forbidden to take assignments that provided a strong challenge to their capacities? If such decisions were to depend on the circumstances, how and on which circumstances would they depend?

To what federal agency should these tasks be assigned? ACTION seems clearly inappropriate, both because of the vastly greater scale and the involuntary nature of program 4. A strong argument might be made for the Department of Labor. The scale of this program raises the greatest danger of the displacement of current workers from their jobs or the substitution of NSPs for potential new employees, and of all existing federal agencies, the Labor Department would take more seriously the need to operate the program to control those tendencies. State departments of labor or employment might be made responsible for program administration at their level, and the Labor Department, of all federal agencies, has the most effective working relationship with them. The politics of the issue might force that result, in any event.

If the choice were open, a large, novel, difficult, and politically sensitive new program should not, we think, be assigned to an agency whose greatest concern would be to ensure the enforcement of a constraint upon it. If program 4 were enacted, we think a new agency should be established to deal especially with the manifold problems of launching, regulating, and monitoring the new program. We think that 1,000 to 3,000 employees might be required in the first several years, with the staff growing slowly thereafter to a total size of 1,000 or 2,000 more.

State and local administrative arrangements might vary; indeed, they should be encouraged to do so in the early years. A coordinating office, ordinarily reporting to the governor, should be required in all states. In many states, the same agency also would undertake direct responsibility for each of the major state and local operating functions: evaluating proposed positions in public and private nonprofit entities as to their suitability for the assignment of NSPs; assisting new NSPs to choose among the available positions appropriate to them; and (especially) monitoring conditions of employment. In other jurisdictions, departments of labor or employment might be assigned such responsibilities.

These agencies would have to act on complaints from NSPs as to excessive demands, from employing agencies as to nonperformance, and from organized labor and individual unemployed persons as to positions arguably removed from the job market by the assignment of NSPs. These would be burdensome responsibilities. We expect, for example, that in addition to a high volume of complaints about assignment, there would be considerable competition among prospective employers for well-qualified NSPs and considerable maneuvering to avoid (or to isolate and forget, once assigned) less qualified or more difficult NSPs. We thus estimate that the total staffs of state and local agencies administering program 4 (excluding immediate job supervision at NSP work sites) would require very roughly one employee for every twenty-five active NSPs, a doubling of the ratio we estimated in chapter 5 for the administration of high school NSPs in out-of-school assignments. If we are right, by the second year of the program, when accounting for attrition, about 640,000 NSPs might be at work nationwide, total state and local administrative staffs totaling 25,000 persons would be required. By the end of the fifth year, when roughly 1.2 million NSPs would be assigned, those staffs would total just under 50,000.

Costs

The costs of the program would be determined by its size and, to a lesser extent, by the degree to which it offered residential positions. Both factors, of course, are highly uncertain, but a reasonable range of costs, at several points in the history of the program, might be estimated as follows.

In the preceding chapter, we estimated that the total cost of nonresidential voluntary programs might average $14,000 per NSP position per year. Allowing for the substantially greater administrative burden generated by a mandatory program, it seems reasonable to assume that the equivalent costs in program 4 would approximate $15,000. Similarly, the estimate of an average total cost of $18,000 per residential position in program 3 might reasonably be converted to roughly $21,000 for program 4. Since residential programs would likely be filled very largely by the young, we assume that

Table 8–3
Appropriate Costs of Program 4 in Selected Years
(billions of dollars)

	Years of Operation			
	1	*2*	*5*	*50*
Total NSP Positions	320,000	640,000	1,200,000	1,800,000
Number of Residential Positions	48,000	96,000	180,000	180,000
Cost of Residential Positions	$1.01	$2.02	$3.78	$3.78
Number of Nonresidential Positions	272,000	544,000	1,020,000	1,620,000
Cost of Nonresidential Positions	$4.08	$8.16	$15.30	$24.30
Total Cost	$5.09	$10.18	$19.10	$28.10

about 15 percent of NSPs would take residential assignments (in CCC-like settings) during the first 5 years of the program and that thereafter residential positions would be provided for 10 percent of NSPs. Table 8–3 shows the resulting total costs of the nonmilitary components of program 4.

In short, and acknowledging again the very crude nature of these estimates, the cost of the program, apart from those absorbed by the military, would rise from approximately $5 billion in its first year to $10 billion in its fifth, rising more slowly thereafter to a total (still expressed in 1985 dollars) of $28 billion in its fiftieth year, the point at which we project it would reach its full size.

Constitutional Considerations

The constitutionality of program 4 would be hotly debated. The central questions are as follows:

1. Would Congress have the power to enact such a plan?
2. Would the program so restrict personal freedom as to violate the constitutional provisions that proscribe involuntary servitude (Thirteenth Amendment) and taking of property or the deprivation of liberty without due process of law (Fifth Amendment)?
3. Would it be constitutional to distinguish in the first years of the plan between an age group (the young) whose members would be permitted to avoid a tax surcharge by serving and those older members of the population who would not be offered this option?

The answers that first Congress and then the Supreme Court would give to these questions cannot be predicted with confidence. Of the programs described in this book, program 4 would be the most questionable constitutionally. We believe, however, that if the program were otherwise considered desirable, constitutional questions could be resolved in favor of the program.

The Power to Enact Program 4

Congress has the power to tax in support of programs it has the power to undertake.[65] In chapter 6, we discussed Professor Bobbitt's argument that Congress must reference an explicit grant of power to justify a program and that "there is no explicit authority empowering Congress to coerce large-scale labor."[66] We consider this a powerful argument, but on balance we do not think it would prevail if Congress found program 4 otherwise attractive.

Enactment of the program undoubtedly would be supported in part by reference to the Article I, Section 8, Clause 12 authority of Congress to raise and support armies. The positive consequences of the program for the volunteer military would give this reference force, and as we noted in chapter 6, the courts are disinclined to look behind a congressional assertion of motive to challenge a congressional judgment about what is necessary and proper to the conduct of the nation's defense.

However, Congress, no less than the Supreme Court, is sworn to uphold the Constitution, and the mere fact that it could shelter the program under the shield of its power to raise and support armies is not a sufficient discharge of its own obligation to ensure the constitutionality of what it enacts. The military results of program 4 would be collateral to the larger civilian labor force consequences, which are not themselves the principal purpose of the plan. As a result, we doubt the propriety (even though we acknowledge the legal adequacy) of having this tail wag so large a dog. Rather we think proponents of the program should address the constitutionality of the program under the Article I, Section 8, Clause 3 grant of power to Congress to regulate commerce among the states.[67]

In this regard, Bobbitt makes an intuitively attractive point. "I doubt that many persons would think of [a law compelling national service] as the regulation of commerce."[68] But the commerce clause, like the rest of the Constitution, must be read in the light of the nation's experience since it was written and of the case law that has shaped the interpretation of the clause. Through the mid-1930s, there is no doubt that the commerce clause would have been read as narrowly as the layperson would construe it.[69] Since then, however, this approach has been decisively rejected. A broad view has been taken of what commerce is and of how even intrastate events affect commerce among the several states. An early significant signpost on this route was *U.S.* v. *Darby*,[70] which, unanimously overruling an earlier contrary decision, held that the commerce power enabled Congress to restrict the hours of work and wages of those who produced goods for commerce. *Darby*'s conception of the reach of the clause has extended so far as to permit congressional regulation even of the work of window washers, on the theory that the windows they wash belong to companies that are engaged in interstate commerce,[71] and of wheat produced entirely for consumption on the producer's farm, on the theory that "home-consumed wheat could have a substantial influence on price and market conditions"[72] for wheat in interstate commerce. This "house-that-Jack-built chain of causation," as dissenters have put it,[73] is now so well established that it supports Civil Rights acts,[74] federal expenditures on behalf of the handicapped, antipollution and crime control efforts, and other programs equally remote from commerce, local or national.[75]

In this light, we think that if program 4 were thought desirable by Congress, it is the case against it, not the argument for it, that would have to be based on a constitutional revolution. The program's pursuit of improvements in the skills of its participants, and of the environmental and social services they would provide, seem to us to be within the scope of the commerce clause as it has been broadly read over the past 50 years.

Objections

One answer to the contention that the program contravenes the Thirteenth Amendment prohibition of involuntary servitude is that, as the Supreme Court put the point at the end of the nineteenth century, "persons engaged in a public service are not within the amendment."[76] In 1916, this proposition was repeated. The amendment, according to the Supreme Court, "introduced no novel doctrine with respect of services always treated as exceptional, and certainly was not intended to interdict enforcement of those duties which individuals owe to the state, such as service in the army, militia, on the jury, etc."[77] This view is reflected in the opinions on military conscription and on the obligation of conscientious objectors to accept alternative work assignments that were discussed in chapter 6.

This answer admits, however, a counterargument. This is that all save one of the public exceptions to the amendment's reach were established at the time of the amendment[78] and that the exception—permitting a military draft—is so singular as not to form an acceptable basis for other exceptions. As Professor Black has put the matter:

> Large scale coercion of labor is foreign to our traditions and to our Constitution. To this generalization, iron necessity has forced us to admit one mas-

> sive exception—military draft. It is absolutely essential, whether to sound policy or to constitutionalism of spirit as well as of the letter, that we insulate this exception as an exception, and resist every temptation to use it, by analogy or by way of indirect coercion, as a basis for overthrowing the policy itself.[79]

This view has some appeal. As we indicated earlier, we doubt the constitutionality of a plan that would coerce a year of labor on pain of criminal penalty. If Professor Black is correct that new exceptions to the amendment would provide a basis for "overthrowing the policy itself," then perhaps program 4, even without criminal sanctions, should be regarded as unconstitutional.

But if a second exception for national service inevitably or probably legitimizes other exceptions to the Thirteenth Amendment, why does not the first exception (for the military draft) legitimize the second? All Professor Black can say is that the first exception arises from "iron necessity," while the proposed exception for national service presumably is less than necessary. But what in the constitutional text permits an exception born of necessity, but only that exception? And what establishes that a military draft is necessary (even in peacetime) while national service is not?

Moreover, a number of other public compulsions (jury duty, road work, the obligation to be a witness in a case) appear to violate the amendment but have long been tolerated. Although the amendment speaks in absolute terms and this nation is clearly hostile to involuntary servitude, there are instances in which our society has concluded that the public interest demands some form of it.[80]

We think program 4 is reconcilable with the Fifth and Thirteenth Amendments, especially in view of the element of choice that the program leaves to those it would recruit. A tax to support program 4 would neither force servitude nor constrain liberty except insofar as any tax may be said to do so. To the contrary, it would provide more freedom than most taxes because, at least for those under eighteen when it was enacted, it could be paid in cash or avoided by a payment of labor.

If the opportunity to avoid service were illusory because rates were confiscatory or punitive, the plan might be constitutionally intolerable. But this tax would be low enough to permit a choice. It is designed to equalize the costs of service between those who would participate and those who would not. Thus, the program would encourage some to contribute to the national well-being by their labor while permitting others to opt for the more traditional means of dollar payments at tax time. In this way, it is like the road work that was required in many states before the Nineteenth Amendment and was endorsed by the Supreme Court in 1916[81]: It requires service or payment but leaves the choice to the individual involved. Is this an imposition of involuntary servitude or a constitutionally tolerable deprivation of liberty? We think Congress would appropriately decide that it is not.[82]

Equal Protection Issues

Ironically, the most intense and perhaps most novel constitutional objections to program 4 might arise from those not permitted to serve in it. Some of those over eighteen at the time of the program's enactment could object that the program saddled them with a lifetime tax surcharge while permitting those younger than them the option of service in lieu of payment. Because the guarantee of equal protection under the laws has been held to apply to the federal government, arguably this discrimination would render the program constitutionally repugnant.

Although there is good reason for suspecting the propriety of any discrimination by public agencies based on age, the standard to be applied in justifying such a discrimination varies with the vulnerability of the group that is being discriminated against and the importance of the right that is being restrained or forfeited. If a national service program involved, for example, discrimination against those now under eighteen by requiring those youths to undertake a year of national service later, the enacting legislation probably (and in our view properly) would be subject to a highly skeptical review. The right involved—the right to a free allocation of one's own labor—would be fundamental, and the group being deprived of that right would be especially vulnerable because its members would not be a voting constituency at the time the law was passed. In this circumstance, we believe, the Constitution would require a compelling reason to justify the discrimination.[83]

Program 4, however, would pose quite a different situation. The differential based on age discrimination would operate against a population—those who have already come of age—that controls the legislature. It also would be a discrimination that would affect only the tax burden and not a more fundamental circumstance. It seems likely, therefore, that constitutional doctrine would require only a showing that the discrimination against the legislating majority had a rational basis.[84] Our discussion of the design of program 4 has attempted to show that this basis exists: If a distinction based on age were not applied, the program would likely be swamped by applicants from the group of 150 million Americans over eighteen at the time of the program's enactment. Further, a more broadly defined program would be less likely to generate a sense that service was a prevailing choice and a normal part of coming of age in the United States.

We think that the risks of judicial invalidation on this point would be small but that concerns about age discrimination would warrant congressional attention. If the reasons we have given in favor of discrimination were not compelling, the proper remedy, we believe, would be to allow some participation by the older population. Numbers might be limited and admissions regulated by lot, skill, representative categories (for example, age and geography), or on a first-to-apply basis. Thus, even though equal protection contentions probably would not render the program unconstitutional, they might resonate sufficiently to argue for some variation on the form of the program we have proposed.

Conclusion

We believe that of all the plans described in this book, program 4 would be most likely to fulfill the visions of proponents of national service. If successful, almost uniquely among plausible legislative proposals, it could change the character of life in the United States. Service in this program might broaden the outlook and increase the cohesion of U.S. citizens while affording more public services than could otherwise be provided. We also believe that the program's design would minimize many of the costs normally associated with a coercive system of universal service.

The extent of these benefits, however, would be quite uncertain, and they would be accompanied by substantial costs. Program 4 would gain much of its power from its size, but it is not clear that we are correct in our very rough guess about patterns of participation. It is also unclear whether the program would be a positive experience for most of its very diverse participants. High levels of turbulence, waste, and mismatch between participants' skills and assignments might make the program's costs exceed the value of the work produced. Further, the opportunity costs, though hard to measure, inevitably would be very large. Is it sensible to allocate so great a proportion of the nation's labor and budget to national service?

We do not know the answer to this question. In great measure we do not know it because—especially in relation to a program of this scale—the nation's experience with service programs has been small. The careful evaluation of that experience has been more limited still. That being so, program 4 or its equivalents ought probably to be considered only after intermediate steps had been tried, and succeeded.

Notes

1. The director of the Selective Service argued for a system of this type while serving as a member of a presidential committee on manpower problems formed early in President Lyndon Johnson's War on Poverty:

Hershey . . . proposed that all men classified in the new 1-Y category be drafted and rehabilitated in the army, asserting that this experience would teach them teamwork and citizenship. The War on Poverty was fine, said Hershey, but "I think a fellow should be compelled to become better and not let him use his discretion whether he wants to get smarter, more healthy, or more honest. [Flynn, *Lewis B. Hershey, Mr. Selective Service,* 229–31]

2. Arguably, service should be permitted before the age of eighteen, particularly for unemployed youths out of school. The effects of a program on youth unemployment and teenage delinquency are diminished by a later start. On the other hand, the program risks discouraging high school completion if it accepts younger members, and those members also pose substantial supervisory problems.

3. There is a strong interaction between the time when service is to be performed and the sanction applied if it is not performed. A criminal sanction is most compatible with a requirement of service at a sharply defined time. If, for example, national service must be completed by age twenty-one, the time of prosecution is clear. Longer time horizons for permitted service make prosecution less plausible. Would we really threaten to jail sixty-year-olds? Would such a threat induce service from a twenty-year-old? Civil penalties seem to us to be better suited to a program designed to permit service throughout a lifetime.

4. 50 U.S.C. App. §462 (12)(c).

5. Jacobs and McNamara, "Selective Service Without a Draft," 370.

6. In the leading work on the subject, Lawrence Baskir and William Strauss calculate that there were some 570,000 "apparent draft offenders," or roughly 2 percent of the 26.8 million men who were subject to the draft during the Vietnam years. Baskir and Strauss, *Chance and Circumstance,* 5. Their data further indicate, however, that another 15.41 million men did not serve in the military for one reason or another during this period. This avoidance would be certain to recur to some extent under a compulsory national service plan.

7. By comparison, 3,000 draft evasion cases were prosecuted in 1970 and 1971. This constituted 7 percent of the cases in U.S. federal district courts. Blumstein and Nagin, "The Deterrent Effect of Legal Evasion," 250, fn. 48.

8. Quoted in Baskir and Strauss, *Chance and Circumstance,* 7.

9. "About 40 percent of female participants became pregnant either during or shortly after service in the Job Corps. Although this number appears high, it is exactly the same as that of the comparison group." Goldberg, *The Noneconomic Impacts of the Job Corps,* xiv.

10. One enthusiastic report of a rural YACC project notes, for example, that absenteeism "varies from 3 to 25 percent depending on . . . morale levels." "For Youths: Work to Clear the Mind," *U.S. News and World Report,* 25 December 1978, 77.

11. The converse of this point is that attrition and dismissals would be more frequent under program 4 than under a program that utilized criminal sanctions. It also is clear that discipline or dismissal from a program that provided economic benefits would be constrained by a variety of procedures intended to ensure due process. However, the process that was due when economic benefits were impaired normally would be substantially less than the process required if a criminal punishment were imposed.

12. "The 1983 median income for men was $14,631. . . . The median income for women was $6,319." Bureau of the Census, *Money Income and Poverty Status of Families and Persons in the United States: 1983,*" 14, table 8.

13. Nonfarm household tax returns showed a median family income of $24,751 in 1983, while the median farm family income was $18,925. Ibid., 5, table 1.

14. The median money income for families headed by a white householder in 1983 was $25,757, for families headed by someone of Spanish origin, $16,956, and for families headed by a black householder, $14,506. Ibid., 8, table 2.

15. Median family income by region in 1983 ranged from a high of $26,678 in the Northeast to $22,495 in the South. Ibid., 5, table 1.

16. Some states, however, exempt veterans, particularly disabled veterans, from property and a variety of occupational taxes. See generally House Committee on Veterans Affairs "State Veterans' Laws."

17. This also might be true in later decades, but the equity concerns are most relevant in the early decades.

18. Davis, Lauby, and Sheatsley, *Americans View the Military,* 23.

19. This decision might be modified by allowing a limited number of older people to serve each year, particularly if they supplied needed skills.

20. Additionally, the benefits foregone would not be as well proportioned to the wealth of the potential NSP as with a tax surcharge because the social security tax and pay-out systems quickly reach ceilings, while the income tax system does not. At present, an individual with no dependents receives on retirement, at age sixty-seven, 90 percent of his or her average prior earnings up to $254 per month, 32 percent of his or her earnings between $254 and $1,528, and 15 percent of his or her earnings over $1,528 up to a maximum of $2,975 per month. Pellechio and Goodfellow, "Individual Gains and Losses from Social Security Before and After the 1983 Social Security Amendments," 7.

21. We note particularly that the changing economics of the social security system and the resulting 1983 amendments to that system are likely to make today's teen-agers net losers under social security. Relevant data are presented in ibid. The point is stressed in Skaperdas and Capra, "The Social Security System After the 1983 Amendments." While older generations will continue to take out more than they and their employers paid in, under current law today's youth will take out less than those sums. Thus, social security could be said to be, as some might say that national service would be, a tax of the old upon the young. In this light, linking these two systems seems especially disadvantageous.

22. See Rothenberg, *The Neoliberals: Creating the New American Politics,* 215, summarizing a line of thought pressed by Moskos and others.

23. Veterans' Administration, Office of Information, Management and Statistics, "Veterans' Benefits Under Current Educational Programs."

24. Federal student aid, apart from special programs such as veterans' benefits and social security assistance, began with the National Defense Education Act in 1958 and then swelled with the creation of Great Society grant programs from 1963 to 1965. Aid programs created during these years included College Work Study, which subsidized work opportunities for needy students; Educational Opportunity Grants (now called Supplemental Educational Opportunity Grants, SEOG), which gave out-

right grants to low-income students; and Guaranteed Student Loans, which underwrote and guaranteed below-market bank lending to students. These programs were supplemented in 1972 by the Basic Educational Opportunity Grants, BEOG, (later called Pell Grants) expanding direct support, in 1978 by the Middle Income Student Assistant Act (making Pell Grants accessible to middle-income students), and in 1981 by the Parent Loans for Undergraduate Students (PLUS) program.

All of these programs are now authorized under Title IV of the Higher Education Act of 1965, 20 U.S.C. 1070. In the first half of the 1980s, budgetary pressures and a standoff between supporters and opponents of these programs kept them between $10.5 and $11 billion. Rounding numbers for purposes of this discussion, student loans provided $7 billion of assistance each academic year (although the federal appropriation to provide this support was only about 40 percent of this, as the balance of the money comes from the maker of the loan). Pell Grants provided $2.5 billion of support. College Work Study provided $625 million of assistance. Other grant programs (SEOG and SSIG) provided another $425 million of support. For precise numbers and a sketch of these programs, see Gillespie and Carlson, *Trends in Student Aid: 1963 to 1983,* 2–5.

More detailed information may be found in Department of Education, *Program Book, Fiscal Year 1982.* This source notes, on p. 2, that there were 2,583,986 Pell Grant recipients and 2,789,000 guaranteed student loans in fiscal year 1982, as well as several hundred thousand loans under other programs. Unfortunately, no data are provided on the overlap between beneficiaries of these programs. The best estimate of appropriate authorities is that there are about 5 million recipients each year. This figure is derived from telephone interviews with Scott Miller of the American Council on Education (30 November 1984) and Daniel Morrissey of the Department of Education (30 November 1984).

25. This phrase apparently was first advanced by Charles Moskos in *Hearings Before the Senate Committee on the Budget,* 265.

26. An analogous step was taken by the Soloman Amendment to the Department of Defense Authorization Act of 1983, forbidding the award of "assistance or benefit under Title IV of the Higher Education Act" for those who were required to, but failed to, register with the Selective Service System. See Section 1113(f)(1) of PL 97-252 (1982). This law was sustained by the Supreme Court in the face of constitutional challenge in *Selective Service System et al.* versus *Minnesota Public Interest Research Group et al.*

27. See note 41 in this chapter. Some scholarship programs have been used as a recruitment device for the all-volunteer army. To achieve a significant recruitment effect, however, these programs employ a dramatically high level of funding (basic benefits reach $10,800; for some skill groups aid exceeds $20,000). The Congressional Budget Office has estimated that if awarded to all recruits, educational benefits would draw some additional high-quality personnel into the armed services, but at a net cost of $150,000 per additional recruit of this type. This would be as much as six times the cost of attracting such recruits by other means. Congressional Budget Office, "Costs and Recruiting Effects of Alternative Programs of Military Education Benefits."

28. In 1980–1981, 714,000 youths dropped out of school and 3,053,000 grad-

uated from high school. Of the graduates, 1,646,000, or 30 percent of the entire group, are reported to have gone on to full- or part-time postsecondary education. Department of Labor, Bureau of Labor Statistics, "Students, Graduates and Drop-Outs, October 1980–82," 13, table B-3.

29. New York City's experimental service program (described in chapter 7) seeks to moderate this effect by offering the alternative of a cash separation allowance or a scholarship fund worth twice the cash distribution. This still leaves the less advantaged less compensated.

30. In dissenting from the Supreme Court's holding that the Soloman amendment was constitutional, Justice Marshall summarized Department of Education data as follows:

> Although federal education aid is significant for a large segment of postsecondary students, more than three out of four postsecondary students dependent on family incomes under $6000 are receiving Title IV aid. . . . In contrast, only 8 percent of students dependent on families with incomes over $30,000 receive any Department of Education funded financial aid. . . . In the Basic Education Opportunity Grant Program (now known as Pell Grants), 83.1 percent of the recipients are dependent on families with incomes of less than $12,000. . . . In the State Student Incentive Program, 69.4 percent of the recipients are in this category. *Selective Service System, et al.* v. *Minnesota Public Interest Group et al.*, 5140

31. See Hodgkinson, "Student Aid: Its Distribution and Its Impact on College Operating Budgets," 2, table 2. Hodgkinson notes that after accounting for all sources of income, including aid, parents' contributions, and self-help, during the 1980–1981 academic year, expenses exceeded resources by more than $1,000 (or 17.3 percent) for students whose parents made $6,000 a year or less and by $386 (6.2 percent) for students who parents earned between $12,000 and $18,000.

Parents who earned $18,000 to $24,000 met 18 percent of their children's college needs. Those who earned $24,000 to $30,000 contributed 30 percent. Parents who earned $30,000 to $36,000 contributed 42 percent, and those who earned above that contributed about three-quarters of their children's resources. Not surprisingly, the parental contribution of the poorest students (those with incomes under $12,000) was only about 4 percent. Children of parents with incomes of more than $36,000 have about 30 percent more resources than expenses. Students from middle-income families find their resources roughly in balance.

32. Manski and Wise, *College Choice in America*, 21.

33. Ibid., 119.

34. Ibid., 21.

35. In 1982, the estimated average Pell Grant was $918, and the average Guaranteed Student Loan was $2,217. U.S. Department of Education, *Program Book, Fiscal Year 1982*, 33, 40.

36. The failure to account for such support is an important omission in the proposals to make federal aid conditional on national service. Recently, state expenditures on student aid and support of public colleges and universities was calculated at $31 billion per year, three times the federal expenditure. *The Chronicle of Higher Education* 31 (30 October 1985): 9.

37. Congressional Budget Office, *Improving Military Education Benefits: Effects on Costs, Recruiting and Retention*, 72. This suggests a further objection to

making student aid conditional on service: Such a change likely would have a severe negative effect on private colleges through a loss of students who switched to public institutions. Proponents of making aid conditional on service must address whether they would admit sutdents to public institutions if they had not served. These institutions typically pay for one-half to two-thirds of a student's education with funds provided directly by government sources. Private colleges receive only 2 to 4 percent of their income this way, but one-half of their income (three times that of public universities) comes through tuition. Gillespie and Carlson, *Trends in Student Aid: 1963 to 1983,* 10. To be effective and equitable, it would seem imperative to treat admission to public universities as synonymous with government tuition assistance and thus under these proposals to make it conditional on public service.

38. Manski and Wise, *College Choice in America,* 21.

39. Ibid., 21.

40. Ibid., 21–22.

41. See generally Congressional Budget Office, *Improving Military Education Benefits: Effects on Costs, Recruiting and Retention.* It is for this reason that the Pentagon has consistently opposed numerous efforts to reinstate the G.I. Bill after it expired in 1976. Several Veterans Education Assistance programs are operated and legislatively supported by the Pentagon (including a Super-VEAP and an Army Education Fund with potential benefits accumulating to more than $20,000). But these are rationalized as compensating for their negative reenlistment effects by drawing a higher quality, more education-oriented recruit into the military. If civilian national service also offered this benefit, the military's recruiting advantage would be eliminated, and the net effect on the armed services would be negative.

Some commentators have urged that educational benefits be provided only to those who have undertaken military service. We have not seen any of these proposals address the question of how they would deal with educational benefits for those who could not enter the military (for example the handicapped, those who did not meet quality standards) and the three out of four qualified men for whom the military would have no need if the entire cohort of qualified men applied for service.

42. A national service program could offer educational incentives only to those who entered civilian service and financial incentives to those who entered the military, but this would adversely affect military recruitment and would differentiate military service from other forms of national service, making the military seem more mercenary.

43. One could structure educational support predominantly as loans and arrange forgiveness of those loans in return for posteducational service. This would induce more service immediately after completing an education, but it would not induce service from those who had not taken loans to begin with. Further, it would exacerbate class differences if service were merely an option and an alternative to repayment. Those with higher income expectations would be most likely to repay the loan. If posteducation service were required in return for a loan or grant, substantial enforcement difficulties would arise. What of the woman who had children or the individual who became the sole support of parents or held a private sector job otherwise in the national interest?

44. Reserve commitments require, on average, 15 weeks of entry training, 2

weekends of monthly drills each month, and 2 weeks of summer camp each year. This accumulates to about 265 work days over a 4-year period, compared with about 230 work days in a year of civilian national service. Nelson, Hale, and Slackman, "National Service and the Military," VI-9. We assume that the tax surcharge would not be lifted until service was completed.

45. Alternative forms of the program could minimize attrition and the opportunity costs of participation by permitting service in discontinuous 3-month terms or by requiring only 6 or 9 months of service. Of course, the value of the service rendered and the impact of the experience on the NSP would then be diminished. A program also could permit an accumulation of hours given at will over a period of years. This would, however, tend to bureaucratize the existing system of charitable work. In this description of program 4, we assume that a year of continuous service is required.

46. In 1983, the median family income for the United States as a whole was $24,580. Bureau of the Census, *Money Income and Poverty Status of Families and Persons in the United States: 1983,* 5, table I.

47. Few taxpayers, with the possible exception of the very rich and those with accountants, would be likely to calculate carefully the economic costs and benefits of serving early versus late or not at all. Still, it may be instructive to show the results of several examples of such calculations.

Assuming a real interest rate (the excess of nominal interest over inflation) of 2.5 percent, a twenty-year-old anticipating a 40-year income-earning career should estimate that the present value of avoiding a dollar's surtax every year for 40 years would be $25.10. Ignoring bracket creep, someone who anticipated constantly earning under $5,000 in real terms would thus value the avoidance of a surtax over the course of his or her 40-year working life at about $177 ($7.05 × $25.10). For another twenty-year-old anticipating annual income in real terms of between $10,000 and $14,999, avoidance of a surtax would have a present value of about $1,545 ($61.55 anticipated average surtax × $25.10). A couple anticipating approximately the present median familly income would value avoiding the surtax at about $4,267. A graduate of medical school who anticipated real earnings of $30,000 to $40,000 for the first 10 years, $50,000 to $75,000 for the next 10 years, and $100,000 to $200,000 for the last 20 years of his or her career would assign a present value of $26,831 to spending 1 year in national service immediately and thus avoiding the surcharge thereafter.

Polling data, more sophisticated modeling, and trial and error would be warranted before setting the surcharge at a given rate. Considerable argument could be had about the proper real interest rates to be assumed and different discount rates that might be used by the old and the young. It is possible that we have significantly underpriced the incentive that is required.

48. Marini, in "The Transition to Adulthood," analyzed data from high school students who were surveyed in 1957–1958 and then resurveyed later. Marini calculated that 25 percent of the female members of this cohort had their first child by age 19.86 and 75 percent by age 26.74. 494–5, table 1. It is indicative of the difficulties in using social science data to predict experience with a national service program that the data in this instance must be used to predict the likely behavior of a cohort 30 years later. Moreover, apart from changes in female labor force participation, a national service program might itself change patterns of child bearing and rearing.

49. Ibid., 494–495.

50. Attrition from the military is twice as high among high school nongraduates as among graduates. Analogous experience in civilian programs is discussed in Lacy and Kleindienst, "NYC National Service Demonstration Project—Attrition Prospects and Implications," unpublished memorandum, 5 April 1984, 1.

51. Public/Private Ventures, "A Profile of Past and Present Youth Conservation Corps Programs," unpublished manuscript, 1983.

52. Preliminary data provided orally by the National Criminal Justice Reference Center, 1984.

53. Rabinovitz, "National Service Other Services Study," 19 (citing American Correctional Association guidelines). The inefficiencies associated with 1-year workers noted in respect to previous programs would occur and cause NSPs to achieve somewhat less than a halving of the professional workload.

54. Research Triangle Institute, "Youth Attitude Tracking Survey II," 146.

55. Congressional Budget Office, *Economic Budget Outlook, 1983.*

56. Estimate based on a calculation that about $6.2 billion per year is spent on first term (less than 3 years in service) enlisted pay. This figure was provided in 1986 by the Office of the Assistant Secretary of Defense for Force Management.

57. Ibid., VI-9.

58. Thurman, "Sustaining the All-Volunteer Force, 1983–1992: The Second Decade," in Bowman, Little and Sicilia, *The All-Volunteer Force after a Decade* (forthcoming 1986).

59. Ibid., 32.

60. There are reasonable arguments to be made that this figure both understates and overstates the potential military benefit. Those who regard the likely gain as less might note that if given $350 million on an unrestricted basis, the military probably would not choose to spend most, or even much, of it in this way. Reserve recruitment rates, for example, now meet stated requirements, and the draw of higher quality college students might even be counterproductive if they had little interest in unit drills and little prospect of reenlistment. Money might better be spent on improving training and retaining those already in reserve units. Similar judgments might be made about active-force labor power expenditures, particularly given the likelihood that recruits prodded to serve by program 4 likely would reenlist at lower rates than recruits with a true preference for military service. One also could argue that reenlistment of quality recruits is more critical to the military than is recruitment in the first place.

61. Ashenfelter and Oaxaca, "Potential Labor Market Effects of National Service Programs," table 6.

62. Ibid., table 4.1.

63. Ibid., Table 4.3.

64. In 1982, employment in state and local government agencies exceeded that in federal agencies by a margin of roughly four and a half to one, according to the Bureau of the Census, *Statistical Abstract: 1984,* 303. The opportunities for augmenting those staffs with NSPs would likely favor state and especially local government by even wider margins. Federal agencies would be more likely to be engaged in policymaking, standard-setting, and other activities inappropriate for NSPs, while local entities would be more likely to be devoted to the direct provision of services.

65. See Article 1, Section 8, Clause 1, and the Sixteenth Amendment to the Constitution.

66. Bobbitt, "National Service: Unwise or Unconstitutional?," 312.

67. Article I, Section 8, Clause 1, providing that Congress may levy taxes to "provide for the . . . general welfare," may provide an alternative basis for the program. Costello, "Military and Civilian Conscription: The Constitutional Issues," 25–26, discusses this provision and concludes that it would authorize spending but not conscription. It is not clear which of these categories would apply to program 4.

68. Bobbitt, "National Service: Unwise or Unconstitutional?," 315.

69. See, for example, *U.S.* v. *Butler* 401 U.S. 297 (1936).

70. *U.S.* v. *Darby* 312 U.S. 100 (1938).

71. *Martino* v. *Mich. Window Cleaning Co.* 327 U.S. 173 (1946).

72. *Wickard* v. *Filburn* 317 U.S. 111, 128–29 (1942).

73. *Borden Co.* v. *Borella* 325 U.S. 679, 685 (Chief Justice Stone, dissenting).

74. The leading opinion is *Heart of Atlanta Model* v. *U.S.* 379 U.S. 241 (1964). There the court said: "The only questions are (1) whether Congress had a national basis for finding that racial discrimination by motels affected commerce, and (2) if it had such a basis, whether the means it selected to eliminate that evil are reasonable and appropriate." Ibid., 242, 258.

75. See generally Corwin, *The Constitution and What It Means Today,* 47–50.

76. *Robertson* v. *U.S.* 165 U.S. 275, 282 (1897).

77. *Butler* v. *Perry* 240 U.S. 328, 332 (1916).

78. In *Robertson,* the Court was concerned with a practice—the return of sailors who deserted—that "from time immemorial" had been treated as exceptional. The *Butler* Court was similarly dealing with long-established "services always treated as exceptional."

79. Black, "Constitutional Problems in Compulsory National Service," 21.

80. Besides the cases noted earlier, see *Pollack* v. *Williams* 332 U.S. 4, 17–18 (1943): "[F]orced labor in some special circumstances may be consistent with the general basic system of free labor. . . . [t]here are duties such as work on highways which society may compel." And see *Wiedenfeller* v. *Kidulis* 380 F. Supp. 445, 450 (E.D. Wis., 1974): "[E]ven upon a showing that labor was performed involuntarily . . . Courts have held that such labor is not violative of the Thirteenth Amendment if it serves a compelling state interest."

81. *Butler* v. *Perry* 240 U.S. 328 (1916). The opinion notes that all but one of the states that constituted the Northwest Territory compelled road work even while the Northwest Ordinance—the model for the Thirteenth Amendment—forbade involuntary servitude. Moreover, by 1889, twenty-seven states had laws requiring road work.

82. "Moreover, to the extent that the Congress is empowered to define slavery by section 2 of the Thirteenth Amendment, it cannot be irrelevant that any system of compulsory national service will have been ordered by Congress." McGrew, "The Constitutionality of Compulsory National Service," 262.

83. The Supreme Court's approach in this regard is best illustrated in *Plyer* v. *Doe* where the court bestowed "extraordinary protection from the majoritarian political process" upon those in "a position of political powerlessness." Of course, the

military draft provides an example of a compelling reason constitutionally justifying a compulsion confined to a particular age group. In regard to age discrimination, see generally Tribe, *American Constitutional Law,* 1077ff.

84. "[E]ven old age does not define a 'discrete' and insular group . . . in need of 'extraordinary protection from the majoritarian political process.' Instead, it marks a stage that each of us will reach if we live out our normal span. Even if the statute could be said to impose a penalty upon a class defined as the aged, it would not impose a distinction sufficiently akin to those classifications that we have found suspect to call for strict judicial scrutiny." *Mass. Bd. of Retirement* v. *Murgia* 427 U.S. 307, 313–14 (1976).

9
Conclusions

In this final chapter, we draw together thirteen judgments that we regard as central to thinking about national service. Some of these judgments flow directly from the analysis presented in the earlier chapters. Others are simply our assessments of political or administrative feasibility. One is the premise from which we began.

Neither separately nor together do these considerations determine whether some form of national service should be adopted. They do, however, suggest which benefits one might reasonably expect from particular forms of national service, and which should not be expected; they suggest the human and financial costs associated with various forms of national service; and they help clarify, we hope, the degree to which differing forms of national service would be consistent or inconsistent with the political and social values of our society.

National Service Is an Ideal, Not a Program

We began our work from the premise that national service is not an idea, and still less a plan, but rather an ideal encompassing a variety of often inconsistent ideas. The core of the concept is the conviction that the nation and its citizens would be better off if more persons devoted a portion of their lives to public service. On that much the various proponents of national service agree. But outside that core conviction, there is little agreement.

The three most significant disagreements concern whether a program should be voluntary or compulsory, whether it should benefit mainly the servers or those served, and whether it should be designed for the disadvantaged or make special efforts and expenditures to engage the middle class. On much else, too, there is disagreement: the age or ages at which service should be undertaken; the length of service required; the character of service activities; the relationship between civilian and military service; the rate of pay and extent of postservice benefits, if any; the degree to which national service should be centrally or locally planned and managed. Our first proposition, therefore, was and is that national service cannot be assessed—indeed can hardly be usefully discussed—until particular forms of the idea have been specified. We have tried to provide such a specification by positing four alternative programs, or models, of national service.

To review, the first is a school-based program. States would be free to participate or not. Those that did would require 240 hours of unpaid service from high school seniors as a prerequisite to a high school diploma. States (or school districts) could specify whether service would be performed in lieu of classroom time or as an after-school or summer activity. Students would be free to select the nature of their service from among a variety of tasks certified as acceptable by local authorities. For those who chose it and were accepted, military training would meet the service requirement. The federal government would bear 75 percent of the program's cost (100 percent in the case of military training).

Program 2 is draft-based; it assumes that a 2-year military draft would be reinstituted. This model would then offer all persons actually called to military service the opportunity to choose instead 2 years of civilian service. Participants would choose assignments from among those approved as socially useful by a federal agency under rules similar to those historically applied to conscientious objectors. Pay would approximate that for military recruits but without the full postservice benefits of the military.

The third model is evolutionary and voluntary. It would base national service on the political support and operational experience of existing service programs. It would exploit the fact that the diversity of those programs would make it possible to match different kinds of service requirements to the differing skills, needs, and interests of participants. This model envisions the establishment of a federal conservation corps, the expansion of state conservation corps, an enlargement of the Peace Corps and VISTA, and the development of state and local community service programs that together would provide 180,000 positions, most of them likely to be filled by eighteen- to twenty-three-year-olds. Together with military recruitment, this program would create service opportunities for one-sixth of the youth population and would engage a broadly representative (though male dominated) portion of that population. The subsistence allowances paid during the course of the program together with the termination payment at its end would provide total compensation equivalent to the minimum wage. Service commitments generally would be for 1 year, although the Peace Corps would continue to require a 2-year commitment.

Our fourth model is universal. It represents the form many people seem to assume national service would necessarily take: a system in which a year of service, civil or military, is expected of every citizen regardless of circumstances or capacities. In our formulation, however, the year could be served at any time after the age of eighteen, and the requirement would be enforced not by criminal sanctions, but by the imposition of an income tax surcharge of 5 percent of net taxable income in each year, after age twenty, until service was completed.

These four programs do not begin to exhaust the possible forms of national service. But readers can develop alternative plans by recombining the characteristics of the programs discussed here or by devising entirely new systems of service. The articulation of such additional alternatives is desireable, and we hope that the analysis of our four models can help illuminate the costs and benefits of such new alternatives as well. What we fear is the reverse, that public discussion will continue to focus on an abstract and ambiguous ideal. In that event, either the ideal will remain unrealized, or a program of national service will someday be adopted with little agreement on its purpose and little understanding of its likely consequences.

We emphasize this point not because no other specific programs have ever been proposed; many have. We emphasize it because we think the political temptation is to keep the debate unparticularized. The basis for that temptation is that, as an ideal, national service appeals to strange bedfellows: to persons who wish to improve social services through cheap additional labor power and others who seek intensive remedial education or job training for the participants, to some who wish to stimulate military enlistment and others who seek alternatives to it, to those who want youth to pay its dues, and to others who hope to enlarge the opportunities for retired persons to volunteer. As an ideal, therefore, national service has relatively broad political appeal; reduced to a particular plan, it may have considerably less appeal.

Similarly, problems with the concept will arise from efforts to realize it: from opportunities foregone; transaction costs incurred; risks of misassignment, poor supervision, and bad performance; the costs of administration, including, in a compulsory plan, the costs of enforcement. These costs, and the magnitude of related benefits, can begin to be appreciated only when visions are reduced to plans. Only then can the debate over national service, a debate now three-quarters of a century old, approach resolution.

Many Forms of National Service Are Constitutionally Permissible and Politically Plausible

It often has been asserted that national service probably would be unconstitutional, politically impossible, or both, or that it would create an intrusive federal bureaucracy or portend a police state. Those who have taken such positions seem to assume that national service must be universal, mandatory, and enforced by criminal penalties. Such a form of national service would indeed be questionable. But we believe that many national service alternatives are constitutionally tolerable, consistent with the central values of U.S. society, and politically plausible. This conclusion rests on three findings.

First, effective inducements to service can be achieved without using criminal penalties. Program 1 would do this by requiring service as a prerequisite to the award of a high school diploma. Assuming the reimposition of a draft, program 2 would offer a civilian alternative to a military service. Program 3 simply would expand a variety of existing programs, one or more of which would likely be attractive, on a voluntary basis to many prospective participants. Program 4 would afford tax benefits for those who had served or, viewed from the opposite perspective, impose tax penalties on those who had not. None of these techniques seems to us to contravene the Thirteenth Amendment's prohibition of involuntary servitude or to be clearly beyond the political pale.

Second, many forms of national service need not intrude deeply into individual freedoms. A mandatory universal plan, like our fourth program, would, over time, affect the personal lives of much of the population. Even this program, however, would leave much choice about whether, when, and how to serve. We estimate that more than 25 percent of those affected by our model would not, in fact, serve. The school-based program need add no demands on the participants' time to those now made by the educational system. The draft-based program would result in larger draft calls but would simultaneously enlarge the freedom of choice of those who were called. Program 3, as noted, would be entirely voluntary.

Third, although any mandatory universal form of national service would spawn a large bureaucracy, many service programs could be run in ways that minimized both federal intrusion on state prerogatives and bureaucratic overhead. The school-based program we describe would receive federal funding, but the states or school districts would decide whether to participate, and the program would be operated by the schools. The other programs all envision a large measure of self-placement in national service jobs. Programs 2 and 3, each affecting fewer than a quarter of a million youths per year, probably could be administered by a total staff of fewer than 10,000 persons.

This is not to say that the value of national service would outweigh its costs. Our point is simply that the questions of costs versus benefits are the right questions to address; they are not rendered moot by insuperable constitutional barriers or binding political constraints.

The Work Is There to Do

One premise of all national service proposals is clearly correct: There is useful social and environmental work that national service participants (NSPs) could do. Indeed, there is so much work to be done, and of such variety, that carefully administered programs, even if very large, probably could offer most participants a considerable choice of tasks.

Some forms of national service would be better suited to particular kinds of public work than others, and some would be more productive than others. As we have pointed out, for example, the students in program 1 could usefully undertake many tasks in schools, but their limited time, availability and other factors would reduce their utility elsewhere. Conversely, participants in programs 2 and 4 might be less useful in schools but could more effectively care for the elderly, help staff government agencies, and undertake environmental conservation tasks. Participants in programs 2 and 4 would be much more valuable, on average, than those in program 1. The contribution of program 3 workers would depend greatly on the nature of the subprograms in which they were enrolled. Overall, the value of their work probably would exceed that of program 1 but not reach that of programs 2 or 4.

All NSPs could perform some useful work, and the tasks to be performed would be sufficiently numerous and diverse as to allow even the largest program of national service to match most participants to tasks.

Most Forms of National Service Would Not Accomplish Public Service Tasks Cheaply

Notwithstanding the previous conclusion, national service would not be an inexpensive means of performing public work. Those who assume the contrary tend, we think, to exaggerate either the productivity of NSPs or the economies that might be achieved by paying subminimum wages.

We think that, except in school-based service, NSPs in each program would and should be paid no less than the equivalent of a minimum wage. Even if participants were paid only two-thirds of the minimum wage, however, we doubt that an economic bonus would result. For most forms of service, short terms of participation, high attrition rates, and a high proportion of immature NSPs with limited skills would keep the value of labor relatively low. National service programs that sought to teach basic skills to youths who lack them, or offered substantial job training, or housed many NSPs in residential camps would increase that value but also considerably increase costs. In all the programs, the overhead expenses associated with assignment, training, supervision, and general administration would be substantial.

National service workers, in short, seem to us to be like solar energy: ample in supply and attractive in their potential power but costly to bring to bear on the tasks at hand. The notion that national service programs would accomplish public work at bargain prices is, we conclude, an illusion.

National Service Would Meet Some Needs of Youth but Only Partially and at High Cost

The needs of chronically unemployed youths, a special and especially important problem, we discuss below. As for all other youths, we believe that it is simply undemonstrated that national service would meet their needs or that the costs of meeting them—at least in the programs involving some degree of compulsion—would not be disproportionately high.

One asserted need of youth generally is contact with the world of work. However, as we have seen, more than 80 percent of today's sixteen- to nineteen-year-olds have had some substantial experience of employment. The chronically unemployed aside, contact with the world of work is not a major unmet need of youth.

Would national service jobs provide more useful experience than currently available private sector jobs? We see little reason to believe so. In the main, we think such jobs would involve tasks very like those in existing positions. To the extent that national service work diverges from the prevailing norm, moreover, it risks doing so at the cost of not providing NSPs with skills, experience, seniority, credentials, and contacts likely to be useful in postprogram jobs. At least in the short term, those who have completed service in the Peace Corps and the military have lagged economically behind their counterparts who did not serve. In short, national service would be a doubtful means of facilitating a transition to the world of work.

Nor would many national service assignments necessarily provide good alternative settings for self-definition. Some national service work settings—particularly in schools—would be familiar; the tasks in some others, as we have discussed, would be menial and possibly demeaning. At least in large programs, relatively few positions would provide that combination of novelty and challenge that enables military service, the Peace Corps, or highly disciplined (and expensive) residential service programs like the California Conservation Corps to give young people a much broader view of their interests, capacities, and potential.

With respect to asserted needs of youth for broader acquaintanceship, the picture is more mixed. Many forms of national service likely would leave youths in their own communities. Acquaintanceship with persons from different parts of the country would not arise. In small and homogeneous communities, relationships across racial or ethnic lines would not develop. Most forms of service would, however, expand the familiarity of youths with persons not part of their families, schools, and immediate neighborhoods. Especially in cities, a real expansion of perspective would be possible.

Similarly, some NSPs, whether assigned to schools, hospitals, day care centers, or precinct houses, would find themselves depended upon rather than dependent, perhaps for the first time in their lives; that should prove a maturing experience. Yet most bureaucracies to which NSPs were assigned would tend to give NSPs the least interesting and least responsible tasks. Alert and forceful administration could constrain that tendency but would not be likely to overcome it.

Although much would depend on the size and nature of the program and on the quality of its administration, we do not believe that a very high proportion of national service assignments would generate the satisfaction derived from collective action toward common goals. The goals in some cases might seem trivial, and the collectivity in others might not be evident. Only where stable groups of NSPs worked together would it be clear that participants shared a goal and were working jointly toward it.

Moreover, any form of national service would experience high attrition. Apart from systems that impose military discipline, as in program 2, the dropout rates would exceed one-quarter and might reach two-thirds of the participants. For this substantial fraction, the program might prove a negative experience.

More broadly, we note again the uncertainty as to how genuine, how pressing, and how universal are some asserted needs of youth. The evidence that youth feels them is slim. The evidence is voluminous that they are not so much the needs of youth as the needs society feels with respect to youth and that each generation of adults defines such needs differently. Moreover, however defined, the needs of youth vary immensely. A national service program must at least implicitly make hard choices as to which needs it would meet and therefore which segments of the youth population it would predominantly serve and attract.

Finally, many youths and their families feel quite pressing needs that national service may preclude. About 15 percent of women under age twenty are single mothers. Despite their much higher unemployment rates, minority youths contribute larger fractions of their families' total income than do majority youth. Some young people care for disabled parents; others simply want to get established as rapidly as possible in a career. For all such youths, the opportunity costs of service would be high.

National Service Is a Poor Solution to Youth Unemployment

Most Americans probably expect that any program of national service would provide chronically unemployed youths with meaningful tasks during their period of service and with improved chances for nonmenial employment thereafter. Not surprisingly, these youths themselves cite improvement of their employment prospects as their first priority, even in joining programs with a high service component. Some forms of service would indeed contribute to these ends, but national service likely would prove less effective in this regard than more traditional employment training programs.

The reason is that converting the unemployed into the employed is not made easier by superimposing a service requirement. Current programs demonstrate that a service experience can improve employability, but as employment and service goals are mixed, three complications arise.

The first complication is expense. Service-oriented programs that focus on the disadvantaged and provide intense supervision and training are costly. The most successful are residential programs with average annual costs approaching $20,000 per position. Nonresidential programs can be run for perhaps two-thirds that amount, but even this cost causes one to question whether it would not be better to focus on training alone.

The second complication is that of targeting. Programs designed for the unemployed normally do not attract the more fortunate. Nor would such programs meet the needs of readily employable youth were they arbitrarily assigned to it. Short of a depression of the scale that drew impoverished working- and middle-class young men together into the CCC of the 1930s, programs designed to improve employability would be unlikely to integrate participants of differing classes or levels of education.

If powerfully articulated and steadily honored, the ideal of universal service might change matters: It might draw advantaged youths into a national program. If so, program participation would be less stigmatizing, and completion of service would become a more useful and more accepted credential. But such gains would be achieved at the cost of inducing or requiring large numbers of youths whose employment prospects were good to defer employment. Reducing youth unemployment, in short, would not likely be addressed efficiently through a national service system that devoted much of its budget and organizational energy to persons who were already employable or who, like many in our program 4, were not young.

Finally, there is the problem noted in the preceding section: Service work normally does not lead to private sector jobs. Some public service work—in nursing homes and day care centers, for example—may open (mostly low-wage) follow-on opportunities. But many of the public service tasks we have described—in conservation, tutoring, and public health prophylactic work, for example—do not provide good prospects for follow-on jobs. The service orientation of a national service program not only makes it hard to reject projects that offer poor employment prospects later, but it also biases the program toward activities in which work is not being done by public and private sector employers. Well-run service programs would provide to some disadvantaged participants socialization to the demands of the workplace, including discipline, teamwork, and punctuality. This would be a valuable achievement. But the comparative question remains: Would the disadvantaged be better served by such programs or by job training that made no pretense of service? The answer is unclear, but we think the evidence favors the latter hypothesis.

Their Elders May Need It More

National service programs limited to youths not only would serve some youths poorly, they also would ignore the capacities and interests of older people. Among persons in middle life, national service opportunities might meet a number of needs. They could ease a transition from dead-end employment to a changed career; offer a socially approved means of absorbing a period of unemployment; or provide an opportunity, perhaps especially useful for women entering the labor market after a long absence, to become socialized or resocialized to work and to experience various work settings through the halfway house of volunteering.

Persons at or beyond retirement age may have more to give and more reason to benefit from national service than any other age group. The United States now possesses the largest, healthiest, best educated, and most skilled population of elderly in the history of the world—and probably the least useful. It is a population whose most common needs are a greater sense of purpose and self-esteem, increased income, and new sources of acquaintanceship. Many forms of national service might supply each of these. Indeed, national service would likely meet the needs of the elderly more than it could satisfy the corresponding requirements of youth. Many of the elderly likely would be more satisfied with relatively routine tasks, gain more discretionary income from relatively modest payments for service, and take pleasure from a broader diversity of new acquaintances than would youth. Moreover, by including older persons, national service would not only help reintegrate elderly participants into the mainstream of society, it also would bring into service a repertoire of skills, knowledge, maturity, and supervisory experience that very few youths possess.

The possibilities for combining the elderly and youth in service programs are the most promising and the most underexplored issues associated with national service. We urge more attention to them.

National Service Would Provide Little Benefit to the Military

We conclude that most forms of national service would not improve the quality or representativeness of either the all-volunteer or a draft-based military.

Assuming the AVF

If the AVF continued, program 1 would draw some high school juniors and seniors into 3-month military training programs to fulfill their national service requirements. These students would be more likely than average students to become reserve or active-duty soldiers and probably would require less training when they enlisted. But that benefit would be small as against the dollars and labor power spent to secure it. Roughly 1 percent of the active-duty Army personnel would have to be allocated to the training of such national service participants, and more than $10,000 would be spent for each ultimate recruit.

Program 2 and similar programs that established civilian service as an alternative to military service would depend on the existence of a draft. By definition, then, they could not help sustain an AVF.

Our voluntary program 3 would have a negative effect on the AVF. Arguably, it would help AVF recruiting by establishing an expectation that a period of service is a normal interlude either in the progression from school to the work force or later. But we conclude that this advantage would be more than offset by the establishment of more than 100,000 new civilian jobs against whose attractions military recruiters would have to compete.

Assuming a Draft

We are not impressed with the military gains that might be achieved by supplementing a military draft with national service. If conscription were reestablished, program 1's military training option for high school students would decrease their later training time and therefore increase the utility of a small fraction of those drafted. But even more clearly than under an all-volunteer system, this gain would be bought dearly. Since it inducts more recruits for shorter periods than an AVF, a draft places especially high demands on the training establishment. Given a draft, it would make little sense to devote additional training resources to high school students, some of whom would neither enlist nor be drafted.

By providing a civilian alternative to military service, program 2 might facilitate acceptance of a military draft. Once in operation, however, the program probably would have negative effects on the military. The evidence is that better educated conscripts would disproportionately choose civilian service and that civilian service would attract relatively more whites than blacks. Thus, the program would produce a less qualified and less racially representative military than would be created by a straightforward draft. Program 3, establishing a large number of civilian jobs that would not afford a draft deferral, would have no significant effect on a conscription system.

The universal mandatory program 4 would almost certainly have a positive effect on the military. By making all citizens face an obligation to serve, it probably would encourage enlistment and might lessen the sense of grievance or ill luck among those conscripted to military duty. That gain seems quite small, however, when measured against the costs and disruptions of a universal mandatory system.

Program 4 and an AVF

The only circumstance in which national service might yield important military manpower gains would be one in which an all-volunteer system coexisted with program 4. Since everyone would face an obligation to serve in some capacity, a military tour, even though longer than the civilian service period, would involve a shorter diversion from self-directed career plans than would be the case in the absence of a service requirement. Program 4, with its 5 percent tax surcharge for failure to serve, would cause military service to yield the additional benefit of a lifetime 5 percent tax advantage as against those who did not serve at all. This recruiting advantage could be exploited to improve the representativeness and the quality of those entering the military, to extend the terms of recruit service, or to reduce the costs of recruitment.

Opportunity Costs Are Critical, and They Vary

The question of whether some form of national service should be adopted cannot be answered by examining national service alone. A comparative judgment is involved. The value of national service, for its participants and for the country, would depend significantly on its opportunity costs—that is, on the nature and value of the activities in which its participants otherwise would have been engaged. These activities would vary enormously. They would vary among individuals, they would be different for the same individuals at different times in their lives, and they would vary for the country as a whole depending on the state of the economy, the age distribution of the population, the degree of need for military manpower, and the nation's social priorities.

The extent of variation over time is suggested by the history of the most often cited U.S. precedent for national service, the Civilian Conservation Corps which operated from 1933 to 1942. During the early Depression years, the CCC offered income and a chance to be useful when both such opportunities were in short supply. As the Depression receded, however, and ordinary job opportunities increased, the CCC's focus shifted: It gave much more emphasis to education and training, and it was notably less popular. World

War II brought a more dramatic change: The bulk of the youth cohort was preempted for military purposes. Civilian national service became irrelevant for all but COs, and the program was abandoned. Despite its great success, it was not reestablished in the booming economy of the postwar period. Labor in that period had other, richer opportunities and (with the Korean War) other responsibilities.

This history suggests that a large-scale national service program would likely be enacted only when alternative economic and educational opportunities were so poor and military manpower demands so low as to leave a large portion of the population, and especially of youth, without an obviously useful occupation. Further, one may infer that continued support of any large-scale service program would depend on the nation's economic, demographic, and military circumstances. National service is no program for all seasons.

Choices Lower the Costs

Although the opportunity costs of national service to society at large would shift over time, those costs would vary even more dramatically among individuals and for most individuals at different stages in their lives.

The ideal of national service traditionally has implied comprehensiveness, uniformity, and perhaps compulsion. The ideal suggests that all should participate and at roughly the same young age. In that way, the experience would be truly national, and service would mark the passage into adulthood.

That vision ignores the extraordinary diversity of the group that would be affected. The 3.5 to 4 million young people in each year-of-birth group differ in every dimension: skill, temperament, interest, experience, strength, opportunities, family situation, maturity, personal obligations. The intense manual labor of a conservation program that was novel and challenging to an aimless middle-class urban male may be pointless to a farm boy and severely disruptive to a teenage mother, a talented musician, or a young secretary contributing a needed increment to her family's income. Similarly, although the obligation to serve may be repugnant to many young people, opportunities to serve during periods of unemployment later in their lives or at retirement may be far more welcome.

This is a strong and perhaps decisive argument against programs that would induct all citizens into service for a defined period at a prescribed age. Forms of national service, like our programs 3 and 4, that left individuals considerable choice as to when to enter service would greatly mitigate the opportunity costs and also might enlarge the personal benefits of the program. Programs like our programs 1 and 2, which substitute national service for other obligations (as program 1 might substitute service for time in school and program 2 would substitute civilian service for military conscription), would minimize opportunity costs in other ways.

Despite the conceptual appeal of universal service at a single age, programs that leave open the choice at least as to when and probably also as to whether to serve, and that offer a variety of kinds of assignments, would provide the highest aggregate benefits to participants and impose the lowest opportunity costs. They also would accord best with our society's preference for local control, diversity, and experimentation. Paradoxically, national service might be most attractive if it were least national—that is, least uniform and comprehensive. Noncoercive, diverse, locally defined opportunities for service still could meet nationally established objectives, deserve national financial support, and advance the ideal of serving the nation's needs.

Ultimately, Less Obvious Benefits May Be the Most Important

Here we enter the realm of sheer speculation, but it may be that, were national service to be enacted, the most important benefits would be subtler and more difficult to measure than those on which we now have data.

First, national service might give its graduates the sense that they had paid their dues, that through some modest sacrifice they had become full participants in a nation that, on the whole, offers much and asks very little. Military veterans, Peace Corps alumni, and ironically, immigrants are now virtually the only Americans who experience a sense of citizenship earned rather than simply received. As a result, they often value themselves and their country more highly. Forms of national service that required sacrifice, intensive effort, or some risk might offer that sense to all.

National service also might, over time, have a profound effect on large bureaucratic institutions now largely closed to public view. Experience suggests a tendency for at least some hospitals, schools, nursing homes, social service agencies, and other bureaucracies to drift toward meeting the convenience of their staffs more than toward maximizing benefits to their clients. A continuing flow of national service participants would interrupt the privacy in which such distortions of purpose flourish. Although some NSPs would become socialized to the norms of the institution, others would not; they would open to society a window on those institutions. Over time, in much the same way that many former Peace Corps volunteers remain concerned about less developed nations, large numbers of former NSPs might retain an interest in the improvement of the institutions in which they served. Many previously insulated institutions might thereby be made more responsive, in some cases quite substantially so.

Another collateral benefit—for some it may be a dominating benefit—

would be that any large-scale system of national service would create a pool of human resources that might enable an expanded national effort in day care, conservation, assistance to the aged, or other social tasks. As we have argued, national service probably would not be a cost-effective means for performing most such tasks, but it may be politically effective. By virtue of the many and divergent sources of its appeal, national service may be more likely to be enacted than any more direct means of achieving those ends. And once in being, it would require that work for NSPs be found. Thus, needs that some would argue now receive too low a national priority would be met—not efficiently, perhaps, but met nonetheless.

Finally, national service might stimulate and encourage volunteering generally. As an expression of the value the nation attributed to service, the enactment of a national service program might strengthen the norm of constructive voluntary service throughout society and in all age groups. It might thereby deepen the personal satisfactions of those who already serve, increase the number who would serve independently of the national program, improve the quality of the services to which the volunteers contributed, and perhaps diminish feelings of isolation and purposelessness throughout society. Conceivably, such broader opportunities and wider participation in service might absorb into productive and satisfying work so substantial a portion of otherwise destructive social energies as to amount, in time, to "a moral equivalent to war."

Implementation Would Be Difficult and Crucial

The most important and best established lessons to be learned from the many youth and service programs of the past quarter century are that their impact has depended on the match between participants' interests and their work, on the quality and quantity of supervision, and for employment programs, on the availability of later job opportunities for which the programs were effective preparation.

It is noteworthy that these particulars are not determined by the questions of program architecture that are the central concern of this book. We have attempted mainly to illuminate the sharp differences among several major types of national service programs, but they have one characteristic in common: Their effect would depend as much on the care with which they were administered, the dedication of their staffs, and the public support they generated as on their conceptual design. It is tempting to assume that the quality of training and supervision would be high and that work experience would be rewarding. But U.S. youth programs have in fact varied around a mean of mediocrity. Striking successes have been mostly local, transitory, and rare. Successes have been difficult to replicate and have faded when charismatic leaders left or budget priorities changed.

It follows, then, that decisions as to whether one form or another of national service should be enacted would be followed by at least equally vexing and no less important questions of implementation. How should selection, assignment, training, and supervision be carried out? By whom? At what levels? Through what processes? At what cost? What rules of behavior would be set for participants? How rigorously would they be enforced? How could vulnerable clients—an old woman living alone, three-year-olds in a day care center—be protected from NSPs who may prove unstable, abusive, or merely irresponsible?

The difficulty and the importance of hundreds of such questions suggest that the administration of any large-scale service program might be well advised to start small, begin with what works, encourage diversity, monitor results closely, terminate failures as promptly as possible, reward success, expand slowly, and anticipate that the overhead costs of operating a successful national service program will be high.

Experimentation Is Needed

In the last analysis, we are struck by how much is still unknown about national service. The opportunity costs of service are consistently unclear, whether we consider the relatively simple problem of what activities high school seniors would sacrifice if service were required after school or the complex one of society's losses under program 4. The effects of service remain similarly debatable. In the short term, the economic consequences seem negative; in the long term, they may be positive, but we do not know the net consequences. The psychological effects of service are even less clear. Virtually nothing has been written on the different effects of service on different age groups (especially the elderly) and income classes. Little evaluation has been done of the impact of mixing groups or of team as compared with individual service. Well-monitored experiments with national service, and especially with models like our programs 1 and 3,[1] would be illuminating, especially if the comparative effects of service were tested through the use of control groups.

Since we think forms of national service like program 2 are likely to receive serious public attention over the next decade, we believe the development of such data would be well justified.

Perhaps after local experiments were assessed, the nation would wish to adopt some system of national service. Whether the national judgment is positive or negative, however, we urge policymakers to reach conclusions only through incremental judgments. National service, we hope we have made clear, is not simple or unitary; it is a host of possibilities that might be realized in a host of ways, each with promise, each with difficulties, each with a mix of cost and benefits that is very hard to anticipate. The evocative ideal of national service now justifies neither more nor less than deliberate experiment and clear-eyed sequential judgments about whether the promise of various proposals can be realized in practice.

Note

1. Polling data also might provide insight into plans like our programs 2 and 4. A relatively modest investment might cast light on those who would select military over civilian service, on what that choice might depend, and on whether and when persons would serve in a program like our program 4.

References

ACTION, *Annual Report, 1981*. Washington, DC: ACTION, 1981.

ACTION, "Candid Admissions," *Synergist* 10, no. 1 (Spring 1981), 2–5.

ACTION, "National Youth Service Demonstrations" (1980).

ACTION, *Senior Companion Program Impact Evaluation: 1980 Summary Report*. Washington, DC: ACTION, 1980.

ACTION, Office of Policy and Planning, Evaluation Division, *A Survey of Former Peace Corps and VISTA Volunteers*. Vol. 1, *The Post-Peace Corps Experience*. Washington, DC: ACTION, 1979.

ACTION, "Two Demonstrations of National Service." An updated mimeographed report.

ACTION, *Youth Community Service: Non-Traditional Projects and Tasks for Volunteers*. Washington, DC: ACTION, 1978.

Agnew, V.C., "Better Education Through Application," *Synergist* 10, 3 (1982), 44–48.

Alden, J., ed., *Volunteers in Education: Future Public Policy*. Alexandria, VA: National School Volunteers Program, 1979.

Allen, K., I. Chapin, S. Keller, and D. Hill, *Volunteers from the Workplace*. Arlington, VA: National Center for Voluntary Action, 1979.

Allen, V.L., and R.S. Feldman, "Learning through Tutoring: Low Achieving Children as Tutors," *Journal of Experiential Education* 42 (1974), 1–5.

American Enterprise Institute, "A Conversation with Robert Pirie: The Manpower Problems of the 1980s." Washington, D.C.: American Enterprise Institute, 1980.

American Jewish Committee, "National Service," *National Affairs Backgrounder*, October 1983. New York: American Jewish Committee.

American Library Association, "Guidelines for Using Volunteers in Libraries." Chicago: American Library Association, 1971.

Appelbaum, E., *Back to Work: Determinants of Women's Successful Re-entry*. Boston: Auburn House Publishing Company, 1981.

Arkell, R.N., "Are Student-Helpers Helped?" *Psychology in the Schools*, January 1975, 113–15.

Ashenfelter, O., and R. Oaxaca, "Potential Labor Market Effects of National Service Programs." Unpublished paper prepared for the National Service Study Project, September 1983.

Atlanta Public Schools, Office of Planning and Extended Services, "Community Service Requirement: Class of 1988 Duties to the Community," October 1984.

Babic, A., "The Older Volunteer: Expectations and Satisfactions," *The Gerontologist* (Spring 1972), 87–90.

Bachman, J., L. Johnston, and P. O'Malley, *Monitoring the Future: 1982*. Ann Arbor: Institute for Social Research, University of Michigan Press, 1984.

Bachman, J., P. O'Malley, and L. Johnston, *Youth in Transition*. Vol. 6, *Adolescence to Adulthood: Change and Stability in the Lives of Young Men*. Ann Arbor: Institute for Social Research, University of Michigan Press, 1978.

Bailin, M., and N. Jaffe, *The California Conservation Corps: A Case Study*. Working Paper #5. The State Youth Initiatives Project. Philadelphia: Public/Private Ventures, 1982.

Baskir, L., and W. Strauss, *Chance and Circumstance*. New York: Alfred A. Knopf, 1978.

Benson, C., "The Real Costs of National Service," in *National Service: A Report of a Conference,* edited by Donald Eberly, 15–27. New York: Russell Sage Foundation, 1968.

Berlin, Gordon, *Not Working: Unskilled Youth and Displaced Adults,* New York: Ford Foundation, 1983.

Beverly, V.E., "The Double-Barreled Impact of Volunteer Services," *Geriatrics* 30, no. 7: 132–41.

Bingham, Jonathan, "Replacing the Draft," *The New Republic,* 16 January 1971, 17–21.

Binkin, M., "Military Manpower Issues in the 1980s: Issues and Choices," *International Security Review* 5, no. 3 (1980), 347–74.

Binkin, M., M. Eitelberg, A. Schexnider, and M. Smith, *Blacks and the Military.* Washington, DC: Brookings Institution, 1982.

Bird, R., "The Case for Voluntary Service," in *National Service: A Report of a Conference,* edited by Donald Eberly, 485–502. New York: Russell Sage Foundation, 1968.

Birman, B., and A. Ginsburg, "The Federal Role in Elementary and Secondary Education: New Directions and Continuing Concerns," *The Urban Lawyer* 14, no. 3 (1982), 471–500.

Black, C.L. Jr., "Constitutional Problems in Compulsory National Service," Yale Law Reports 13, no. 19 (Summer 1967), 9–21.

Blackmer, A., and P. Irwin. "A Study of Off-Campus Education." Boston: National Association of Independent Schools, 1977.

Blum, H., "A Model of Transition Mainstreaming: A Cross-Cognitive Tutor Program." Unpublished doctoral dissertation, 1978.

Blumstein, N., and D. Nagin, "The Deterrent Effect of Legal Evasion," *Stanford Law Review* 29(1977), 241–70.

Bobbitt, P., "National Service: Unwise or Unconstitutional?" in *Registration and the Draft,* edited by M. Anderson, 299–342. Stanford, CA: Hoover Institution, 1982.

Bobilin v. *Board of Education, State of Hawaii* 403 F. Supp. 1095 (District Court, Hawaii, 1975).

Borden Co. v. *Borella* 325 U.S. 679, 685 (Chief Justice Stone, dissenting).

Borus, M.E., "Willingness to Work Among Youth," *The Journal of Human Resources,* 17, no. 4, 592.

Boyer, E.L., *High School: A Report on Secondary Education in America.* A study funded by the Carnegie Foundation for the Advancement of Teaching. New York: Harper & Row, Publishers, Inc., 1983.

Bramson, L., "Social Impact of Voluntary National Service," in *National Service: A Report of a Conference,* edited by Donald Eberly, 105–30. New York: Russell Sage Foundation, 1968.

Brinkerhoff, J.R., and D.W. Grissmer, *The Reserve Forces in an All-Volunteer Environment.* Santa Monica, CA: Rand Corporation, 1984.

Bronx River Restoration, *Report on a 1-Year Experience Working with Young Adult Conservation Corps Workers.* New York: Bronx River Restoration, June 1980.

Browning, H.L., S.C. Lopreato, and D.L. Poston, Jr., "Income and Veteran Status: Variations Among Mexican Americans, Blacks and Anglos," *American Sociological Review* 31, no. 1 February 1973, 74–85.

Bucknam, R., "Experience-Based Career Education: A Study of the Research, Development, Implementation, Dissemination and Institutionalization Process." Unpublished draft paper. Washington, DC: National Institute of Education, 1978.

Bucknam, R., and S.G. Brand, "EBCE Really Works: A Meta-analysis on Experience Based Career Education," *Educational Leadership,* March 1983, 121.

Butler, E.P., and J. Darr, *Lessons from Experience: An Interim Review of the Youth Employment and Demonstration Projects Act.* The Vice President's Task Force on Youth Employment. Waltham, MA: Center for Public Service, The Florence Heller Graduate School, Brandeis University, March 1980.

Butler v. *Perry* 240 U.S. 328 (1916).

California Conservation Corps, *1976–79 Report to the Legislature.* Sacramento, CA.

Carp, A., "The Organization of National Service: The Peace Corps Today" in *National Service: A Report of a Conference,* edited by Donald Eberly, 319–22. New York: The Russell Sage Foundation, 1968.

Chambers, J., *Draftees or Volunteers.* New York: Garland, 1975.

Charner, I., and B. Fraser, "Fast Foods Jobs." National Institute for Work and Learning. Washington, D.C.: 1984.

The Children's Foundation, "Child Care Food Program: Umbrella Sponsorship for Family Day Care Homes." A fact sheet from the Children's Foundation, Washington, DC, 1984.

The Children's Foundation, "Facts About the Child Care Food Program in Family Day Care." Washington, DC, 1984.

Clay v. *U.S.* 403 U.S. 698, 700 (1971).

Cloward, R., "Studies in Tutoring," *Journal of Experimental Education* 36 (1967), 14–25.

College Entrance Examination Board, *On Further Examination.* Report of the Advisory Panel on the Scholastic Aptitude Test Score Decline. New York: College Entrance Examination Board, 1977.

Coleman, J., et al., *Youth: Transition to Adulthood.* The Report of the Panel on Youth of the President's Science Advisory Committee. Chicago: University of Chicago Press, 1974.

Colombatto, E., Foreign Evidence Relevant to the Proposed Nationwide Social Service in the United Kingdom, London: Centre for Labour Economics, 1981.

Committee for the Study of National Service, *Youth and the Needs of the Nation*. Washington, DC: Potomac Institute, 1979.

Community Service Society of New York: *Proceedings of the Fourth Annual SERVE Volunteer Training Institute*. New York: 1970.

Conrad, D., "The Differential Impact of Experiential Learning Programs on Secondary School Students." A doctoral thesis from the University of Minnesota. Ann Arbor: University Microfilms International, 1980.

Conrad, D., and D. Hedin, "Are Experiential Learning Programs Effective?" *NASSP Bulletin* 62, no. 421 (1978), 102–7.

Conrad, D., and D. Hedin, "Citizenship Education Through Participation," in *Education for Responsible Citizenship,* edited by B.F. Brown, 133–55. New York: McGraw Hill, 1977.

Conrad, D., and D. Hedin, "Executive Summary: Experiential Education Evaluation Project." Center for Youth Development and Research, University of Minnesota, St. Paul, MN.

Conrad, D., and D. Hedin, "National Assessment of Experiential Education." University of Minnesota, 1981. Unpublished paper.

Cooper, R., *Military Manpower and the All-Volunteer Force,* Santa Monica, CA: The Rand Corporation, 1977.

Cooper, R., "Military Manpower Procurement Policy in the 1980s," in *Military Service in the United States,* edited by Brent Scowcroft, 151–94. New York: The American Assembly, Columbia University, 1982.

Corwin, *The Constitution and What It Means Today,* 14th ed. Princeton, NJ: Princeton University Press, 1978.

Costello, "Military and Civilian Conscription: The Constitutional Issues." Congressional Research Service Report. Washington, DC, 1980.

Couto, R.A., *Streams of Idealism and Health Care Innovation: An Assessment of Service-Learning and Community Mobilization*. New York: Teachers College Press, 1982.

Cullinan, T., *Attitudes of Returning Peace Corps Volunteers Concerning Impact of Peace Corps Interlude on Subsequent Academic Work*. Menlo Park, CA: Stanford Research Institute, 1969.

Cullinan, T., "National Service and the American Educational System," in *The Draft: A Handbook of Facts and Alternatives,* edited by Sol Tax, 91–98. Chicago: University of Chicago Press, 1967.

Cutright, P., "The Civilian Earnings of White and Black Draftees and Non Veterans," *American Sociological Review* 39, no. 3 (June 1974), 317–27.

Dale, C., and C. Gilroy, "Determinants of Enlistments: A Macroeconomic Time-Series View," *Armed Services in Society* 10, no. 2 (February 1984), 192–210.

Davis, J., J. Lauby, and P. Sheatsley, *Americans View the Military: Public Opinion in 1982*. The National Opinion Research Center Report no. 131. Chicago: University of Chicago Press, 1985.

de Toqueville, A. *Democracy in America,* vol. 2, book 2. New York: Vintage Books, 1958.

Detroit Public School System, *High School Graduation Requirement #7: Outside of Class Learning Experience*. Detroit Public School System, 1978.

Devin-Sheehan, L., R.S. Feldman, and V.L. Allen, "Research on Children Tutoring Children: A Critical Review," *Review of Educational Research* 46, no. 3 (Summer 1976), 355–85.

Diaz, W.A., J. Ball, and C. Wolfhagen, *Linking School and Work for Disadvantaged Youths*. The YIEPP Demonstration Final Implementation Report. Washington, DC: Manpower Demonstration Research Corporation, 1982.

Dickson, A., "Community Service and the Curriculum." An updated mimeograph. London: Community Service Volunteer.

Dickson, A., "Reflecting on a Contemporary Taboo," *Chronicle* 2 (1982), 25–31. London: The Dag Hammarskjold Information Centre on the Study of Violence and Peace.

Dickson, A., "Youth Call: The Real Questions," *Community Care,* 16 July 1981. London.

Dorring and Hutzler, *Description of Officers and Enlisted Personnel in the U.S. Armed Forces*. Santa Monica, CA: Rand Corporation, 1982.

Eberly, D., *The Estimated Effect of a National Service Program on Public Service Manpower Needs, Youth Unemployment, College Attendance, and Marriage Rates*. New York: Russell Sage Foundation, 1970.

Eberly, D., ed., *National Service: A Report of a Conference*. New York: Russell Sage Foundation, 1968.

Eberly, D., "A National Service Model Based on Experience and Research." A paper presented for the annual convention of the American Political Science Association in Washington, D.C., August 1984.

Eberly, D., "Service Experience and Educational Growth," *Educational Record* 1 (Spring 1968), 197–205.

Edelman, M.W., Prepared statement of testimony presented to the House Select Committee on Children, Youth and Families, Hearings on Child Care, 4 April 1984.

Ellington, J. "The Effects of Three Curriculum Strategies Upon High School Seniors' Attitudes Towards the Elderly." A University of Mississippi doctoral dissertation. Ann Arbor: University Microfilms International, 1978.

Elliot, D.S., and B.A. Knowles, "Development and Employment: An Evaluation of the Oakland Youth Work Experience Program," *UCLA Educator* 21, no. 1 (Fall 1979), 64–73.

Etzioni, A., *An Immodest Agenda*. New York: McGraw Hill, 1983.

Etzioni, A., "National Service for Youth" *Human Behavior,* August 1976, volume 5, no. 8, p. 13.

Evaluation Technologies, Inc., *A Trend Study of Offerings and Enrollments*. Arlington, VA: National Center for Education Statistics (Contract Report), 1984.

Ezekiel, R.S., "The Personal Future and Peace Corps Competence," *Journal of Personality and Social Psychology,* Monograph Supplement vol. 8, no. 2, part 2 (February 1968) 62.

Fallows, James, *National Defense*. New York: Random House, 1981.

Federal Register, "The Selective Service Regulations: Alternative Service, 32 C.F.R. Parts 1656 and 1660," *Federal Register,* 48 (1983), 16,675–880

Feller, B., "Americans Needing Help to Function at Home," National Center for Health Statistics. *Advance Data,* Number 92. Washington, DC: Department of Health and Human Services, 14 September 1983.

Firman, J., D. Gelfand, and C. Ventura, "Students as Resources to the Aging Network," in *The Gerontologist* 23, no. 2 (1983), 185–91.

Flynn, G. *Lewis B. Hershey, Mr. Selective Service*. Chapel Hill: University of North Carolina Press, 1985.

Foley, J., T. Freeman, and J.L. Schwartz, *The Peace Corps: More Today than Twenty Years Ago*. Washington, DC: Youth Policy Institute, 1984.

Foley, J., M. Maneker, and J.L. Schwartz, *National Service and America's Future*. Washington, DC: Youth Policy Institute, 1984.

Friedman, H., "Conscription and the Constitution: The Original Understanding," *Mich. L. Rev.* 67 (1969), 1493.

Friends Committee on National Legislation, "National Service—A National Disservice," *Washington Newsletter of the Friends Committee on National Legislation*, July 1981, 2, 4.

Gallup Organization, Inc., *Americans Volunteer: 1981. A Survey conducted for the Independent Sector*. Princeton, NJ: 1981.

Gallup, G., "The 1983 Gallup Survey on Volunteering," *Voluntary Action Leadership*, Winter 1984, 20–22.

Gallup, G., "Eight in Ten Opinion Leaders Back Compulsory National Service." Public information release, 25 November 1984. Princeton, NJ: Gallup Organization, Inc.

Gallup, G., "Most Teens Favor National Youth Service." Public Information Release, 3 October 1984. Princeton, NJ: Gallup Organization, Inc.

Gallup, G., "Majority of Teens Favor National Youth Service." Public Information Release, 26 September 1984. Princeton, NJ: Gallup Organization, Inc.

Gallup, G., "Two in Three Favor National Service in Exchange for Educational Benefits." Public Information Release, 12 February 1984. Princeton, NJ: Gallup Organization, Inc.

Gallup, G., and C. Robinson, "American Institute of Public Opinion—Surveys, 1935–38," *Public Opinion Quarterly* 2, no. 3 (July 1938), 373–98.

General Accounting Office, Comptroller General, *CETA Demonstration Provides Lessons on Implementing Youth Programs*. A Report to the Congress of the United States. Washington, DC: General Accounting Office, 1980.

Gilantz, A., D. Coelen, and C. Calore, *Day Care Centers in the United States: A National Profile, 1976–77*. Cambridge, MA: ABT Associates, 1978.

Gilinsky, R.M., "When Helping Others is Part of Learning," *The New York Times*, Higher Education Supplement, 6 January 1985.

Gillespie, D., and N. Carlson, *Trends in Student Aid: 1963 to 1983*. Washington, DC: The College Board, 1983.

Gilsinan, James F., and E. Allan Tomey, "Public Versus Private Sector Jobs Demonstration Project." St. Louis University, Center for Urban Programs, 1981.

Gittell, M., M. Beardsley, and M. Weissman, *Final Evaluation Report on Syracuse Youth Community Service*. Washington, DC: ACTION, 1981.

Goldberg, J., *The Noneconomic Impacts of the Job Corps*. R&D Monograph #64. Prepared by Abt Associates, Inc., for the Employment and Training Administration of the Department of Labor. Washington, DC, 1978.

Greenberger, E., L. Steinberg, and M. Ruggiero, "A Job Is a Job Is a Job . . . or Is It? Behavioral Observations in the Adolescent Workplace," *Work and Occupations* 9, no. 1 (February 1982), 79–96.

Gueron, J., *The Youth Incentive Entitlement Pilot Projects: Lessons from a Job Guarantee,* Princeton, NJ: Manpower Demonstration Research Corporation, 1984.

Haan, N., "Changes in Young Adults After Peace Corps Experiences: Political-Social Views, Moral Reasoning, and Perceptions of Self and Parents," *Journal of Youth and Adolescence* 3, no. 3 (1974), 177–94.

Hagenstein, P., "National Service: Conservation and Environmental Aspects." Unpublished paper prepared for the National Service Study Project, September 1983.

Hahn, A., and R. Lehrman, *What Works in Youth Employment Policy?* Brandeis University Center for Human Resources, The Florence Heller Graduate School. Washington, DC: National Planning Association, 1985.

Hanson v. *Cushman* 490 F. Supp. 109 (1980) 490.

Heart of Atlanta Motel v. *U.S.* 379 U.S. 241 (1964).

Hedin, D., J. Arneson, M. Resnick, and H. Wolfe, *Minnesota Youth Poll: Youth's View on National Service and the Draft.* Miscellaneous Report no. 158. University of Minnesota, 1980.

Heflin v. *Sanford* 142 F.2d. 798,800 (5th Circuit Court of Appeals, 1944).

Hodgkinson, V., "Student Aid: Its Distribution and its Impact on College Operating Budgets," in *Perspectives and Projections: Student Aid Planning and Educational Policy,* edited by Virginia Hodgkinson. Washington, DC: National Institute of Independent Colleges and Universities, 1982, 1–12.

Hollingshead, A., *Elmtown's Youth: The Impact of Social Class in Adolescents* (1949).

Hopkins, B., *The Law of Tax Exempt Organizations.* Washington, DC: Lerner Law Book Co., 1977.

Houck, O., "With Charity for All," *Yale Law Journal* 93 (1984), 1415–63.

Hovey, H., *The Costs and Benefits of Universal and National Service Programs.* New York: Fund For the City of New York, 1982.

Howze v. *United States,* 272 F. 2d. 146, 148 (9th Circuit Court of Appeals, 1959).

Huda, F., "Special Study on VISTA Attrition." Washington, DC: ACTION, 24 July 1978.

Human Environment Center, "Conservation and Service Corps Profiles." Washington, DC: Human Environment Center, November 1984.

Human Environment Center, *Youth Conservation Jobs and Service—A New National Corps?* Report of a Conference. Washington, D.C., 4–5 May 1981.

Hunter, K.I., and M.W. Linn. "Psycho-Social Differences Between Elderly Volunteers and Non-Volunteers," *International Journal of Aging and Human Development* 12, no. 3 (1981), 205–13.

Internal Revenue Service, *Statistics of Income Bulletin* 2 (Winter 1982–3), 2.

Jacobs, J., and D. McNamara, "Selective Service Without a Draft," *Armed Forces and Society* 10, no. 3, 361–367.

James, W. "The Moral Equivalent of War," in *The Moral Equivalent of War and Other Essays and Selections from Some Problems of Philosophy,* edited by John K. Roth, pp. 3–16. New York: Harper & Row Publishers, 1971.

Janowitz, M., "The Logic of National Service," in *The Draft: A Handbook of Facts and Alternatives,* edited by Sol Tax, 73–90. Chicago: University of Chicago Press, 1967.

Janowitz, M., *The Reconstruction of Patriotism: Education for Civic Consciousness.* Chicago: University of Chicago Press, 1983.

Johnson, L.A., W. Lynn and B.L. Driver, *Final Report of Pilot Study of the Perceived Long-Term Benefits of the Youth Conservation Corps.* Fort Collins Colorado: Colorado State University and the Rocky Mountain Forest and Range Experiment Station, 1982.

Johnson and Associates, Inc., *Profile of State Day-Care Licensing Regulations.* Washington, DC: Office of Program Development of the Administration of Children, Youth and Families, Office of Human Development Services, Department of Health and Human Services, 1982.

Johnston, L.D., P.M. O'Malley, and J.G. Bachman, *Highlights from Drugs and American High School Students, 1975–83.* Work done at University of Michigan, Institute for Social Research, under a grant from the National Institue of Drug Abuse, Department of Health and Human Services. Washington, DC: Government Printing Office, 1984.

Kaplan, B.H., "Role Continuity in the Older Volunteer Role." Dissertation presented to the faculty of the School of Social Work, University of Southern California, January 1978.

Kassing, D., "Military Experience as a Determinant of Veterans' Earnings." Study #8 of the studies prepared for the President's Commission on an All-Volunteer Force, Washington, DC, November 1970.

Kelley, B., "Many College Students Show an Inclination to Get Involved," *The Christian Science Monitor,* 7 September 1984, 21.

Kemper, P., Long, D. and C. Thornton, *The Supported Work Evaluation: Final Benefit-Cost Analysis.* New York: Manpower Demonstration Research Corporation, 1980.

Kerr, C., *Giving Youth a Better Chance: Options for Education, Work and Service.* Princeton, NJ: Carnegie Council on Policy Studies in Education, 1979.

Kotin, L., and Aikman, *Legal Foundations of Compulsory School Attendance.* Port Washington, NY: Kennikat Press, 1980.

Kuhlman, J., "Linkages Between Military Service and Alternative National Service in West Germany." Paper presented at the Inter-University Seminar on Armed Forces and Society, Chicago, 1983.

Lacy, J. "National Service as an Alternative or Complement to the All-Volunteer Force." Draft paper prepared for the President's Military Manpower Task Force. Washington, DC, February 1982.

Lacy, J., "National Service: The Origins and Evolution in Theory and Practice." Unpublished paper prepared as part of a preliminary study of National Service submitted to the Ford Foundation by the National Service Study Project in 1982.

Lacy, J., "The Draft," unpublished manuscript in possession of the author, Washington, DC, 1981.

Landrum, R., "National Service in West Germany and France," in *National Service: Social, Economic and Military Impact,* edited by Michael Sherraden and Donald Eberly, 71–80. Elmsford, New York: Pergamon Press, Inc., 1982.

Landrum, R., "National Service: A Grass Roots Expansion," *Youth Policy,* September 1985, 24.

Landrum, R., "Service for Society: The Missing Dimension for American Youth," in *Youth and the Needs of the Nation,* 23–138. Washington, DC: Potomac Institute, 1979.

Landrum, R., (ed.), *National Youth Service: What's at Stake?* Washington, DC: Potomac Institute, 1980.

Laurence, M.T., and S. Bridges, *Youth Attitude Tracking Survey: Historical Evolution and Characteristics.* A technical note. Arlington, VA: Defense Manpower Data Center, 1985.

Lee, P., et al., "Study of Service and Social Needs in the Health Sector." Unpublished paper prepared for the National Service Study Project, September 1983.

Levi Strauss Foundation, *1982 Annual Report.* San Francisco: Levi Strauss, Inc., 1983.

Levin, L.S., and E. Idler, *The Hidden Health Care System: Mediating Structures and Medicine.* Cambridge, MA: Ballinger Publishing Co., 1981.

Levine, A., *When Dreams and Heroes Die: A Portrait of Today's College Student.* Carnegie Council on Policy Studies in Higher Education: 1980.

Levitan, S., and B. Johnston, *The Job Corps:* A Social Experiment That Works. Baltimore: Johns Hopkins University Press, 1975.

Levitan, S., and C. Johnson, *Beyond the Safety Net.* Cambridge, MA: Ballinger Publishing Co., 1984.

Levitan, S., and B. Johnston, *The Job Corps:* A Social Experiment that Works. Baltimore: The Johns Hopkins University Press, 1975.

Levitan, S., and G. Magnum, *The "T" in CETA.* Kalamazoo, MI: Upjohn Institute, 1981.

Lewin-Epstein, Noah, *Youth Employment During High School.* An Analysis of High School and Beyond: A National Longitudinal Study for the 1980's. Washington, DC: National Center for Education Statistics, 1981.

Little, R.D., and J.E. Fredlund, "Veteran Status Earnings and Race: Some Long Term Results," *Armed Forces and Society* 5, no. 2 (February 1979), 244–60.

Louis Harris and Associates, Inc., *Aging in the Eighties: America in Transition.* A study for the National Council on the Aging, Inc. Washington, DC, 1981.

Louis Harris and Associates, Inc., "A Survey of Returned Peace Corps Volunteers." Study no. 1929 conducted for the Peace Corps. Washington, DC, 1969.

Lopreato, S.C., and D.L. Poston, Jr., "Differences in Earnings and Earnings Ability Between Black Veterans and Non Veterans in the United States," *Social Science Quarterly* 57 (March 1977), 750–66.

Low, A.M., *Dust Bowl Diary.* Lincoln, NE: University of Nebraska Press, 1984.

Luchs, K.P., "Selected Changes in Urban High School Students After Participation in Community Based Learning and Service Activities." Doctoral dissertation submitted to the Faculty of the Graduate School of the University of Maryland, College Park, MD, 1981.

Maccoby, M., and C.E. Margolies, "The Psychological Effects on Youth of National Service." Unpublished paper prepared for the National Service Study Project, September 1983.

Magnum, G., and J. Walsh, *Employment and Training Programs for Youth: What Works Best for Whom?* Washington, DC: Department of Labor, 1978.

Maller, C., et al., *Evaluation of the Economic Impact of the Job Corps Program*. Washington, DC: Department of Labor, 1982.

Manski, C.F., and D.A. Wise, *College Choice in America*. Cambridge, MA: Harvard University Press, 1983.

Marans, R.W., B.L. Driver, and J.C. Scott, *Youth and the Environment: An Evaluation of the 1971 Youth Conservation Corps*. Ann Arbor: Institute for Social Research, University of Michigan Press, 1972.

Marini, M.M., "The Transition to Adulthood: Sex Differences in Educational Attainment and Age at Marriage," *American Sociological Review* 43 (August 1978), 483–507.

Mark Battle and Associates, Inc., "Local Mixed Income Testing." Youth Knowledge Development Report 4.1, 1980.

Mark Battle and Associates, Inc., "Mixed Income Experiment, Phase III, Report II: Participant Status Eight Months After Program Completion." Submitted to Department of Labor, Washington, D.C., 1981.

Mark Battle and Associates, Inc., "The Mixed Income Experiment, Report III: Test Results by Site." Submitted to Department of Labor, Washington, DC, 1981.

Market Facts, Inc., "Youth Attitude Tracking Study, Fall 1982." Arlington, VA: Defense Manpower Data Center, May 1983.

Martino v. *Mich. Window Cleaning Co.* 327 U.S. 173 (1946).

Mason, R. *Preliminary Analysis of the Social Attainment of White Males in the CPS Sample of the 1964 Department of Defense Surveys*. Washington, DC: Department of Defense, 1966.

Mass. Bd. of Retirement v. *Murgia* 427 U.S. 307, 313–14 (1976).

Maza, P., "Characteristics of Children in Foster Care," "Child Welfare Research Notes #1." Unpublished paper available from the Administration on Children, Youth and Families, Washington, DC, December 1983.

McEntee, J.J., *Final Report of the Director of the Civilian Conservation Corps: April 1933 through June 30, 1942*. Washington, D.C.: Federal Security Agency, 1942.

McGrew, T., "The Constitutionality of Compulsory National Service," *Public Law Forum,* Volume IV, 259–267 (Fall 1984).

Mead, M., "A National Service System as a Solution to a Variety of National Problems," in *The Draft: A Handbook of Facts and Alternatives,* edited by Sol Tax, 99–109. Chicago: University of Chicago Press, 1967.

Menacker, J., and E.A. Wynne, "Helping Students to Serve Society," *Phi Delta Kappan,* February 1982, 381–84.

Meyer, T., "More Students Finding Time to Give the Needy a Hand," *The Chronicle of Higher Education,* 27 February 1985.

The Military Manpower Task Force, *A Report to the President on the Status and Prospects of the All-Volunteer Force,* rev. ed. November 1982.

Millis, W., *Arms and Men*. New York: Putnam, 1956.

Mirengoff, W., and L. Rindler, "CETA: Manpower Programs Under Local Control." Washington, DC: National Academy of Sciences, 1978.

Monk, A., and A. Cryns, "Predictors of Voluntaristic Intent Among the Aged," *The Gerontologist* 14, no. 5 (1974), 425–29.

Mortimer, J., and M. D. Finch, "The Development of Self-Esteem in the Early Work Career." Unpublished paper, University of Minnesota, 1984.

Moskos, C., "How to Save the All-Volunteer Force," *The Public Interest* 61 (Fall 1980), 74–89.

Moskos, C., "Making the All-Volunteer Force Work: A National Service Approach," *Foreign Affairs,* Fall 1981, 17–34.

Moskos, C., "Social Considerations of the All-Volunteer Force," in *Military Service in the United States,* edited by Brent Scowcroft, 129–50. New York: The American Assembly, Columbia University, 1982.

National Center for Clinical Infant Programs, "Who Will Mind the Babies?" A public policy paper. Washington, DC, undated.

National Center for Service Learning, *National Survey of High School Student Community Service Programs.* Washington, DC: ACTION, 1979.

The National Commission on Excellence in Education, *A Nation at Risk: The Imperative for Educational Reform.* A report to the nation and the secretary of education. Washington, DC: Government Printing Office, April 1983.

National Commission on Resources for Youth, Inc., "An Evaluation of the Youth Tutoring Youth Model for In-School Neighborhood Youth Corps." 1982.

National Council on Employment Policy, "Investing in America's Future." Alexandria, VA, Remediation and Training Institute, 1984.

National Service Secretariat, *A Plan for National Service.* Washington, DC: National Service Secretariat, 1966.

Nelson, G., R. Hale and J. Slackman, "National Service and the Military." Unpublished paper prepared for the National Service Project, September 1983.

Newman, F., *Higher Education and the American Resurgence.*A study sponsored by the Carnegie Foundation for the Advancement of Teaching. Princeton, NJ: Princeton University Press, 1985.

Newmann, F., and R. Rutter, "The Effects of High School Community Service Programs on Students' Social Development." N.I.E. Final Report on Grant No. NIE-G-81-0009. Washington, DC: National Institute of Education, 1983.

Nye, D.E., *The History of the Youth Conservation Corps.* Washington, DC: Department of Agriculture, Forest Service, 1980.

O'Connell, M., and C. Rogers, *Child Care Arrangements of Working Mothers, June 1982.* Current Population Reports, Special Studies Series, p-23, no. 129. Washington, DC: Bureau of the Census, November 1983.

Office of Management and Budget, *Midsession Review of the 1985 Budget.* September, 1984.

Office of Naval Research, *First-Term Enlisted Attrition, Volume I: Papers.* June, 1977.

Patchen, M., *Black-White Contact in Schools: Its Social and Academic Effects.* Purdue, IN: Purdue University Press, 1982.

Pellechio, A.J., and G.P. Goodfellow, "Individual Gains and Losses from Social Security Before and After the 1983 Social Security Amendments." Prepared for the CATO Institute Conference on Social Security, July 1983.

Pierce v. *Society of Sisters,* 268 U.S. 510 (1925).

Pilisuk, M., and M. Minkler, "Supportive Networks: Life Ties for the Elderly," *Journal of Social Issues* 36, 2 (1980), 95–116.

Pinkau, I. *Services for Development,* Dayton, OH, C.F. Kettering Foundation, 1978.

Plisko, V.W., ed., *The Condition of Education, 1983 Edition.* Statistical Report, National Center for Education Statistics. Washington, DC: Government Printing Office, 1983.

Plisko, V.W., ed., *The Condition of Education, 1984 Edition*. Statistical Report, National Center for Education Statistics. Washington, DC: Government Printing Office, 1984.

Pollack v. *Williams* 332 U.S. 4, 17–18 (1943).

Public/Private Ventures, "A Profile of Past and Present Youth Conservation Corps Programs." An unpublished comparative chart. Philadelphia, PA: Public/Private Ventures, 1983.

Public/Private Ventures, "The California Conservation Corps: An Analysis of Participant Characteristics." Philadelphia, PA: Public/Private Ventures, 1983.

Public/Private Ventures, "Ventures in Community Improvement: Final Report of the Demonstration." Philadelphia, PA: Public/Private Ventures, 1982.

Quinn, R.P., and G.L. Staines, *The 1977 Quality of Employment Survey*. Descriptive statistics with comparison data from the 1969–70 and the 1972–73 surveys. Ann Arbor: Institute for Social Research, University of Michigan, 1979.

Rabinovitz, F., "National Service Other Services Study." Unpublished paper prepared for the National Service Study Project, September 1983.

Rafuse, J., "United States Experience with Volunteer and Conscript Forces," in *Studies Prepared for the President's Commission on an All-Volunteer Force,* Vol. 2, ??. Washington, DC: Government Printing Office, 1970.

Raphael, E., "Youth Employment and its Effects on Performance in High School." A paper presented at the Kennedy School of Government, Harvard University, 1982.

Research Triangle Institute, *Youth Attitude Tracking Survey II, Fall 1983*. A contract report for the Department of Defense. Arlington, VA: Defense Manpower Data Center, 1984.

Reskin, Lauren R., "Law Poll," *American Bar Association Journal* 71 (November 1985), 42–45.

Reubens, B., J.M. Harrison, and K. Rupp, *The Youth Labor Force, 1945–1995* Totowa, NJ: Allanheld, 1981.

Robertson v. *U.S.* 165 U.S. 275, 282 (1897).

Rock, D.A., et al., *Factors Associated with the Test Score Decline*. A briefing paper prepared under contract no. 300-83-0247, for the Department of Education, National Center for Education Statistics. Princeton, NJ: Educational Testing Service, 1984.

Roosevelt Centennial Youth Project, *A Policy Blueprint for Community Service and Youth Employment*. Washington, DC: Roosevelt Centennial Youth Project, 1984.

Rostker, B., "How Can the Draft be Fair?," *Washington Post,* 5 August 1981, A–23.

Rostker v. *Goldberg* 453 U.S. 57 (1981).

Rothenberg, R., *The Neoliberals: Creating the New American Politics*. New York: Simon and Schuster, Inc., 1984.

Ruggiero, M., E. Greenberger, and L. Steinberg, "Occupational Deviance Among Adolescent Workers," *Youth and Society* 13 (June 1982), 423–48.

Sachnoff, I.S., *High School Peer Resource Programs: A Director's Perspective*. (Booklet) Copyrighted by Ira Sachnoff. San Francisco, 1984.

San Antonio School District v. *Rodriguez* 411 U.S. 1, 28 (1973).

Seeley, R. "Three Hundred Years: The Struggle for Conscience in America." Unpaginated, undated pamphlet, published by Coordinating Council of Conscientious Objectors, 2016 Walnut Street, Philadelphia, PA.

Segal, D.R., and M.W. Segal, "The Impact of Military Service on Trust in Government, International Attitudes, and Social Status," in *The Social Psychology of Military Service,* edited by N. Goldman and D.R. Segal. Beverly Hills, CA: Sage Publications, 1976, 262–281.

Select Panel for the Promotion of Child Health, *Better Health for Our Children: A National Strategy,* Vol. 3, A Statistical Profile. Washington, DC: Government Printing Office, 1981.

Selective Draft Law Cases 245 U.S. 366, 390 (1981).

Selective Service System et al. v. *Minnesota Public Interest Research Group et al.,* 104 S.Ct. 3348 (1984).

Selective Service System, *Conscientious Objection.* Special Monograph #11. Washington, DC: Government Printing Office, 1950.

Sheehan, S., *Kate Quinton's Days.* Boston: Houghton-Mifflin Co., 1984.

Sherraden, M.W., and D.J. Eberly, eds., *National Service: Social, Economic and Military Impacts.* Elmsford, NY: Pergamon Press, 1982.

Sherraden, M., *The Civilian Conservation Corps: Effectiveness of the Camps.* Doctoral dissertation, Ann Arbor: University of Michigan, 1979.

Sibley, M.W., and P.E. Jacobs, *Conscription of Conscience: The American State and the Conscientious Objector.* Ithaca, NY: Cornell University Press, 1952.

Sigler, E., and E.W. Gordon, *Day Care: Scientific and Social Policy Issues.* Boston: Auburn House Publishing Company, 1982.

Silver Flash II, "How to Sharpen Uncle Sam's Defense Sword, Increase Home-Front Human Services, Shrink the Government, Cut Taxes, Reduce the Budget and Get America Off its Apathy," *Armed Forces Journal,* November 1980, 11.

Sizer, T.R., "National Service Education Study." Unpublished paper prepared for the National Service Study Project, September 1983.

Skaperdas, P., and J.R. Capra, "The Social Security System After the 1983 Amendments." A paper published by the Federal Reserve Bank of New York, July 1983.

Smith, D.H., "The Impact of Voluntary Action Upon the Volunteer/Participant," in *Voluntary Action Research: 1973,* edited by D.H. Smith, Lexington, MA: Lexington Books, D.C. Heath and Co., 1973.

Smith, D.H., and W. Baldwin, "Voluntary Associations and Volunteering in the United States" in *Voluntary Action Research: 1973,* edited by D.H. Smith, Lexington, MA: Lexington Books, D.C. Heath and Co., 1973.

Smith, E., J.B. Hunter, and P. Zildjian, "The Impact of Peace Corps and VISTA Service on Former Volunteers and American Society." A survey of former Peace Corps and VISTA volunteers, Peace Corps decliners and early terminees. Prepared for ACTION under Contract #76-043-1068. Belmont, MA: CRC Education and Human Development, Inc., 1978.

Sohlberg, R., "Defense Manpower Policies in Seven Northern and Central European NATO Countries: Part II." Santa Monica, CA: Rand Corporation, 1977.

Soldo, B., "The Elderly Home Care Population: National Prevalence Rates, Select Characteristics and Alternative Sources of Assistance." Washington, DC: Urban Institute, May 1983.

State v. *Bailey* 157 Ind. 324, 61 N.E. 730 (1901).

State v. *Jackson* 71 N.H. 552, 53A. 1021 (1923).

Stein, M.I., *Volunteers for Peace*. New York: John Wiley and Sons, 1966.

Steinberg, L.D., E. Greenberger, L. Garduque, M. Ruggiero, and A. Vaux, "Effects of Working on Adolescent Development," *Developmental Psychology* 18, no. 3 (1982), 385–95.

Steinberg, L.D., E. Greenberger, L. Garduque, and S. McAuliffe, "High School Students in the Labor Force: Some Costs and Benefits to Schooling and Learning," *Educational Evaluation and Policy Analysis* 4, no. 3 (Fall 1982), 363–72.

Stephens v. *Bongart* 189 A. 131 (1937).

Stockhaus, S.H., "The Effects of a Community Involvement Program on Adolescent Students' Citizenship Attitudes." A doctoral dissertation presented to the University of Minnesota, 1976.

The Student Conservation Association, Inc., "1984 High School Work Groups." A brochure for prospective members. Charlestown, NH, 1984.

Sum, Andrew, Paul Harrington, and Bill Goedicke, "One Fifth of the Nation's Teenagers: Employment Problems of Poor Youth in America, 1981–1984." Prepared by Center for Labor Market Studies, Northeastern University, for Ford Foundation, 1985.

Taggart, R., *A Fisherman's Guide: An Assessment of Training and Remediation Strategies*. Kalamazoo, Mich.: 1981.

Thorndike, W., and G. Hagen, "Attitudes, Educational Programs, and Job Experiences of Airmen Who Did Not Reenlist."

Thurman, M., "Sustaining the All-Volunteer Force 1983–1992: The Second Decade," in *The All-Volunteer Force After a Decade*, edited by W. Bowman, R. Little and T. Sicilia, Elmsford, NY: Pergamon Press (forthcoming, 1986).

Tribe, L., *American Constitutional Law*. Mineola, NY: Foundation Press, 1978.

United Way of America, *Management Assistance Programs: A Closer Look*. Alexandria, VA: United Way of America, 1983.

U.S. Air Force, *An Analysis of the Effects of Varying Male/Female Force Levels*, Annex 3, *The Prospects for Military Enlistments* Washington, DC: Department of Defense (March 1985).

U.S. Congress. Congressional Budget Office. *Costs of the National Service Act (H.R. 2206): A Technical Analysis*. Washington, DC: Congressional Budget Office, 1980.

U.S. Congress. Congressional Budget Office. "Costs and Recruiting Effects of Alternative Programs of Military Education." An unpublished paper. Washington, DC: Congressional Budget Office, 1984.

U.S. Congress. Congressional Budget Office. *Economic Budget Outlook, 1983 Edition*. Washington, D.C.: 1983.

U.S. Congress. Congressional Budget Office. *Improving Military Education Benefits: Effects on Costs, Recruiting and Retention*. Washington, D.C.: Congressional Budget Office, 1982.

U.S. Congress. House. Armed Services Committee. Military Personnel Subcommittee. *Hearings on National Service Legislation*. 96th Congress, 2d Session, 1980.

U.S. Congress. House. Committee on Veteran's Affairs. "State Veterans' Laws." 98th Congress, 2nd Session. Washington, D.C. Government Printing Office, 1984.

U.S. Congress. House. H.R. 999, *The American Conservation Corps Act of 1984,* 98th Congress, 2nd Session, October 1984.

U.S. Congress. House. H.R. 99, *The American Conservation Corps Act of 1985,* 99th Congress, 1st Session, January, 1985.

U.S. Congress. House. H.R. 18025, *National Service Act of 1970.*91st Congress, 2nd Session, June 1970.

U.S. Congress. House. H.R. 2206, *The National Service Act of 1979.* 96th Congress, 1st Session. February 1979.

U.S. Congress. House. H.R. 888, *Voluntary Youth Service Act.* 99th Congress, 1st Session, January, 1985.

U.S. Congress. House. Hearings Before the Select Committee on Children, Youth and Families. *Child Care: Beginning a National Initiative.* 98th Congress, 2d Session, 1984.

U.S. Congress. House. Select Committee on Children, Youth and Families. *Families and Child Care: Improving the Options.* 98th Congress, 2d Session, 1984.

U.S. Congress. House. Committee on Education and Labor. Special Subcommittee on Labor. *Hearings on H.R. 5625: A Bill to Strengthen Community Service Programs in the U.S.* 88th Congress, 1st Session, 1963.

U.S. Congress. Senate. Committee on Labor and Human Resources. Subcommittee on Child and Human Development. *Hearings on Presidential Commission on National Service and National Commission on Volunteerism,* 96th Congress, 2d Session, 1980.

U.S. Congress. Senate. Committee on Labor and Public Welfare. Subcommittee on Employment and Manpower. *Youth Conservation Corps and Youth Public Service.* 87th Congress, 1st Session, 1961.

U.S. Congress. Senate. *Hearings Before the Senate Committee on the Budget,* Vol. 1. 96th Congress, 2d Session, 1980.

U.S. Department of Agriculture. U.S. Forest Service, *Youth Conservation Corps: Tenth Anniversary Report.*

U.S. Department of the Army. Office of the Comptroller of the Army. *Pocket Data Supplement.* Washington, D.C.: GPO.

U.S. Department of the Army, U.S. Army Recruiting Command, *Fact Sheet: Prime Market Calculation,* Washington, DC: 1984.

U.S. Department of Commerce. Bureau of the Census. 1980 Census Subject Report 4-C. *Marital Statistics.* Washington, DC: Government Printing Office, 1980.

U.S. Department of Commerce. Bureau of the Census. March 1983 Current Population Reports, Series P-20, No. 389. *Marital Status and Living Arrangements.* Washington, DC: Government Printing Office, 1984.

U.S. Department of Commerce. Bureau of the Census. Current Population Reports, Series P-60, No. 140. *Money Income and Poverty Status of Families and Persons in the United States: 1982* (Advance Data from the March 1983 Current Population Survey). Washington, DC: Government Printing Office, 1983.

U.S. Department of Commerce. Bureau of the Census. Current Population Reports, Series P-60, No. 145. *Money Income and Poverty Status of Families and Persons in the United States: 1983.* Washington, DC: Government Printing Office, 1984.

U.S. Department of Commerce. Bureau of the Census. Current Population Survey,

March 1984 supplement. Washington, DC: Government Printing Office, 1984.

U.S. Department of Commerce. Bureau of the Census. Current Population Reports, Series P-25, No. 949. *Estimates of the Population of the United States by Age, Sex and Race: 1980–83*. Washington, DC: Government Printing Office, 1984.

U.S. Department of Commerce. Bureau of the Census. Current Population Reports, Series P-20, No. 394. *School Enrollment—Social and Economic Characteristics of Students: October 1983 Advanced Report*. Washington, DC: Government Printing Office, 1984.

U.S. Department of Commerce. Bureau of the Census. Fifteenth Census of the United States. *1930 Population General Report, (Vol. 2), Statistics by Subject*. Washington, DC: Government Printing Office, 1933.

U.S. Department of Commerce. Bureau of the Census. *Projections of the Population of the United States: 1977–2050*. Washington, DC: Government Printing Office, 1977.

U.S. Department of Commerce. Bureau of the Census. Current Population Reports, Series P-25, No. 952. *Projection of the Population of the United States by Age, Sex and Race: 1983–2080*. Washington, DC: Government Printing Office, 1984.

U.S. Department of Commerce. Bureau of the Census. *Statistical Abstract of the United States: 1984*. Washington, DC, Government Printing Office, 1983.

U.S. Department of Commerce. Bureau of the Census. *Statistical Abstract of the United States: 1985*. Washington, DC, Government Printing Office, 1984.

U.S. Department of Defense. *Defense 84 Almanac*. Washington, DC: Department of Defense, 1984.

U.S. Department of Defense. *America's Volunteers: A Report on the All-Volunteer Armed Forces*. Washington, DC: Department of Defense, 1978.

U.S. Department of Defense. Office of the Assistant Secretary of Defense for Manpower, Reserve Affairs and Logistics. *Educational Incentives Study*. Washington, DC: Department of Defense, 1980.

U.S. Department of Defense. News Release No. 596-79. "Remarks of Richard Danzig at the Hoover-Rochester Conference on the All-Volunteer Force." 13 December 1979.

U.S. Departemnt of Defense. News Release No. 528-81. "Secretary of Defense Weinberger Announces Year-End Results of Volunteer Force Accessions; Reenlistments are Encouraging," 1981.

U.S. Department of Education. Office of Student Financial Assistance. *Program Book, Fiscal Year 1982*. Washington, DC: Government Printing Office, 1982.

U.S. Department of Education. National Center for Education Statistics. Bulletin No. 81-246B. *High School Seniors Will Work for Less Than The Minimum Wage*. Washington, DC: 10 April 1981.

U.S. Department of Education. National Center for Education Statistics. Bulletin No. 82-110. *A Comparison of Selected Characteristics of Private and Public Schools*. Washington, DC: 1982.

U.S. Department of Education. National Center for Education Statistics. "Bi-Annual Survey of Education in the United States: Statistics of State School Systems." Unpublished data, 1983.

U.S. Department of Justice. National Institute of Law Enforcement and Criminal Justice. *The National Manpower Survey of the Criminal Justice System.* Washington, DC: Government Printing Office, 1978.

U.S. Department of Labor. Bureau of Labor Statistics. Special Labor Force Report 217. *Children of Working Mothers: March 1977.* Washington, DC: Government Printing Office, 1979.

U.S. Department of Labor. Bureau of Labor Statistics. Current Population Survey. "Metropolitan and non-Metropolitan Area Tables." Unpublished data tables; annual averages for 1983.

U.S. Department of Labor. Bureau of Labor Statistics. Bulletin No. 2192. *Students, Graduates and Drop-outs, October 1980–82.* Washington, DC: Government Printing Office, 1983.

U.S. Department of Labor. Bureau of Labor Statistics. *Employment and Earnings (April 1985).* Washington, DC: Government Printing Office, 1985.

U.S. Department of Labor. Bureau of Labor Statistics. Bulletin No. 2096. *Labor Force Statistics Derived from Current Population Survey.* Washington, DC: Government Printing Office, 1982.

U.S. Department of Labor. Bureau of Labor Statistics. Bulletin 2175. *Handbook of Labor Statistics.* Washington, DC: Government Printing Office, 1983.

U.S. Department of Labor. News Release No. 84-321. "Number of Working Mothers Now at Record Levels." Washington, DC, 26 June 1984.

U.S. Department of the Treasury. Internal Revenue Service. *Statistics of Income Bulletin* 2 (Winter 1982–83). Washington, DC: Government Printing Office, 1983.

U.S. Veterans' Administration, Office of Information, Management and Statistics. "Veterans' Benefits Under Current Educational Programs," Washington, DC, 1985.

U.S. v. *Butler* 401 U.S. 297 (1936).

U.S. v. *Darby* 312 U.S. 100 (1938).

U.S. v. *Holmes,* 387 F.2d. 781, 784 (7th Circuit Court of Appeals, 1968); *cert. denied* 391 U.S. 936 (1960).

U.S. v. *MacIntosh* 283 U.S. 605, 623 (1931).

U.S. v. *O'Brien* 391 U.S. 367 (1968).

The Urban Institute and American Institutes for Research, *Assessing the Feasibility of Large-Scale Counter-Cyclical Public Job Creation,* Vols. 1–3. A report submitted to the Department of Labor under Contract No. 20-11-77-18. Washington, DC: Urban Institute, 1978.

Van House, N., N. Roderer, and M. Cooper, "Librarians: A Study of Supply and Demand," *American Libraries* 14 (June 1983), 361–70.

Vance, G.W., and T.D. Snyder, *Digest of Education Statistics, 1983–84.* A publication of the Department of Education. National Center for Education Statistics. Washington, DC: Government Printing Office, 1983.

Ventura, C., and P. Newman, *Voluntary Action and Older Americans: A Catalogue of Program Profiles.* Washington, DC: The National Council on Aging, Inc., 1982.

VISTA, Office of Planning and Evaluation, "VISTA Volunteer Sponsor Survey." Washington, DC: VISTA, 1976.

VISTA, *VISTA,* Washington, DC: VISTA, 1980.

VISTA, *Volunteer Handbook*. Washington, DC: ACTION, 1981.

Winkler, A. and P. Thompson, "Post-Service Utilization of Air Force–Gained Skills." Alexandria, VA.: Air Force Systems Command, 1971.

Welsh v. *United States,* 398 U.S. 333 (1970).

Wickard v. *Filburn* 317 U.S. 111, 128–29 (1942).

Wiedenfeller v. *Kidulis* 380 F. Supp. 445, 450 (E.D. Wis., 1974).

Winn, Ralph B., ed., *John Dewey: Dictionary of Education*. New York: Philosophical Library, 1952.

Wilson, D.P., and J. Horack, "Military Experience as a Determinant of Veterans' Attitudes." Study #7 of the studies prepared for the President's Commission on an All-Volunteer Force, Washington, D.C.: November 1970.

Winslow, E., "A Survey of Returned Peace Corps Volunteers." Washington, DC: ACTION, 1977.

Wisconsin v. *Yoder* 406 U.S. 205 (1972).

Woolsey, S., and S. Gutchess, "Child Care Jobs for National Service Participants." An unpublished paper prepared for the National Service Study Project, September 1983.

Wynne, E., ed., *Developing Character: Transmitting Knowledge,* A Thanksgiving Day Statement by Twenty-Seven Americans. Posen, IL: Thanksgiving Day Statement Group (c/o ARL, 2605 W. 147th Street, Posen, IL 60649), 1984.

Yarmolinsky, Adam, "National Service Program," in *National Compulsory Service,* U.S. Military Academy 1977 Senior Conference, Final Report. West Point: U.S. Military Academy, 1977.

Yee, R., "A Report of: The Summer Cross Age Tutoring Program—1980." An unpublished paper provided by the Detroit Public Schools, Detroit, MI, 1980.

Yogev, A., and R. Ronen, "Cross-Age Tutoring: Effects on Tutors' Attributes," *Journal of Educational Research* 75, no. 5 (May–June 1982), 261–68.

Young Adult Conservation Corps. Department of Labor, *Annual Reports, 1978–82*. Washington, DC: Government Printing Office, 1979–1982.

Zigler, E., and E.W. Gordon, *Day Care: Scientific and Social Policy Issues*. Boston: Auburn House Publishing Company, 1982.

Zimmerman, D.J., "A Study of the value of Output of Participants in the Summer Youth Employment Program." Washington, DC: Office of Youth Programs, Department of Labor, 1980.

Zimmerman, D.J., R. Egan, and R. Ross, "A Study of the Value of Output of Participants in Youth Demonstrations and CETA programs in New York State." Preliminary draft of the final report. Washington, DC: Office of Youth Programs, Department of Labor, 1981.

Zimmerman, D.J., and S. Masters, "A Pilot Study of the Value of Output of Youth Employment Programs." Special Report #21. Washington, DC: Office of Youth Programs, Department of Labor, 1979.

Index

About the Authors

Richard Danzig is a partner in the Washington, D.C. office of the law firm of Latham, Watkins and Hills. During the Carter Administration he was the Principal Deputy Assistant Secretary of Defense for Management and Logistics. Before that he was a Prize Fellow of the Harvard Society of Fellows, a Rockefeller Foundation Fellow, and an Associate Professor of Law at Stanford University. He has written extensively in the fields of law, public policy, and history.

Peter Szanton heads a Washington-based policy and management consulting firm. He was an Associate Director of the Office of Management and Budget in the Carter Administration, and served as the first President of the New York City-RAND Institute. He is the author of *Not Well Advised;* the co-author, with Graham Allison, of *Remaking Foreign Policy: the Organizational Connection,* and the author of numerous articles on issues of public policy.